The American Book of Prayer

Expanded and Revised

Second Edition

Edited by Justin Trask Haskins
ISBN: 978-0-9997355-1-0

Published in Durham, North Carolina

Copyright for original material held by Justin Haskins, 2018. Content compiled and edited by Justin Haskins.

Cover design by Justin Haskins. Cross on cover attributed to: http://graphicssoft.about.com/

All rights to original material reserved, 2018.

All material contained in this book that is not the original work of the author is material considered to be in the public domain under United States copyright law as of January 1, 2018. Sections of this book containing scripture use a slightly modified version of the *The King James Bible*, specifically the 1769 edition of the 1611 text, or the *World English Bible*. Both *The King James Bible* and the *World English Bible* are in the public domain in the United States of America.

This book is not intended to be sold or distributed outside of the United States.

Published in Durham, North Carolina in the United States of America by Justin Haskins and the New Revere Daily Press.

Second Edition of *The American Book of Prayer*, expanded and revised version, paperback, January 2018.

ISBN: 978-0-9997355-1-0

For the two most powerful forces in my life:
God and Jacquelyn.
For Glenn, my father and closest friend.
For my mother Deborah, for her dedication to her family.
For my sister Lindsey, for her endless perseverance.
For Robert Corley, who tirelessly preached the Gospel to me.

Contents

1. Introduction (p. i)
    Thoughts on Prayer Books (pg. i)
    Why This Prayer Book Is Different (pg. ii)
    How Were Prayers Selected? (pg. v)
    Before You Get Started (pg. vi)
    About the Editor (pg. viii)
    Abbreviations (pg. ix)
    Now You Are Ready (pg. ix)

2. Daily Prayer (p. 1)
3. Book of Acts (p. 323)
4. Holy Week Prayer (p. 387)
5. Prayers and Readings for Christmas (p. 435)
    Twas the Night Before Christmas by Clement Clarke Moore (p. 441)
6. Prayers for Daily Life (p. 453)
    A Prayer for the Final Abolition of Slavery
    A Prayer for the End of War
    A Prayer for Soldiers
    A Prayer for the Families of Soldiers
    A Prayer for Those Seeking Employment
    A Prayer for the End of Sin

- A Prayer for the Protection of God's Creation
- A Prayer for the Impoverished of the World
- A Prayer for the Homeless
- A Prayer for Doctors, Nurses, and Other Medical Staff
- A Prayer for Police Officers, Firefighters, Teachers, and Public Servants
- A Prayer for Good Government
- A Prayer in Preparation for Baptism
- A Prayer for the Baptized
- A Prayer in Preparation for the Lord's Supper
- A Prayer for the Clergy
- A Prayer in Preparation for a Wedding
- A Prayer for a Married Couple
- A Prayer in the Hope of Children
- A Prayer for Your Children
- A Prayer for the Faithless
- A Prayer for the Departed

7. A Treatise on the State of Man and God (p. 463)
8. End Notes (p. 473)

The American Book of Prayer

Introduction

Thoughts on Prayer Books

Like many throughout the history of Christianity, I did not start out as a believer. In fact, I have spent most of my life far from Christianity. But once I couldn't ignore the evidence any longer and my stubbornness was beaten down by what I am convinced must have been an act of God Himself, I became a small "s" saint and a passionate Christian.

Accepting Christ, I later found, proved to be much easier than finding the right "version" of Christianity. In the pursuit of the truth, a story worthy of its own book, I fell in love with Christian prayer and prayer books in particular. Not all Christian denominations have them, but of the ones that do, the *Book of Common Prayer* was always my favorite. First formulated by the hand of the famous (or infamous, depending upon your religious views and beliefs) Thomas Cranmer following the separation of the Church of England from the Roman Catholic Church in 1534, the *Book of Common Prayer* was a revolutionary idea. It brought a structured and manageable prayer life to anyone in England who could read English. Some of the most famous phrases in the English language come from the *Book of Common Prayer*, and Shakespeare himself is said by some scholars to have been heavily influenced by its writings.

I instantly connected with works like the *Book of Common Prayer* and immediately set out to find the best prayer book available. No matter where I looked, however, I kept seeing major flaws in the design of prayer books.

Because most of them are bound by liturgical church calendars and/or the desire to include readings that covered most of both the Old Testament and New Testament, prayer books are generally cumbersome to use. I would find myself reading along normally and then having to flip to a totally different section of the book to read a Psalm, then back to the prayer section I started on, then to a separate Bible for scripture readings, and back to the Psalms, and on and on. It is a tiring process, not very intuitive, and creates far too many distractions.

Additionally, prayer books are generally structured so that you are reading the same relatively small set of prayers every single day (or week).

Some books are less burdensome than others (one of my favorites is the *Lutheran Book of Prayer*, published by Concordia Publishing House), but in the end, they all lack one important aspect or another.

Why This Prayer Book Is Different

My goal for this book is to take a great idea (prayer books) and improve on it in ways others have rarely (or never) done before. The overarching purpose behind this book, however, isn't to win a prize for "best prayer book," it's to bring people closer to God by providing a structured, modern, easy-to-use system for studying scripture and praying.

Some of you may be wondering, "Who the heck needs a prayer book?" I will be the first to acknowledge that no one actually *must* have a prayer book, but I have found in my own life that prayer without a prayer book is like making a cross-country drive without a map. Can you get

Introduction

from Virginia to California without one? Of course, but a map sure does have its benefits!

What makes this prayer book different from all the other prayer books out there? For starters, I have structured my prayer book to operate separately from the traditional Christian calendar (or any other calendar). The downside to this is that your readings won't align with the readings you will get at church (if you go to a liturgical church like the the Anglican Church in North America or the Lutheran Church-Missouri Synod). The benefit is that you can start reading from the beginning of the "Daily Prayers" section at any time, beginning with "Day One," and you can continue through the entire 40-day cycle without worrying about the Christian calendar. Further, if you miss a day or two, it won't throw you off at all, because you can pick right back up where you left off.

Second, this is by far the easiest and most intuitive prayer book available today. You simply pick it up and start reading, beginning on "Day One." You follow the order of the book and you don't have to worry about flipping through different sections like you do with most other prayer books.

Third, unlike other "easy-to-use" prayer books that are pretty much just a collection of prayers thrown into various sections, usually compiled by category, this book offers a complete package. Every day, you will read a short prayer, a psalm or proverb, a substantial reading from the Gospel (or Book of Genesis), a confession of sin, and the Lord's Prayer. Of course, you can add numerous other private prayers to each day, but you don't have to get a good experience every time you pick the book up.

Fourth, one of the most frustrating parts of using other prayer books is the need to switch between a Bible and the prayer book when you get to the "scripture" section of the day. This is largely done for practical purposes. A prayer book cannot reasonably contain an entire Bible within it, so editors and writers expect you to have one with you when using their book. While this certainly isn't impossible today with all of the technology out there, I found this to be incredibly distracting and something I really detested about using prayer books. This book eliminates this problem by putting the scripture readings in the book itself, broken down by day, so there is no page-turning, no moving between one book and another, and you have the added benefit of sticking to a structured reading plan.

The downside to this model is that I couldn't fit the entire Bible into the book, so I had to pick and choose which readings were most important and which were not. At this point in the discussion, I should mention that this prayer book is obviously not a replacement for the Bible. While much of the four gospels and some of the Book of Genesis appear in this book as part of the daily readings, there are sections that were left out, including all of the New Testament Epistles, much of the Old Testament, and small sections of the Gospel. (Note: In this revised and expanded version, I've added the entire Book of Acts in a later section in the book. It can be used to substitute assigned scripture readings once you've read through those multiple times and want to add some variety to the daily readings.)

So, what does appear in this book? I tried to build a prayerful experience with my selection of scripture, so I started with the story of Adam and Eve and the creation. I think it's always important to think about God's creative power regularly and the Adam and Eve story is essential in understanding the story of mankind and its relationship with God.

Once Adam and Eve are expelled from the Garden of Eden, the readings jump ahead to important figures of the Old Testament: Noah and Abraham. The reason I included these stories is to show examples of the pattern that exists in salvation history. Reasonable people could

Introduction

argue I should have chosen different figures to highlight or that I should have included more Old Testament readings. However, unavoidable constraints, such as the size of the book and cost, kept me from including additional Old Testament readings.

The bulk of the scripture readings come from the four Gospel books. I include as much of the story of Jesus as possible by weaving together all four Gospels in chronological order, rather than working through each Gospel account and then moving to the next one.

What are the benefits of this system? With every cycle you go through, you will read the story of creation, man's fall from the Garden of Eden, the stories of Noah and Abraham, and the story of Christ in its entirety (nearly). Lots of important information is obviously missing from these readings (which is why I stressed the point that this prayer book is not a replacement for the Bible), but this book still offers you a wealth of readings that will allow you to pray the Psalms or Proverbs each day while reading through significant portions of the Bible.

Future editions may switch the formatting up a bit, but for now, this was the best system I could come up with that allowed the book to remain small enough to be carried around and affordable.

How Were Prayers Selected?

In the "Daily Readings" section of the book are prayers to start each day. They were written by famous (and often influential) Americans or individuals who have heavily influenced American Christianity.

How did I choose one prayer over another? I picked the prayers based on a few factors. First, I chose prayers I liked and felt were spiritually rich. Second, I tried to choose prayers that fit the theme of this book, which is "America's place in Christian history."

Why did I choose to write a prayer book with "America" as a theme? For several reasons. For starters, most prayer books are very old and reflect the time and place in which they were written. Americans, however, are *not* English, German, or ancient Romans. We are distinctly American and have our own culture and religious history. No other nation in the world today has more influence over Christianity, except for arguably the Vatican, than America does, and yet, we are still reading from prayer books that do not reflect our American past.

This prayer book is entirely different. There are ancient prayers included in this book, but many of the prayers are distinctly American or were written by men or women who greatly influenced some element of America's Christian heritage.

Before You Get Started

Before getting started, there are a few other things to note. As it was already suggested, this prayer book is easy to use and requires no training to put to good use, unlike many other prayer books. Just start on page 1 and take it from there.

Second, this book also contains numerous short prayers, known in some liturgical churches as "collects," located toward the back of the book. Here you will find prayers for weddings, baptisms, finding a job, etc. It's not a complete group of prayers, but I hope it's enough to contribute to your prayer life.

Third, there are numerous notes listing attributions when necessary, but all the prayers contained throughout this book were either written by myself or an anonymous individual, if no attribution is listed. If an attribution is listed, then the attribution is correct as far as I know. I have included notes when authorship is questioned (which is the case with some of the George Washington prayers, for instance).

Introduction

Fourth, although this prayer book does not follow the Christian calendar, I did include a special week of prayers for Holy Week, beginning on Palm Sunday, so that readers can follow a relevant reading plan during the most important week in the Christian calendar. Prayers for Christmas, as well as the famous poem *Twas the Night Before Christmas*, are also included in a section following the "Holy Week" portion of this book. All of this can easily be found in the Table of Contents.

Fifth, I tried very hard to compile a prayer book that evangelical Christians of all denominations could use. It doesn't matter if you identify as a Baptist, Lutheran, Presbyterian, nondenominational Christian, Methodist, or with some other denomination; you should be able to use this prayer book without too many issues.

One negative aspect of having a prayer book designed for many different Christian denominations is that some of the language in certain sections of the prayer book is purposefully vague. For instance, I deliberately made the language in prayers about baptism and the Lord's Supper neutral so that you can use them whether you believe in the bodily Real Presence and baptismal regeneration or a symbolic meal and symbolic baptism. This means that some prayers are not as theologically rich as I would like, which is an unfortunate part of living in a time when the church is so divided. I should point out, however, that the prayers here are absolutely orthodox and have been influenced heavily by ancient sources. You will find no uneasy or squeamish questions about who Jesus is, why He died for us, or if God really exists in this book. This book is designed to be used by evangelical, in the traditional sense of the word, users. If you're looking for a more theologically liberal prayer book, I'd recommend *Common Prayer*, published by Zondervan.

Sixth, there are two different note sections: end notes and footnotes. For all sections of the book outside of the scripture reading sections, I used end notes, which can be found toward the back of the book. This is because most people likely won't be regularly looking up the noted material in those sections. For the scripture sections, however, I wanted to make accessing the notes as easy as possible, because I don't want anyone flipping pages during prayer and contemplation, so footnotes were used in all scripture sections.

Seventh, at the very end of the book is an apologetic essay I wrote regarding God's existence. It's titled "A Treatise on the State of Man and God." It's a short and very concise series of logical arguments against the claims of atheism. I hope you find it to be useful in your own life.

Eighth, you might notice that I've left page numbers on blank pages throughout the book. This isn't something most books do, but I included those additional page numbers because some readers may choose to use those pages for handwritten notes.

About the Editor

Justin Haskins is the executive editor of The Heartland Institute, one of the nation's leading free-market think tanks. It's headquartered in Arlington Heights, Illinois. Justin graduated summa cum laude with a B.A.S. from the University of Richmond (Richmond, VA) in 2010 and from Regent University (Virginia Beach, VA) with an M.A. in government, with a focus on international relations, in 2011. Haskins finished his second M.A. from Regent University, this time in journalism, in 2015.

Haskins has been published hundreds of times in major digital and print publications, including *The Wall Street Journal*, *New York Post*, *Forbes*, FoxNews.com, *Newsweek*, and *National Review*, among many others. His writing has also been featured or discussed by the White House, *The Rush Limbaugh Show*, *Glenn Beck Radio Program*, Fox News Channel, *The New York Times*, *Drudge Report*, and *Newsmax*,

Introduction

which named Haskins one of "Top 30 Republicans Under 30" in 2017. In 2016, Haskins was named to MediaDC's "30 Under 30" list of young and influential leaders on the right.

He's currently a contributing writer for *Washington Examiner*, a columnist for *Townhall*, and he writes regularly for *The Blaze*.

Haskins lives in North Carolina with his wife, Dr. Jacquelyn, and his dog Roxy.

Abbreviations

As explained by the *World English Bible* editors, "In the [scripture] footnotes, MT refers to the Greek Majority Text New Testament, which is the authoritative basis for the WEB translation. TR stands for Textus Receptus, which is the Greek Text from which the *King James Version* New Testament was translated. NU stands for the Nestle-Aland/UBS critical text of the Greek New Testament, which is used as a basis for some other Bible translations."

Now You Are Ready

Now that you have some background information about the book, why it was written, and what it contains, it's time to get in there and start a new cycle of prayer in your life. I wish you the best in whatever journey you are on and sincerely hope you find this book to be helpful in your prayer life.

God Bless.

-J

Day One

Daily Prayer

Almighty God, Who has given us this good land for our heritage; We humbly beseech Thee that we may always prove ourselves a people mindful of Thy favor and glad to do Thy will. Bless our land with honorable ministry, sound learning, and pure manners. Save us from violence, discord, and confusion, from pride and arrogance, and from every evil way. Defend our liberties, and fashion into one united people, the multitude brought hither out of many kindreds and tongues. Endow with Thy spirit of wisdom those whom in Thy name we entrust the authority of government, that there may be justice and peace at home, and that through obedience to Thy law, we may show forth Thy praise among the nations of the earth. In time of prosperity fill our hearts with

> *"In time of prosperity, fill our hearts with thankfulness, and in the day of trouble, suffer not our trust in Thee to fail; all of which we ask through Jesus Christ our Lord."*

thankfulness, and in the day of trouble, suffer not our trust in Thee to fail; all of which we ask through Jesus Christ our Lord.
-U.S. *Book of Common Prayer, 1928 edition.*[1]

Prayer of Confession

Almighty and most merciful Father; we have erred, and strayed from your ways like lost sheep. We have followed too much the devices and desires of our own hearts. We have offended against your holy laws. We have left undone those things which we ought to have done; and we have done those things which we ought not to have done; and there is no health in us. O Lord, have mercy upon us, miserable offenders. Spare those, O God, who confess their faults. Restore those who are penitent; according to your promises declared unto mankind in Christ Jesus our Lord. And grant, O most merciful Father, for his sake; that we may hereafter live a godly, righteous, and sober life, to the glory of thy holy Name. Amen.
-Revised prayer from *The Book of Common Prayer*, 1662

Daily Wisdom[3]

1 Blessed is the man that walks not in the counsel of the ungodly, nor stands in the way of sinners, nor sits in the seat of the scornful.
2 But his delight is in the law of the LORD; and in his law does he meditate day and night.
3 And he shall be like a tree planted by the rivers of water, that brings forth his fruit in his season; his leaf also shall not wither; and whatsoever he does shall prosper.
4 The ungodly are not so: but are like the chaff which the wind drives away.

Day One

5 Therefore the ungodly shall not stand in the judgment, nor sinners in the congregation of the righteous.
6 For the LORD knows the way of the righteous: but the way of the ungodly shall perish.
-Psalm 1, *The King James Bible*, 1769 edition of 1611 text

Readings from the Holy Bible[4]

The Book of Genesis, Chapters 1 & 2

1 In the beginning, God[1] created the heavens and the earth. **2** The earth was formless and empty. Darkness was on the surface of the deep and God's Spirit was hovering over the surface of the waters. **3** God said, "Let there be light," and there was light. **4** God saw the light, and saw that it was good. God divided the light from the darkness. **5** God called the light "day", and the darkness he called "night". There was evening and there was morning, the first day.
6 God said, "Let there be an expanse in the middle of the waters, and let it divide the waters from the waters." **7** God made the expanse, and divided the waters which were under the expanse from the waters which were above the expanse; and it was so. **8** God called the expanse "sky". There was evening and there was morning, a second day.
9 God said, "Let the waters under the sky be gathered together to one place, and let the dry land appear;" and it was so. **10** God called the dry land "earth", and the gathering together of the waters he called "seas". God saw that it was good. **11** God said, "Let the earth yield grass, herbs yielding seeds, and fruit trees bearing fruit after their kind, with their seeds in it, on the earth;" and it was so. **12** The earth yielded grass, herbs yielding seed after their kind, and trees bearing fruit, with their seeds in it, after their kind; and God saw that it was good.
13 There was evening and there was morning, a third day.
14 God said, "Let there be lights in the expanse of the sky to divide the day from the night; and let them be for signs to mark seasons,

---

[1]1:1 1:1 The Hebrew word rendered "God" is "אֱלֹהִים" (Elohim).

days, and years; ¹⁵ and let them be for lights in the expanse of the sky to give light on the earth;" and it was so. ¹⁶ God made the two great lights: the greater light to rule the day, and the lesser light to rule the night. He also made the stars. ¹⁷ God set them in the expanse of the sky to give light to the earth, ¹⁸ and to rule over the day and over the night, and to divide the light from the darkness. God saw that it was good. ¹⁹ There was evening and there was morning, a fourth day.

²⁰ God said, "Let the waters abound with living creatures, and let birds fly above the earth in the open expanse of the sky." ²¹ God created the large sea creatures and every living creature that moves, with which the waters swarmed, after their kind, and every winged bird after its kind. God saw that it was good. ²² God blessed them, saying, "Be fruitful, and multiply, and fill the waters in the seas, and let birds multiply on the earth." ²³ There was evening and there was morning, a fifth day.

²⁴ God said, "Let the earth produce living creatures after their kind, livestock, creeping things, and animals of the earth after their kind;" and it was so. ²⁵ God made the animals of the earth after their kind, and the livestock after their kind, and everything that creeps on the ground after its kind. God saw that it was good.

²⁶ God said, "Let's make man in our image, after our likeness. Let them have dominion over the fish of the sea, and over the birds of the sky, and over the livestock, and over all the earth, and over every creeping thing that creeps on the earth." ²⁷ God created man in his own image. In God's image he created him; male and female he created them. ²⁸ God blessed them. God said to them, "Be fruitful, multiply, fill the earth, and subdue it. Have dominion over the fish of the sea, over the birds of the sky, and over every living thing that moves on the earth." ²⁹ God said, "Behold,² I have given you every herb yielding seed, which is on the surface of all the earth, and every tree, which bears fruit yielding seed. It will be your food. ³⁰ To every animal of the earth, and to every bird of the sky, and to everything that creeps on the earth, in which there is life, I have given every green herb for food;" and it was so.

---

²1:29 1:29 "Behold", from "הִנֵּה", means look at, take notice, observe, see, or gaze at. It is often used as an interjection.

Day One

¹31 God saw everything that he had made, and, behold, it was very good. There was evening and there was morning, a sixth day.

2

²1 The heavens, the earth, and all their vast array were finished. ²2 On the seventh day God finished his work which he had done; and he rested on the seventh day from all his work which he had done. ²3 God blessed the seventh day, and made it holy, because he rested in it from all his work of creation which he had done. ²4 This is the history of the generations of the heavens and of the earth when they were created, in the day that Yahweh[3] God made the earth and the heavens. ²5 No plant of the field was yet in the earth, and no herb of the field had yet sprung up; for Yahweh God had not caused it to rain on the earth. There was not a man to till the ground, ²6 but a mist went up from the earth, and watered the whole surface of the ground. ²7 Yahweh God formed man from the dust of the ground, and breathed into his nostrils the breath of life; and man became a living soul. ²8 Yahweh God planted a garden eastward, in Eden, and there he put the man whom he had formed. ²9 Out of the ground Yahweh God made every tree to grow that is pleasant to the sight, and good for food, including the tree of life in the middle of the garden and the tree of the knowledge of good and evil. ²10 A river went out of Eden to water the garden; and from there it was parted, and became the source of four rivers. ²11 The name of the first is Pishon: it flows through the whole land of Havilah, where there is gold; ²12 and the gold of that land is good. Bdellium[4] and onyx stone are also there. ²13 The name of the second river is Gihon. It is the same river that flows through the whole land of Cush. ²14 The name of the third river is Hiddekel. This is the one which flows in front of Assyria. The fourth river is the Euphrates. ²15 Yahweh God took the man, and put him into the garden of Eden to cultivate and keep it. ²16 Yahweh God commanded the man, saying, "You may freely eat of every tree of the garden; ²17 but you shall not eat of the tree of the

---

[3] 2:4 2:4 "Yahweh" is God's proper Name, sometimes rendered "LORD" (all caps) in other translations.
[4] 2:12 2:12 or, aromatic resin

knowledge of good and evil; for in the day that you eat of it, you will surely die."

²18 Yahweh God said, "It is not good for the man to be alone. I will make him a helper comparable to[5] him."

²19 Out of the ground Yahweh God formed every animal of the field, and every bird of the sky, and brought them to the man to see what he would call them. Whatever the man called every living creature became its name. ²20 The man gave names to all livestock, and to the birds of the sky, and to every animal of the field; but for man there was not found a helper comparable to him.

²21 Yahweh God caused the man to fall into a deep sleep. As the man slept, he took one of his ribs, and closed up the flesh in its place.

²22 Yahweh God made a woman from the rib which he had taken from the man, and brought her to the man.

²23 The man said, "This is now bone of my bones, and flesh of my flesh. She will be called 'woman,' because she was taken out of Man."

²24 Therefore a man will leave his father and his mother, and will join with his wife, and they will be one flesh.

²25 The man and his wife were both naked, and they were not ashamed.

The Lord's Prayer

Our Father, who art in heaven,
Hallowed be thy name.
Thy Kingdom come.
Thy will be done on Earth, as it is in heaven.
Give us this day our daily bread.
And forgive us our trespasses,
As we forgive those that trespass against us.
And lead us not into temptation,
But deliver us from evil.
For thine is the kingdom,

---

[5]2:18 2:18 or, suitable for, or appropriate for.

Day One

The power, and the glory,
Forever.
AMEN

Day Two

Daily Prayer

To preserve our blessed land, we must look to God ... It is time to realize that we need God more than He needs us ... We also have His promise that we could take to heart with regard to our country, that "If my people, which are called by my name shall humble themselves, and pray and seek my face, and turn from their wicked ways; then I will hear from heaven and will forgive their sin, and will heal their land." Let us, young and old, join together, as did the First Continental Congress, in the first step, in humble heartfelt prayer. Let us do so for the love of God and His great goodness, in search of His guidance and the grace of repentance, in seeking His blessings, His peace, and the resting of His kind and holy hands on ourselves, our nation, our friends in the defense of freedom, and all mankind, now and always. The time has come to turn to God and reassert our trust in Him for the healing of America ... Our country is in need of and ready for a

> *"To preserve our blessed land we must look to God... It is time to realize that we need God more than He needs us..."*

spiritual renewal. Today, we utter no prayer more fervently than the ancient prayer for peace on Earth. If I had a prayer for you today, among those that have all been uttered, it is that one we're so familiar with: "The Lord bless you and keep you; the Lord make His face to shine upon you and be gracious unto you; the Lord lift up His countenance upon you and give you peace. ..." And God bless you all.
-*Ronald Reagan, 40th U.S. President, in a speech on February 6, 1986*[5]

Prayer of Confession

Almighty and most merciful Father; we have erred, and strayed from your ways like lost sheep. We have followed too much the devices and desires of our own hearts. We have offended against your holy laws. We have left undone those things which we ought to have done; and we have done those things which we ought not to have done; and there is no health in us. O Lord, have mercy upon us, miserable offenders. Spare those, O God, who confess their faults. Restore those who are penitent; according to your promises declared unto mankind in Christ Jesus our Lord. And grant, O most merciful Father, for his sake; that we may hereafter live a godly, righteous, and sober life, to the glory of thy holy Name. Amen.
-Revised prayer from *The Book of Common Prayer*, 1662[6]

Day Two

Daily Wisdom

1 My son, if thou will receive my words, and hide my commandments with thee;
2 So that thou incline thine ear unto wisdom, and apply thine heart to understanding;
3 Yea, if thou cry after knowledge, and lift up thy voice for understanding;
4 If thou seek her as silver, and search for her as for hid treasures;
5 Then shalt thou understand the fear of the LORD, and find the knowledge of God.
6 For the LORD giveth wisdom: out of his mouth cometh knowledge and understanding.
7 He layeth up sound wisdom for the righteous: he is a buckler to them that walk uprightly.
8 He keeps the paths of judgment, and preserves the way of his saints.
-Proverbs 2:1-8, *The King James Bible*, 1769 edition of 1611 text

Readings from the Holy Bible

The Book of Genesis, Chapter 3

3

³1 Now the serpent was more subtle than any animal of the field which Yahweh God had made. He said to the woman, "Has God really said, 'You shall not eat of any tree of the garden'?"
³2 The woman said to the serpent, "We may eat fruit from the trees of the garden, **³3** but not the fruit of the tree which is in the middle of the garden. God has said, 'You shall not eat of it. You shall not touch it, lest you die.'"
³4 The serpent said to the woman, "You won't really die, **³5** for God knows that in the day you eat it, your eyes will be opened, and you will be like God, knowing good and evil."

The American Book of Prayer

³6 When the woman saw that the tree was good for food, and that it was a delight to the eyes, and that the tree was to be desired to make one wise, she took some of its fruit, and ate. Then she gave some to her husband with her, and he ate it, too. ³7 Their eyes were opened, and they both knew that they were naked. They sewed fig leaves together, and made coverings for themselves. ³8 They heard Yahweh God's voice walking in the garden in the cool of the day, and the man and his wife hid themselves from the presence of Yahweh God among the trees of the garden.

³9 Yahweh God called to the man, and said to him, "Where are you?"
³10 The man said, "I heard your voice in the garden, and I was afraid, because I was naked; so I hid myself."
³11 God said, "Who told you that you were naked? Have you eaten from the tree that I commanded you not to eat from?"
³12 The man said, "The woman whom you gave to be with me, she gave me fruit from the tree, and I ate it."
³13 Yahweh God said to the woman, "What have you done?"
The woman said, "The serpent deceived me, and I ate."
³14 Yahweh God said to the serpent,
"Because you have done this,
you are cursed above all livestock,
and above every animal of the field.
You shall go on your belly
and you shall eat dust all the days of your life.
³15 I will put hostility between you and the woman,
and between your offspring and her offspring.
He will bruise your head,
and you will bruise his heel."
³16 To the woman he said,
"I will greatly multiply your pain in childbirth.
You will bear children in pain.
Your desire will be for your husband,
and he will rule over you."
³17 To Adam he said,
"Because you have listened to your wife's voice,
and ate from the tree,
about which I commanded you, saying, 'You shall not eat of it,'
the ground is cursed for your sake.

Day Two

You will eat from it with much labor all the days of your life.
³18 It will yield thorns and thistles to you;
and you will eat the herb of the field.
³19 You will eat bread by the sweat of your face until you return to the ground, for you were taken out of it.
For you are dust,
and you shall return to dust."
³20 The man called his wife Eve because she would be the mother of all the living.
³21 Yahweh God made garments of animal skins for Adam and for his wife, and clothed them.
³22 Yahweh God said, "Behold, the man has become like one of us, knowing good and evil. Now, lest he reach out his hand, and also take of the tree of life, and eat, and live forever—"
³23 Therefore Yahweh God sent him out from the garden of Eden, to till the ground from which he was taken.
³24 So he drove out the man; and he placed cherubim[6] at the east of the garden of Eden, and a flaming sword which turned every way, to guard the way to the tree of life.

The Lord's Prayer

Our Father, who art in heaven,
Hallowed be thy name.
Thy Kingdom come.
Thy will be done on Earth, as it is in heaven.
Give us this day our daily bread.
And forgive us our trespasses,
As we forgive those that trespass against us.
And lead us not into temptation,
But deliver us from evil.
For thine is the kingdom,

---

[6]3:24 3:24 cherubim are powerful angelic creatures, messengers of God with wings. See Ezekiel 10.

The American Book of Prayer

The power, and the glory,
For ever and ever.
AMEN

Day Three

Daily Prayer

Whereas the Congress of the United States, by a joint resolution of the two Houses, have signified a request that a day may be recommended to be observed by the people of the United States with religious solemnity as a day of public humiliation and prayer; and Whereas such a recommendation will enable the several religious denominations and societies so disposed to offer at one and the same time their common vows and adorations to Almighty God on the solemn occasion produced by the war in which He has been pleased to permit the injustice of a foreign power to involve these United States:

> "I do therefore recommend the third Thursday in August next as a convenient day to be set apart for the devout purposes of rendering the Sovereign of the Universe and the Benefactor of Mankind the public homage due to His holy attributes ..."

I do therefore recommend the third Thursday in August next as a convenient day to be set apart for the devout purposes of rendering the Sovereign of the Universe and the Benefactor of Mankind the public homage due to His holy attributes; of acknowledging the transgressions which

might justly provoke the manifestations of His divine displeasure; of seeking His merciful forgiveness and His assistance in the great duties of repentance and amendment, and especially of offering fervent supplications that in the present season of calamity and war He would take the American people under His peculiar care and protection; that He would guide their public councils, animate their patriotism, and bestow His blessing on their arms; that He would inspire all nations with a love of justice and of concord and with a reverence for the unerring precept of our holy religion to do to others as they would require that others should do to them; and, finally, that, turning the hearts of our enemies from the violence and injustice which sway their councils against us, He would hasten a restoration of the blessings of peace.
-*Proclamation of Day of Fasting and Prayer, delivered on July 9, 1812, by President James Madison.*

Prayer of Confession

Almighty and most merciful Father; we have erred, and strayed from your ways like lost sheep. We have followed too much the devices and desires of our own hearts. We have offended against your holy laws. We have left undone those things which we ought to have done; and we have done those things which we ought not to have done; and there is no health in us. O Lord, have mercy upon us, miserable offenders. Spare those, O God, who confess their faults. Restore those who are penitent; according to your promises declared unto mankind in Christ Jesus our Lord. And grant, O most merciful Father, for his sake; that we may hereafter live a godly, righteous, and sober life, to the glory of thy holy Name. Amen.
-Revised prayer from *The Book of Common Prayer, 1662*[7]

Day Three

Daily Wisdom

1 A good name is rather to be chosen than great riches, and loving favour rather than silver and gold.
2 The rich and poor meet together: the LORD is the maker of them all.
3 A prudent man foreseeth the evil, and hideth himself: but the simple pass on, and are punished.
4 By humility and the fear of the LORD are riches, and honor, and life.
5 Thorns and snares are in the way of the froward: he that doth keep his soul shall be far from them.
6 Train up a child in the way he should go: and when he is old, he will not depart from it.
7 The rich ruleth over the poor, and the borrower is servant to the lender.
8 He that soweth iniquity shall reap vanity: and the rod of his anger shall fail.
9 He that hath a bountiful eye shall be blessed; for he giveth of his bread to the poor.
-Proverbs 22:1-9, *The King James Bible*, 1769 edition of 1611 text

Readings from the Holy Bible

The Book of Genesis, Chapters 6:9-9:29

⁶**9** This is the history of the generations of Noah: Noah was a righteous man, blameless among the people of his time. Noah walked with God. ⁶**10** Noah became the father of three sons: Shem, Ham, and Japheth. ⁶**11** The earth was corrupt before God, and the earth was filled with violence. ⁶**12** God saw the earth, and saw that it was corrupt, for all flesh had corrupted their way on the earth.
⁶**13** God said to Noah, "I will bring an end to all flesh, for the earth is filled with violence through them. Behold, I will destroy them and the

earth. ⁶14 Make a ship of gopher wood. You shall make rooms in the ship, and shall seal it inside and outside with pitch. ⁶15 This is how you shall make it. The length of the ship shall be three hundred cubits,⁷ its width fifty cubits, and its height thirty cubits. ⁶16 You shall make a roof in the ship, and you shall finish it to a cubit upward. You shall set the door of the ship in its side. You shall make it with lower, second, and third levels. ⁶17 I, even I, will bring the flood of waters on this earth, to destroy all flesh having the breath of life from under the sky. Everything that is in the earth will die. ⁶18 But I will establish my covenant with you. You shall come into the ship, you, your sons, your wife, and your sons' wives with you. ⁶19 Of every living thing of all flesh, you shall bring two of every sort into the ship, to keep them alive with you. They shall be male and female. ⁶20 Of the birds after their kind, of the livestock after their kind, of every creeping thing of the ground after its kind, two of every sort will come to you, to keep them alive. ⁶21 Take with you some of all food that is eaten, and gather it to yourself; and it will be for food for you, and for them." ⁶22 Thus Noah did. He did all that God commanded him. ⁶

7

⁷1 Yahweh said to Noah, "Come with all of your household into the ship, for I have seen your righteousness before me in this generation. ⁷2 You shall take seven pairs of every clean animal with you, the male and his female. Of the animals that are not clean, take two, the male and his female. ⁷3 Also of the birds of the sky, seven and seven, male and female, to keep seed alive on the surface of all the earth. ⁷4 In seven days, I will cause it to rain on the earth for forty days and forty nights. I will destroy every living thing that I have made from the surface of the ground."
⁷5 Noah did everything that Yahweh commanded him.
⁷6 Noah was six hundred years old when the flood of waters came on the earth. ⁷7 Noah went into the ship with his sons, his wife, and his sons' wives, because of the floodwaters. ⁷8 Clean animals, unclean animals, birds, and everything that creeps on the ground ⁷9 went by pairs to Noah into the ship, male and female, as God commanded

---

⁷6:15 6:15 A cubit is the length from the tip of the middle finger to the elbow on a man's arm, or about 18 inches or 46 centimeters.

Day Three

Noah. ⁷10 After the seven days, the floodwaters came on the earth. ⁷11 In the six hundredth year of Noah's life, in the second month, on the seventeenth day of the month, on that day all the fountains of the great deep burst open, and the sky's windows opened. ⁷12 It rained on the earth forty days and forty nights.

⁷13 In the same day Noah, and Shem, Ham, and Japheth—the sons of Noah—and Noah's wife and the three wives of his sons with them, entered into the ship— ⁷14 they, and every animal after its kind, all the livestock after their kind, every creeping thing that creeps on the earth after its kind, and every bird after its kind, every bird of every sort. ⁷15 Pairs from all flesh with the breath of life in them went into the ship to Noah. ⁷16 Those who went in, went in male and female of all flesh, as God commanded him; then Yahweh shut him in. ⁷17 The flood was forty days on the earth. The waters increased, and lifted up the ship, and it was lifted up above the earth. ⁷18 The waters rose, and increased greatly on the earth; and the ship floated on the surface of the waters. ⁷19 The waters rose very high on the earth. All the high mountains that were under the whole sky were covered. ⁷20 The waters rose fifteen cubits[8] higher, and the mountains were covered. ⁷21 All flesh died that moved on the earth, including birds, livestock, animals, every creeping thing that creeps on the earth, and every man. ⁷22 All on the dry land, in whose nostrils was the breath of the spirit of life, died. ⁷23 Every living thing was destroyed that was on the surface of the ground, including man, livestock, creeping things, and birds of the sky. They were destroyed from the earth. Only Noah was left, and those who were with him in the ship. ⁷24 The waters flooded the earth one hundred fifty days. ⁷

8

⁸1 God remembered Noah, all the animals, and all the livestock that were with him in the ship; and God made a wind to pass over the earth. The waters subsided. ⁸2 The deep's fountains and the sky's windows were also stopped, and the rain from the sky was restrained. ⁸3 The waters continually receded from the earth. After the end of one hundred fifty days the waters receded. ⁸4 The ship rested in the

---

[8]7:20 7:20 A cubit is the length from the tip of the middle finger to the elbow on a man's arm, or about 18 inches or 46 centimeters.

seventh month, on the seventeenth day of the month, on Ararat's mountains. ⁸5 The waters receded continually until the tenth month. In the tenth month, on the first day of the month, the tops of the mountains were visible.

⁸6 At the end of forty days, Noah opened the window of the ship which he had made, ⁸7 and he sent out a raven. It went back and forth, until the waters were dried up from the earth. ⁸8 He himself sent out a dove to see if the waters were abated from the surface of the ground, ⁸9 but the dove found no place to rest her foot, and she returned into the ship to him, for the waters were on the surface of the whole earth. He put out his hand, and took her, and brought her to him into the ship. ⁸10 He waited yet another seven days; and again he sent the dove out of the ship. ⁸11 The dove came back to him at evening and, behold, in her mouth was a freshly plucked olive leaf. So Noah knew that the waters were abated from the earth. ⁸12 He waited yet another seven days, and sent out the dove; and she didn't return to him any more.

⁸13 In the six hundred first year, in the first month, the first day of the month, the waters were dried up from the earth. Noah removed the covering of the ship, and looked. He saw that the surface of the ground was dry. ⁸14 In the second month, on the twenty-seventh day of the month, the earth was dry.

⁸15 God spoke to Noah, saying, ⁸16 "Go out of the ship, you, your wife, your sons, and your sons' wives with you. ⁸17 Bring out with you every living thing that is with you of all flesh, including birds, livestock, and every creeping thing that creeps on the earth, that they may breed abundantly in the earth, and be fruitful, and multiply on the earth."

⁸18 Noah went out, with his sons, his wife, and his sons' wives with him. ⁸19 Every animal, every creeping thing, and every bird, whatever moves on the earth, after their families, went out of the ship.

⁸20 Noah built an altar to Yahweh, and took of every clean animal, and of every clean bird, and offered burnt offerings on the altar.

⁸21 Yahweh smelled the pleasant aroma. Yahweh said in his heart, "I will not again curse the ground any more for man's sake because the imagination of man's heart is evil from his youth. I will never again strike every living thing, as I have done. ⁸22 While the earth remains,

Day Three

seed time and harvest, and cold and heat, and summer and winter, and day and night will not cease." 8

9

⁹1 God blessed Noah and his sons, and said to them, "Be fruitful, multiply, and replenish the earth. ⁹2 The fear of you and the dread of you will be on every animal of the earth, and on every bird of the sky. Everything that moves along the ground, and all the fish of the sea, are delivered into your hand. ⁹3 Every moving thing that lives will be food for you. As I gave you the green herb, I have given everything to you. ⁹4 But flesh with its life, that is, its blood, you shall not eat. ⁹5 I will surely require accounting for your life's blood. At the hand of every animal I will require it. At the hand of man, even at the hand of every man's brother, I will require the life of man. ⁹6 Whoever sheds man's blood, his blood will be shed by man, for God made man in his own image. ⁹7 Be fruitful and multiply. Increase abundantly in the earth, and multiply in it."

⁹8 God spoke to Noah and to his sons with him, saying, ⁹9 "As for me, behold, I establish my covenant with you, and with your offspring after you, ⁹10 and with every living creature that is with you: the birds, the livestock, and every animal of the earth with you, of all that go out of the ship, even every animal of the earth. ⁹11 I will establish my covenant with you: All flesh will not be cut off any more by the waters of the flood. There will never again be a flood to destroy the earth." ⁹12 God said, "This is the token of the covenant which I make between me and you and every living creature that is with you, for perpetual generations: ⁹13 I set my rainbow in the cloud, and it will be a sign of a covenant between me and the earth. ⁹14 When I bring a cloud over the earth, that the rainbow will be seen in the cloud, ⁹15 I will remember my covenant, which is between me and you and every living creature of all flesh, and the waters will no more become a flood to destroy all flesh. ⁹16 The rainbow will be in the cloud. I will look at it, that I may remember the everlasting covenant between God and every living creature of all flesh that is on the earth." ⁹17 God said to Noah, "This is the token of the covenant which I have established between me and all flesh that is on the earth."

⁹18 The sons of Noah who went out from the ship were Shem, Ham, and Japheth. Ham is the father of Canaan. ⁹19 These three were the sons of Noah, and from these the whole earth was populated.
⁹20 Noah began to be a farmer, and planted a vineyard. ⁹21 He drank of the wine and got drunk. He was uncovered within his tent.
⁹22 Ham, the father of Canaan, saw the nakedness of his father, and told his two brothers outside.
⁹23 Shem and Japheth took a garment, and laid it on both their shoulders, went in backwards, and covered the nakedness of their father. Their faces were backwards, and they didn't see their father's nakedness. ⁹24 Noah awoke from his wine, and knew what his youngest son had done to him.
⁹25 He said,
"Canaan is cursed.
He will be a servant of servants to his brothers."
⁹26 He said,
"Blessed be Yahweh, the God of Shem.
Let Canaan be his servant.
⁹27 May God enlarge Japheth.
Let him dwell in the tents of Shem.
Let Canaan be his servant."
⁹28 Noah lived three hundred fifty years after the flood. ⁹29 All the days of Noah were nine hundred fifty years, and then he died.

The Lord's Prayer

Our Father, who art in heaven,
Hallowed be thy name.
Thy Kingdom come.
Thy will be done on Earth, as it is in heaven.
Give us this day our daily bread.
And forgive us our trespasses,
As we forgive those that trespass against us.
And lead us not into temptation,

Day Three

But deliver us from evil.
For thine is the kingdom,
The power, and the glory,
For ever and ever.
AMEN

Day Four

Calvin Coolidge on Christianity

I hope it is true [that Howard University was the outgrowth of the inspiration of a prayer meeting], and I shall choose to believe it, for it makes of this scene and this occasion a new testimony that prayers are answered. Here has been established a great university, a sort of educational laboratory for the production of intellectual and spiritual leadership among a people. ...

The accomplishments of the colored people in the United States, in the brief historic period since they were brought here from the restrictions of their native continent, cannot but make us realize that there is something essential in our civilization which gives it a special power. I think we shall be able to agree that this particular element is the Christian religion, whose influence always and everywhere has been a force

> *"I think we shall be able to agree that this particular element is the Christian religion, whose influence always and everywhere has been a force for the illumination and advancement of the peoples who have come under its sway."*

for the illumination and advancement of the peoples who have come under its sway.
-*Address given to attendees at Howard University by President Calvin Coolidge, June 6, 1924.*

Prayer of Confession

Almighty and most merciful Father; we have erred, and strayed from your ways like lost sheep. We have followed too much the devices and desires of our own hearts. We have offended against your holy laws. We have left undone those things which we ought to have done; and we have done those things which we ought not to have done; and there is no health in us. O Lord, have mercy upon us, miserable offenders. Spare those, O God, who confess their faults. Restore those who are penitent; according to your promises declared unto mankind in Christ Jesus our Lord. And grant, O most merciful Father, for his sake; that we may hereafter live a godly, righteous, and sober life, to the glory of thy holy Name. Amen.
-Revised prayer from *The Book of Common Prayer*, 1662[8]

Daily Wisdom

9 If a wise man goes to court with a foolish man,
the fool rages or scoffs, and there is no peace.
10 The bloodthirsty hate a man of integrity;
and they seek the life of the upright.
11 A fool vents all of his anger,
but a wise man brings himself under control.
12 If a ruler listens to lies,
all of his officials are wicked.
13 The poor man and the oppressor have this in common:
Yahweh gives sight to the eyes of both.
14 The king who fairly judges the poor,

Day Four

his throne shall be established forever.
15 The rod of correction gives wisdom,
but a child left to himself causes shame to his mother.
16 When the wicked increase, sin increases;
but the righteous will see their downfall.
17 Correct your son, and he will give you peace;
yes, he will bring delight to your soul.
18 Where there is no revelation, the people cast off restraint;
but one who keeps the law is blessed.
19 A servant can't be corrected by words.
Though he understands, yet he will not respond.
20 Do you see a man who is hasty in his words?
There is more hope for a fool than for him.
21 He who pampers his servant from youth
will have him become a son in the end.
22 An angry man stirs up strife,
and a wrathful man abounds in sin.
23 A man's pride brings him low,
but one of lowly spirit gains honor.
24 Whoever is an accomplice of a thief is an enemy of his own soul.
He takes an oath, but dares not testify.
25 The fear of man proves to be a snare,
but whoever puts his trust in Yahweh is kept safe.
26 Many seek the ruler's favor,
but a man's justice comes from Yahweh.
27 A dishonest man detests the righteous, [29]
and the upright in their ways detest the wicked.
-Proverbs 29:9-27, *World English Bible*

The American Book of Prayer

Readings from the Holy Bible

The Book of Genesis, Abraham's Role in God's Plan, Chapters 11:27-14:24

11:27 Now this is the history of the generations of Terah. Terah became the father of Abram, Nahor, and Haran. Haran became the father of Lot. **11:28** Haran died in the land of his birth, in Ur of the Chaldees, while his father Terah was still alive. **11:29** Abram and Nahor married wives. The name of Abram's wife was Sarai, and the name of Nahor's wife was Milcah, the daughter of Haran, who was also the father of Iscah. **11:30** Sarai was barren. She had no child. **11:31** Terah took Abram his son, Lot the son of Haran, his son's son, and Sarai his daughter-in-law, his son Abram's wife. They went from Ur of the Chaldees, to go into the land of Canaan. They came to Haran and lived there. **11:32** The days of Terah were two hundred five years. Terah died in Haran.

12

12:1 Now Yahweh said to Abram, "Leave your country, and your relatives, and your father's house, and go to the land that I will show you. **12:2** I will make of you a great nation. I will bless you and make your name great. You will be a blessing. **12:3** I will bless those who bless you, and I will curse him who treats you with contempt. All the families of the earth will be blessed through you."
12:4 So Abram went, as Yahweh had told him. Lot went with him. Abram was seventy-five years old when he departed from Haran.
12:5 Abram took Sarai his wife, Lot his brother's son, all their possessions that they had gathered, and the people whom they had acquired in Haran, and they went to go into the land of Canaan. They entered into the land of Canaan. **12:6** Abram passed through the land to the place of Shechem, to the oak of Moreh. At that time, Canaanites were in the land.
12:7 Yahweh appeared to Abram and said, "I will give this land to your offspring."
He built an altar there to Yahweh, who had appeared to him. **12:8** He left from there to go to the mountain on the east of Bethel and

Day Four

pitched his tent, having Bethel on the west, and Ai on the east. There he built an altar to Yahweh and called on Yahweh's name. ¹²9 Abram traveled, still going on toward the South.

¹²10 There was a famine in the land. Abram went down into Egypt to live as a foreigner there, for the famine was severe in the land.

¹²11 When he had come near to enter Egypt, he said to Sarai his wife, "See now, I know that you are a beautiful woman to look at. ¹²12 It will happen, when the Egyptians see you, that they will say, 'This is his wife.' They will kill me, but they will save you alive. ¹²13 Please say that you are my sister, that it may be well with me for your sake, and that my soul may live because of you."

¹²14 When Abram had come into Egypt, Egyptians saw that the woman was very beautiful. ¹²15 The princes of Pharaoh saw her, and praised her to Pharaoh; and the woman was taken into Pharaoh's house. ¹²16 He dealt well with Abram for her sake. He had sheep, cattle, male donkeys, male servants, female servants, female donkeys, and camels. ¹²17 Yahweh afflicted Pharaoh and his house with great plagues because of Sarai, Abram's wife. ¹²18 Pharaoh called Abram and said, "What is this that you have done to me? Why didn't you tell me that she was your wife? ¹²19 Why did you say, 'She is my sister,' so that I took her to be my wife? Now therefore, see your wife, take her, and go your way."

¹²20 Pharaoh commanded men concerning him, and they escorted him away with his wife and all that he had.

13

¹³1 Abram went up out of Egypt—he, his wife, all that he had, and Lot with him—into the South. ¹³2 Abram was very rich in livestock, in silver, and in gold. ¹³3 He went on his journeys from the South as far as Bethel, to the place where his tent had been at the beginning, between Bethel and Ai, ¹³4 to the place of the altar, which he had made there at the first. There Abram called on Yahweh's name.

¹³5 Lot also, who went with Abram, had flocks, herds, and tents. ¹³6 The land was not able to bear them, that they might live together; for their possessions were so great that they couldn't live together. ¹³7 There was strife between the herdsmen of Abram's livestock and the herdsmen of Lot's livestock. The Canaanites and the Perizzites

lived in the land at that time. ¹³8 Abram said to Lot, "Please, let there be no strife between you and me, and between your herdsmen and my herdsmen; for we are relatives. ¹³9 Isn't the whole land before you? Please separate yourself from me. If you go to the left hand, then I will go to the right. Or if you go to the right hand, then I will go to the left."

¹³10 Lot lifted up his eyes, and saw all the plain of the Jordan, that it was well-watered everywhere, before Yahweh destroyed Sodom and Gomorrah, like the garden of Yahweh, like the land of Egypt, as you go to Zoar. ¹³11 So Lot chose the Plain of the Jordan for himself. Lot traveled east, and they separated themselves from one other.

¹³12 Abram lived in the land of Canaan, and Lot lived in the cities of the plain, and moved his tent as far as Sodom. ¹³13 Now the men of Sodom were exceedingly wicked and sinners against Yahweh.

¹³14 Yahweh said to Abram, after Lot was separated from him, "Now, lift up your eyes, and look from the place where you are, northward and southward and eastward and westward, ¹³15 for I will give all the land which you see to you and to your offspring forever. ¹³16 I will make your offspring as the dust of the earth, so that if a man can count the dust of the earth, then your offspring may also be counted. ¹³17 Arise, walk through the land in its length and in its width; for I will give it to you."

¹³18 Abram moved his tent, and came and lived by the oaks of Mamre, which are in Hebron, and built an altar there to Yahweh.

14

¹⁴1 In the days of Amraphel, king of Shinar; Arioch, king of Ellasar; Chedorlaomer, king of Elam; and Tidal, king of Goiim, ¹⁴2 they made war with Bera, king of Sodom; Birsha, king of Gomorrah; Shinab, king of Admah; Shemeber, king of Zeboiim; and the king of Bela (also called Zoar). ¹⁴3 All these joined together in the valley of Siddim (also called the Salt Sea). ¹⁴4 They served Chedorlaomer for twelve years, and in the thirteenth year they rebelled. ¹⁴5 In the fourteenth year Chedorlaomer came, and the kings who were with him, and struck the Rephaim in Ashteroth Karnaim, the Zuzim in Ham, the Emim in Shaveh Kiriathaim, ¹⁴6 and the Horites in their Mount Seir, to El Paran, which is by the wilderness. ¹⁴7 They returned, and came to En

Day Four

Mishpat (also called Kadesh), and struck all the country of the Amalekites, and also the Amorites, that lived in Hazazon Tamar. ¹⁴8 The king of Sodom, and the king of Gomorrah, the king of Admah, the king of Zeboiim, and the king of Bela (also called Zoar) went out; and they set the battle in array against them in the valley of Siddim ¹⁴9 against Chedorlaomer king of Elam, Tidal king of Goiim, Amraphel king of Shinar, and Arioch king of Ellasar; four kings against the five. ¹⁴10 Now the valley of Siddim was full of tar pits; and the kings of Sodom and Gomorrah fled, and some fell there. Those who remained fled to the hills. ¹⁴11 They took all the goods of Sodom and Gomorrah, and all their food, and went their way. ¹⁴12 They took Lot, Abram's brother's son, who lived in Sodom, and his goods, and departed.

¹⁴13 One who had escaped came and told Abram, the Hebrew. At that time, he lived by the oaks of Mamre, the Amorite, brother of Eshcol and brother of Aner. They were allies of Abram. ¹⁴14 When Abram heard that his relative was taken captive, he led out his three hundred eighteen trained men, born in his house, and pursued as far as Dan. ¹⁴15 He divided himself against them by night, he and his servants, and struck them, and pursued them to Hobah, which is on the left hand of Damascus. ¹⁴16 He brought back all the goods, and also brought back his relative Lot and his goods, and the women also, and the other people.

¹⁴17 The king of Sodom went out to meet him after his return from the slaughter of Chedorlaomer and the kings who were with him, at the valley of Shaveh (that is, the King's Valley). ¹⁴18 Melchizedek king of Salem brought out bread and wine. He was priest of God Most High. ¹⁴19 He blessed him, and said, "Blessed be Abram of God Most High, possessor of heaven and earth. ¹⁴20 Blessed be God Most High, who has delivered your enemies into your hand."

Abram gave him a tenth of all.

¹⁴21 The king of Sodom said to Abram, "Give me the people, and take the goods for yourself."

¹⁴22 Abram said to the king of Sodom, "I have lifted up my hand to Yahweh, God Most High, possessor of heaven and earth, ¹⁴23 that I will not take a thread nor a sandal strap nor anything that is yours, lest you should say, 'I have made Abram rich.' ¹⁴24 I will accept nothing from you except that which the young men have eaten, and the

portion of the men who went with me: Aner, Eshcol, and Mamre. Let them take their portion."

The Lord's Prayer

Our Father, who art in heaven,
Hallowed be thy name.
Thy Kingdom come.
Thy will be done on Earth, as it is in heaven.
Give us this day our daily bread.
And forgive us our trespasses,
As we forgive those that trespass against us.
And lead us not into temptation,
But deliver us from evil.
For thine is the kingdom,
The power, and the glory,
For ever and ever.
AMEN

Day Five

George Whitefield on the Gospel

Whoever reads the gospel with a single eye, and sincere intentions, will find, that our blessed Lord took all opportunities of reminding his disciples that His Kingdom was not of this world; that His doctrine was a doctrine of the Cross; and that their professing themselves to be His followers, would call them to a constant state of voluntary suffering and self-denial.

> "... His doctrine was a doctrine of the Cross; and that their professing themselves to be His followers, would call them to a constant state of voluntary suffering and self-denial."

-George Whitefield, one of the most prominent pastors in American history, in the sermon "The Extent and Reasonableness of Self-Denial."

Prayer of Confession

Almighty and most merciful Father; we have erred, and strayed from your ways like lost sheep. We have followed

too much the devices and desires of our own hearts. We have offended against your holy laws. We have left undone those things which we ought to have done; and we have done those things which we ought not to have done; and there is no health in us. O Lord, have mercy upon us, miserable offenders. Spare those, O God, who confess their faults. Restore those who are penitent; according to your promises declared unto mankind in Christ Jesus our Lord. And grant, O most merciful Father, for his sake; that we may hereafter live a godly, righteous, and sober life, to the glory of thy holy Name. Amen.
-Revised prayer from *The Book of Common Prayer*, 1662[9]

Daily Wisdom

1 Be not thou envious against evil men, neither desire to be with them.
2 For their heart studieth destruction, and their lips talk of mischief.
3 Through wisdom is an house builded; and by understanding it is established:
4 And by knowledge shall the chambers be filled with all precious and pleasant riches.
5 A wise man is strong; yea, a man of knowledge increaseth strength.
6 For by wise counsel thou shalt make thy war: and in multitude of counsellers there is safety.
7 Wisdom is too high for a fool: he openeth not his mouth in the gate.
8 He that deviseth to do evil shall be called a mischievous person.
9 The thought of foolishness is sin: and the scorner is an abomination to men.
10 If thou faint in the day of adversity, thy strength is small.
11 If thou forbear to deliver them that are drawn unto death, and those that are ready to be slain;

Day Five

12 If thou sayest, Behold, we knew it not; doth not he that pondereth the heart consider it? and he that keepeth thy soul, doth not he know it? and shall not he render to every man according to his works?
13 My son, eat thou honey, because it is good; and the honeycomb, which is sweet to thy taste:
14 So shall the knowledge of wisdom be unto thy soul: when thou hast found it, then there shall be a reward, and thy expectation shall not be cut off.
15 Lay not wait, O wicked man, against the dwelling of the righteous; spoil not his resting place:
16 For a just man falleth seven times, and riseth up again: but the wicked shall fall into mischief.
17 Rejoice not when thine enemy falleth, and let not thine heart be glad when he stumbleth:
18 Lest the LORD see it, and it displease him, and he turn away his wrath from him.
-Proverbs 24:1-18, *The King James Bible,* 1769 edition of 1611 text

Readings from the Holy Bible

The Book of Genesis, God's Promise to Abraham, Chapters 15:1-17:27

15

15:1 After these things Yahweh's word came to Abram in a vision, saying, "Don't be afraid, Abram. I am your shield, your exceedingly great reward."
15:2 Abram said, "Lord[9] Yahweh, what will you give me, since I go childless, and he who will inherit my estate is Eliezer of Damascus?"
15:3 Abram said, "Behold, you have given no children to me: and, behold, one born in my house is my heir."

---

[9]15:2 15:2 The word translated "Lord" is "Adonai".

The American Book of Prayer

¹⁵4 Behold, Yahweh's word came to him, saying, "This man will not be your heir, but he who will come out of your own body will be your heir." ¹⁵5 Yahweh brought him outside, and said, "Look now toward the sky, and count the stars, if you are able to count them." He said to Abram, "So your offspring will be." ¹⁵6 He believed in Yahweh, who credited it to him for righteousness. ¹⁵7 He said to Abram, "I am Yahweh who brought you out of Ur of the Chaldees, to give you this land to inherit it."

¹⁵8 He said, "Lord Yahweh, how will I know that I will inherit it?"

¹⁵9 He said to him, "Bring me a heifer three years old, a female goat three years old, a ram three years old, a turtledove, and a young pigeon." ¹⁵10 He brought him all these, and divided them in the middle, and laid each half opposite the other; but he didn't divide the birds. ¹⁵11 The birds of prey came down on the carcasses, and Abram drove them away.

¹⁵12 When the sun was going down, a deep sleep fell on Abram. Now terror and great darkness fell on him. ¹⁵13 He said to Abram, "Know for sure that your offspring will live as foreigners in a land that is not theirs, and will serve them. They will afflict them four hundred years. ¹⁵14 I will also judge that nation, whom they will serve. Afterward they will come out with great wealth; ¹⁵15 but you will go to your fathers in peace. You will be buried at a good old age. ¹⁵16 In the fourth generation they will come here again, for the iniquity of the Amorite is not yet full." ¹⁵17 It came to pass that, when the sun went down, and it was dark, behold, a smoking furnace and a flaming torch passed between these pieces. ¹⁵18 In that day Yahweh made a covenant with Abram, saying, "I have given this land to your offspring, from the river of Egypt to the great river, the river Euphrates: ¹⁵19 the land of the Kenites, the Kenizzites, the Kadmonites, ¹⁵20 the Hittites, the Perizzites, the Rephaim, ¹⁵21 the Amorites, the Canaanites, the Girgashites, and the Jebusites." ¹⁵

16

¹⁶1 Now Sarai, Abram's wife, bore him no children. She had a servant, an Egyptian, whose name was Hagar. ¹⁶2 Sarai said to Abram, "See now, Yahweh has restrained me from bearing. Please go in to my servant. It may be that I will obtain children by her." Abram listened

Day Five

to the voice of Sarai. ¹⁶3 Sarai, Abram's wife, took Hagar the Egyptian, her servant, after Abram had lived ten years in the land of Canaan, and gave her to Abram her husband to be his wife. ¹⁶4 He went in to Hagar, and she conceived. When she saw that she had conceived, her mistress was despised in her eyes. ¹⁶5 Sarai said to Abram, "This wrong is your fault. I gave my servant into your bosom, and when she saw that she had conceived, she despised me. May Yahweh judge between me and you."

¹⁶6 But Abram said to Sarai, "Behold, your maid is in your hand. Do to her whatever is good in your eyes." Sarai dealt harshly with her, and she fled from her face.

¹⁶7 Yahweh's angel found her by a fountain of water in the wilderness, by the fountain on the way to Shur. ¹⁶8 He said, "Hagar, Sarai's servant, where did you come from? Where are you going?"

She said, "I am fleeing from the face of my mistress Sarai."

¹⁶9 Yahweh's angel said to her, "Return to your mistress, and submit yourself under her hands." ¹⁶10 Yahweh's angel said to her, "I will greatly multiply your offspring, that they will not be counted for multitude." ¹⁶11 Yahweh's angel said to her, "Behold, you are with child, and will bear a son. You shall call his name Ishmael, because Yahweh has heard your affliction. ¹⁶12 He will be like a wild donkey among men. His hand will be against every man, and every man's hand against him. He will live opposed to all of his brothers."

¹⁶13 She called the name of Yahweh who spoke to her, "You are a God who sees," for she said, "Have I even stayed alive after seeing him?"

¹⁶14 Therefore the well was called Beer Lahai Roi.[10] Behold, it is between Kadesh and Bered.

¹⁶15 Hagar bore a son for Abram. Abram called the name of his son, whom Hagar bore, Ishmael. ¹⁶16 Abram was eighty-six years old when Hagar bore Ishmael to Abram. ¹⁶

17

¹⁷1 When Abram was ninety-nine years old, Yahweh appeared to Abram and said to him, "I am God Almighty. Walk before me and be

---

[10] 16:14 16:14 Beer Lahai Roi means "well of the one who lives and sees me".

blameless. ¹⁷2 I will make my covenant between me and you, and will multiply you exceedingly."
¹⁷3 Abram fell on his face. God talked with him, saying, ¹⁷4 "As for me, behold, my covenant is with you. You will be the father of a multitude of nations. ¹⁷5 Your name will no more be called Abram, but your name will be Abraham; for I have made you the father of a multitude of nations. ¹⁷6 I will make you exceedingly fruitful, and I will make nations of you. Kings will come out of you. ¹⁷7 I will establish my covenant between me and you and your offspring after you throughout their generations for an everlasting covenant, to be a God to you and to your offspring after you. ¹⁷8 I will give to you, and to your offspring after you, the land where you are traveling, all the land of Canaan, for an everlasting possession. I will be their God."
¹⁷9 God said to Abraham, "As for you, you will keep my covenant, you and your offspring after you throughout their generations. ¹⁷10 This is my covenant, which you shall keep, between me and you and your offspring after you. Every male among you shall be circumcised.
¹⁷11 You shall be circumcised in the flesh of your foreskin. It will be a token of the covenant between me and you. ¹⁷12 He who is eight days old will be circumcised among you, every male throughout your generations, he who is born in the house, or bought with money from any foreigner who is not of your offspring. ¹⁷13 He who is born in your house, and he who is bought with your money, must be circumcised. My covenant will be in your flesh for an everlasting covenant. ¹⁷14 The uncircumcised male who is not circumcised in the flesh of his foreskin, that soul shall be cut off from his people. He has broken my covenant."
¹⁷15 God said to Abraham, "As for Sarai your wife, you shall not call her name Sarai, but her name will be Sarah. ¹⁷16 I will bless her, and moreover I will give you a son by her. Yes, I will bless her, and she will be a mother of nations. Kings of peoples will come from her."
¹⁷17 Then Abraham fell on his face, and laughed, and said in his heart, "Will a child be born to him who is one hundred years old? Will Sarah, who is ninety years old, give birth?" ¹⁷18 Abraham said to God, "Oh that Ishmael might live before you!"

Day Five

17:19 God said, "No, but Sarah, your wife, will bear you a son. You shall call his name Isaac.[11] I will establish my covenant with him for an everlasting covenant for his offspring after him. **17:20** As for Ishmael, I have heard you. Behold, I have blessed him, and will make him fruitful, and will multiply him exceedingly. He will become the father of twelve princes, and I will make him a great nation. **17:21** But I will establish my covenant with Isaac, whom Sarah will bear to you at this set time next year."

17:22 When he finished talking with him, God went up from Abraham. **17:23** Abraham took Ishmael his son, all who were born in his house, and all who were bought with his money: every male among the men of Abraham's house, and circumcised the flesh of their foreskin in the same day, as God had said to him. **17:24** Abraham was ninety-nine years old when he was circumcised in the flesh of his foreskin. **17:25** Ishmael, his son, was thirteen years old when he was circumcised in the flesh of his foreskin. **17:26** In the same day both Abraham and Ishmael, his son, were circumcised. **17:27** All the men of his house, those born in the house, and those bought with money from a foreigner, were circumcised with him. 17

The Lord's Prayer

Our Father, who art in heaven,
Hallowed be thy name.
Thy Kingdom come.
Thy will be done on Earth, as it is in heaven.
Give us this day our daily bread.
And forgive us our trespasses,
As we forgive those that trespass against us.
And lead us not into temptation,
But deliver us from evil.
For thine is the kingdom,

---

[11] 17:19 17:19 Isaac means "he laughs".

The American Book of Prayer

The power, and the glory,
For ever and ever.
AMEN

Day Six

Daily Prayer

Fondly do we hope, fervently do we pray, that this mighty scourge of war may speedily pass away. Yet if God wills that it continues… until every drop of blood drawn with the lash shall be paid another drawn with the sword… so still it must be said that the judgments of the Lord are true and righteous altogether. With malice toward none, with charity for all, with firmness in the right as God gives us to see the right, let us finish the work we are in, to bind up the nation's wounds, to care for him who shall have borne the battle, and for his widow and for his orphans, to do all which may achieve and cherish a just and a lasting peace among ourselves and with all nations.
— *16th U.S. President Abraham Lincoln, Second Inaugural Address, March 4, 1865*

> "With malice toward none, with charity for all, with firmness in the right as God gives us to see the right, let us finish the work we are in…"

Prayer of Confession

Almighty and most merciful Father; we have erred, and strayed from your ways like lost sheep. We have followed too much the devices and desires of our own hearts. We have offended against your holy laws. We have left undone those things which we ought to have done; and we have done those things which we ought not to have done; and there is no health in us. O Lord, have mercy upon us, miserable offenders. Spare those, O God, who confess their faults. Restore those who are penitent; according to your promises declared unto mankind in Christ Jesus our Lord. And grant, O most merciful Father, for his sake; that we may hereafter live a godly, righteous, and sober life, to the glory of thy holy Name. Amen.
-Revised prayer from *The Book of Common Prayer*, 1662

Daily Wisdom

1 Why do the heathen rage, and the people imagine a vain thing?
2 The kings of the earth set themselves, and the rulers take counsel together, against the LORD, and against his anointed, *saying*,
3 Let us break their bands asunder, and cast away their cords from us.
4 He that sitteth in the heavens shall laugh: the Lord shall have them in derision.
5 Then shall he speak unto them in his wrath, and vex them in his sore displeasure.
6 Yet have I set my king upon my holy hill of Zion.
7 I will declare the decree: the LORD hath said unto me, Thou *art* my Son; this day have I begotten thee.

Day Six

8 Ask of me, and I shall give *thee* the heathen *for* thine inheritance, and the uttermost parts of the earth *for* thy possession.
9 Thou shalt break them with a rod of iron; thou shalt dash them in pieces like a potter's vessel.
10 Be wise now therefore, O ye kings: be instructed, ye judges of the earth.
11 Serve the LORD with fear, and rejoice with trembling.
12 Kiss the Son, lest he be angry, and ye perish *from* the way, when his wrath is kindled but a little. Blessed *are* all they that put their trust in him.
-Psalm 3, *The King James Bible*, 1769 edition of 1611 text

Readings from the Holy Bible

The Holy Gospel According to Luke, Chapter 1:1-31

1

¹1 Since many have undertaken to set in order a narrative concerning those matters which have been fulfilled among us, **¹2** even as those who from the beginning were eyewitnesses and servants of the word delivered them to us, **¹3** it seemed good to me also, having traced the course of all things accurately from the first, to write to you in order, most excellent Theophilus; **¹4** that you might know the certainty concerning the things in which you were instructed.
¹5 There was in the days of Herod, the king of Judea, a certain priest named Zacharias, of the priestly division of Abijah. He had a wife of the daughters of Aaron, and her name was Elizabeth. **¹6** They were both righteous before God, walking blamelessly in all the commandments and ordinances of the Lord. **¹7** But they had no child, because Elizabeth was barren, and they both were well advanced in years. **¹8** Now while he executed the priest's office before God in the order of his division, **¹9** according to the custom of the priest's office, his lot was to enter into the temple of the Lord and burn incense. **¹10** The whole multitude of the people were praying outside at the hour of incense.

The American Book of Prayer

11 An angel of the Lord appeared to him, standing on the right side of the altar of incense. **12** Zacharias was troubled when he saw him, and fear fell upon him. **13** But the angel said to him, "Don't be afraid, Zacharias, because your request has been heard, and your wife, Elizabeth, will bear you a son, and you shall call his name John.
14 You will have joy and gladness; and many will rejoice at his birth.
15 For he will be great in the sight of the Lord, and he will drink no wine nor strong drink. He will be filled with the Holy Spirit, even from his mother's womb. **16** He will turn many of the children of Israel to the Lord, their God. **17** He will go before him in the spirit and power of Elijah, 'to turn the hearts of the fathers to the children,'# and the disobedient to the wisdom of the just; to prepare a people prepared for the Lord."
18 Zacharias said to the angel, "How can I be sure of this? For I am an old man, and my wife is well advanced in years."
19 The angel answered him, "I am Gabriel, who stands in the presence of God. I was sent to speak to you, and to bring you this good news. **20** Behold,¹² you will be silent and not able to speak, until the day that these things will happen, because you didn't believe my words, which will be fulfilled in their proper time."
21 The people were waiting for Zacharias, and they marveled that he delayed in the temple. **22** When he came out, he could not speak to them, and they perceived that he had seen a vision in the temple. He continued making signs to them, and remained mute. **23** When the days of his service were fulfilled, he departed to his house. **24** After these days Elizabeth, his wife, conceived, and she hid herself five months, saying, **25** "Thus has the Lord done to me in the days in which he looked at me, to take away my reproach among men."
26 Now in the sixth month, the angel Gabriel was sent from God to a city of Galilee, named Nazareth, **27** to a virgin pledged to be married to a man whose name was Joseph, of David's house. The virgin's name was Mary. **28** Having come in, the angel said to her, "Rejoice, you highly favored one! The Lord is with you. Blessed are you among women!"

#1:17 1:17 Malachi 4:6
¹²1:20 1:20 "Behold", from "ἰδοὺ", means look at, take notice, observe, see, or gaze at. It is often used as an interjection.

Day Six

¹²⁹ But when she saw him, she was greatly troubled at the saying, and considered what kind of salutation this might be. ¹³⁰ The angel said to her, "Don't be afraid, Mary, for you have found favor with God. ¹³¹ Behold, you will conceive in your womb, and give birth to a son, and will call his name 'Jesus.'"

The Lord's Prayer

Our Father, who art in heaven,
Hallowed be thy name.
Thy Kingdom come.
Thy will be done on Earth, as it is in heaven.
Give us this day our daily bread.
And forgive us our trespasses,
As we forgive those that trespass against us.
And lead us not into temptation,
But deliver us from evil.
For thine is the kingdom,
The power, and the glory,
For ever and ever.
AMEN

Day Seven

Daily Prayer

Almighty God: Our sons, pride of our nation, this day have set upon a mighty endeavor, a struggle to preserve our Republic, our religion and our civilization, and to set free a suffering humanity… Lead them straight and true; give strength to their arms, stoutness to their hearts, steadfastness in their faith. They will need Thy blessings. Their road will be long and hard. For the enemy is strong. He may hurl back our forces. Success may not come with rushing speed, but we shall return again and again; and we know by Thy grace, and by the righteousness of our cause, our sons will triumph… Embrace these, Father, and receive them, Thy heroic servants, into Thy kingdom. And for us at home—fathers, mothers, children, wives, sisters, and brothers of brave men overseas, whose thoughts and prayers are ever with them—help us, Almighty God, to rededicate ourselves in

> *"Their road will be long and hard. For the enemy is strong. He may hurl back our forces. Success may not come with rushing speed, but we shall return again and again; and we know by Thy grace, and by the righteousness of our cause, our sons will triumph…"*

renewed faith in Thee in this hour of great sacrifice... Give us strength, too–strength in our daily tasks, to redouble the contributions we make in the physical and the material support of our armed forces. With Thy blessing, we shall prevail over the unholy forces of our enemy. Help us to conquer the apostles of greed and racial arrogances. Lead us to the saving of our country, and with our sister nations into a world unity that will spell a sure peace–a peace invulnerable to the schemings of unworthy men. And a peace that will let all men live in freedom, reaping the just rewards of their honest toil.
–President Franklin D. Roosevelt, D-Day, June 6, 1944

Prayer of Confession

Almighty and most merciful Father; we have erred, and strayed from your ways like lost sheep. We have followed too much the devices and desires of our own hearts. We have offended against your holy laws. We have left undone those things which we ought to have done; and we have done those things which we ought not to have done; and there is no health in us. O Lord, have mercy upon us, miserable offenders. Spare those, O God, who confess their faults. Restore those who are penitent; according to your promises declared unto mankind in Christ Jesus our Lord. And grant, O most merciful Father, for his sake; that we may hereafter live a godly, righteous, and sober life, to the glory of thy holy Name. Amen.
-Revised prayer from *The Book of Common Prayer*, 1662

Day Seven

Daily Wisdom

1 Hear me when I call, O God of my righteousness: thou hast enlarged me *when I was* in distress; have mercy upon me, and hear my prayer.
2 O ye sons of men, how long *will ye turn* my glory into shame? *how long* will ye love vanity, *and* seek after leasing? Selah.
3 But know that the LORD hath set apart him that is godly for himself: the LORD will hear when I call unto him.
4 Stand in awe, and sin not: commune with your own heart upon your bed, and be still. Selah.
5 Offer the sacrifices of righteousness, and put your trust in the LORD.
6 *There be* many that say, Who will shew us *any* good? LORD, lift thou up the light of thy countenance upon us.
7 Thou hast put gladness in my heart, more than in the time *that* their corn and their wine increased.
8 I will both lay me down in peace, and sleep: for thou, LORD, only makest me dwell in safety.
-Psalm 4, *The King James Bible*, 1769 edition of 1611 text

Readings from the Holy Bible

The Holy Gospel According to Luke, Chapter 1:32-80

¹32 He will be great, and will be called the Son of the Most High. The Lord God will give him the throne of his father, David, **¹33** and he will reign over the house of Jacob forever. There will be no end to his Kingdom."
¹34 Mary said to the angel, "How can this be, seeing I am a virgin?"
¹35 The angel answered her, "The Holy Spirit will come on you, and the power of the Most High will overshadow you. Therefore also the holy one who is born from you will be called the Son of God.
¹36 Behold, Elizabeth, your relative, also has conceived a son in her

old age; and this is the sixth month with her who was called barren. **¹³⁷** For nothing spoken by God is impossible."¹³

¹³⁸ Mary said, "Behold, the servant of the Lord; let it be done to me according to your word."

The angel departed from her. **¹³⁹** Mary arose in those days and went into the hill country with haste, into a city of Judah, **¹⁴⁰** and entered into the house of Zacharias and greeted Elizabeth. **¹⁴¹** When Elizabeth heard Mary's greeting, the baby leaped in her womb, and Elizabeth was filled with the Holy Spirit. **¹⁴²** She called out with a loud voice, and said, "Blessed are you among women, and blessed is the fruit of your womb! **¹⁴³** Why am I so favored, that the mother of my Lord should come to me? **¹⁴⁴** For behold, when the voice of your greeting came into my ears, the baby leaped in my womb for joy! **¹⁴⁵** Blessed is she who believed, for there will be a fulfillment of the things which have been spoken to her from the Lord!"

¹⁴⁶ Mary said,

"My soul magnifies the Lord.

¹⁴⁷ My spirit has rejoiced in God my Savior,

¹⁴⁸ for he has looked at the humble state of his servant.

For behold, from now on, all generations will call me blessed.

¹⁴⁹ For he who is mighty has done great things for me.

Holy is his name.

¹⁵⁰ His mercy is for generations of generations on those who fear him.

¹⁵¹ He has shown strength with his arm.

He has scattered the proud in the imagination of their hearts.

¹⁵² He has put down princes from their thrones.

And has exalted the lowly.

¹⁵³ He has filled the hungry with good things.

He has sent the rich away empty.

¹⁵⁴ He has given help to Israel, his servant, that he might remember mercy,

¹⁵⁵ as he spoke to our fathers,

to Abraham and his offspring¹⁴ forever."

¹⁵⁶ Mary stayed with her about three months, and then returned to her house. **¹⁵⁷** Now the time that Elizabeth should give birth was fulfilled,

---

¹³1:37 1:37 or, "For everything spoken by God is possible."
¹⁴1:55 1:55 or, seed

Day Seven

and she gave birth to a son. **158** Her neighbors and her relatives heard that the Lord had magnified his mercy toward her, and they rejoiced with her. **159** On the eighth day, they came to circumcise the child; and they would have called him Zacharias, after the name of his father. **160** His mother answered, "Not so; but he will be called John."
161 They said to her, "There is no one among your relatives who is called by this name." **162** They made signs to his father, what he would have him called.
163 He asked for a writing tablet, and wrote, "His name is John." They all marveled. **164** His mouth was opened immediately, and his tongue freed, and he spoke, blessing God. **165** Fear came on all who lived around them, and all these sayings were talked about throughout all the hill country of Judea. **166** All who heard them laid them up in their heart, saying, "What then will this child be?" The hand of the Lord was with him. **167** His father, Zacharias, was filled with the Holy Spirit, and prophesied, saying,
168 "Blessed be the Lord, the God of Israel,
for he has visited and redeemed his people;
169 and has raised up a horn of salvation for us in the house of his servant David
170 (as he spoke by the mouth of his holy prophets who have been from of old),
171 salvation from our enemies, and from the hand of all who hate us;
172 to show mercy toward our fathers,
to remember his holy covenant,
173 the oath which he swore to Abraham, our father,
174 to grant to us that we, being delivered out of the hand of our enemies,
should serve him without fear,
175 in holiness and righteousness before him all the days of our life.
176 And you, child, will be called a prophet of the Most High,
for you will go before the face of the Lord to prepare his ways,
177 to give knowledge of salvation to his people by the remission of their sins,
178 because of the tender mercy of our God,
by which the dawn from on high will visit us,
179 to shine on those who sit in darkness and the shadow of death;

to guide our feet into the way of peace."
[80] The child was growing, and becoming strong in spirit, and was in the desert until the day of his public appearance to Israel.

The Lord's Prayer

Our Father, who art in heaven,
Hallowed be thy name.
Thy Kingdom come.
Thy will be done on Earth, as it is in heaven.
Give us this day our daily bread.
And forgive us our trespasses,
As we forgive those that trespass against us.
And lead us not into temptation,
But deliver us from evil.
For thine is the kingdom,
The power, and the glory,
For ever and ever.
AMEN

Day Eight

Daily Prayer

Let us therefore proclaim our gratitude to Providence for manifold blessings—let us be humbly thankful for inherited ideals—and let us resolve to share those blessings and those ideals with our fellow human beings throughout the world. On that day let us gather in sanctuaries dedicated to worship and in homes blessed by family affection to express our gratitude for the glorious gifts of God; and let us earnestly and humbly pray that He will continue to guide and sustain us in the great unfinished tasks of achieving peace, justice, and understanding among all men and nations and of ending misery and suffering wherever they exist.
—*President John F. Kennedy, Thanksgiving Day, 1963*[10]

> "On that day let us gather in sanctuaries dedicated to worship and in homes blessed by family affection to express our gratitude for the glorious gifts of God..."

Prayer of Confession

Almighty and most merciful Father; we have erred, and strayed from your ways like lost sheep. We have followed too much the devices and desires of our own hearts. We have offended against your holy laws. We have left undone those things which we ought to have done; and we have done those things which we ought not to have done; and there is no health in us. O Lord, have mercy upon us, miserable offenders. Spare those, O God, who confess their faults. Restore those who are penitent; according to your promises declared unto mankind in Christ Jesus our Lord. And grant, O most merciful Father, for his sake; that we may hereafter live a godly, righteous, and sober life, to the glory of thy holy Name. Amen.
-Revised prayer from *The Book of Common Prayer*, 1662

Daily Wisdom

1 Give ear to my words, O LORD, consider my meditation.
2 Hearken unto the voice of my cry, my King, and my God: for unto thee will I pray.
3 My voice shalt thou hear in the morning, O LORD; in the morning will I direct *my prayer* unto thee, and will look up.
4 For thou *art* not a God that hath pleasure in wickedness: neither shall evil dwell with thee.
5 The foolish shall not stand in thy sight: thou hatest all workers of iniquity.
6 Thou shalt destroy them that speak leasing: the LORD will abhor the bloody and deceitful man.
7 But as for me, I will come *into* thy house in the multitude of thy mercy: *and* in thy fear will I worship toward thy holy temple.
8 Lead me, O LORD, in thy righteousness because of mine enemies; make thy way straight before my face.

Day Eight

9 For *there is* no faithfulness in their mouth; their inward part *is* very wickedness; their throat *is* an open sepulchre; they flatter with their tongue.
10 Destroy thou them, O God; let them fall by their own counsels; cast them out in the multitude of their transgressions; for they have rebelled against thee.
11 But let all those that put their trust in thee rejoice: let them ever shout for joy, because thou defendest them: let them also that love thy name be joyful in thee.
12 For thou, LORD, wilt bless the righteous; with favour wilt thou compass him as *with* a shield.
-Psalm 5, *The King James Bible*, 1769 edition of 1611 text

Readings from the Holy Bible

The Holy Gospel According to Matthew, Luke, and John (MATT 1:1-17; LUKE 3:23-38; JOHN 1:1-18)

MATT 1:1-17, THE GENEALOGY OF CHRIST

1

1 The book of the generation of Jesus Christ, the son of David, the son of Abraham.
2 Abraham begat Isaac; and Isaac begat Jacob; and Jacob begat Judas and his brethren;
3 And Judas begat Phares and Zara of Thamar; and Phares begat Esrom; and Esrom begat Aram;
4 And Aram begat Aminadab; and Aminadab begat Naasson; and Naasson begat Salmon;
5 And Salmon begat Booz of Rachab; and Booz begat Obed of Ruth; and Obed begat Jesse;
6 And Jesse begat David the king; and David the king begat Solomon of her *that had been the wife* of Urias;
7 And Solomon begat Roboam; and Roboam begat Abia; and Abia begat Asa;
8 And Asa begat Josaphat; and Josaphat begat Joram; and Joram begat Ozias;

The American Book of Prayer

9 And Ozias begat Joatham; and Joatham begat Achaz; and Achaz begat Ezekias;
10 And Ezekias begat Manasses; and Manasses begat Amon; and Amon begat Josias;
11 And Josias begat Jechonias and his brethren, about the time they were carried away to Babylon:
12 And after they were brought to Babylon, Jechonias begat Salathiel; and Salathiel begat Zorobabel;
13 And Zorobabel begat Abiud; and Abiud begat Eliakim; and Eliakim begat Azor;
14 And Azor begat Sadoc; and Sadoc begat Achim; and Achim begat Eliud;
15 And Eliud begat Eleazar; and Eleazar begat Matthan; and Matthan begat Jacob;
16 And Jacob begat Joseph the husband of Mary, of whom was born Jesus, who is called Christ.
17 So all the generations from Abraham to David are fourteen generations; and from David until the carrying away into Babylon are fourteen generations; and from the carrying away into Babylon unto Christ are fourteen generations.

LUKE 3: 23-38, THE GENEALOGY OF CHRIST

23 [PARTIAL VERSE] ... being (as was supposed) the son of Joseph, which was *the son* of Heli,
24 Which was *the son* of Matthat, which was *the son* of Levi, which was *the son* of Melchi, which was *the son* of Janna, which was *the son* of Joseph,
25 Which was *the son* of Mattathias, which was *the son* of Amos, which was *the son* of Naum, which was *the son* of Esli, which was *the son* of Nagge,
26 Which was *the son* of Maath, which was *the son* of Mattathias, which was *the son* of Semei, which was *the son* of Joseph, which was *the son* of Juda,
27 Which was *the son* of Joanna, which was *the son* of Rhesa, which was *the son* of Zorobabel, which was *the son* of Salathiel, which was *the son* of Neri,
28 Which was *the son* of Melchi, which was *the son* of Addi, which was *the son* of Cosam, which was *the son* of Elmodam, which was *the son* of

Day Eight

Er, **29** Which was *the son* of Jose, which was *the son* of Eliezer, which was *the son* of Jorim, which was *the son* of Matthat, which was *the son* of Levi,
30 Which was *the son* of Simeon, which was *the son* of Juda, which was *the son* of Joseph, which was *the son* of Jonan, which was *the son* of Eliakim,
31 Which was *the son* of Melea, which was *the son* of Menan, which was *the son* of Mattatha, which was *the son* of Nathan, which was *the son* of David,
32 Which was *the son* of Jesse, which was *the son* of Obed, which was *the son* of Booz, which was *the son* of Salmon, which was *the son* of Naasson,
33 Which was *the son* of Aminadab, which was *the son* of Aram, which was *the son* of Esrom, which was *the son* of Phares, which was *the son* of Juda,
34 Which was *the son* of Jacob, which was *the son* of Isaac, which was *the son* of Abraham, which was *the son* of Thara, which was *the son* of Nachor,
35 Which was *the son* of Saruch, which was *the son* of Ragau, which was *the son* of Phalec, which was *the son* of Heber, which was *the son* of Sala,
36 Which was *the son* of Cainan, which was *the son* of Arphaxad, which was *the son* of Sem, which was *the son* of Noe, which was *the son* of Lamech,
37 Which was *the son* of Mathusala, which was *the son* of Enoch, which was *the son* of Jared, which was *the son* of Maleleel, which was *the son* of Cainan,
38 Which was *the son* of Enos, which was *the son* of Seth, which was *the son* of Adam, which was *the son* of God.

JOHN 1:1-18, THE WORD IS FLESH

1

11 In the beginning was the Word, and the Word was with God, and the Word was God. **2** The same was in the beginning with God. **3** All things were made through him. Without him, nothing was made that has been made. **4** In him was life, and the life was the light of men. **5** The light shines in the darkness, and the darkness hasn't overcome

[15] it. [6] There came a man, sent from God, whose name was John. [7] The same came as a witness, that he might testify about the light, that all might believe through him. [8] He was not the light, but was sent that he might testify about the light. [9] The true light that enlightens everyone was coming into the world.

[10] He was in the world, and the world was made through him, and the world didn't recognize him. [11] He came to his own, and those who were his own didn't receive him. [12] But as many as received him, to them he gave the right to become God's children, to those who believe in his name: [13] who were born not of blood, nor of the will of the flesh, nor of the will of man, but of God. [14] The Word became flesh, and lived among us. We saw his glory, such glory as of the one and only Son of the Father, full of grace and truth. [15] John testified about him. He cried out, saying, "This was he of whom I said, 'He who comes after me has surpassed me, for he was before me.'"

[16] From his fullness we all received grace upon grace. [17] For the law was given through Moses. Grace and truth were realized through Jesus Christ. [18] No one has seen God at any time. The one and only Son,[16] who is in the bosom of the Father, has declared him.

The Lord's Prayer

Our Father, who art in heaven,
Hallowed be thy name.
Thy Kingdom come.
Thy will be done on Earth, as it is in heaven.
Give us this day our daily bread.
And forgive us our trespasses,
As we forgive those that trespass against us.
And lead us not into temptation,
But deliver us from evil.

---

[15]1:5 1:5 The word translated "overcome" (κατέλαβεν) can also be translated "comprehended." It refers to getting a grip on an enemy to defeat him.
[16]1:18 1:18 NU reads "God"

Day Eight

For thine is the kingdom,
The power, and the glory,
For ever and ever.
AMEN

Day Nine

Daily Prayer

My first act as President is a prayer. I ask you to bow your heads. Heavenly Father, we bow our heads and thank You for Your love. Accept our thanks for the peace that yields this day and the shared faith that makes its continuance likely. Make us strong to do Your work, willing to heed and hear Your will, and write on our hearts these words: "Use power to help people." For we are given power not to advance our own purposes, nor to make a great show in the world, nor a name. There is but one just use of power, and it is to serve people. Help us to remember it, Lord. The Lord our God be with us, as He was with our fathers; may He not leave us or forsake us; so that He may incline our hearts to Him, to walk in all His ways... that all peoples of the earth may know that the Lord is God; there is no other.
–President George H. W. Bush, Inaugural Address, January 20, 1989.

> "The Lord our God be with us, as He was with our fathers; may He not leave us or forsake us; so that He may incline our hearts to Him, to walk in all His ways..."

Prayer of Confession

Almighty and most merciful Father; we have erred, and strayed from your ways like lost sheep. We have followed too much the devices and desires of our own hearts. We have offended against your holy laws. We have left undone those things which we ought to have done; and we have done those things which we ought not to have done; and there is no health in us. O Lord, have mercy upon us, miserable offenders. Spare those, O God, who confess their faults. Restore those who are penitent; according to your promises declared unto mankind in Christ Jesus our Lord. And grant, O most merciful Father, for his sake; that we may hereafter live a godly, righteous, and sober life, to the glory of thy holy Name. Amen.
-Revised prayer from *The Book of Common Prayer*, 1662

Daily Wisdom

1 O LORD, rebuke me not in thine anger, neither chasten me in thy hot displeasure.
2 Have mercy upon me, O LORD; for I am weak: O LORD, heal me; for my bones are vexed.
3 My soul is also sore vexed: but thou, O LORD, how long?
4 Return, O LORD, deliver my soul: oh save me for thy mercies' sake.
5 For in death there is no remembrance of thee: in the grave who shall give thee thanks?
6 I am weary with my groaning; all the night make I my bed to swim; I water my couch with my tears.
7 Mine eye is consumed because of grief; it waxeth old because of all mine enemies.
8 Depart from me, all ye workers of iniquity; for the LORD hath heard the voice of my weeping.

Day Nine

9 The LORD hath heard my supplication; the LORD will receive my prayer.
10 Let all mine enemies be ashamed and sore vexed: let them return and be ashamed suddenly.
-Psalm 6, *The King James Bible*, 1769 edition of 1611 text

Readings from the Holy Bible

The Holy Gospel According to Matthew and Luke (MATT 1:18-2:23; LUKE 2:1-41)

MATT 1:18-2:23, A KING IS BORN
18 Now the birth of Jesus Christ was like this: After his mother, Mary, was engaged to Joseph, before they came together, she was found pregnant by the Holy Spirit. **19** Joseph, her husband, being a righteous man, and not willing to make her a public example, intended to put her away secretly. **20** But when he thought about these things, behold,[17] an angel of the Lord appeared to him in a dream, saying, "Joseph, son of David, don't be afraid to take to yourself Mary, your wife, for that which is conceived in her is of the Holy Spirit. **21** She shall give birth to a son. You shall call his name Jesus,[18] for it is he who shall save his people from their sins."
22 Now all this has happened that it might be fulfilled which was spoken by the Lord through the prophet, saying,
23 "Behold, the virgin shall be with child,
and shall give birth to a son.
They shall call his name Immanuel;"
which is, being interpreted, "God with us."[#]
24 Joseph arose from his sleep, and did as the angel of the Lord commanded him, and took his wife to himself; **25** and didn't know her sexually until she had given birth to her firstborn son. He named him Jesus.

---

[17]1:20 1:20 "Behold", from "ἰδοὺ", means look at, take notice, observe, see, or gaze at. It is often used as an interjection.
[18]1:21 1:21 "Jesus" means "Salvation".
[#]1:23 1:23 Isaiah 7:14

The American Book of Prayer

2

²1 Now when Jesus was born in Bethlehem of Judea in the days of King Herod, behold, wise men¹⁹ from the east came to Jerusalem, saying, ²2 "Where is he who is born King of the Jews? For we saw his star in the east, and have come to worship him." ²3 When King Herod heard it, he was troubled, and all Jerusalem with him. ²4 Gathering together all the chief priests and scribes of the people, he asked them where the Christ would be born. ²5 They said to him, "In Bethlehem of Judea, for this is written through the prophet,
²6 'You Bethlehem, land of Judah,
are in no way least among the princes of Judah:
for out of you shall come a governor,
who shall shepherd my people, Israel.'"#
²7 Then Herod secretly called the wise men, and learned from them exactly what time the star appeared. ²8 He sent them to Bethlehem, and said, "Go and search diligently for the young child. When you have found him, bring me word, so that I also may come and worship him."
²9 They, having heard the king, went their way; and behold, the star, which they saw in the east, went before them, until it came and stood over where the young child was. ²10 When they saw the star, they rejoiced with exceedingly great joy. ²11 They came into the house and saw the young child with Mary, his mother, and they fell down and worshiped him. Opening their treasures, they offered to him gifts: gold, frankincense, and myrrh. ²12 Being warned in a dream not to return to Herod, they went back to their own country another way.
²13 Now when they had departed, behold, an angel of the Lord appeared to Joseph in a dream, saying, "Arise and take the young child and his mother, and flee into Egypt, and stay there until I tell you, for Herod will seek the young child to destroy him."
²14 He arose and took the young child and his mother by night, and departed into Egypt, ²15 and was there until the death of Herod; that it

---

¹⁹2:1 2:1 The word for "wise men" (magoi) can also mean teachers, scientists, physicians, astrologers, seers, interpreters of dreams, or sorcerers.
#2:6 2:6 Micah 5:2

Day Nine

might be fulfilled which was spoken by the Lord through the prophet, saying, "Out of Egypt I called my son."#

²16 Then Herod, when he saw that he was mocked by the wise men, was exceedingly angry, and sent out, and killed all the male children who were in Bethlehem and in all the surrounding countryside, from two years old and under, according to the exact time which he had learned from the wise men. ²17 Then that which was spoken by Jeremiah the prophet was fulfilled, saying,

²18 "A voice was heard in Ramah,
lamentation, weeping and great mourning,
Rachel weeping for her children;
she wouldn't be comforted,
because they are no more."#

²19 But when Herod was dead, behold, an angel of the Lord appeared in a dream to Joseph in Egypt, saying, ²20 "Arise and take the young child and his mother, and go into the land of Israel, for those who sought the young child's life are dead."

²21 He arose and took the young child and his mother, and came into the land of Israel. ²22 But when he heard that Archelaus was reigning over Judea in the place of his father, Herod, he was afraid to go there. Being warned in a dream, he withdrew into the region of Galilee, ²23 and came and lived in a city called Nazareth; that it might be fulfilled which was spoken through the prophets: "He will be called a Nazarene."

LUKE 2:1-41, ANOTHER ACCOUNT OF THE BIRTH OF CHRIST

2

²1 Now in those days, a decree went out from Caesar Augustus that all the world should be enrolled. ²2 This was the first enrollment made when Quirinius was governor of Syria. ²3 All went to enroll themselves, everyone to his own city. ²4 Joseph also went up from Galilee, out of the city of Nazareth, into Judea, to David's city, which is called Bethlehem, because he was of the house and family of David;

#2:15 2:15 Hosea 11:1
#2:18 2:18 Jeremiah 31:15

²5 to enroll himself with Mary, who was pledged to be married to him as wife, being pregnant.
²6 While they were there, the day had come for her to give birth.
²7 She gave birth to her firstborn son. She wrapped him in bands of cloth, and laid him in a feeding trough, because there was no room for them in the inn. ²8 There were shepherds in the same country staying in the field, and keeping watch by night over their flock. ²9 Behold, an angel of the Lord stood by them, and the glory of the Lord shone around them, and they were terrified. ²10 The angel said to them, "Don't be afraid, for behold, I bring you good news of great joy which will be to all the people. ²11 For there is born to you today, in David's city, a Savior, who is Christ the Lord. ²12 This is the sign to you: you will find a baby wrapped in strips of cloth, lying in a feeding trough."
²13 Suddenly, there was with the angel a multitude of the heavenly army praising God, and saying,
²14 "Glory to God in the highest,
on earth peace, good will toward men."
²15 When the angels went away from them into the sky, the shepherds said to one another, "Let's go to Bethlehem, now, and see this thing that has happened, which the Lord has made known to us." ²16 They came with haste, and found both Mary and Joseph, and the baby was lying in the feeding trough. ²17 When they saw it, they publicized widely the saying which was spoken to them about this child. ²18 All who heard it wondered at the things which were spoken to them by the shepherds. ²19 But Mary kept all these sayings, pondering them in her heart. ²20 The shepherds returned, glorifying and praising God for all the things that they had heard and seen, just as it was told them.
²21 When eight days were fulfilled for the circumcision of the child, his name was called Jesus, which was given by the angel before he was conceived in the womb.
²22 When the days of their purification according to the law of Moses were fulfilled, they brought him up to Jerusalem, to present him to the Lord ²23 (as it is written in the law of the Lord, "Every male who opens the womb shall be called holy to the Lord"),# ²24 and to offer a

---

#2:23 2:23 Exodus 13:2,12

Day Nine

sacrifice according to that which is said in the law of the Lord, "A pair of turtledoves, or two young pigeons."#
²25 Behold, there was a man in Jerusalem whose name was Simeon. This man was righteous and devout, looking for the consolation of Israel, and the Holy Spirit was on him. ²26 It had been revealed to him by the Holy Spirit that he should not see death before he had seen the Lord's Christ.²⁰ ²27 He came in the Spirit into the temple. When the parents brought in the child, Jesus, that they might do concerning him according to the custom of the law, ²28 then he received him into his arms, and blessed God, and said,
²29 "Now you are releasing your servant, Master, according to your word, in peace;
²30 for my eyes have seen your salvation,
²31 which you have prepared before the face of all peoples;
²32 a light for revelation to the nations,
and the glory of your people Israel."
²33 Joseph and his mother were marveling at the things which were spoken concerning him, ²34 and Simeon blessed them, and said to Mary, his mother, "Behold, this child is set for the falling and the rising of many in Israel, and for a sign which is spoken against.
²35 Yes, a sword will pierce through your own soul, that the thoughts of many hearts may be revealed."
²36 There was one Anna, a prophetess, the daughter of Phanuel, of the tribe of Asher (she was of a great age, having lived with a husband seven years from her virginity, ²37 and she had been a widow for about eighty-four years), who didn't depart from the temple, worshiping with fastings and petitions night and day. ²38 Coming up at that very hour, she gave thanks to the Lord, and spoke of him to all those who were looking for redemption in Jerusalem.
²39 When they had accomplished all things that were according to the law of the Lord, they returned into Galilee, to their own city, Nazareth. ²40 The child was growing, and was becoming strong in spirit, being filled with wisdom, and the grace of God was upon him. ²41 His parents went every year to Jerusalem at the feast of the Passover.

#2:24 2:24 Leviticus 12:8
²⁰2:26 2:26 "Christ" (Greek) and "Messiah" (Hebrew) both mean "Anointed One"

The American Book of Prayer

The Lord's Prayer

Our Father, who art in heaven,
Hallowed be thy name.
Thy Kingdom come.
Thy will be done on Earth, as it is in heaven.
Give us this day our daily bread.
And forgive us our trespasses,
As we forgive those that trespass against us.
And lead us not into temptation,
But deliver us from evil.
For thine is the kingdom,
The power, and the glory,
For ever and ever.
AMEN

Day Ten

Daily Prayer

We come before God to pray for the missing and the dead, and for those who love them... On this national day of prayer and remembrance, we ask Almighty God to watch over our nation, and grant us patience and resolve in all that is to come. We pray that He will comfort and console those who now walk in sorrow. We thank Him for each life we now must mourn, and the promise of a life to come. As we have been assured, neither death nor life, nor angels nor principalities nor powers, nor things present nor things to come, nor height nor depth, can separate us from God's love. May He bless the souls of the departed. May He comfort our own. And may He always guide our country.
– President George W. Bush, On the World Trade Center Attacks, September 14, 2001[11]

> "We pray that He will comfort and console those who now walk in sorrow. We thank Him for each life we now must mourn, and the promise of a life to come."

Prayer of Confession

Almighty and most merciful Father; we have erred, and strayed from your ways like lost sheep. We have followed too much the devices and desires of our own hearts. We have offended against your holy laws. We have left undone those things which we ought to have done; and we have done those things which we ought not to have done; and there is no health in us. O Lord, have mercy upon us, miserable offenders. Spare those, O God, who confess their faults. Restore those who are penitent; according to your promises declared unto mankind in Christ Jesus our Lord. And grant, O most merciful Father, for his sake; that we may hereafter live a godly, righteous, and sober life, to the glory of thy holy Name. Amen.
-Revised prayer from *The Book of Common Prayer*, 1662

Daily Wisdom

1 O LORD my God, in thee do I put my trust: save me from all them that persecute me, and deliver me:
2 Lest he tear my soul like a lion, rending *it* in pieces, while *there is* none to deliver.
3 O LORD my God, if I have done this; if there be iniquity in my hands;
4 If I have rewarded evil unto him that was at peace with me; (yea, I have delivered him that without cause is mine enemy:)
5 Let the enemy persecute my soul, and take *it*; yea, let him tread down my life upon the earth, and lay mine honor in the dust. Selah.
6 Arise, O LORD, in thine anger, lift up thyself because of the rage of mine enemies: and awake for me *to* the judgment *that* thou hast commanded.

Day Ten

7 So shall the congregation of the people compass thee about: for their sakes therefore return thou on high.
8 The LORD shall judge the people: judge me, O LORD, according to my righteousness, and according to mine integrity *that is* in me.
9 Oh let the wickedness of the wicked come to an end; but establish the just: for the righteous God trieth the hearts and reins.
10 My defence *is* of God, which saveth the upright in heart.
11 God judgeth the righteous, and God is angry *with the wicked* every day.
12 If he turn not, he will whet his sword; he hath bent his bow, and made it ready.
13 He hath also prepared for him the instruments of death; he ordaineth his arrows against the persecutors.
14 Behold, he travaileth with iniquity, and hath conceived mischief, and brought forth falsehood.
15 He made a pit, and digged it, and is fallen into the ditch *which* he made.
16 His mischief shall return upon his own head, and his violent dealing shall come down upon his own pate.
17 I will praise the LORD according to his righteousness: and will sing praise to the name of the LORD most high.
-Psalm 7, *The King James Bible*, 1769 edition of 1611 text

The American Book of Prayer

Readings from the Holy Bible

The Holy Gospel According to Luke (LUKE 3:1-23; 4:1-13)

LUKE 3:1-23; 4:1-13, JOHN THE BAPTIST PREPARES THE WAY AND JESUS PREPARES FOR HIS MINISTRY

3

3:1 Now in the fifteenth year of the reign of Tiberius Caesar, Pontius Pilate being governor of Judea, and Herod being tetrarch of Galilee, and his brother Philip tetrarch of the region of Ituraea and Trachonitis, and Lysanias tetrarch of Abilene, 3:2 in the high priesthood of Annas and Caiaphas, the word of God came to John, the son of Zacharias, in the wilderness. 3:3 He came into all the region around the Jordan, preaching the baptism of repentance for remission of sins. 3:4 As it is written in the book of the words of Isaiah the prophet,
"The voice of one crying in the wilderness,
'Make ready the way of the Lord.
Make his paths straight.
3:5 Every valley will be filled.
Every mountain and hill will be brought low.
The crooked will become straight,
and the rough ways smooth.
3:6 All flesh will see God's salvation.'"#
3:7 He said therefore to the multitudes who went out to be baptized by him, "You offspring of vipers, who warned you to flee from the wrath to come? 3:8 Therefore produce fruits worthy of repentance, and don't begin to say among yourselves, 'We have Abraham for our father;' for I tell you that God is able to raise up children to Abraham from these stones! 3:9 Even now the ax also lies at the root of the trees. Every tree therefore that doesn't produce good fruit is cut down, and thrown into the fire."
3:10 The multitudes asked him, "What then must we do?"

#3:6 3:6 Isaiah 40:3-5

Day Ten

³11 He answered them, "He who has two coats, let him give to him who has none. He who has food, let him do likewise."
³12 Tax collectors also came to be baptized, and they said to him, "Teacher, what must we do?"
³13 He said to them, "Collect no more than that which is appointed to you."
³14 Soldiers also asked him, saying, "What about us? What must we do?"
He said to them, "Extort from no one by violence, neither accuse anyone wrongfully. Be content with your wages."
³15 As the people were in expectation, and all men reasoned in their hearts concerning John, whether perhaps he was the Christ, ³16 John answered them all, "I indeed baptize you with water, but he comes who is mightier than I, the strap of whose sandals I am not worthy to loosen. He will baptize you in the Holy Spirit and fire, ³17 whose fan is in his hand, and he will thoroughly cleanse his threshing floor, and will gather the wheat into his barn; but he will burn up the chaff with unquenchable fire."
³18 Then with many other exhortations he preached good news to the people, ³19 but Herod the tetrarch,[21] being reproved by him for Herodias, his brother's [22] wife, and for all the evil things which Herod had done, ³20 added this also to them all, that he shut up John in prison. ³21 Now when all the people were baptized, Jesus also had been baptized, and was praying. The sky was opened, ³22 and the Holy Spirit descended in a bodily form like a dove on him; and a voice came out of the sky, saying "You are my beloved Son. In you I am well pleased."
³23 Jesus himself, when he began to teach, was about thirty years old…

4

⁴1 Jesus, full of the Holy Spirit, returned from the Jordan, and was led by the Spirit into the wilderness ⁴2 for forty days, being tempted by the devil. He ate nothing in those days. Afterward, when they were

---

[21]3:19 3:19 a tetrarch is one of four governors of a province
[22]3:19 3:19 TR reads "brother Philip's" instead of "brother's"

The American Book of Prayer

completed, he was hungry. **⁴3** The devil said to him, "If you are the Son of God, command this stone to become bread."
⁴4 Jesus answered him, saying, "It is written, 'Man shall not live by bread alone, but by every word of God.'"
⁴5 The devil, leading him up on a high mountain, showed him all the kingdoms of the world in a moment of time. **⁴6** The devil said to him, "I will give you all this authority, and their glory, for it has been delivered to me; and I give it to whomever I want. **⁴7** If you therefore will worship before me, it will all be yours."
⁴8 Jesus answered him, "Get behind me Satan! For it is written, 'You shall worship the Lord your God, and you shall serve him only.'"
⁴9 He led him to Jerusalem, and set him on the pinnacle of the temple, and said to him, "If you are the Son of God, cast yourself down from here, **⁴10** for it is written,
'He will put his angels in charge of you, to guard you;'
⁴11 and,
'On their hands they will bear you up,
lest perhaps you dash your foot against a stone.'"#
⁴12 Jesus answering, said to him, "It has been said, 'You shall not tempt the Lord your God.'"#
⁴13 When the devil had completed every temptation, he departed from him until another time.

The Lord's Prayer

Our Father, who art in heaven,
Hallowed be thy name.
Thy Kingdom come.
Thy will be done on Earth, as it is in heaven.
Give us this day our daily bread.
And forgive us our trespasses,
As we forgive those that trespass against us.

#4:11 4:11 Psalm 91:11-12
#4:12 4:12 Deuteronomy 6:16

Day Ten

And lead us not into temptation,
But deliver us from evil.
For thine is the kingdom,
The power, and the glory,
For ever and ever.
AMEN

Day Eleven

Daily Prayer

I would like to have my frequent prayer answered that God let my life be meaningful in the enhancement of His kingdom and that my life might be meaningful in the enhancement of the lives of my fellow human beings. I call upon all the people of our Nation to give thanks on that day for the blessings Almighty God has bestowed upon us, and to join the fervent prayer of George Washington, who as President asked God to "impart all the blessings we possess, or ask for ourselves to the whole family of mankind."
—*President Jimmy Carter, 1977 Inaugural Address.*

> "I call upon all the people of our Nation to give thanks on that day for the blessings Almighty God has bestowed upon us..."

Prayer of Confession

Almighty and most merciful Father; we have erred, and strayed from your ways like lost sheep. We have followed too much the devices and desires of our own hearts. We

have offended against your holy laws. We have left undone those things which we ought to have done; and we have done those things which we ought not to have done; and there is no health in us. O Lord, have mercy upon us, miserable offenders. Spare those, O God, who confess their faults. Restore those who are penitent; according to your promises declared unto mankind in Christ Jesus our Lord. And grant, O most merciful Father, for his sake; that we may hereafter live a godly, righteous, and sober life, to the glory of thy holy Name. Amen.
-Revised prayer from *The Book of Common Prayer*, 1662

Daily Wisdom

1 O LORD our Lord, how excellent *is* thy name in all the earth! who hast set thy glory above the heavens.
2 Out of the mouth of babes and sucklings hast thou ordained strength because of thine enemies, that thou mightest still the enemy and the avenger.
3 When I consider thy heavens, the work of thy fingers, the moon and the stars, which thou hast ordained;
4 What is man, that thou art mindful of him? and the son of man, that thou visitest him?
5 For thou hast made him a little lower than the angels, and hast crowned him with glory and honor.
6 Thou madest him to have dominion over the works of thy hands; thou hast put all *things* under his feet:
7 All sheep and oxen, yea, and the beasts of the field;
8 The fowl of the air, and the fish of the sea, *and whatsoever* passeth through the paths of the seas.
9 O LORD our Lord, how excellent *is* thy name in all the earth!
-Psalm 8, *The King James Bible*, 1769 edition of 1611 text

Day Eleven

Readings from the Holy Bible

The Holy Gospel According to Matthew, Luke, and John (MATT 4:12-22; 9:9-14; LUKE 5:1-11; JOHN 1:35-51)

MATTHEW 4:12-22, JESUS BEGINS HIS MINISTRY

4:12 Now when Jesus heard that John was delivered up, he withdrew into Galilee. **4:13** Leaving Nazareth, he came and lived in Capernaum, which is by the sea, in the region of Zebulun and Naphtali, **4:14** that it might be fulfilled which was spoken through Isaiah the prophet, saying,

4:15 "The land of Zebulun and the land of Naphtali,
toward the sea, beyond the Jordan,
Galilee of the Gentiles,

4:16 the people who sat in darkness saw a great light,
to those who sat in the region and shadow of death,
to them light has dawned."#

4:17 From that time, Jesus began to preach, and to say, "Repent! For the Kingdom of Heaven is at hand."

4:18 Walking by the sea of Galilee, he[23] saw two brothers: Simon, who is called Peter, and Andrew, his brother, casting a net into the sea; for they were fishermen. **4:19** He said to them, "Come after me, and I will make you fishers for men."

4:20 They immediately left their nets and followed him. **4:21** Going on from there, he saw two other brothers, James the son of Zebedee, and John his brother, in the boat with Zebedee their father, mending their nets. He called them. **4:22** They immediately left the boat and their father, and followed him.

LUKE 5:1-11, JESUS BEGINS HIS MINISTRY

1

5:1 Now while the multitude pressed on him and heard the word of God, he was standing by the lake of Gennesaret. **5:2** He saw two boats

---

#4:16 4:16 Isaiah 9:1-2
[23]4:18 4:18 TR reads "Jesus" instead of "he"

standing by the lake, but the fishermen had gone out of them, and were washing their nets. ⁵3 He entered into one of the boats, which was Simon's, and asked him to put out a little from the land. He sat down and taught the multitudes from the boat. ⁵4 When he had finished speaking, he said to Simon, "Put out into the deep, and let down your nets for a catch."
⁵5 Simon answered him, "Master, we worked all night, and took nothing; but at your word I will let down the net." ⁵6 When they had done this, they caught a great multitude of fish, and their net was breaking. ⁵7 They beckoned to their partners in the other boat, that they should come and help them. They came, and filled both boats, so that they began to sink. ⁵8 But Simon Peter, when he saw it, fell down at Jesus' knees, saying, "Depart from me, for I am a sinful man, Lord." ⁵9 For he was amazed, and all who were with him, at the catch of fish which they had caught; ⁵10 and so also were James and John, sons of Zebedee, who were partners with Simon.
Jesus said to Simon, "Don't be afraid. From now on you will be catching people alive."
⁵11 When they had brought their boats to land, they left everything, and followed him.

MATTHEW 9:9-14, JESUS CALLS MATTHEW
⁹9 As Jesus passed by from there, he saw a man called Matthew sitting at the tax collection office. He said to him, "Follow me." He got up and followed him. ⁹10 As he sat in the house, behold, many tax collectors and sinners came and sat down with Jesus and his disciples. ⁹11 When the Pharisees saw it, they said to his disciples, "Why does your teacher eat with tax collectors and sinners?"
⁹12 When Jesus heard it, he said to them, "Those who are healthy have no need for a physician, but those who are sick do. ⁹13 But you go and learn what this means: 'I desire mercy, and not sacrifice,'# for I came not to call the righteous, but sinners to repentance."²⁴
⁹14 Then John's disciples came to him, saying, "Why do we and the Pharisees fast often, but your disciples don't fast?"

#9:13 9:13 Hosea 6:6
²⁴9:13 9:13 NU omits "to repentance".

Day Eleven

JOHN 1:35-51, JESUS BEGINS HIS MINISTRY

35 Again, the next day, John was standing with two of his disciples, **36** and he looked at Jesus as he walked, and said, "Behold, the Lamb of God!" **37** The two disciples heard him speak, and they followed Jesus. **38** Jesus turned and saw them following, and said to them, "What are you looking for?"

They said to him, "Rabbi" (which is to say, being interpreted, Teacher), "where are you staying?"

39 He said to them, "Come, and see."

They came and saw where he was staying, and they stayed with him that day. It was about the tenth hour.[25] **40** One of the two who heard John and followed him was Andrew, Simon Peter's brother. **41** He first found his own brother, Simon, and said to him, "We have found the Messiah!" (which is, being interpreted, Christ[26]). **42** He brought him to Jesus. Jesus looked at him, and said, "You are Simon the son of Jonah. You shall be called Cephas" (which is by interpretation, Peter).[27] **43** On the next day, he was determined to go out into Galilee, and he found Philip. Jesus said to him, "Follow me." **44** Now Philip was from Bethsaida, of the city of Andrew and Peter. **45** Philip found Nathanael, and said to him, "We have found him, of whom Moses in the law, and the prophets, wrote: Jesus of Nazareth, the son of Joseph."

46 Nathanael said to him, "Can any good thing come out of Nazareth?"

Philip said to him, "Come and see."

47 Jesus saw Nathanael coming to him, and said about him, "Behold, an Israelite indeed, in whom is no deceit!"

48 Nathanael said to him, "How do you know me?"

Jesus answered him, "Before Philip called you, when you were under the fig tree, I saw you."

49 Nathanael answered him, "Rabbi, you are the Son of God! You are King of Israel!"

50 Jesus answered him, "Because I told you, 'I saw you underneath the fig tree,' do you believe? You will see greater things than these!"

---

[25] 1:39 1:39 4:00 p.m.
[26] 1:41 1:41 "Messiah" (Hebrew) and "Christ" (Greek) both mean "Anointed One".
[27] 1:42 1:42 "Cephas" (Aramaic) and "Peter" (Greek) both mean "Rock".

151 He said to him, [1]"Most certainly, I tell you all, hereafter you will see heaven opened, and the angels of God ascending and descending on the Son of Man."

The Lord's Prayer

Our Father, who art in heaven,
Hallowed be thy name.
Thy Kingdom come.
Thy will be done on Earth, as it is in heaven.
Give us this day our daily bread.
And forgive us our trespasses,
As we forgive those that trespass against us.
And lead us not into temptation,
But deliver us from evil.
For thine is the kingdom,
The power, and the glory,
For ever and ever.
AMEN

Day Twelve

Daily Prayer

Almighty God, and most merciful father, who didst command the children of Israel to offer a daily sacrifice to thee, that thereby they might glorify and praise thee for thy protection both night and day, receive, O Lord, my morning sacrifice which I now offer up to thee; I yield thee humble and hearty thanks that thou has preserved me from the danger of the night past, and brought me to the light of the day, and the comforts thereof, a day which is consecrated at thine own service and for thine own honor. Let my heart, therefore, Gracious God, be so affected with the glory and majesty of it, that I may not do mine own works, but wait on thee, and discharge those weighty duties thou requirest of me, and since thou art a God of pure eyes, and wilt be sanctified in all who draw near unto thee, who doest not regard the sacrifice of fools, nor hear sinners who tread in

> "Let my heart, therefore, Gracious God, be so affected with the glory and majesty of it, that I may not do mine own works, but wait on thee, and discharge those weighty duties thou requirest of me..."

thy courts, pardon, I beseech thee, my sins, remove them from thy presence, as far as the east is from the west, and accept of me for the merits of thy son Jesus Christ, that when I come into thy temple, and compass thine altar, my prayers may come before thee as incense; and as thou wouldst hear me calling upon thee in my prayers, so give me grace to hear thee calling on me in thy word, that it may be wisdom, righteousness, reconciliation and peace to the saving of the soul in the day of the Lord Jesus. Grant that I may hear it with reverence, receive it with meekness, mingle it with faith, and that it may accomplish in me, Gracious God, the good work for which thou has sent it. Bless my family, kindred, friends and country, be our God and guide this day and for ever for his sake, who ay down in the Grave and arose again for us, Jesus Christ our Lord, Amen.
–Attributed to American hero George Washington. Discovered in Washington's Prayer Journal *in a prayer entitled "Sunday Morning Prayer." Likely a prayer from a resident at Mt. Vernon, but it's not clear if George Washington is the true author.*[12,13]

Prayer of Confession

Almighty and most merciful Father; we have erred, and strayed from your ways like lost sheep. We have followed too much the devices and desires of our own hearts. We have offended against your holy laws. We have left undone those things which we ought to have done; and we have done those things which we ought not to have done; and there is no health in us. O Lord, have mercy upon us, miserable offenders. Spare those, O God, who confess their faults. Restore those who are penitent;
according to your promises declared unto mankind in Christ Jesus our Lord. And grant, O most merciful Father,

Day Twelve

for his sake; that we may hereafter live a godly, righteous, and sober life, to the glory of thy holy Name. Amen.
-Revised prayer from *The Book of Common Prayer*, 1662

Daily Wisdom

1 I will praise *thee*, O LORD, with my whole heart; I will shew forth all thy marvellous works.
2 I will be glad and rejoice in thee: I will sing praise to thy name, O thou most High.
3 When mine enemies are turned back, they shall fall and perish at thy presence.
4 For thou hast maintained my right and my cause; thou satest in the throne judging right.
5 Thou hast rebuked the heathen, thou hast destroyed the wicked, thou hast put out their name for ever and ever.
6 O thou enemy, destructions are come to a perpetual end: and thou hast destroyed cities; their memorial is perished with them.
7 But the LORD shall endure forever: he hath prepared his throne for judgment.
8 And he shall judge the world in righteousness, he shall minister judgment to the people in uprightness.
9 The LORD also will be a refuge for the oppressed, a refuge in times of trouble.
10 And they that know thy name will put their trust in thee: for thou, LORD, hast not forsaken them that seek thee.
11 Sing praises to the LORD, which dwelleth in Zion: declare among the people his doings.
12 When he maketh inquisition for blood, he remembereth them: he forgetteth not the cry of the humble.
13 Have mercy upon me, O LORD; consider my trouble *which I suffer* of them that hate me, thou that liftest me up from the gates of death:
14 That I may shew forth all thy praise in the gates of the daughter of Zion: I will rejoice in thy salvation.

15 The heathen are sunk down in the pit *that* they made: in the net which they hid is their own foot taken.
16 The LORD is known *by* the judgment *which* he executeth: the wicked is snared in the work of his own hands. Higgaion. Selah.
17 The wicked shall be turned into hell, *and* all the nations that forget God.
18 For the needy shall not always be forgotten: the expectation of the poor shall *not* perish forever.
19 Arise, O LORD; let not man prevail: let the heathen be judged in thy sight.
20 Put them in fear, O LORD: *that* the nations may know themselves *to be but* men. Selah.
-Psalm 9, *The King James Bible,* 1769 edition of 1611 text

Readings from the Holy Bible

The Holy Gospel According to Mark, John, and Matthew (MARK 3:14-21; JOHN 2:1-25; MATTHEW 4:23-25)

MARK 3:14-21,   ETERNAL LIFE
³**14** As Moses lifted up the serpent in the wilderness, even so must the Son of Man be lifted up, ³**15** that whoever believes in him should not perish, but have eternal life. ³**16** For God so loved the world, that he gave his one and only Son, that whoever believes in him should not perish, but have eternal life. ³**17** For God didn't send his Son into the world to judge the world, but that the world should be saved through him. ³**18** He who believes in him is not judged. He who doesn't believe has been judged
already, because he has not believed in the name of the one and only Son of God. ³**19** This is the judgment, that the light has come into the world, and men loved the darkness rather than the light; for their works were evil. ³**20** For everyone who does evil hates the light, and doesn't come to the light, lest his works would be exposed. ³**21** But he who does the truth comes to the light, that his works may be revealed, that they have been done in God."

Day Twelve

JOHN 2:1-25, JESUS' FIRST MIRACLE AND EARLY TEACHINGS

2

²1 The third day, there was a wedding in Cana of Galilee. Jesus' mother was there. ²2 Jesus also was invited, with his disciples, to the wedding. ²3 When the wine ran out, Jesus' mother said to him, "They have no wine."
²4 Jesus said to her, "Woman, what does that have to do with you and me? My hour has not yet come."
²5 His mother said to the servants, "Whatever he says to you, do it."
²6 Now there were six water pots of stone set there after the Jews' way of purifying, containing two or three metretes²⁸ apiece. ²7 Jesus said to them, "Fill the water pots with water." So they filled them up to the brim. ²8 He said to them, "Now draw some out, and take it to the ruler of the feast." So they took it. ²9 When the ruler of the feast tasted the water now become wine, and didn't know where it came from (but the servants who had drawn the water knew), the ruler of the feast called the bridegroom ²10 and said to him, "Everyone serves the good wine first, and when the guests have drunk freely, then that which is worse. You have kept the good wine until now!" ²11 This beginning of his signs Jesus did in Cana of Galilee, and revealed his glory; and his disciples believed in him.
²12 After this, he went down to Capernaum, he, and his mother, his brothers, and his disciples; and they stayed there a few days. ²13 The Passover of the Jews was at hand, and Jesus went up to Jerusalem.
²14 He found in the temple those who sold oxen, sheep, and doves, and the changers of money sitting. ²15 He made a whip of cords, and threw all out of the temple, both the sheep and the oxen; and he poured out the changers' money and overthrew their tables. ²16 To those who sold the doves, he said, "Take these things out of here! Don't make my Father's house a marketplace!" ²17 His disciples remembered that it was written, "Zeal for your house will eat me up."#

---

²⁸2:6 2:6 2 to 3 metretes is about 20 to 30 U. S. Gallons, or 75 to 115 liters.
#2:17 2:17 Psalm 69:9

²18 The Jews therefore answered him, "What sign do you show us, seeing that you do these things?"
²19 Jesus answered them, "Destroy this temple, and in three days I will raise it up."
²20 The Jews therefore said, "It took forty-six years to build this temple! Will you raise it up in three days?" ²21 But he spoke of the temple of his body. ²22 When therefore he was raised from the dead, his disciples remembered that he said this, and they believed the Scripture, and the word which Jesus had said.
²23 Now when he was in Jerusalem at the Passover, during the feast, many believed in his name, observing his signs which he did. ²24 But Jesus didn't entrust himself to them, because he knew everyone, ²25 and because he didn't need for anyone to testify concerning man; for he himself knew what was in man.

MATTHEW 4:23-25, JESUS HEALS THE SICK

⁴23 Jesus went about in all Galilee, teaching in their synagogues, preaching the Good News of the Kingdom, and healing every disease and every sickness among the people. ⁴24 The report about him went out into all Syria. They brought to him all who were sick, afflicted with various diseases and torments, possessed with demons, epileptics, and paralytics; and he healed them. ⁴25 Great multitudes from Galilee, Decapolis, Jerusalem, Judea and from beyond the Jordan followed him.

The Lord's Prayer

Our Father, who art in heaven,
Hallowed be thy name.
Thy Kingdom come.
Thy will be done on Earth, as it is in heaven.
Give us this day our daily bread.
And forgive us our trespasses,
As we forgive those that trespass against us.

Day Twelve

And lead us not into temptation,
But deliver us from evil.
For thine is the kingdom,
The power, and the glory,
For ever and ever.
AMEN

Day Thirteen

Daily Prayer

I now make it my earnest prayer, that God would have you, and the State over which you preside, in his holy protection, that he would incline the hearts of the Citizens to cultivate a spirit of subordination and obedience to Government, to entertain a brotherly affection and love for one another, for their fellow Citizens of the United States at large, and particularly for their brethren who have served in the Field, and finally, that he would most graciously be pleased to dispose us all, to do Justice, to love mercy, and to demean ourselves with that Charity, humility and pacific temper of mind, which were the Characteristicks of the Divine Author of our blessed Religion, and without an humble imitation of whose example in these things, we can never hope to be a happy Nation.

—American hero George Washington, Circular to the States, Sunday, June 08, 1783.

Prayer of Confession

Almighty and most merciful Father; we have erred, and strayed from your ways like lost sheep. We have followed too much the devices and desires of our own hearts. We have offended against your holy laws. We have left undone those things which we ought to have done; and we have done those things which we ought not to have done; and there is no health in us. O Lord, have mercy upon us, miserable offenders. Spare those, O God, who confess their faults. Restore those who are penitent; according to your promises declared unto mankind in Christ Jesus our Lord. And grant, O most merciful Father, for his sake; that we may hereafter live a godly, righteous, and sober life, to the glory of thy holy Name. Amen.
-Revised prayer from *The Book of Common Prayer*, 1662

Daily Wisdom

1 Why standest thou afar off, O LORD? *Why* hidest thou *thyself* in times of trouble?
2 The wicked in *his* pride doth persecute the poor: let them be taken in the devices that they have imagined.
3 For the wicked boasteth of his heart's desire, and blesseth the covetous, *whom* the LORD abhorreth.
4 The wicked, through the pride of his countenance, will not seek *after God*: God *is* not in all his thoughts.
5 His ways are always grievous; thy judgments *are* far above out of his sight: *as for* all his enemies, he puffeth at them.
6 He hath said in his heart, I shall not be moved: for *I shall* never *be* in adversity.
7 His mouth is full of cursing and deceit and fraud: under his tongue *is* mischief and vanity.

Day Thirteen

8 He sitteth in the lurking places of the villages: in the secret places doth he murder the innocent: his eyes are privily set against the poor.
9 He lieth in wait secretly as a lion in his den: he lieth in wait to catch the poor: he doth catch the poor, when he draweth him into his net.
10 He croucheth, *and* humbleth himself, that the poor may fall by his strong ones.
11 He hath said in his heart, God hath forgotten: he hideth his face; he will never see *it*.
12 Arise, O LORD; O God, lift up thine hand: forget not the humble.
13 Wherefore doth the wicked condemn God? he hath said in his heart, Thou wilt not require *it*.
14 Thou hast seen *it*; for thou beholdest mischief and spite, to requite *it* with thy hand: the poor committeth himself unto thee; thou art the helper of the fatherless.
15 Break thou the arm of the wicked and the evil *man*: seek out his wickedness *till* thou find none.
16 The LORD *is* King for ever and ever: the heathen are perished out of his land.
17 LORD, thou hast heard the desire of the humble: thou wilt prepare their heart, thou wilt cause thine ear to hear:
18 To judge the fatherless and the oppressed, that the man of the earth may no more oppress.
-Psalm 10, *The King James Bible*, 1769 edition of 1611 text

The American Book of Prayer

Readings from the Holy Bible

The Holy Gospel According to Matthew (MATTHEW 5:1-6:34)

MATTHEW 5:1-6:34, LIVING A CHRISTIAN LIFE

5

⁵1 Seeing the multitudes, he went up onto the mountain. When he had sat down, his disciples came to him. ⁵2 He opened his mouth and taught them, saying,
⁵3 "Blessed are the poor in spirit,
for theirs is the Kingdom of Heaven.
⁵4 Blessed are those who mourn,
for they shall be comforted.[#]
⁵5 Blessed are the gentle,
for they shall inherit the earth.[29][#]
⁵6 Blessed are those who hunger and thirst after righteousness,
for they shall be filled.
⁵7 Blessed are the merciful,
for they shall obtain mercy.
⁵8 Blessed are the pure in heart,
for they shall see God.
⁵9 Blessed are the peacemakers,
for they shall be called children of God.
⁵10 Blessed are those who have been persecuted for righteousness' sake,
for theirs is the Kingdom of Heaven.
⁵11 "Blessed are you when people reproach you, persecute you, and say all kinds of evil against you falsely, for my sake. ⁵12 Rejoice, and be exceedingly glad, for great is your reward in heaven. For that is how they persecuted the prophets who were before you.

[#]5:4 5:4 Isaiah 61:2; 66:10,13
[29]5:5 5:5 or, land.
[#]5:5 5:5 Psalm 37:11

Day Thirteen

⁵13 "You are the salt of the earth, but if the salt has lost its flavor, with what will it be salted? It is then good for nothing, but to be cast out and trodden under the feet of men. ⁵14 You are the light of the world. A city located on a hill can't be hidden. ⁵15 Neither do you light a lamp, and put it under a measuring basket, but on a stand; and it shines to all who are in the house. ⁵16 Even so, let your light shine before men; that they may see your good works, and glorify your Father who is in heaven.

⁵17 "Don't think that I came to destroy the law or the prophets. I didn't come to destroy, but to fulfill. ⁵18 For most certainly, I tell you, until heaven and earth pass away, not even one smallest letter[30] or one tiny pen stroke[31] shall in any way pass away from the law, until all things are accomplished. ⁵19 Whoever, therefore, shall break one of these least commandments, and teach others to do so, shall be called least in the Kingdom of Heaven; but whoever shall do and teach them shall be called great in the Kingdom of Heaven. ⁵20 For I tell you that unless your righteousness exceeds that of the scribes and Pharisees, there is no way you will enter into the Kingdom of Heaven.

⁵21 "You have heard that it was said to the ancient ones, 'You shall not murder;'[#] and 'Whoever murders will be in danger of the judgment.' ⁵22 But I tell you that everyone who is angry with his brother without a cause [32] will be in danger of the judgment. Whoever says to his brother, 'Raca!' [33] will be in danger of the council. Whoever says, 'You fool!' will be in danger of the fire of Gehenna. [34]

⁵23 "If therefore you are offering your gift at the altar, and there remember that your brother has anything against you, ⁵24 leave your gift there before the altar, and go your way. First be reconciled to your brother, and then come and offer your gift. ⁵25 Agree with your adversary quickly, while you are with him on the way; lest perhaps the prosecutor deliver you to the judge, and the judge deliver you to the officer, and you be cast into prison. ⁵26 Most certainly I tell you, you

---

[30]5:18 5:18 literally, iota
[31]5:18 5:18 or, serif
[#]5:21 5:21 Exodus 20:13
[32]5:22 5:22 NU omits "without a cause".
[33]5:22 5:22 "Raca" is an Aramaic insult, related to the word for "empty" and conveying the idea of empty-headedness.
[34]5:22 5:22 or, Hell

shall by no means get out of there, until you have paid the last penny."[35]

[527] "You have heard that it was said,[36] 'You shall not commit adultery;'[#] [528] but I tell you that everyone who gazes at a woman to lust after her has committed adultery with her already in his heart. [529] If your right eye causes you to stumble, pluck it out and throw it away from you. For it is more profitable for you that one of your members should perish, than for your whole body to be cast into Gehenna.[37] [530] If your right hand causes you to stumble, cut it off, and throw it away from you. For it is more profitable for you that one of your members should perish, than for your whole body to be cast into Gehenna.[38]

[531] "It was also said, 'Whoever shall put away his wife, let him give her a writing of divorce,'[#] [532] but I tell you that whoever puts away his wife, except for the cause of sexual immorality, makes her an adulteress; and whoever marries her when she is put away commits adultery.

[533] "Again you have heard that it was said to the ancient ones, 'You shall not make false vows, but shall perform to the Lord your vows,'[#] [534] but I tell you, don't swear at all: neither by heaven, for it is the throne of God; [535] nor by the earth, for it is the footstool of his feet; nor by Jerusalem, for it is the city of the great King. [536] Neither shall you swear by your head, for you can't make one hair white or black. [537] But let your 'Yes' be 'Yes' and your 'No' be 'No.' Whatever is more than these is of the evil one.

[538] "You have heard that it was said, 'An eye for an eye, and a tooth for a tooth.'[#] [539] But I tell you, don't resist him who is evil; but whoever strikes you on your right cheek, turn to him the other also. [540] If anyone sues you to take away your coat, let him have your cloak also.

---

[35]5:26 5:26 literally, kodrantes. A kodrantes was a small copper coin worth about 2 lepta (widow's mites)—not enough to buy very much of anything.
[36]5:27 5:27 TR adds "to the ancients".
[#]5:27 5:27 Exodus 20:14
[37]5:29 5:29 or, Hell
[38]5:30 5:30 or, Hell
[#]5:31 5:31 Deuteronomy 24:1
[#]5:33 5:33 Numbers 30:2; Deuteronomy 23:21; Ecclesiastes 5:4
[#]5:38 5:38 Exodus 21:24; Leviticus 24:20; Deuteronomy 19:21

Day Thirteen

⁵41 Whoever compels you to go one mile, go with him two. ⁵42 Give to him who asks you, and don't turn away him who desires to borrow from you.

⁵43 "You have heard that it was said, 'You shall love your neighbor # and hate your enemy.'³⁹ ⁵44 But I tell you, love your enemies, bless those who curse you, do good to those who hate you, and pray for those who mistreat you and persecute you, ⁵45 that you may be children of your Father who is in heaven. For
he makes his sun to rise on the evil and the good, and sends rain on the just and the unjust. ⁵46 For if you love those who love you, what reward do you have? Don't even the tax collectors do the same? ⁵47 If you only greet your friends, what more do you do than others? Don't even the tax collectors⁴⁰ do the same? ⁵48 ⁵Therefore you shall be perfect, just as your Father in heaven is perfect.

6

⁶1 "Be careful that you don't do your charitable giving⁴¹ before men, to be seen by them, or else you have no reward from your Father who is in heaven. ⁶2 Therefore when you do merciful deeds, don't sound a trumpet before yourself, as the hypocrites do in the synagogues and in the streets, that they may get glory from men. Most certainly I tell you, they have received their reward. ⁶3 But when you do merciful deeds, don't let your left hand know what your right hand does, ⁶4 so that your merciful deeds may be in secret, then your Father who sees in secret will reward you openly.

⁶5 "When you pray, you shall not be as the hypocrites, for they love to stand and pray in the synagogues and in the corners of the streets, that they may be seen by men. Most certainly, I tell you, they have received their reward. ⁶6 But you, when you pray, enter into your inner room, and having shut your door, pray to your Father who is in secret, and your Father who sees in secret will reward you openly. ⁶7 In praying, don't use vain repetitions, as the Gentiles do; for they think that they will be heard for their much speaking. ⁶8 Therefore don't be like

---

#5:43 5:43 Leviticus 19:18
³⁹5:43 5:43 not in the Bible, but see Qumran Manual of Discipline Ix, 21-26
⁴⁰5:47 5:47 NU reads "Gentiles" instead of "tax collectors".
⁴¹6:1 6:1 NU reads "acts of righteousness" instead of "charitable giving"

them, for your Father knows what things you need, before you ask him. **⁶9** Pray like this: 'Our Father in heaven, may your name be kept holy. **⁶10** Let your Kingdom come. Let your will be done on earth as it is in heaven. **⁶11** Give us today our daily bread. **⁶12** Forgive us our debts, as we also forgive our debtors. **⁶13** Bring us not into temptation, but deliver us from the evil one. For yours is the Kingdom, the power, and the glory forever. Amen.'[42]

⁶14 "For if you forgive men their trespasses, your heavenly Father will also forgive you. **⁶15** But if you don't forgive men their trespasses, neither will your Father forgive your trespasses.

⁶16 "Moreover when you fast, don't be like the hypocrites, with sad faces. For they disfigure their faces, that they may be seen by men to be fasting. Most certainly I tell you, they have received their reward. **⁶17** But you, when you fast, anoint your head, and wash your face; **⁶18** so that you are not seen by men to be fasting, but by your Father who is in secret, and your Father, who sees in secret, will reward you.

⁶19 "Don't lay up treasures for yourselves on the earth, where moth and rust consume, and where thieves break through and steal; **⁶20** but lay up for yourselves treasures in heaven, where neither moth nor rust consume, and where thieves don't break through and steal; **⁶21** for where your treasure is, there your heart will be also.

⁶22 "The lamp of the body is the eye. If therefore your eye is sound, your whole body will be full of light. **⁶23** But if your eye is evil, your whole body will be full of darkness. If therefore the light that is in you is darkness, how great is the darkness!

⁶24 "No one can serve two masters, for either he will hate the one and love the other; or else he will be devoted to one and despise the other. You can't serve both God and Mammon. **⁶25** Therefore I tell you, don't be anxious for your life: what you will eat, or what you will drink; nor yet for your body, what you will wear. Isn't life more than food, and the body more than clothing? **⁶26** See the birds of the sky, that they don't sow, neither do they reap, nor gather into barns. Your heavenly Father feeds them. Aren't you of much more value than they?

---

[42]6:13 6:13 NU omits "For yours is the Kingdom, the power, and the glory forever. Amen."

Day Thirteen

6:27 "Which of you, by being anxious, can add one moment[43] to his lifespan?

6:28 Why are you anxious about clothing? Consider the lilies of the field, how they grow. They don't toil, neither do they spin, **6:29** yet I tell you that even Solomon in all his glory was not dressed like one of these. **6:30** But if God so clothes the grass of the field, which today exists, and tomorrow is thrown into the oven, won't he much more clothe you, you of little faith?

6:31 "Therefore don't be anxious, saying, 'What will we eat?', 'What will we drink?' or, 'With what will we be clothed?'

6:32 For the Gentiles seek after all these things; for your heavenly Father knows that you need all these things. **6:33** But seek first God's Kingdom, and his righteousness; and all these things will be given to you as well. **6:34** ⁶Therefore don't be anxious for tomorrow, for tomorrow will be anxious for itself. Each day's own evil is sufficient.

The Lord's Prayer

Our Father, who art in heaven,
Hallowed be thy name.
Thy Kingdom come.
Thy will be done on Earth, as it is in heaven.
Give us this day our daily bread.
And forgive us our trespasses,
As we forgive those that trespass against us.
And lead us not into temptation,
But deliver us from evil.
For thine is the kingdom,
The power, and the glory,
For ever and ever.
AMEN

---

[43]6:27 6:27 literally, cubit

Day Fourteen

Washington's Orders for 'a Day of Public Thanksgiving'

The Honorable the Legislature of this Colony having thought fit to set apart Thursday the 23d of November Instant, as a day of public thanksgiving 'to offer up our praises, and prayers to Almighty God, the Source and Benevolent Bestower of all good; That he would be pleased graciously to continue, to smile upon our Endeavours, to restore peace, preserve our Rights, and Privileges, to the latest posterity; prosper the American Arms, preserve and strengthen the Harmony of the United Colonies, and avert the Calamities of a civil war.' The General therefore commands that day to be observed with all the Solemnity directed by the Legislative Proclamation, and all Officers, Soldiers and others, are hereby directed, with the most unfeigned Devotion, to obey the same."
—Gen. George Washington. General Orders, Headquarters, Cambridge, Massachusetts, November 18, 1775.

Prayer of Confession

Almighty and most merciful Father; we have erred, and strayed from your ways like lost sheep. We have followed too much the devices and desires of our own hearts. We have offended against your holy laws. We have left undone those things which we ought to have done; and we have done those things which we ought not to have done; and there is no health in us. O Lord, have mercy upon us, miserable offenders. Spare those, O God, who confess their faults. Restore those who are penitent; according to your promises declared unto mankind in Christ Jesus our Lord. And grant, O most merciful Father, for his sake; that we may hereafter live a godly, righteous, and sober life, to the glory of thy holy Name. Amen.
-Revised prayer from *The Book of Common Prayer*, 1662

Daily Wisdom

1 In the LORD put I my trust: how say ye to my soul, Flee *as* a bird to your mountain?
2 For, lo, the wicked bend *their* bow, they make ready their arrow upon the string, that they may privily shoot at the upright in heart.
3 If the foundations be destroyed, what can the righteous do?
4 The LORD *is* in his holy temple, the LORD'S throne *is* in heaven: his eyes behold, his eyelids try, the children of men.
5 The LORD trieth the righteous: but the wicked and him that loveth violence his soul hateth.
6 Upon the wicked he shall rain snares, fire and brimstone, and an horrible tempest: *this shall be* the portion of their cup.
7 For the righteous LORD loveth righteousness; his countenance doth behold the upright.
-Psalm 11, *The King James Bible*, 1769 edition of 1611 text

Day Fourteen

Readings from the Holy Bible

The Holy Gospel According to Matthew and John (MATTHEW 7:1-29; JOHN 4:1-38)

MATTHEW 7:1-29, JESUS TEACHES HIS FOLLOWERS

7

7:1 "Don't judge, so that you won't be judged. **7:2** For with whatever judgment you judge, you will be judged; and with whatever measure you measure, it will be measured to you. **7:3** Why do you see the speck that is in your brother's eye, but don't consider the beam that is in your own eye? **7:4** Or how will you tell your brother, 'Let me remove the speck from your eye;' and behold, the beam is in your own eye? **7:5** You hypocrite! First remove the beam out of your own eye, and then you can see clearly to remove the speck out of your brother's eye. **7:6** "Don't give that which is holy to the dogs, neither throw your pearls before the pigs, lest perhaps they trample them under their feet, and turn and tear you to pieces.
7:7 "Ask, and it will be given you. Seek, and you will find. Knock, and it will be opened for you. **7:8** For everyone who asks receives. He who seeks finds. To him who knocks it will be opened. **7:9** Or who is there among you, who, if his son asks him for bread, will give him a stone? **7:10** Or if he asks for a fish, who will give him a serpent? **7:11** If you then, being evil, know how to give good gifts to your children, how much more will your Father who is in heaven give good things to those who ask him! **7:12** Therefore whatever you desire for men to do to you, you shall also do to them; for this is the law and the prophets.
7:13 "Enter in by the narrow gate; for wide is the gate and broad is the way that leads to destruction, and many are those who enter in by it. **7:14** How[44] narrow is the gate, and restricted is the way that leads to life! Few are those who find it.
7:15 "Beware of false prophets, who come to you in sheep's clothing, but inwardly are ravening wolves. **7:16** By their fruits you will know

---

[44]7:14 7:14 TR reads "Because" instead of "How"

them. Do you gather grapes from thorns, or figs from thistles? ⁷17 Even so, every good tree produces good fruit; but the corrupt tree produces evil fruit. ⁷18 A good tree can't produce evil fruit, neither can a corrupt tree produce good fruit. ⁷19 Every tree that doesn't grow good fruit is cut down, and thrown into the fire. ⁷20 Therefore by their fruits you will know them. ⁷21 Not everyone who says to me, 'Lord, Lord,' will enter into the Kingdom of Heaven; but he who does the will of my Father who is in heaven. ⁷22 Many will tell me in that day, 'Lord, Lord, didn't we prophesy in your name, in your name cast out demons, and in your name do many mighty works?' ⁷23 Then I will tell them, 'I never knew you. Depart from me, you who work iniquity.'

⁷24 "Everyone therefore who hears these words of mine, and does them, I will liken him to a wise man, who built his house on a rock. ⁷25 The rain came down, the floods came, and the winds blew, and beat on that house; and it didn't fall, for it was founded on the rock. ⁷26 Everyone who hears these words of mine, and doesn't do them will be like a foolish man, who built his house on the sand. ⁷27 The rain came down, the floods came, and the winds blew, and beat on that house; and it fell—and great was its fall."

⁷28 When Jesus had finished saying these things, the multitudes were astonished at his teaching, ⁷29 for he taught them with authority, and not like the scribes. ⁷

JOHN 4:1-38, JESUS IS REJECTED AT NAZARETH

4

⁴1 Therefore when the Lord knew that the Pharisees had heard that Jesus was making and baptizing more disciples than John ⁴2 (although Jesus himself didn't baptize, but his disciples), ⁴3 he left Judea and departed into Galilee. ⁴4 He needed to pass through Samaria. ⁴5 So he came to a city of Samaria, called Sychar, near the parcel of ground that Jacob gave to his son, Joseph. ⁴6 Jacob's well was there. Jesus therefore, being tired from his journey, sat down by the well. It was about the sixth hour.⁴⁵ ⁴7 A woman of Samaria came to draw water.

---

⁴⁵4:6 4:6 noon

Day Fourteen

Jesus said to her, "Give me a drink." ⁸ For his disciples had gone away into the city to buy food.

⁹ The Samaritan woman therefore said to him, "How is it that you, being a Jew, ask for a drink from me, a Samaritan woman?" (For Jews have no dealings with Samaritans.)

¹⁰ Jesus answered her, "If you knew the gift of God, and who it is who says to you, 'Give me a drink,' you would have asked him, and he would have given you living water."

¹¹ The woman said to him, "Sir, you have nothing to draw with, and the well is deep. So where do you get that living water? ¹² Are you greater than our father, Jacob, who gave us the well and drank from it himself, as did his children and his livestock?"

¹³ Jesus answered her, "Everyone who drinks of this water will thirst again, ¹⁴ but whoever drinks of the water that I will give him will never thirst again; but the water that I will give him will become in him a well of water springing up to eternal life."

¹⁵ The woman said to him, "Sir, give me this water, so that I don't get thirsty, neither come all the way here to draw."

¹⁶ Jesus said to her, "Go, call your husband, and come here."

¹⁷ The woman answered, "I have no husband."

Jesus said to her, "You said well, 'I have no husband,' ¹⁸ for you have had five husbands; and he whom you now have is not your husband. This you have said truly."

¹⁹ The woman said to him, "Sir, I perceive that you are a prophet. ²⁰ Our fathers worshiped in this mountain, and you Jews say that in Jerusalem is the place where people ought to worship."

²¹ Jesus said to her, "Woman, believe me, the hour comes, when neither in this mountain, nor in Jerusalem, will you worship the Father. ²² You worship that which you don't know. We worship that which we know; for salvation is from the Jews. ²³ But the hour comes, and now is, when the true worshipers will worship the Father in spirit and truth, for the Father seeks such to be his worshipers. ²⁴ God is spirit, and those who worship him must worship in spirit and truth."

²⁵ The woman said to him, "I know that Messiah comes, he who is called Christ. When he has come, he will declare to us all things."

426 Jesus said to her, "I am he, the one who speaks to you." **427** At this, his disciples came. They marveled that he was speaking with a woman; yet no one said, "What are you looking for?" or, "Why do you speak with her?" **428** So the woman left her water pot, went away into the city, and said to the people, **429** "Come, see a man who told me everything that I did. Can this be the Christ?"

430 They went out of the city, and were coming to him. **431** In the meanwhile, the disciples urged him, saying, "Rabbi, eat."

432 But he said to them, "I have food to eat that you don't know about."

433 The disciples therefore said to one another, "Has anyone brought him something to eat?"

434 Jesus said to them, "My food is to do the will of him who sent me and to accomplish his work. **435** Don't you say, 'There are yet four months until the harvest?' Behold, I tell you, lift up your eyes and look at the fields, that they are white for harvest already. **436** He who reaps receives wages and gathers fruit to eternal life; that both he who sows and he who reaps may rejoice together. **437** For in this the saying is true, 'One sows, and another reaps.' **438** I sent you to reap that for which you haven't labored. Others have labored, and you have entered into their labor."

The Lord's Prayer

Our Father, who art in heaven,
Hallowed be thy name.
Thy Kingdom come.
Thy will be done on Earth, as it is in heaven.
Give us this day our daily bread.
And forgive us our trespasses,
As we forgive those that trespass against us.
And lead us not into temptation,
But deliver us from evil.

Day Fourteen

For thine is the kingdom,
The power, and the glory,
For ever and ever.
AMEN

Day Fifteen

Daily Prayer

In recurring to the internal situation of our country since I had last the pleasure to address you, I find ample reason for a renewed expression of that gratitude to the Ruler of the Universe which a continued series of prosperity has so often and so justly called forth. ...

The situation in which I now stand for the last time, in the midst of the representatives of the people of the United States, naturally recalls the period when the administration of the present form of government commenced, and I cannot omit the occasion to congratulate you and my country on the success of the experiment, nor to repeat my fervent supplications to the Supreme Ruler of the Universe and Sovereign Arbiter of Nations that His providential care may still be extended to the United States, that the virtue and happiness of the people may be preserved, and that

> "I cannot omit the occasion to congratulate you and my country on the success of the experiment, nor to repeat my fervent supplications to the Supreme Ruler of the Universe ..."

the Government which they have instituted for the protection of their liberties may be perpetual.
—*George Washington's Eighth Annual Address to Congress, December 7, 1796.*

Prayer of Confession

Almighty and most merciful Father; we have erred, and strayed from your ways like lost sheep. We have followed too much the devices and desires of our own hearts. We have offended against your holy laws. We have left undone those things which we ought to have done; and we have done those things which we ought not to have done; and there is no health in us. O Lord, have mercy upon us, miserable offenders. Spare those, O God, who confess their faults. Restore those who are penitent; according to your promises declared unto mankind in Christ Jesus our Lord. And grant, O most merciful Father, for his sake; that we may hereafter live a godly, righteous, and sober life, to the glory of thy holy Name. Amen.
-Revised prayer from *The Book of Common Prayer*, 1662

Daily Wisdom

1 Help, LORD; for the godly man ceaseth; for the faithful fail from among the children of men.
2 They speak vanity every one with his neighbour: *with* flattering lips *and* with a double heart do they speak.
3 The LORD shall cut off all flattering lips, *and* the tongue that speaketh proud things:
4 Who have said, With our tongue will we prevail; our lips *are* our own: who *is* lord over us?
5 For the oppression of the poor, for the sighing of the needy, now will I arise, saith the LORD; I will set *him* in safety *from him that* puffeth at him.

Day Fifteen

6 The words of the LORD *are* pure words: *as* silver tried in a furnace of earth, purified seven times.
7 Thou shalt keep them, O LORD, thou shalt preserve them from this generation for ever.
8 The wicked walk on every side, when the vilest men are exalted.
-Psalm 12, *The King James Bible,* 1769 edition of 1611 text

Readings from the Holy Bible

The Holy Gospel According to Matthew (MATTHEW 8:1-9:38)

MATTHEW 8:1-9:38

8

⁸**1** When he came down from the mountain, great multitudes followed him. ⁸**2** Behold, a leper came to him and worshiped him, saying, "Lord, if you want to, you can make me clean."
⁸**3** Jesus stretched out his hand, and touched him, saying, "I want to. Be made clean." Immediately his leprosy was cleansed. ⁸**4** Jesus said to him, "See that you tell nobody, but go, show yourself to the priest, and offer the gift that Moses commanded, as a testimony to them."
⁸**5** When he came into Capernaum, a centurion came to him, asking him, ⁸**6** and saying, "Lord, my servant lies in the house paralyzed, grievously tormented."
⁸**7** Jesus said to him, "I will come and heal him."
⁸**8** The centurion answered, "Lord, I'm not worthy for you to come under my roof. Just say the word, and my servant will be healed.
⁸**9** For I am also a man under authority, having under myself soldiers. I tell this one, 'Go,' and he goes; and tell another, 'Come,' and he comes; and tell my servant, 'Do this,' and he does it."
⁸**10** When Jesus heard it, he marveled, and said to those who followed, "Most certainly I tell you, I haven't found so great a faith, not even in Israel. ⁸**11** I tell you that many will come from the east and the west, and will sit down with Abraham, Isaac, and Jacob in the Kingdom of

Heaven, ⁸12 but the children of the Kingdom will be thrown out into the outer darkness. There will be weeping and gnashing of teeth."
⁸13 Jesus said to the centurion, "Go your way. Let it be done for you as you have believed." His servant was healed in that hour.
⁸14 When Jesus came into Peter's house, he saw his wife's mother lying sick with a fever. ⁸15 He touched her hand, and the fever left her. She got up and served him. [46] ⁸16 When evening came, they brought to him many possessed with demons. He cast out the spirits with a word, and healed all who were sick; ⁸17 that it might be fulfilled which was spoken through Isaiah the prophet, saying, "He took our infirmities, and bore our diseases."# ⁸18 Now when Jesus saw great multitudes around him, he gave the order to depart to the other side.
⁸19 A scribe came, and said to him, "Teacher, I will follow you wherever you go."
⁸20 Jesus said to him, "The foxes have holes, and the birds of the sky have nests, but the Son of Man has nowhere to lay his head."
⁸21 Another of his disciples said to him, "Lord, allow me first to go and bury my father."
⁸22 But Jesus said to him, "Follow me, and leave the dead to bury their own dead."
⁸23 When he got into a boat, his disciples followed him. ⁸24 Behold, a violent storm came up on the sea, so much that the boat was covered with the waves, but he was asleep. ⁸25 They came to him, and woke him up, saying, "Save us, Lord! We are dying!"
⁸26 He said to them, "Why are you fearful, O you of little faith?" Then he got up, rebuked the wind and the sea, and there was a great calm.
⁸27 The men marveled, saying, "What kind of man is this, that even the wind and the sea obey him?"
⁸28 When he came to the other side, into the country of the Gergesenes, [47] two people possessed by demons met him there, coming out of the tombs, exceedingly fierce, so that nobody could pass that way. ⁸29 Behold, they cried out, saying, "What do we have to do with you, Jesus, Son of God? Have you come here to torment us

---

[46]8:15 8:15 TR reads "them" instead of "him"
#8:17 8:17 Isaiah 53:4
[47]8:28 8:28 NU reads "Gadarenes"

Day Fifteen

before the time?" ⁸30 Now there was a herd of many pigs feeding far away from them. ⁸31 The demons begged him, saying, "If you cast us out, permit us to go away into the herd of pigs."
⁸32 He said to them, "Go!"
They came out, and went into the herd of pigs: and behold, the whole herd of pigs rushed down the cliff into the sea, and died in the water. ⁸33 Those who fed them fled, and went away into the city, and told everything, including what happened to those who were possessed with demons. ⁸34 Behold, all the city came out to meet Jesus. When they saw him, they begged that he would depart from their borders. ⁸

9

⁹1 He entered into a boat, and crossed over, and came into his own city. ⁹2 Behold, they brought to him a man who was paralyzed, lying on a bed. Jesus, seeing their faith, said to the paralytic, "Son, cheer up! Your sins are forgiven you."
⁹3 Behold, some of the scribes said to themselves, "This man blasphemes."
⁹4 Jesus, knowing their thoughts, said, "Why do you think evil in your hearts? ⁹5 For which is easier, to say, 'Your sins are forgiven;' or to say, 'Get up, and walk?' ⁹6 But that you may know that the Son of Man has authority on earth to forgive sins-" (then he said to the paralytic), "Get up, and take up your mat, and go to your house."
⁹7 He arose and departed to his house. ⁹8 But when the multitudes saw it, they marveled and glorified God, who had given such authority to men.
⁹9 As Jesus passed by from there, he saw a man called Matthew sitting at the tax collection office. He said to him, "Follow me." He got up and followed him. ⁹10 As he sat in the house, behold, many tax collectors and sinners came and sat down with Jesus and his disciples. ⁹11 When the Pharisees saw it, they said to his disciples, "Why does your teacher eat with tax collectors and sinners?"
⁹12 When Jesus heard it, he said to them, "Those who are healthy have no need for a physician, but those who are sick do. ⁹13 But you go

and learn what this means: 'I desire mercy, and not sacrifice,'# for I came not to call the righteous, but sinners to repentance."⁴⁸

⁹14 Then John's disciples came to him, saying, "Why do we and the Pharisees fast often, but your disciples don't fast?"

⁹15 Jesus said to them, "Can the friends of the bridegroom mourn, as long as the bridegroom is with them? But the days will come when the bridegroom will be taken away from them, and then they will fast. ⁹16 No one puts a piece of unshrunk cloth on an old garment; for the patch would tear away from the garment, and a worse hole is made. ⁹17 Neither do people put new wine into old wine skins, or else the skins would burst, and the wine be spilled, and the skins ruined. No, they put new wine into fresh wine skins, and both are preserved."

⁹18 While he told these things to them, behold, a ruler came and worshiped him, saying, "My daughter has just died, but come and lay your hand on her, and she will live."

⁹19 Jesus got up and followed him, as did his disciples. ⁹20 Behold, a woman who had a discharge of blood for twelve years came behind him, and touched the fringe⁴⁹ of his garment; ⁹21 for she said within herself, "If I just touch his garment, I will be made well."

⁹22 But Jesus, turning around and seeing her, said, "Daughter, cheer up! Your faith has made you well." And the woman was made well from that hour.

⁹23 When Jesus came into the ruler's house, and saw the flute players, and the crowd in noisy disorder, ⁹24 he said to them, "Make room, because the girl isn't dead, but sleeping."

They were ridiculing him. ⁹25 But when the crowd was put out, he entered in, took her by the hand, and the girl arose. ⁹26 The report of this went out into all that land. ⁹27 As Jesus passed by from there, two blind men followed him, calling out and saying, "Have mercy on us, son of David!"

⁹28 When he had come into the house, the blind men came to him. Jesus said to them, "Do you believe that I am able to do this?"

They told him, "Yes, Lord."

#9:13 9:13 Hosea 6:6
⁴⁸9:13 9:13 NU omits "to repentance".
⁴⁹9:20 9:20 or, tassel

Day Fifteen

⁹29 Then he touched their eyes, saying, "According to your faith be it done to you." ⁹30 Their eyes were opened. Jesus strictly commanded them, saying, "See that no one knows about this." ⁹31 But they went out and spread abroad his fame in all that land.
⁹32 As they went out, behold, a mute man who was demon possessed was brought to him. ⁹33 When the demon was cast out, the mute man spoke. The multitudes marveled, saying, "Nothing like this has ever been seen in Israel!"
⁹34 But the Pharisees said, "By the prince of the demons, he casts out demons."
⁹35 Jesus went about all the cities and the villages, teaching in their synagogues, and preaching the Good News of the Kingdom, and healing every disease and every sickness among the people. ⁹36 But when he saw the multitudes, he was moved with compassion for them, because they were harassed[50] and scattered, like sheep without a shepherd. ⁹37 Then he said to his disciples, "The harvest indeed is plentiful, but the laborers are few. ⁹38 ⁹Pray therefore that the Lord of the harvest will send out laborers into his harvest."

The Lord's Prayer

Our Father, who art in heaven,
Hallowed be thy name.
Thy Kingdom come.
Thy will be done on Earth, as it is in heaven.
Give us this day our daily bread.
And forgive us our trespasses,
As we forgive those that trespass against us.
And lead us not into temptation,
But deliver us from evil.
For thine is the kingdom,

---

[50]9:36 9:36 TR reads "weary" instead of "harassed"

The American Book of Prayer

The power, and the glory,
For ever and ever.
AMEN

Day Sixteen

Daily Prayer

O Lord our God, most mighty and merciful father, I thine unworthy creature and servant, do once more approach thy presence. Though not worthy to appear before thee, because of my natural corruptions, and the many sins and transgressions which I have committed against thy divine majesty; yet I beseech thee, for the sake of him in whom thou art well pleased, the Lord Jesus Christ, to admit me to render thee deserved thanks and praises for thy manifold mercies extended toward me, for the quiet rest & repose of the past night, for food, rainment, health, peace, liberty, and the hopes of a better life through the merits of thy dear son's bitter passion. And O kind father continue thy mercy and favor to me this day, and ever hereafter; purpose all my lawful undertakings; let me have all my directions from thy holy spirit; and success from thy bountiful hand. Let the bright beams of thy light so shine into my heart, and enlighten my mind in understanding thy

> "And O kind father continue thy mercy and favor to me this day, and ever hereafter; purpose all my lawful undertakings; let me have all my directions from thy holy spirit; and success from thy bountiful hand."

blessed word, that I may be enabled to perform thy will in all things, and effectually resist all temptations of the world, the flesh and the devil. Preserve and defend our rulers in church and state. Bless the people of this land, be a father to the fatherless, a comforter to the comfortless, a deliverer to the captives, and a physician to the sick. Let thy blessings guide this day and forever through Jesus Christ in whose blessed form of prayer I conclude my weak petitions.
—*Attributed to American hero George Washington. Discovered in* Washington's Prayer Journal *in a prayer entitled "Tuesday Morning Prayer." Likely a prayer from a resident at Mt. Vernon, but it's not clear if George Washington is the true author.*

Prayer of Confession

Almighty and most merciful Father; we have erred, and strayed from your ways like lost sheep. We have followed too much the devices and desires of our own hearts. We have offended against your holy laws. We have left undone those things which we ought to have done; and we have done those things which we ought not to have done; and there is no health in us. O Lord, have mercy upon us, miserable offenders. Spare those, O God, who confess their faults. Restore those who are penitent; according to your promises declared unto mankind in Christ Jesus our Lord. And grant, O most merciful Father, for his sake; that we may hereafter live a godly, righteous, and sober life, to the glory of thy holy Name. Amen.
-Revised prayer from *The Book of Common Prayer*, 1662

Day Sixteen

Daily Wisdom

1 How long wilt thou forget me, O LORD? for ever? how long wilt thou hide thy face from me?
2 How long shall I take counsel in my soul, *having* sorrow in my heart daily? how long shall mine enemy be exalted over me?
3 Consider *and* hear me, O LORD my God: lighten mine eyes, lest I sleep the *sleep of* death;
4 Lest mine enemy say, I have prevailed against him; *and* those that trouble me rejoice when I am moved.
5 But I have trusted in thy mercy; my heart shall rejoice in thy salvation.
6 I will sing unto the LORD, because he hath dealt bountifully with me.
-Psalm 13, *The King James Bible*, 1769 edition of 1611 text

Readings from the Holy Bible

The Holy Gospel According to Matthew and John (MATTHEW 10:1-39; JOHN 3:1-21)

MATTHEW 10:1-39, JESUS' MISSION FOR THE TWELVE

10

[10]1 He called to himself his twelve disciples, and gave them authority over unclean spirits, to cast them out, and to heal every disease and every sickness. [10]2 Now the names of the twelve apostles are these. The first, Simon, who is called Peter; Andrew, his brother; James the son of Zebedee; John, his brother; [10]3 Philip; Bartholomew; Thomas; Matthew the tax collector; James the son of Alphaeus; Lebbaeus, who was also called[51] Thaddaeus; [10]4 Simon the Canaanite; and Judas Iscariot, who also betrayed him.

---

[51]10:3 10:3 NU omits "Lebbaeus, who was also called"

The American Book of Prayer

¹⁰5 Jesus sent these twelve out, and commanded them, saying, "Don't go among the Gentiles, and don't enter into any city of the Samaritans. ¹⁰6 Rather, go to the lost sheep of the house of Israel. ¹⁰7 As you go, preach, saying, 'The Kingdom of Heaven is at hand!' ¹⁰8 Heal the sick, cleanse the lepers,[52] and cast out demons. Freely you received, so freely give. ¹⁰9 Don't take any gold, silver, or brass in your money belts. ¹⁰10 Take no bag for your journey, neither two coats, nor shoes, nor staff: for the laborer is worthy of his food. ¹⁰11 Into whatever city or village you enter, find out who in it is worthy; and stay there until you go on. ¹⁰12 As you enter into the household, greet it. ¹⁰13 If the household is worthy, let your peace come on it, but if it isn't worthy, let your peace return to you. ¹⁰14 Whoever doesn't receive you, nor hear your words, as you go out of that house or that city, shake the dust off your feet. ¹⁰15 Most certainly I tell you, it will be more tolerable for the land of Sodom and Gomorrah in the day of judgment than for that city.

¹⁰16 "Behold, I send you out as sheep among wolves. Therefore be wise as serpents, and harmless as doves. ¹⁰17 But beware of men: for they will deliver you up to councils, and in their synagogues they will scourge you. ¹⁰18 Yes, and you will be brought before governors and kings for my sake, for a testimony to them and to the nations. ¹⁰19 But when they deliver you up, don't be anxious how or what you will say, for it will be given you in that hour what you will say. ¹⁰20 For it is not you who speak, but the Spirit of your Father who speaks in you. ¹⁰21 "Brother will deliver up brother to death, and the father his child. Children will rise up against parents, and cause them to be put to death. ¹⁰22 You will be hated by all men for my name's sake, but he who endures to the end will be saved. ¹⁰23 But when they persecute you in this city, flee into the next, for most certainly I tell you, you will not have gone through the cities of Israel until the Son of Man has come.

¹⁰24 "A disciple is not above his teacher, nor a servant above his lord. ¹⁰25 It is enough for the disciple that he be like his teacher, and the servant like his lord. If they have called the master of the house Beelzebul,[53] how much more those of his household! ¹⁰26 Therefore

---

[52] 10:8 10:8 TR adds "raise the dead,"
[53] 10:25 10:25 Literally, Lord of the Flies, or the devil

Day Sixteen

don't be afraid of them, for there is nothing covered that will not be revealed; and hidden that will not be known. ¹⁰27 What I tell you in the darkness, speak in the light; and what you hear whispered in the ear, proclaim on the housetops. ¹⁰28 Don't be afraid of those who kill the body, but are not able to kill the soul. Rather, fear him who is able to destroy both soul and body in Gehenna. ⁵⁴

¹⁰29 "Aren't two sparrows sold for an assarion coin?⁵⁵ Not one of them falls on the ground apart from your Father's will, ¹⁰30 but the very hairs of your head are all numbered. ¹⁰31 Therefore don't be afraid. You are of more value than many sparrows. ¹⁰32 Everyone therefore who confesses me before men, I will also confess him before my Father who is in heaven. ¹⁰33 But whoever denies me before men, I will also deny him before my Father who is in heaven. ¹⁰34 "Don't think that I came to send peace on the earth. I didn't come to send peace, but a sword. ¹⁰35 For I came to set a man at odds against his father, and a daughter against her mother, and a daughter-in-law against her mother-in-law. ¹⁰36 A man's foes will be those of his own household.# ¹⁰37 He who loves father or mother more than me is not worthy of me; and he who loves son or daughter more than me isn't worthy of me. ¹⁰38 He who doesn't take his cross and follow after me, isn't worthy of me. ¹⁰39 He who seeks his life will lose it; and he who loses his life for my sake will find it. ¹⁰40 He who receives you receives me, and he who receives me receives him who sent me. ¹⁰41 He who receives a prophet in the name of a prophet will receive a prophet's reward. He who receives a righteous man in the name of a righteous man will receive a righteous man's reward. ¹⁰42 ¹⁰Whoever gives one of these little ones just a cup of cold water to drink in the name of a disciple, most certainly I tell you he will in no way lose his reward."

---

⁵⁴10:28 10:28 or, Hell.
⁵⁵10:29 10:29 An assarion is a small coin worth one tenth of a drachma or a sixteenth of a denarius. An assarion is approximately the wages of one half hour of agricultural labor.
#10:36 10:36 Micah 7:6

The American Book of Prayer

JOHN 3:1-21, JESUS AND NICODEMUS

3

³1 Now there was a man of the Pharisees named Nicodemus, a ruler of the Jews. ³2 The same came to him by night, and said to him, "Rabbi, we know that you are a teacher come from God, for no one can do these signs that you do, unless God is with him."

³3 Jesus answered him, "Most certainly, I tell you, unless one is born anew,[56] he can't see God's Kingdom."

³4 Nicodemus said to him, "How can a man be born when he is old? Can he enter a second time into his mother's womb, and be born?"

³5 Jesus answered, "Most certainly I tell you, unless one is born of water and spirit, he can't enter into God's Kingdom. ³6 That which is born of the flesh is flesh. That which is born of the Spirit is spirit. ³7 Don't marvel that I said to you, 'You must be born anew.' ³8 The wind[57] blows where it wants to, and you hear its sound, but don't know where it comes from and where it is going. So is everyone who is born of the Spirit."

³9 Nicodemus answered him, "How can these things be?"

³10 Jesus answered him, "Are you the teacher of Israel, and don't understand these things? ³11 Most certainly I tell you, we speak that which we know, and testify of that which we have seen, and you don't receive our witness. ³12 If I told you earthly things and you don't believe, how will you believe if I tell you heavenly things? ³13 No one has ascended into heaven but he who descended out of heaven, the Son of Man, who is in heaven. ³14 As Moses lifted up the serpent in the wilderness, even so must the Son of Man be lifted up, ³15 that whoever believes in him should not perish, but have eternal life. ³16 For God so loved the world, that he gave his one and only Son, that whoever believes in him should not perish, but have eternal life. ³17 For God didn't send his Son into the world to judge the world, but that the world should be saved through him. ³18 He who believes in him is not judged. He who doesn't believe has been judged already, because he has not believed in the name of the one and only Son of

---

[56]3:3 3:3 The word translated "anew" here and in John 3:7 (ἄνωθεν) also means "again" and "from above".
[57]3:8 3:8 The same Greek word (πνεῦμα) means wind, breath, and spirit.

Day Sixteen

God. ³¹⁹ This is the judgment, that the light has come into the world, and men loved the darkness rather than the light; for their works were evil. ³²⁰ For everyone who does evil hates the light, and doesn't come to the light, lest his works would be exposed. ³²¹ But he who does the truth comes to the light, that his works may be revealed, that they have been done in God.

The Lord's Prayer

Our Father, who art in heaven,
Hallowed be thy name.
Thy Kingdom come.
Thy will be done on Earth, as it is in heaven.
Give us this day our daily bread.
And forgive us our trespasses,
As we forgive those that trespass against us.
And lead us not into temptation,
But deliver us from evil.
For thine is the kingdom,
The power, and the glory,
For ever and ever.
AMEN

Day Seventeen

Daily Prayer

I now make it my earnest prayer, that God would have you and the State over which you preside, in his holy protection, that he would incline the hearts of the Citizens to cultivate a spirit of subordination and obedience to Government—to entertain a brotherly affection and love for one another, for their fellow Citizens of the United States at large, and particularly for their Brethren who have served in the Field, and finally, that he would most graciously be pleased to dispose us all, to do Justice, to love Mercy, and to demean ourselves with that Charity, Humility, and Pacific temper of mind which were the Characteristicks of the Divine Author of our blessed Religion, and without an humble imitation of whose example in these things, we can never hope to be a Happy Nation. I have the honor to be with the greatest esteem & respect Sir Your Excellency's Most Obedient and very Humble Servant.
—*George Washington to John Hancock, June 11, 1783.*

> "I now make it my earnest prayer, that God would have you and the State over which you preside, in his holy protection."

Prayer of Confession

Almighty and most merciful Father; we have erred, and strayed from your ways like lost sheep. We have followed too much the devices and desires of our own hearts. We have offended against your holy laws. We have left undone those things which we ought to have done; and we have done those things which we ought not to have done; and there is no health in us. O Lord, have mercy upon us, miserable offenders. Spare those, O God, who confess their faults. Restore those who are penitent; according to your promises declared unto mankind in Christ Jesus our Lord. And grant, O most merciful Father, for his sake; that we may hereafter live a godly, righteous, and sober life, to the glory of thy holy Name. Amen.
-Revised prayer from *The Book of Common Prayer*, 1662

Daily Wisdom

1 The fool hath said in his heart, *There is* no God. They are corrupt, they have done abominable works, *there is* none that doeth good.
2 The LORD looked down from heaven upon the children of men, to see if there were any that did understand, *and* seek God.
3 They are all gone aside, they are *all* together become filthy: *there is* none that doeth good, no, not one.
4 Have all the workers of iniquity no knowledge? Who eat up my people *as* they eat bread, and call not upon the LORD.
5 There were they in great fear: for God *is* in the generation of the righteous.
6 Ye have shamed the counsel of the poor, because the LORD *is* his refuge.

Day Seventeen

7 Oh that the salvation of Israel *were come* out of Zion! when the LORD bringeth back the captivity of his people, Jacob shall rejoice, *and* Israel shall be glad.
-Psalm 14, *The King James Bible*, 1769 edition of 1611 text

Readings from the Holy Bible

The Holy Gospel According to Matthew and John (MATTHEW 11:1-19; JOHN 3:22-4:54)

MATTHEW 11:1-19, JOHN THE BAPTIST

11

¹¹1 When Jesus had finished directing his twelve disciples, he departed from there to teach and preach in their cities. ¹¹2 Now when John heard in the prison the works of Christ, he sent two of his disciples ¹¹3 and said to him, "Are you he who comes, or should we look for another?"
¹¹4 Jesus answered them, "Go and tell John the things which you hear and see: ¹¹5 the blind receive their sight, the lame walk, the lepers are cleansed, the deaf hear,# the dead are raised up, and the poor have good news preached to them.# ¹¹6 Blessed is he who finds no occasion for stumbling in me."
¹¹7 As these went their way, Jesus began to say to the multitudes concerning John, "What did you go out into the wilderness to see? A reed shaken by the wind? ¹¹8 But what did you go out to see? A man in soft clothing? Behold, those who wear soft clothing are in kings' houses. ¹¹9 But why did you go out? To see a prophet? Yes, I tell you, and much more than a prophet. ¹¹10 For this is he, of whom it is written, 'Behold, I send my messenger before your face, who will prepare your way before you.'# ¹¹11 Most certainly I tell you, among those who are born of women there has not arisen anyone greater

---

#11:5 11:5 Isaiah 35:5
#11:5 11:5 Isaiah 61:1-4
#11:10 11:10 Malachi 3:1

than John the Baptizer; yet he who is least in the Kingdom of Heaven is greater than he. **11:12** From the days of John the Baptizer until now, the Kingdom of Heaven suffers violence, and the violent take it by force.[58] **11:13** For all the prophets and the law prophesied until John. **11:14** If you are willing to receive it, this is Elijah, who is to come. **11:15** He who has ears to hear, let him hear.

11:16 "But to what shall I compare this generation? It is like children sitting in the marketplaces, who call to their companions **11:17** and say, 'We played the flute for you, and you didn't dance. We mourned for you, and you didn't lament.' **11:18** For John came neither eating nor drinking, and they say, 'He has a demon.' **11:19** The Son of Man came eating and drinking, and they say, 'Behold, a gluttonous man and a drunkard, a friend of tax collectors and sinners!' But wisdom is justified by her children."[59]

JOHN 3:22-4:54

3:22 After these things, Jesus came with his disciples into the land of Judea. He stayed there with them and baptized. **3:23** John also was baptizing in Enon near Salim, because there was much water there. They came, and were baptized; **3:24** for John was not yet thrown into prison. **3:25** Therefore a dispute arose on the part of John's disciples with some Jews about purification. **3:26** They came to John and said to him, "Rabbi, he who was with you beyond the Jordan, to whom you have testified, behold, he baptizes, and everyone is coming to him." **3:27** John answered, "A man can receive nothing unless it has been given him from heaven. **3:28** You yourselves testify that I said, 'I am not the Christ,' but, 'I have been sent before him.' **3:29** He who has the bride is the bridegroom; but the friend of the bridegroom, who stands and hears him, rejoices greatly because of the bridegroom's voice. This, my joy, therefore is made full. **3:30** He must increase, but I must decrease. **3:31** He who comes from
above is above all. He who is from the earth belongs to the earth and speaks of the earth. He who comes from heaven is above all. **3:32** What he has seen and heard, of that he testifies; and no one receives his

---

[58]11:12 11:12 or, plunder it.
[59]11:19 11:19 NU reads "actions" instead of "children"

Day Seventeen

witness. **333** He who has received his witness has set his seal to this, that God is true. **334** For he whom God has sent speaks the words of God; for God gives the Spirit without measure. **335** The Father loves the Son, and has given all things into his hand. **336** One who believes in the Son has eternal life, but one who disobeys [360] the Son won't see life, but the wrath of God remains on him."

The Lord's Prayer

Our Father, who art in heaven,
Hallowed be thy name.
Thy Kingdom come.
Thy will be done on Earth, as it is in heaven.
Give us this day our daily bread.
And forgive us our trespasses,
As we forgive those that trespass against us.
And lead us not into temptation,
But deliver us from evil.
For thine is the kingdom,
The power, and the glory,
For ever and ever.
AMEN

---

[60]3:36 3:36 The same word can be translated "disobeys" or "disbelieves" in this context.

Day Eighteen

Daily Prayer

Search, therefore, the scriptures, my dear brethren; taste and see how good the word of God is, and then you will never leave that heavenly manna, that angel's food, to feed on dry husks, that light bread, those trifling, sinful compositions, in which men of false taste delight themselves: no, you will then disdain such poor entertainment, and blush that yourselves once were fond of it. The word of God will then be sweeter to you than honey, and the honey-comb, and dearer than gold and silver; your souls by reading it, will be filled as it were, with marrow and fatness, and your hearts insensibly molded into the spirit of its blessed Author. In short, you will be guided by God's wisdom here, and conducted by the light of his divine word into glory hereafter.
– *George Whitefield, one of the most prominent pastors in American history, Sermon: "The Duty of Searching the Scriptures."*

> "The word of God will then be sweeter to you than honey, and the honey-comb, and dearer than gold and silver ..."

Prayer of Confession

Almighty and most merciful Father; we have erred, and strayed from your ways like lost sheep. We have followed too much the devices and desires of our own hearts. We have offended against your holy laws. We have left undone those things which we ought to have done; and we have done those things which we ought not to have done; and there is no health in us. O Lord, have mercy upon us, miserable offenders. Spare those, O God, who confess their faults. Restore those who are penitent; according to your promises declared unto mankind in Christ Jesus our Lord. And grant, O most merciful Father, for his sake; that we may hereafter live a godly, righteous, and sober life, to the glory of thy holy Name. Amen.
-Revised prayer from *The Book of Common Prayer*, 1662

Daily Wisdom

1 My son, forget not my law; but let thine heart keep my commandments:
2 For length of days, and long life, and peace, shall they add to thee.
3 Let not mercy and truth forsake thee: bind them about thy neck; write them upon the table of thine heart:
4 So shalt thou find favour and good understanding in the sight of God and man.
5 Trust in the LORD with all thine heart; and lean not unto thine own understanding.
6 In all thy ways acknowledge him, and he shall direct thy paths.
7 Be not wise in thine own eyes: fear the LORD, and depart from evil.
8 It shall be health to thy navel, and marrow to thy bones.

Day Eighteen

9 Honor the LORD with thy substance, and with the firstfruits of all thine increase:
10 So shall thy barns be filled with plenty, and thy presses shall burst out with new wine.
11 My son, despise not the chastening of the LORD; neither be weary of his correction:
12 For whom the LORD loveth he correcteth; even as a father the son *in whom* he delighteth.
13 Happy *is* the man *that* findeth wisdom, and the man *that* getteth understanding.
-Proverbs 3:1-13, *The King James Bible*, 1769 edition of 1611 text

Readings from the Holy Bible

The Holy Gospel According to John (JOHN 5:1-47)

JOHN 5:1-47

5

5:1 After these things, there was a feast of the Jews, and Jesus went up to Jerusalem. **5:2** Now in Jerusalem by the sheep gate, there is a pool, which is called in Hebrew, "Bethesda", having five porches. **5:3** In these lay a great multitude of those who were sick, blind, lame, or paralyzed, waiting for the moving of the water; **5:4** for an angel went down at certain times into the pool and stirred up the water. Whoever stepped in first after the stirring of the water was healed of whatever disease he had.[61] **5:5** A certain man was there who had been sick for thirty-eight years. **5:6** When Jesus saw him lying there, and knew that he had been sick for a long time, he asked him, "Do you want to be made well?"
5:7 The sick man answered him, "Sir, I have no one to put me into the pool when the water is stirred up, but while I'm coming, another steps down before me."

---

[61]5:4 5:4 NU omits from "waiting" in verse 3 to the end of verse 4.

⁸ Jesus said to him, "Arise, take up your mat, and walk."
⁹ Immediately, the man was made well, and took up his mat and walked.
Now it was the Sabbath on that day. ¹⁰ So the Jews said to him who was cured, "It is the Sabbath. It is not lawful for you to carry the mat."
¹¹ He answered them, "He who made me well said to me, 'Take up your mat and walk.'"
¹² Then they asked him, "Who is the man who said to you, 'Take up your mat and walk'?"
¹³ But he who was healed didn't know who it was, for Jesus had withdrawn, a crowd being in the place.
¹⁴ Afterward Jesus found him in the temple, and said to him, "Behold, you are made well. Sin no more, so that nothing worse happens to you."
¹⁵ The man went away, and told the Jews that it was Jesus who had made him well. ¹⁶ For this cause the Jews persecuted Jesus, and sought to kill him, because he did these things on the Sabbath. ¹⁷ But Jesus answered them, "My Father is still working, so I am working, too." ¹⁸ For this cause therefore the Jews sought all the more to kill him, because he not only broke the Sabbath, but also called God his own Father, making himself equal with God. ¹⁹ Jesus therefore answered them, "Most certainly, I tell you, the Son can do nothing of himself, but what he sees the Father doing. For whatever things he does, these the Son also does likewise. ²⁰ For the Father has affection for the Son, and shows him all things that he himself does. He will show him greater works than these, that you may marvel. ²¹ For as the Father raises the dead and gives them life, even so the Son also gives life to whom he desires. ²² For the Father judges no one, but he has given all judgment to the Son, ²³ that all may honor the Son, even as they honor the Father. He who doesn't honor the Son doesn't honor the Father who sent him.
²⁴ "Most certainly I tell you, he who hears my word and believes him who sent me has eternal life, and doesn't come into judgment, but has passed out of death into life. ²⁵ Most certainly I tell you, the hour comes, and now is, when the dead will hear the Son of God's voice; and those who hear will live. ²⁶ For as the

Day Eighteen

Father has life in himself, even so he gave to the Son also to have life in himself. ⁵²⁷ He also gave him authority to execute judgment, because he is a son of man. ⁵²⁸ Don't marvel at this, for the hour comes in which all who are in the tombs will hear his voice, ⁵²⁹ and will come out; those who have done good, to the resurrection of life; and those who have done evil, to the resurrection of judgment. ⁵³⁰ I can of myself do nothing. As I hear, I judge, and my judgment is righteous; because I don't seek my own will, but the will of my Father who sent me.

⁵³¹ "If I testify about myself, my witness is not valid. ⁵³² It is another who testifies about me. I know that the testimony which he testifies about me is true. ⁵³³ You have sent to John, and he has testified to the truth. ⁵³⁴ But the testimony which I receive is not from man. However, I say these things that you may be saved. ⁵³⁵ He was the burning and shining lamp, and you were willing to rejoice for a while in his light. ⁵³⁶ But the testimony which I have is greater than that of John, for the works which the Father gave me to accomplish, the very works that I do, testify about me, that the Father has sent me. ⁵³⁷ The Father himself, who sent me, has testified about me. You have neither heard his voice at any time, nor seen his form. ⁵³⁸ You don't have his word living in you; because you don't believe him whom he sent.

⁵³⁹ "You search the Scriptures, because you think that in them you have eternal life; and these are they which testify about me. ⁵⁴⁰ Yet you will not come to me, that you may have life. ⁵⁴¹ I don't receive glory from men. ⁵⁴² But I know you, that you don't have God's love in yourselves. ⁵⁴³ I have come in my Father's name, and you don't receive me. If another comes in his own name, you will receive him. ⁵⁴⁴ How can you believe, who receive glory from one another, and you don't seek the glory that comes from the only God?

⁵⁴⁵ "Don't think that I will accuse you to the Father. There is one who accuses you, even Moses, on whom you have set your hope. ⁵⁴⁶ For if you believed Moses, you would believe me; for he wrote about me. ⁵⁴⁷ ⁵But if you don't believe his writings, how will you believe my words?"

The American Book of Prayer

The Lord's Prayer

Our Father, who art in heaven,
Hallowed be thy name.
Thy Kingdom come.
Thy will be done on Earth, as it is in heaven.
Give us this day our daily bread.
And forgive us our trespasses,
As we forgive those that trespass against us.
And lead us not into temptation,
But deliver us from evil.
For thine is the kingdom,
The power, and the glory,
For ever and ever.
AMEN

Day Nineteen

Daily Prayer

Come, all of you, come, and behold him stretched out for you; see his hands and feet nailed to the cross. O come, come, my brethren, and nail your sins thereto; come, come and see his side pierced; there is a fountain open for sin, and for uncleanness: O wash, wash and be clean: come and see his head crowned with thorns, and all for you. Can you think of a panting, bleeding, dying Jesus, and not be filled with pity towards him? He underwent all this for you. Come unto him by faith; lay hold on him: there is mercy for every soul of you that will come unto him. Then do not delay; fly unto the arms of this Jesus, and you shall be made clean in his blood. ...

> "Show them, O Father, wherein they have offended thee ... and O give them that repentance, we beseech of thee, that they may turn from sin unto thee the living and true God."

Show them, O Father, wherein they have offended thee; make them to see their own vileness, and that they are lost and undone without true repentance; and O give them that

repentance, we beseech of thee, that they may turn from sin unto thee the living and true God. These things, and whatever else thou seest needful for us, we entreat that thou wouldst bestow upon us, on account of what the dear Jesus Christ has done and suffered; to whom, with Thyself, and holy Spirit, three persons, and one God, be ascribed, as is most due, all power, glory, might, majesty, and dominion, now, henceforth, and for evermore. Amen.
– *George Whitefield, one of the most prominent pastors in American history, Sermon: "Christ, the Only Preservative Against a Reprobative Spirit."*

Prayer of Confession

Almighty and most merciful Father; we have erred, and strayed from your ways like lost sheep. We have followed too much the devices and desires of our own hearts. We have offended against your holy laws. We have left undone those things which we ought to have done; and we have done those things which we ought not to have done; and there is no health in us. O Lord, have mercy upon us, miserable offenders. Spare those, O God, who confess their faults. Restore those who are penitent; according to your promises declared unto mankind in Christ Jesus our Lord. And grant, O most merciful Father, for his sake; that we may hereafter live a godly, righteous, and sober life, to the glory of thy holy Name. Amen.
-Revised prayer from *The Book of Common Prayer*, 1662

Daily Wisdom

14 For the merchandise of it *is* better than the merchandise of silver, and the gain thereof than fine gold.
15 She *is* more precious than rubies: and all the things thou canst desire are not to be compared unto her.

Day Nineteen

16 Length of days *is* in her right hand; *and* in her left hand riches and honor.
17 Her ways *are* ways of pleasantness, and all her paths *are* peace.
18 She *is* a tree of life to them that lay hold upon her: and happy *is everyone* that retaineth her.
19 The LORD by wisdom hath founded the earth; by understanding hath he established the heavens.
20 By his knowledge the depths are broken up, and the clouds drop down the dew.
21 My son, let not them depart from thine eyes: keep sound wisdom and discretion:
22 So shall they be life unto thy soul, and grace to thy neck.
23 Then shalt thou walk in thy way safely, and thy foot shall not stumble.
24 When thou liest down, thou shalt not be afraid: yea, thou shalt lie down, and thy sleep shall be sweet.
25 Be not afraid of sudden fear, neither of the desolation of the wicked, when it cometh.
26 For the LORD shall be thy confidence, and shall keep thy foot from being taken.
27 Withhold not good from them to whom it is due, when it is in the power of thine hand to do *it*.
28 Say not unto thy neighbour, Go, and come again, and to morrow I will give; when thou hast it by thee.
29 Devise not evil against thy neighbour, seeing he dwelleth securely by thee.
30 Strive not with a man without cause, if he have done thee no harm.
31 Envy thou not the oppressor, and choose none of his ways.
-Proverbs 3:14-31, *The King James Bible*, 1769 edition of 1611 text

The American Book of Prayer

Readings from the Holy Bible

The Holy Gospel According to Matthew (MATTHEW 11:20-12:50)

MATTHEW 11:20-12:50, BEELZEBOB AND JONAH

11:20 Then he began to denounce the cities in which most of his mighty works had been done, because they didn't repent. **11:21** "Woe to you, Chorazin! Woe to you, Bethsaida! For if the mighty works had been done in Tyre and Sidon which were done in you, they would have repented long ago in sackcloth and ashes. **11:22** But I tell you, it will be more tolerable for Tyre and Sidon on the day of judgment than for you. **11:23** You, Capernaum, who are exalted to heaven, you will go down to Hades. [62] For if the mighty works had been done in Sodom which were done in you, it would have remained until today. **11:24** But I tell you that it will be more tolerable for the land of Sodom, on the day of judgment, than for you."

11:25 At that time, Jesus answered, "I thank you, Father, Lord of heaven and earth, that you hid these things from the wise and understanding, and revealed them to infants. **11:26** Yes, Father, for so it was well-pleasing in your sight. **11:27** All things have been delivered to me by my Father. No one knows the Son, except the Father; neither does anyone know the Father, except the Son, and he to whom the Son desires to reveal him.

11:28 "Come to me, all you who labor and are heavily burdened, and I will give you rest. **11:29** Take my yoke upon you, and learn from me, for I am gentle and humble in heart; and you will find rest for your souls. **11:30** [11]For my yoke is easy, and my burden is light."

12

12:1 At that time, Jesus went on the Sabbath day through the grain fields. His disciples were hungry and began to pluck heads of grain and to eat. **12:2** But the Pharisees, when they saw it, said to him, "Behold, your disciples do what is not lawful to do on the Sabbath."

---

[62]11:23 11:23 or, Hell

Day Nineteen

¹²3 But he said to them, "Haven't you read what David did, when he was hungry, and those who were with him; ¹²4 how he entered into God's house, and ate the show bread, which was not lawful for him to eat, neither for those who were with him, but only for the priests?#
¹²5 Or have you not read in the law, that on the Sabbath day, the priests in the temple profane the Sabbath, and are guiltless? ¹²6 But I tell you that one greater than the temple is here. ¹²7 But if you had known what this means, 'I desire mercy, and not sacrifice,'# you wouldn't have condemned the guiltless. ¹²8 For the Son of Man is Lord of the Sabbath."
¹²9 He departed there, and went into their synagogue. ¹²10 And behold there was a man with a withered hand. They asked him, "Is it lawful to heal on the Sabbath day?" that they might accuse him.
¹²11 He said to them, "What man is there among you, who has one sheep, and if this one falls into a pit on the Sabbath day, won't he grab on to it, and lift it out? ¹²12 Of how much more value then is a man than a sheep! Therefore it is lawful to do good on the Sabbath day."
¹²13 Then he told the man, "Stretch out your hand." He stretched it out; and it was restored whole, just like the other. ¹²14 But the Pharisees went out, and conspired against him, how they might destroy him. ¹²15 Jesus, perceiving that, withdrew from there. Great multitudes followed him; and he healed them all, ¹²16 and commanded them that they should not make him known: ¹²17 that it might be fulfilled which was spoken through Isaiah the prophet, saying,
¹²18 "Behold, my servant whom I have chosen;
my beloved in whom my soul is well pleased:
I will put my Spirit on him.
He will proclaim justice to the nations.
¹²19 He will not strive, nor shout;
neither will anyone hear his voice in the streets.
¹²20 He won't break a bruised reed.
He won't quench a smoking flax,
until he leads justice to victory.
¹²21 In his name, the nations will hope."#

#12:4 12:4 1 Samuel 21:3-6
#12:7 12:7 Hosea 6:6
#12:21 12:21 Isaiah 42:1-4

¹²22 Then one possessed by a demon, blind and mute, was brought to him and he healed him, so that the blind and mute man both spoke and saw. ¹²23 All the multitudes were amazed, and said, "Can this be the son of David?" ¹²24 But when the Pharisees heard it, they said, "This man does not cast out demons, except by Beelzebul, the prince of the demons."
¹²25 Knowing their thoughts, Jesus said to them, "Every kingdom divided against itself is brought to desolation, and every city or house divided against itself will not stand. ¹²26 If Satan casts out Satan, he is divided against himself. How then will his kingdom stand? ¹²27 If I by Beelzebul cast out demons, by whom do your children cast them out? Therefore they will be your judges. ¹²28 But if I by the Spirit of God cast out demons, then God's Kingdom has come upon you.
¹²29 Or how can one enter into the house of the strong man, and plunder his goods, unless he first bind the strong man? Then he will plunder his house.
¹²30 "He who is not with me is against me, and he who doesn't gather with me, scatters. ¹²31 Therefore I tell you, every sin and blasphemy will be forgiven men, but the blasphemy against the Spirit will not be forgiven men. ¹²32 Whoever speaks a word against the Son of Man, it will be forgiven him; but whoever speaks against the Holy Spirit, it will not be forgiven him, neither in this age, nor in that which is to come.
¹²33 "Either make the tree good, and its fruit good, or make the tree corrupt, and its fruit corrupt; for the tree is known by its fruit. ¹²34 You offspring of vipers, how can you, being evil, speak good things? For out of the abundance of the heart, the mouth speaks. ¹²35 The good man out of his good treasure brings out good things, and the evil man out of his evil treasure[63] brings out evil things. ¹²36 I tell you that every idle word that men speak, they will give account of it in the day of judgment. ¹²37 For by your words you will be justified, and by your words you will be condemned."
¹²38 Then certain of the scribes and Pharisees answered, "Teacher, we want to see a sign from you."
¹²39 But he answered them, "An evil and adulterous generation seeks after a sign, but no sign will be given to it but the sign of Jonah the prophet. ¹²40 For as Jonah was three days and three nights in the

---

[63]12:35 12:35 TR adds "of the heart"

Day Nineteen

belly of the whale, so will the Son of Man be three days and three nights in the heart of the earth. [12:41] The men of Nineveh will stand up in the judgment with this generation, and will condemn it, for they repented at the preaching of Jonah; and behold, someone greater than Jonah is here. [12:42] The queen of the south will rise up in the judgment with this generation, and will condemn it, for she came from the ends of the earth to hear the wisdom of Solomon; and behold, someone greater than Solomon is here.

[12:43] When an unclean spirit has gone out of a man, he passes through waterless places, seeking rest, and doesn't find it. [12:44] Then he says, 'I will return into my house from which I came out,' and when he has come back, he finds it empty, swept, and put in order. [12:45] Then he goes, and takes with himself seven other spirits more evil than he is, and they enter in and dwell there. The last state of that man becomes worse than the first. Even so will it be also to this evil generation."

[12:46] While he was yet speaking to the multitudes, behold, his mother and his brothers stood outside, seeking to speak to him. [12:47] One said to him, "Behold, your mother and your brothers stand outside, seeking to speak to you."

[12:48] But he answered him who spoke to him, "Who is my mother? Who are my brothers?" [12:49] He stretched out his hand toward his disciples, and said, "Behold, my mother and my brothers! [12:50] [12]For whoever does the will of my Father who is in heaven, he is my brother, and sister, and mother."

The Lord's Prayer

Our Father, who art in heaven,
Hallowed be thy name.
Thy Kingdom come.
Thy will be done on Earth, as it is in heaven.
Give us this day our daily bread.
And forgive us our trespasses,
As we forgive those that trespass against us.

The American Book of Prayer

And lead us not into temptation,
But deliver us from evil.
For thine is the kingdom,
The power, and the glory,
For ever and ever.
AMEN

Day Twenty

Daily Prayer

If darkness be occasioned by manifold and heavy and unexpected temptations, the best way of removing and preventing this is, to teach believers always to expect temptation, seeing they dwell in an evil world, among wicked, subtle, malicious spirits, and have a heart capable of all evil....

Above all, let them be instructed, when the storm is upon them, not to reason with the devil, but to pray, to pour out their souls before God, and show him of their trouble. And these are the persons unto whom, chiefly, we are to apply the great and precious promises—not to the ignorant, till the ignorance is removed, much less to the impenitent sinner. To these we may largely and affectionately declare the loving kindness of God our Savior, expatiate upon his tender mercies, which have been ever of old. Here we may dwell upon the faithfulness of God, whose "word is tried to the uttermost," and upon the virtue of that blood which

> *"Above all, let them be instructed, when the storm is upon them, not to reason with the devil, but to pray, to pour out their souls before God, and show him of their trouble."*

was shed for us, to "cleanse us from all sin." And God will then bear witness to his word, and bring their souls out of trouble. He will say, "Arise, shine; for thy light is come, and the glory of the Lord is risen upon thee." Yea, and that light, if thou walk humbly and closely with God, will "shine more and more unto the perfect day."
-John Wesley, Sermon: "The Wilderness State."

Prayer of Confession

Almighty and most merciful Father; we have erred, and strayed from your ways like lost sheep. We have followed too much the devices and desires of our own hearts. We have offended against your holy laws. We have left undone those things which we ought to have done; and we have done those things which we ought not to have done; and there is no health in us. O Lord, have mercy upon us, miserable offenders. Spare those, O God, who confess their faults. Restore those who are penitent; according to your promises declared unto mankind in Christ Jesus our Lord. And grant, O most merciful Father, for his sake; that we may hereafter live a godly, righteous, and sober life, to the glory of thy holy Name. Amen.
-Revised prayer from *The Book of Common Prayer*, 1662

Daily Wisdom

1 Hear, ye children, the instruction of a father, and attend to know understanding.
2 For I give you good doctrine, forsake ye not my law.
3 For I was my father's son, tender and only *beloved* in the sight of my mother.
4 He taught me also, and said unto me, Let thine heart retain my words: keep my commandments, and live.

Day Twenty

5 Get wisdom, get understanding: forget *it* not; neither decline from the words of my mouth.

6 Forsake her not, and she shall preserve thee: love her, and she shall keep thee.

7 Wisdom *is* the principal thing; *therefore* get wisdom: and with all thy getting get understanding.

8 Exalt her, and she shall promote thee: she shall bring thee to honor, when thou dost embrace her.

9 She shall give to thine head an ornament of grace: a crown of glory shall she deliver to thee.

10 Hear, O my son, and receive my sayings; and the years of thy life shall be many.

11 I have taught thee in the way of wisdom; I have led thee in right paths.

12 When thou goest, thy steps shall not be straitened; and when thou runnest, thou shalt not stumble.

13 Take fast hold of instruction; let *her* not go: keep her; for she *is* thy life.

14 Enter not into the path of the wicked, and go not in the way of evil *men*.

15 Avoid it, pass not by it, turn from it, and pass away.

16 For they sleep not, except they have done mischief; and their sleep is taken away, unless they cause *some* to fall.

17 For they eat the bread of wickedness, and drink the wine of violence.

18 But the path of the just *is* as the shining light, that shineth more and more unto the perfect day.

19 The way of the wicked *is* as darkness: they know not at what they stumble.

20 My son, attend to my words; incline thine ear unto my sayings.

21 Let them not depart from thine eyes; keep them in the midst of thine heart.

22 For they *are* life unto those that find them, and health to all their flesh.

23 Keep thy heart with all diligence; for out of it *are* the issues of life.

24 Put away from thee a froward mouth, and perverse lips put far from thee.
25 Let thine eyes look right on, and let thine eyelids look straight before thee.
26 Ponder the path of thy feet, and let all thy ways be established.
27 Turn not to the right hand nor to the left: remove thy foot from evil.
-Proverbs 4, *The King James Bible*, 1769 edition of 1611 text

Readings from the Holy Bible

The Holy Gospel According to John (JOHN 11:34-54; JOHN 7:37-8:18)

JOHN 11:34-54, THE LAMP
11**33** When Jesus therefore saw her weeping, and the Jews weeping who came with her, he groaned in the spirit, and was troubled,
11**34** and said, "Where have you laid him?"
They told him, "Lord, come and see."
11**35** Jesus wept.
11**36** The Jews therefore said, "See how much affection he had for him!" **11****37** Some of them said, "Couldn't this man, who opened the eyes of him who was blind, have also kept this man from dying?"
11**38** Jesus therefore, again groaning in himself, came to the tomb. Now it was a cave, and a stone lay against it. **11****39** Jesus said, "Take away the stone."
Martha, the sister of him who was dead, said to him, "Lord, by this time there is a stench, for he has been dead four days."
1**40** Jesus said to her, "Didn't I tell you that if you believed, you would see God's glory?"
11**41** So they took away the stone from the place where the dead man was lying.[64] Jesus lifted up his eyes, and said, "Father, I thank you that you listened to me. **11****42** I know that you always listen to me, but

---

[64]11:41 11:41 NU omits "from the place where the dead man was lying."

Day Twenty

because of the multitude standing around I said this, that they may believe that you sent me." **¹¹43** When he had said this, he cried with a loud voice, "Lazarus, come out!"
¹¹44 He who was dead came out, bound hand and foot with wrappings, and his face was wrapped around with a cloth.
Jesus said to them, "Free him, and let him go."
¹¹45 Therefore many of the Jews who came to Mary and saw what Jesus did believed in him. **¹¹46** But some of them went away to the Pharisees and told them the things which Jesus had done. **¹¹47** The chief priests therefore and the Pharisees gathered a council, and said, "What are we doing? For this man does many signs. **¹¹48** If we leave him alone like this, everyone will believe in him, and the Romans will come and take away both our place and our nation."
¹¹49 But a certain one of them, Caiaphas, being high priest that year, said to them, "You know nothing at all, **¹¹50** nor do you consider that it is advantageous for us that one man should die for the people, and that the whole nation not perish." **¹¹51** Now he didn't say this of himself, but being high priest that year, he prophesied that Jesus would die for the nation, **¹¹52** and not for the nation only, but that he might also gather together into one the children of God who are scattered abroad. **¹¹53** So from that day forward they took counsel that they might put him to death. **¹¹54** Jesus therefore walked no more openly among the Jews, but departed from there into the country near the wilderness, to a city called Ephraim. He stayed there with his disciples.

JOHN 7:37-8:18, THE SINFUL WOMAN AND THE PARABLE OF THE SOWER

⁷37 Now on the last and greatest day of the feast, Jesus stood and cried out, "If anyone is thirsty, let him come to me and drink! **⁷38** He who believes in me, as the Scripture has said, from within him will flow rivers of living water." **⁷39** But he said this about the Spirit, which those believing in him were to receive. For the Holy Spirit was not yet given, because Jesus wasn't yet glorified.
⁷40 Many of the multitude therefore, when they heard these words, said, "This is truly the prophet." **⁷41** Others said, "This is the Christ." But some said, "What, does the Christ come out of Galilee? **⁷42** Hasn't

the Scripture said that the Christ comes of the offspring[65] of David, #
and from Bethlehem,# the village where David was?" **7:43** So a division
arose in the multitude because of him. **7:44** Some of them would have
arrested him, but no one laid hands on him. **7:45** The officers therefore
came to the chief priests and Pharisees, and they said to them, "Why
didn't you bring him?"

7:46 The officers answered, "No man ever spoke like this man!"

7:47 The Pharisees therefore answered them, "You aren't also led
astray, are you? **7:48** Have any of the rulers believed in him, or of the
Pharisees? **7:49** But this multitude that doesn't know the law is cursed."

7:50 Nicodemus (he who came to him by night, being one of them)
said to them, **7:51** "Does our law judge a man, unless it first hears from
him personally and knows what he does?"

7:52 They answered him, "Are you also from Galilee? Search, and see
that no prophet has arisen out of Galilee."#

7:53 Everyone went to his own house, 7

8

8:1 but Jesus went to the Mount of Olives. **8:2** Now very early in the
morning, he came again into the temple, and all the people came to
him. He sat down and taught them. **8:3** The scribes and the Pharisees
brought a woman taken in adultery. Having set her in the middle,
8:4 they told him, "Teacher, we found this woman in adultery, in the
very act. **8:5** Now in our law, Moses commanded us to stone such
women.# What then do you say about her?" **8:6** They said this testing
him, that they might have something to accuse him of.

But Jesus stooped down and wrote on the ground with his finger.
8:7 But when they continued asking him, he looked up and said to
them, "He who is without sin among you, let him throw the first stone
at her." **8:8** Again he stooped down and wrote on the ground with his
finger.

8:9 They, when they heard it, being convicted by their conscience, went
out one by one, beginning from the oldest, even to the last. Jesus was

---

[65]7:42 7:42 or, seed
#7:42 7:42 2 Samuel 7:12
#7:42 7:42 Micah 5:2
#7:52 7:52 See Isaiah 9:1; Matthew 4:13-16
#8:5 8:5 Leviticus 20:10; Deuteronomy 22:22

Day Twenty

left alone with the woman where she was, in the middle. [8]10 Jesus, standing up, saw her and said, "Woman, where are your accusers? Did no one condemn you?"

[8]11 She said, "No one, Lord."

Jesus said, "Neither do I condemn you. Go your way. From now on, sin no more."[66]

[8]12 Again, therefore, Jesus spoke to them, saying, "I am the light of the world.[#] He who follows me will not walk in the darkness, but will have the light of life."

[8]13 The Pharisees therefore said to him, "You testify about yourself. Your testimony is not valid."

[8]14 Jesus answered them, "Even if I testify about myself, my testimony is true, for I know where I came from, and where I am going; but you don't know where I came from, or where I am going.

[8]15 You judge according to the flesh. I judge no one.

[8]16 Even if I do judge, my judgment is true, for I am not alone, but I am with the Father who sent me.

[8]17 It's also written in your law that the testimony of two people is valid. [8]18 I am one who testifies about myself, and the Father who sent me testifies about me."

The Lord's Prayer

Our Father, who art in heaven,
Hallowed be thy name.
Thy Kingdom come.
Thy will be done on Earth, as it is in heaven.
Give us this day our daily bread.
And forgive us our trespasses,
As we forgive those that trespass against us.
And lead us not into temptation,
But deliver us from evil.

---

[66]8:11 8:11 NU includes John 7:53–John 8:11, but puts brackets around it to indicate that the textual critics had less confidence that this was original.
[#]8:12 8:12 Isaiah 60:1

The American Book of Prayer

For thine is the kingdom,
The power, and the glory,
For ever and ever.
AMEN

Day Twenty-One

Daily Prayer

Most gracious and holy God, my wretched soul aches for you, and yet, I continue to separate myself from you in sin. Father, grant me the wisdom and power to overcome my sinful nature. Jesus, provide me strength to live as you have taught the world through your Apostles. Holy Spirit, fill my heart with your wisdom and transform my soul. Guard my heart, God, against the evil of the world—against materialism, violence, profanity, immorality, and anger. For without your love, wisdom, guidance, and Holy Spirit, I could not overcome these qualities of my natural and fallen state. Save me Lord, so that I might save others, all in Your name. Amen.

> "For without your love, wisdom, guidance, and Holy Spirit, I could not overcome these qualities of my natural and fallen state. Save me Lord, so that I might save others, all in Your name."

Prayer of Confession

Almighty and most merciful Father; we have erred, and strayed from your ways like lost sheep. We have followed too much the devices and desires of our own hearts. We have offended against your holy laws. We have left undone those things which we ought to have done; and we have done those things which we ought not to have done; and there is no health in us. O Lord, have mercy upon us, miserable offenders. Spare those, O God, who confess their faults. Restore those who are penitent; according to your promises declared unto mankind in Christ Jesus our Lord. And grant, O most merciful Father, for his sake; that we may hereafter live a godly, righteous, and sober life, to the glory of thy holy Name. Amen.
-Revised prayer from *The Book of Common Prayer*, 1662

Daily Wisdom

18 Let thy fountain be blessed: and rejoice with the wife of thy youth.
19 Let her be as the loving hind and pleasant roe; let her breasts satisfy thee at all times; and be thou ravished always with her love.
20 And why wilt thou, my son, be ravished with a strange woman, and embrace the bosom of a stranger?
21 For the ways of man are before the eyes of the LORD, and he pondereth all his goings.
22 His own iniquities shall take the wicked himself, and he shall be holden with the cords of his sins.
23 He shall die without instruction; and in the greatness of his folly he shall go astray.
-Proverbs 5:18-23, *The King James Bible*, 1769 edition of 1611 text

Day Twenty-One

Readings from the Holy Bible

The Holy Gospel According to Mark and Matthew (MARK 4:26-29; MATTHEW 13:24-14:36)

MARK 4:26-29, THE GROWING SEED
4:26 He said, "God's Kingdom is as if a man should cast seed on the earth, 4:27 and should sleep and rise night and day, and the seed should spring up and grow, though he doesn't know how. 4:28 For the earth bears fruit: first the blade, then the ear, then the full grain in the ear. 4:29 But when the fruit is ripe, immediately he puts in the sickle, because the harvest has come."

MATTHEW 13:24-14:36, PARABLES AND CHRIST WALKS ON WATER

13:24 He set another parable before them, saying, "The Kingdom of Heaven is like a man who sowed good seed in his field, 13:25 but while people slept, his enemy came and sowed darnel weeds[67] also among the wheat, and went away. 13:26 But when the blade sprang up and produced fruit, then the darnel weeds appeared also. 13:27 The servants of the householder came and said to him, 'Sir, didn't you sow good seed in your field? Where did these darnel weeds come from?' 13:28 "He said to them, 'An enemy has done this.'
"The servants asked him, 'Do you want us to go and gather them up?'
13:29 But he said, "No, lest perhaps while you gather up the darnel weeds, you root up the wheat with them. 13:30 Let both grow together until the harvest, and in the harvest time I will tell the reapers, 'First, gather up the darnel weeds, and bind them in bundles to burn them; but gather the wheat into my barn.'"
13:31 He set another parable before them, saying, "The Kingdom of Heaven is like a grain of mustard seed, which a man took, and sowed in his field; 13:32 which indeed is smaller than all seeds. But when it is

---

[67]13:25 13:25 darnel is a weed grass (probably bearded darnel or lolium temulentum) that looks very much like wheat until it is mature, when the difference becomes very apparent.

grown, it is greater than the herbs, and becomes a tree, so that the birds of the air come and lodge in its branches."

13:33 He spoke another parable to them. "The Kingdom of Heaven is like yeast, which a woman took, and hid in three measures[68] of meal, until it was all leavened."

13:34 Jesus spoke all these things in parables to the multitudes; and without a parable, he didn't speak to them, **13:35** that it might be fulfilled which was spoken through the prophet, saying,
"I will open my mouth in parables;
I will utter things hidden from the foundation of the world."[#]

13:36 Then Jesus sent the multitudes away, and went into the house. His disciples came to him, saying, "Explain to us the parable of the darnel weeds of the field."

13:37 He answered them, "He who sows the good seed is the Son of Man, **13:38** the field is the world; and the good seed, these are the children of the Kingdom; and the darnel weeds are the children of the evil one. **13:39** The enemy who sowed them is the devil. The harvest is the end of the age, and the reapers are angels. **13:40** As therefore the darnel weeds are gathered up and burned with fire; so will it be at the end of this age. **13:41** The Son of Man will send out his angels, and they will gather out of his Kingdom all things that cause stumbling, and those who do iniquity, **13:42** and will cast them into the furnace of fire. There will be weeping and the gnashing of teeth. **13:43** Then the righteous will shine like the sun in the Kingdom of their Father. He who has ears to hear, let him hear.

13:44 "Again, the Kingdom of Heaven is like treasure hidden in the field, which a man found, and hid. In his joy, he goes and sells all that he has, and buys that field.

13:45 "Again, the Kingdom of Heaven is like a man who is a merchant seeking fine pearls, **13:46** who having found one pearl of great price, he went and sold all that he had, and bought it.

13:47 "Again, the Kingdom of Heaven is like a dragnet, that was cast into the sea, and gathered some fish of every kind, **13:48** which, when it was filled, they drew up on the beach. They sat down, and gathered

---

[68]13:33 13:33 literally, three sata. Three sata is about 39 liters or a bit more than a bushel
[#]13:35 13:35 Psalm 78:2

Day Twenty-One

the good into containers, but the bad they threw away. **13:49** So will it be in the end of the world.[69] The angels will come and separate the wicked from among the righteous, **13:50** and will cast them into the furnace of fire. There will be the weeping and the gnashing of teeth."
13:51 Jesus said to them, "Have you understood all these things?" They answered him, "Yes, Lord."
13:52 He said to them, "Therefore every scribe who has been made a disciple in the Kingdom of Heaven is like a man who is a householder, who brings out of his treasure new and old things."
13:53 When Jesus had finished these parables, he departed from there. **13:54** Coming into his own country, he taught them in their synagogue, so that they were astonished, and said, "Where did this man get this wisdom, and these mighty works? **13:55** Isn't this the carpenter's son? Isn't his mother called Mary, and his brothers, James, Joses, Simon, and Judas?[70] **13:56** Aren't all of his sisters with us? Where then did this man get all of these things?" **13:57** They were offended by him.
But Jesus said to them, "A prophet is not without honor, except in his own country, and in his own house." **13:58** He didn't do many mighty works there because of their unbelief. **13**

14

14:1 At that time, Herod the tetrarch heard the report concerning Jesus, **14:2** and said to his servants, "This is John the Baptizer. He is risen from the dead. That is why these powers work in him." **14:3** For Herod had arrested John, and bound him, and put him in prison for the sake of Herodias, his brother Philip's wife. **14:4** For John said to him, "It is not lawful for you to have her." **14:5** When he would have put him to death, he feared the multitude, because they counted him as a prophet. **14:6** But when Herod's birthday came, the daughter of Herodias danced among them and pleased Herod. **14:7** Whereupon he promised with an oath to give her whatever she should ask. **14:8** She, being prompted by her mother, said, "Give me here on a platter the head of John the Baptizer."

---

[69]13:49 13:49 or, end of the age.
[70]13:55 13:55 or, Judah

The American Book of Prayer

¹⁴9 The king was grieved, but for the sake of his oaths, and of those who sat at the table with him, he commanded it to be given, ¹⁴10 and he sent and beheaded John in the prison. ¹⁴11 His head was brought on a platter, and given to the young lady; and she brought it to her mother. ¹⁴12 His disciples came, and took the body, and buried it. Then they went and told Jesus. ¹⁴13 Now when Jesus heard this, he withdrew from there in a boat, to a deserted place apart. When the multitudes heard it, they followed him on foot from the cities.

¹⁴14 Jesus went out, and he saw a great multitude. He had compassion on them, and healed their sick. ¹⁴15 When evening had come, his disciples came to him, saying, "This place is deserted, and the hour is already late. Send the multitudes away, that they may go into the villages, and buy themselves food."

¹⁴16 But Jesus said to them, "They don't need to go away. You give them something to eat."

¹⁴17 They told him, "We only have here five loaves and two fish." ¹⁴18 He said, "Bring them here to me." ¹⁴19 He commanded the multitudes to sit down on the grass; and he took the five loaves and the two fish, and looking up to heaven, he blessed, broke and gave the loaves to the disciples, and the disciples gave to the multitudes. ¹⁴20 They all ate, and were filled. They took up twelve baskets full of that which remained left over from the broken pieces. ¹⁴21 Those who ate were about five thousand men, in addition to women and children.

¹⁴22 Immediately Jesus made the disciples get into the boat, and to go ahead of him to the other side, while he sent the multitudes away. ¹⁴23 After he had sent the multitudes away, he went up into the mountain by himself to pray. When evening had come, he was there alone. ¹⁴24 But the boat was now in the middle of the sea, distressed by the waves, for the wind was contrary. ¹⁴25 In the fourth watch of the night,[71] Jesus came to them, walking on the sea.[#] ¹⁴26 When the disciples saw him walking on the sea, they were troubled, saying, "It's

---

[71]14:25 14:25 The night was equally divided into four watches, so the fourth watch is approximately 3:00 a.m. to sunrise.
[#]14:25 14:25 See Job 9:8

Day Twenty-One

a ghost!" and they cried out for fear. ¹⁴27 But immediately Jesus spoke to them, saying, "Cheer up! It is I! [72] Don't be afraid."
¹⁴28 Peter answered him and said, "Lord, if it is you, command me to come to you on the waters."
¹⁴29 He said, "Come!"
Peter stepped down from the boat, and walked on the waters to come to Jesus. ¹⁴30 But when he saw that the wind was strong, he was afraid, and beginning to sink, he cried out, saying, "Lord, save me!"
¹⁴31 Immediately Jesus stretched out his hand, took hold of him, and said to him, "You of little faith, why did you doubt?" ¹⁴32 When they got up into the boat, the wind ceased. ¹⁴33 Those who were in the boat came and worshiped him, saying, "You are truly the Son of God!"
¹⁴34 When they had crossed over, they came to the land of Gennesaret. ¹⁴35 When the people of that place recognized him, they sent into all that surrounding region, and brought to him all who were sick; ¹⁴36 and they begged him that they might just touch the fringe[1473] of his garment. As many as touched it were made whole.

The Lord's Prayer

Our Father, who art in heaven,
Hallowed be thy name.
Thy Kingdom come.
Thy will be done on Earth, as it is in heaven.
Give us this day our daily bread.
And forgive us our trespasses,
As we forgive those that trespass against us.
And lead us not into temptation,
But deliver us from evil.
For thine is the kingdom,

---

[72]14:27 14:27 or, I AM!
[73]14:36 14:36 or, tassel

The American Book of Prayer

The power, and the glory,
For ever and ever.
AMEN

Day Twenty-Two

Daily Prayer

I arise today
Through the strength of heaven;
Light of the sun,
Splendor of fire,
Speed of lightning,
Swiftness of the wind,
Depth of the sea,
Stability of the earth,
Firmness of the rock.
I arise today
Through God's strength to pilot me;
God's might to uphold me,
God's wisdom to guide me,
God's eye to look before me,
God's ear to hear me,
God's word to speak for me,
God's hand to guard me,
God's way to lie before me,
God's shield to protect me,
God's hosts to save me

> *"I arise today through the mighty strength of the Lord of creation."*

Afar and anear,
Alone or in a mulitude.
Christ shield me today
Against wounding
Christ with me, Christ before me, Christ behind me,
Christ in me, Christ beneath me, Christ above me,
Christ on my right, Christ on my left,
Christ when I lie down, Christ when I sit down,
Christ in the heart of everyone who thinks of me,
Christ in the mouth of everyone who speaks of me,
Christ in the eye that sees me,
Christ in the ear that hears me.
I arise today
Through the mighty strength
Of the Lord of creation.
-Patrick, 5th Century Bishop of Ireland

Prayer of Confession

Almighty and most merciful Father; we have erred, and strayed from your ways like lost sheep. We have followed too much the devices and desires of our own hearts. We have offended against your holy laws. We have left undone those things which we ought to have done; and we have done those things which we ought not to have done; and there is no health in us. O Lord, have mercy upon us, miserable offenders. Spare those, O God, who confess their faults. Restore those who are penitent; according to your promises declared unto mankind in Christ Jesus our Lord. And grant, O most merciful Father, for his sake; that we may hereafter live a godly, righteous, and sober life, to the glory of thy holy Name. Amen.
-Revised prayer from *The Book of Common Prayer*, 1662

Day Twenty-Two

Daily Wisdom

11 So shall thy poverty come as one that travelleth, and thy want as an armed man.
12 A naughty person, a wicked man, walketh with a froward mouth.
13 He winketh with his eyes, he speaketh with his feet, he teacheth with his fingers;
14 Frowardness *is* in his heart, he deviseth mischief continually; he soweth discord.
15 Therefore shall his calamity come suddenly; suddenly shall he be broken without remedy.
16 These six *things* doth the LORD hate: yea, seven *are* an abomination unto him:
17 A proud look, a lying tongue, and hands that shed innocent blood,
18 An heart that deviseth wicked imaginations, feet that be swift in running to mischief,
19 A false witness *that* speaketh lies, and he that soweth discord among brethren.
20 My son, keep thy father's commandment, and forsake not the law of thy mother:
21 Bind them continually upon thine heart, *and* tie them about thy neck.
22 When thou goest, it shall lead thee; when thou sleepest, it shall keep thee; and *when* thou awakest, it shall talk with thee.
23 For the commandment *is* a lamp; and the law *is* light; and reproofs of instruction *are* the way of life:
24 To keep thee from the evil woman, from the flattery of the tongue of a strange woman.
25 Lust not after her beauty in thine heart; neither let her take thee with her eyelids.
26 For by means of a whorish woman *a man is brought* to a piece of bread: and the adulteress will hunt for the precious life.

27 Can a man take fire in his bosom, and his clothes not be burned?
28 Can one go upon hot coals, and his feet not be burned?
29 So he that goeth in to his neighbour's wife; whosoever toucheth her shall not be innocent.
-Proverbs 6:11-29, *The King James Bible*, 1769 edition of 1611 text

Readings from the Holy Bible

The Holy Gospel According to John (JOHN 6:1-7:53)

JOHN 6:1-7:53, THE BREAD OF LIFE IS THE CHRIST

6

6:1 After these things, Jesus went away to the other side of the sea of Galilee, which is also called the Sea of Tiberias. **6:2** A great multitude followed him, because they saw his signs which he did on those who were sick. **6:3** Jesus went up into the mountain, and he sat there with his disciples. **6:4** Now the Passover, the feast of the Jews, was at hand. **6:5** Jesus therefore lifting up his eyes, and seeing that a great multitude was coming to him, said to Philip, "Where are we to buy bread, that these may eat?" **6:6** He said this to test him, for he himself knew what he would do.
6:7 Philip answered him, "Two hundred denarii[74] worth of bread is not sufficient for them, that every one of them may receive a little."
6:8 One of his disciples, Andrew, Simon Peter's brother, said to him, **6:9** "There is a boy here who has five barley loaves and two fish, but what are these among so many?"
6:10 Jesus said, "Have the people sit down." Now there was much grass in that place. So the men sat down, in number about five thousand.
6:11 Jesus took the loaves; and having given thanks, he distributed to the disciples, and the disciples to those who were sitting down; likewise also of the fish as much as they desired. **6:12** When they were

---

[74]6:7 6:7 A denarius was a silver coin worth about a day's wages for an agricultural laborer, so 200 denarii would be between 6 and 7 month's pay.

Day Twenty-Two

filled, he said to his disciples, "Gather up the broken pieces which are left over, that nothing be lost." ⁶13 So they gathered them up, and filled twelve baskets with broken pieces from the five barley loaves, which were left over by those who had eaten. ⁶14 When therefore the people saw the sign which Jesus did, they said, "This is truly the prophet who comes into the world." ⁶15 Jesus therefore, perceiving that they were about to come and take him by force to make him king, withdrew again to the mountain by himself.

⁶16 When evening came, his disciples went down to the sea. ⁶17 They entered into the boat, and were going over the sea to Capernaum. It was now dark, and Jesus had not come to them. ⁶18 The sea was tossed by a great wind blowing. ⁶19 When therefore they had rowed about twenty-five or thirty stadia, [75] they saw Jesus walking on the sea,[#] and drawing near to the boat; and they were afraid. ⁶20 But he said to them, "It is I.[76] Don't be afraid." ⁶21 They were willing therefore to receive him into the boat. Immediately the boat was at the land where they were going.

⁶22 On the next day, the multitude that stood on the other side of the sea saw that there was no other boat there, except the one in which his disciples had embarked, and that Jesus hadn't entered with his disciples into the boat, but his disciples had gone away alone. ⁶23 However boats from Tiberias came near to the place where they ate the bread after the Lord had given thanks. ⁶24 When the multitude therefore saw that Jesus wasn't there, nor his disciples, they themselves got into the boats, and came to Capernaum, seeking Jesus. ⁶25 When they found him on the other side of the sea, they asked him, "Rabbi, when did you come here?"

⁶26 Jesus answered them, "Most certainly I tell you, you seek me, not because you saw signs, but because you ate of the loaves, and were filled. ⁶27 Don't work for the food which perishes, but for the food which remains to eternal life, which the Son of Man will give to you. For God the Father has sealed him."

⁶28 They said therefore to him, "What must we do, that we may work the works of God?"

---

[75]6:19 6:19 25 to 30 stadia is about 5 to 6 kilometers or about 3 to 4 miles
[#]6:19 6:19 See Job 9:8
[76]6:20 6:20 or, I AM

The American Book of Prayer

⁶²⁹ Jesus answered them, "This is the work of God, that you believe in him whom he has sent."

⁶³⁰ They said therefore to him, "What then do you do for a sign, that we may see and believe you? What work do you do? ⁶³¹ Our fathers ate the manna in the wilderness. As it is written, 'He gave them bread out of heaven[77] to eat.'"[#]

⁶³² Jesus therefore said to them, "Most certainly, I tell you, it wasn't Moses who gave you the bread out of heaven, but my Father gives you the true bread out of heaven. ⁶³³ For the bread of God is that which comes down out of heaven, and gives life to the world."

⁶³⁴ They said therefore to him, "Lord, always give us this bread."

⁶³⁵ Jesus said to them, "I am the bread of life. Whoever comes to me will not be hungry, and whoever believes in me will never be thirsty. ⁶³⁶ But I told you that you have seen me, and yet you don't believe. ⁶³⁷ All those whom the Father gives me will come to me. He who comes to me I will in no way throw out. ⁶³⁸ For I have come down from heaven, not to do my own will, but the will of him who sent me. ⁶³⁹ This is the will of my Father who sent me, that of all he has given to me I should lose nothing, but should raise him up at the last day. ⁶⁴⁰ This is the will of the one who sent me, that everyone who sees the Son, and believes in him, should have eternal life; and I will raise him up at the last day."

⁶⁴¹ The Jews therefore murmured concerning him, because he said, "I am the bread which came down out of heaven." ⁶⁴² They said, "Isn't this Jesus, the son of Joseph, whose father and mother we know? How then does he say, 'I have come down out of heaven?'"

⁶⁴³ Therefore Jesus answered them, "Don't murmur among yourselves. ⁶⁴⁴ No one can come to me unless the Father who sent me draws him, and I will raise him up in the last day. ⁶⁴⁵ It is written in the prophets, 'They will all be taught by God.' [#] Therefore everyone who hears from the Father and has learned, comes to me. ⁶⁴⁶ Not that anyone has seen the Father, except he who is from God. He has seen the Father. ⁶⁴⁷ Most certainly, I tell you, he who believes

---

[77]6:31 6:31 Greek and Hebrew use the same word for "heaven", "the heavens", "the sky", and "the air".
[#]6:31 6:31 Exodus 16:4; Nehemiah 9:15; Psalm 78:24-25
[#]6:45 6:45 Isaiah 54:13

Day Twenty-Two

in me has eternal life. ⁶48 I am the bread of life. ⁶49 Your fathers ate the manna in the wilderness and they died. ⁶50 This is the bread which comes down out of heaven, that anyone may eat of it and not die. ⁶51 I am the living bread which came down out of heaven. If anyone eats of this bread, he will live forever. Yes, the bread which I will give for the life of the world is my flesh."

⁶52 The Jews therefore contended with one another, saying, "How can this man give us his flesh to eat?"

⁶53 Jesus therefore said to them, "Most certainly I tell you, unless you eat the flesh of the Son of Man and drink his blood, you don't have life in yourselves. ⁶54 He who eats my flesh and drinks my blood has eternal life, and I will raise him up at the last day. ⁶55 For my flesh is food indeed, and my blood is drink indeed. ⁶56 He who eats my flesh and drinks my blood lives in me, and I in him. ⁶57 As the living Father sent me, and I live because of the Father; so he who feeds on me, he will also live because of me. ⁶58 This is the bread which came down out of heaven—not as our fathers ate the manna, and died. He who eats this bread will live forever." ⁶59 He said these things in the synagogue, as he taught in Capernaum.

⁶60 Therefore many of his disciples, when they heard this, said, "This is a hard saying! Who can listen to it?"

⁶61 But Jesus knowing in himself that his disciples murmured at this, said to them, "Does this cause you to stumble? ⁶62 Then what if you would see the Son of Man ascending to where he was before? ⁶63 It is the spirit who gives life. The flesh profits nothing. The words that I speak to you are spirit, and are life. ⁶64 But there are some of you who don't believe." For Jesus knew from the beginning who they were who didn't believe, and who it was who would betray him. ⁶65 He said, "For this cause I have said to you that no one can come to me, unless it is given to him by my Father."

⁶66 At this, many of his disciples went back, and walked no more with him. ⁶67 Jesus said therefore to the twelve, "You don't also want to go away, do you?"

⁶68 Simon Peter answered him, "Lord, to whom would we go? You have the words of eternal life. ⁶69 We have come to believe and know that you are the Christ, the Son of the living God."

⁶⁷⁰ Jesus answered them, "Didn't I choose you, the twelve, and one of you is a devil?" ⁶⁷¹ Now he spoke of Judas, the son of Simon Iscariot, for it was he who would betray him, being one of the twelve. ⁶

7

⁷¹ After these things, Jesus was walking in Galilee, for he wouldn't walk in Judea, because the Jews sought to kill him. ⁷² Now the feast of the Jews, the Feast of Booths, was at hand. ⁷³ His brothers therefore said to him, "Depart from here and go into Judea, that your disciples also may see your works which you do. ⁷⁴ For no one does anything in secret while he seeks to be known openly. If you do these things, reveal yourself to the world." ⁷⁵ For even his brothers didn't believe in him.

⁷⁶ Jesus therefore said to them, "My time has not yet come, but your time is always ready. ⁷⁷ The world can't hate you, but it hates me, because I testify about it, that its works are evil. ⁷⁸ You go up to the feast. I am not yet going up to this feast, because my time is not yet fulfilled."

⁷⁹ Having said these things to them, he stayed in Galilee. ⁷¹⁰ But when his brothers had gone up to the feast, then he also went up, not publicly, but as it were in secret. ⁷¹¹ The Jews therefore sought him at the feast, and said, "Where is he?" ⁷¹² There was much murmuring among the multitudes concerning him. Some said, "He is a good man." Others said, "Not so, but he leads the multitude astray." ⁷¹³ Yet no one spoke openly of him for fear of the Jews. ⁷¹⁴ But when it was now the middle of the feast, Jesus went up into the temple and taught. ⁷¹⁵ The Jews therefore marveled, saying, "How does this man know letters, having never been educated?"

⁷¹⁶ Jesus therefore answered them, "My teaching is not mine, but his who sent me. ⁷¹⁷ If anyone desires to do his will, he will know about the teaching, whether it is from God, or if I am speaking from myself. ⁷¹⁸ He who speaks from himself seeks his own glory, but he who seeks the glory of him who sent him is true, and no unrighteousness is in him. ⁷¹⁹ Didn't Moses give you the law, and yet none of you keeps the law? Why do you seek to kill me?"

⁷²⁰ The multitude answered, "You have a demon! Who seeks to kill you?"

Day Twenty-Two

⁷²¹ Jesus answered them, "I did one work and you all marvel because of it. ⁷²² Moses has given you circumcision (not that it is of Moses, but of the fathers), and on the Sabbath you circumcise a boy. ⁷²³ If a boy receives circumcision on the Sabbath, that the law of Moses may not be broken, are you angry with me, because I made a man completely healthy on the Sabbath? ⁷²⁴ Don't judge according to appearance, but judge righteous judgment."

⁷²⁵ Therefore some of them of Jerusalem said, "Isn't this he whom they seek to kill? ⁷²⁶ Behold, he speaks openly, and they say nothing to him. Can it be that the rulers indeed know that this is truly the Christ? ⁷²⁷ However we know where this man comes from, but when the Christ comes, no one will know where he comes from."

⁷²⁸ Jesus therefore cried out in the temple, teaching and saying, "You both know me, and know where I am from. I have not come of myself, but he who sent me is true, whom you don't know. ⁷²⁹ I know him, because I am from him, and he sent me."

⁷³⁰ They sought therefore to take him; but no one laid a hand on him, because his hour had not yet come. ⁷³¹ But of the multitude, many believed in him. They said, "When the Christ comes, he won't do more signs than those which this man has done, will he?" ⁷³² The Pharisees heard the multitude murmuring these things concerning him, and the chief priests and the Pharisees sent officers to arrest him. ⁷³³ Then Jesus said, "I will be with you a little while longer, then I go to him who sent me. ⁷³⁴ You will seek me, and won't find me. You can't come where I am."

⁷³⁵ The Jews therefore said among themselves, "Where will this man go that we won't find him? Will he go to the Dispersion among the Greeks, and teach the Greeks? ⁷³⁶ What is this word that he said, 'You will seek me, and won't find me;' and 'Where I am, you can't come'?"

⁷³⁷ Now on the last and greatest day of the feast, Jesus stood and cried out, "If anyone is thirsty, let him come to me and drink! ⁷³⁸ He who believes in me, as the Scripture has said, from within him will flow rivers of living water." ⁷³⁹ But he said this about the Spirit, which those believing in him were to receive. For the Holy Spirit was not yet given, because Jesus wasn't yet glorified.

⁷⁴⁰ Many of the multitude therefore, when they heard these words, said, "This is truly the prophet." ⁷⁴¹ Others said, "This is the Christ."

But some said, "What, does the Christ come out of Galilee? [742] Hasn't the Scripture said that the Christ comes of the offspring of David, and from Bethlehem, the village where David was?" [743] So a division arose in the multitude because of him. [744] Some of them would have arrested him, but no one laid hands on him. [745] The officers therefore came to the chief priests and Pharisees, and they said to them, "Why didn't you bring him?"
[746] The officers answered, "No man ever spoke like this man!"
[747] The Pharisees therefore answered them, "You aren't also led astray, are you? [748] Have any of the rulers believed in him, or of the Pharisees? [749] But this multitude that doesn't know the law is cursed." [750] Nicodemus (he who came to him by night, being one of them) said to them, [751] "Does our law judge a man, unless it first hears from him personally and knows what he does?"
[752] They answered him, "Are you also from Galilee? Search, and see that no prophet has arisen out of Galilee."

The Lord's Prayer

Our Father, who art in heaven,
Hallowed be thy name.
Thy Kingdom come.
Thy will be done on Earth, as it is in heaven.
Give us this day our daily bread.
And forgive us our trespasses,
As we forgive those that trespass against us.
And lead us not into temptation,
But deliver us from evil.
For thine is the kingdom,
The power, and the glory,
For ever and ever.
AMEN

Day Twenty-Three

Daily Prayer

You are holy, Lord, the only God,
and Your deeds are wonderful.
You are strong.
You are great.
You are the Most High.
You are Almighty.
You, Holy Father are King
of heaven and earth.
You are Three and One,
Lord God, all Good.
You are Good, all Good,
supreme Good,
Lord God, living and true.
You are love. You are
wisdom.
You are humility. You are
endurance.
You are rest. You are peace.
You are joy and gladness.
You are justice and moderation.
You are all our riches, and You suffice for us.
You are beauty.
You are gentleness.

> "You are Three and One, Lord God, all Good. You are Good, all Good, supreme Good, Lord God, living and true."

You are our protector.
You are our guardian and defender.
You are our courage. You are our haven and our hope.
You are our faith, our great consolation.
You are our eternal life, Great and Wonderful Lord,
God Almighty, Merciful Savior.
-Francis of Assisi (1181–1226)

Prayer of Confession

Almighty and most merciful Father; we have erred, and strayed from your ways like lost sheep. We have followed too much the devices and desires of our own hearts. We have offended against your holy laws. We have left undone those things which we ought to have done; and we have done those things which we ought not to have done; and there is no health in us. O Lord, have mercy upon us, miserable offenders. Spare those, O God, who confess their faults. Restore those who are penitent; according to your promises declared unto mankind in Christ Jesus our Lord. And grant, O most merciful Father, for his sake; that we may hereafter live a godly, righteous, and sober life, to the glory of thy holy Name. Amen.
-Revised prayer from *The Book of Common Prayer*, 1662

Daily Wisdom

4 Say unto wisdom, Thou *art* my sister; and call understanding *thy* kinswoman:
5 That they may keep thee from the strange woman, from the stranger *which* flattereth with her words.
6 For at the window of my house I looked through my casement,
7 And beheld among the simple ones, I discerned among the youths, a young man void of understanding,

Day Twenty-Three

8 Passing through the street near her corner; and he went the way to her house,

9 In the twilight, in the evening, in the black and dark night:

10 And, behold, there met him a woman *with* the attire of an harlot, and subtil of heart.

11 (She *is* loud and stubborn; her feet abide not in her house:

12 Now *is she* without, now in the streets, and lieth in wait at every corner.)

13 So she caught him, and kissed him, *and* with an impudent face said unto him,

14 *I have* peace offerings with me; this day have I payed my vows.

15 Therefore came I forth to meet thee, diligently to seek thy face, and I have found thee.

16 I have decked my bed with coverings of tapestry, with carved *works*, with fine linen of Egypt.

17 I have perfumed my bed with myrrh, aloes, and cinnamon.

18 Come, let us take our fill of love until the morning: let us solace ourselves with loves.

19 For the goodman *is* not at home, he is gone a long journey:

20 He hath taken a bag of money with him, *and* will come home at the day appointed.

21 With her much fair speech she caused him to yield, with the flattering of her lips she forced him.

22 He goeth after her straightway, as an ox goeth to the slaughter, or as a fool to the correction of the stocks;

23 Till a dart strike through his liver; as a bird hasteth to the snare, and knoweth not that it *is* for his life.

24 Hearken unto me now therefore, O ye children, and attend to the words of my mouth.

25 Let not thine heart decline to her ways, go not astray in her paths.

26 For she hath cast down many wounded: yea, many strong *men* have been slain by her.

27 Her house *is* the way to hell, going down to the chambers of death.
-Proverbs 7:4-27, *The King James Bible*, 1769 edition of 1611 text

Readings from the Holy Bible

The Holy Gospel According to Mark (MARK 7:1-8:26)

MARK 7:1-8:26, LIFE AND MIRACLES

7

7:1 Then the Pharisees and some of the scribes gathered together to him, having come from Jerusalem. **7:2** Now when they saw some of his disciples eating bread with defiled, that is unwashed, hands, they found fault. **7:3** (For the Pharisees and all the Jews don't eat unless they wash their hands and forearms, holding to the tradition of the elders. **7:4** They don't eat when they come from the marketplace unless they bathe themselves, and there are many other things, which they have received to hold to: washings of cups, pitchers, bronze vessels, and couches.) **7:5** The Pharisees and the scribes asked him, "Why don't your disciples walk according to the tradition of the elders, but eat their bread with unwashed hands?"
7:6 He answered them, "Well did Isaiah prophesy of you hypocrites, as it is written,
'This people honors me with their lips,
but their heart is far from me.
7:7 But they worship me in vain, teaching as doctrines the commandments of men.'#
7:8 "For you set aside the commandment of God, and hold tightly to the tradition of men—the washing of pitchers and cups, and you do many other such things." **7:9** He said to them, "Full well do you reject the commandment of God, that you may keep your tradition. **7:10** For Moses said, 'Honor your father and your mother;'# and, 'He who

---

#7:7 7:7 Isaiah 29:13
#7:10 7:10 Exodus 20:12; Deuteronomy 5:16

Day Twenty-Three

speaks evil of father or mother, let him be put to death.'[#] 7:11 But you say, 'If a man tells his father or his mother, "Whatever profit you might have received from me is Corban,"'[78] that is to say, given to God, 7:12 "then you no longer allow him to do anything for his father or his mother, 7:13 making void the word of God by your tradition, which you have handed down. You do many things like this."

7:14 He called all the multitude to himself, and said to them, "Hear me, all of you, and understand. 7:15 There is nothing from outside of the man, that going into him can defile him; but the things which proceed out of the man are those that defile the man. 7:16 If anyone has ears to hear, let him hear!"[79]

7:17 When he had entered into a house away from the multitude, his disciples asked him about the parable. 7:18 He said to them, "Are you also without understanding? Don't you perceive that whatever goes into the man from outside can't defile him, 7:19 because it doesn't go into his heart, but into his stomach, then into the latrine, making all foods clean?"[80] 7:20 He said, "That which proceeds out of the man, that defiles the man. 7:21 For from within, out of the hearts of men, proceed evil thoughts, adulteries, sexual sins, murders, thefts, 7:22 covetings, wickedness, deceit, lustful desires, an evil eye, blasphemy, pride, and foolishness. 7:23 All these evil things come from within, and defile the man."

7:24 From there he arose, and went away into the borders of Tyre. And when He had entered a house, He wanted no one to know of it, but he couldn't escape notice. 7:25 For a woman, whose little daughter had an unclean spirit, having heard of him, came and fell down at his feet. 7:26 Now the woman was a Greek, a Syrophoenician by race. She begged him that he would cast the demon out of her daughter. 7:27 But Jesus said to her, "Let the children be filled first, for it is not appropriate to take the children's bread and throw it to the dogs." 7:28 But she answered him, "Yes, Lord. Yet even the dogs under the table eat the children's crumbs."

[#]7:10 7:10 Exodus 21:17; Leviticus 20:9
[78]7:11 7:11 Corban is a Hebrew word for an offering devoted to God.
[79]7:16 7:16 NU omits verse 16.
[80]7:19 7:19 NU ends Jesus' direct quote and question after "latrine", ending the verse with "Thus he declared all foods clean.

⁷²⁹ He said to her, "For this saying, go your way. The demon has gone out of your daughter."
⁷³⁰ She went away to her house, and found the child having been laid on the bed, with the demon gone out.
⁷³¹ Again he departed from the borders of Tyre and Sidon, and came to the sea of Galilee, through the middle of the region of Decapolis.
⁷³² They brought to him one who was deaf and had an impediment in his speech. They begged him to lay his hand on him. ⁷³³ He took him aside from the multitude, privately, and put his fingers into his ears, and he spat, and touched his tongue. ⁷³⁴ Looking up to heaven, he sighed, and said to him, "Ephphatha!" that is, "Be opened!"
⁷³⁵ Immediately his ears were opened, and the impediment of his tongue was released, and he spoke clearly. ⁷³⁶ He commanded them that they should tell no one, but the more he commanded them, so much the more widely they proclaimed it. ⁷³⁷ They were astonished beyond measure, saying, "He has done all things well. He makes even the deaf hear, and the mute speak!" ⁷

8

⁸¹ In those days, when there was a very great multitude, and they had nothing to eat, Jesus called his disciples to himself, and said to them,
⁸² "I have compassion on the multitude, because they have stayed with me now three days, and have nothing to eat. ⁸³ If I send them away fasting to their home, they will faint
on the way, for some of them have come a long way."
⁸⁴ His disciples answered him, "From where could one satisfy these people with bread here in a deserted place?"
⁸⁵ He asked them, "How many loaves do you have?"
They said, "Seven."
⁸⁶ He commanded the multitude to sit down on the ground, and he took the seven loaves. Having given thanks, he broke them, and gave them to his disciples to serve, and they served the multitude. ⁸⁷ They had a few small fish. Having blessed them, he said to serve these also.
⁸⁸ They ate, and were filled. They took up seven baskets of broken pieces that were left over. ⁸⁹ Those who had eaten were about four thousand. Then he sent them away.

Day Twenty-Three

⁸10 Immediately he entered into the boat with his disciples, and came into the region of Dalmanutha. ⁸11 The Pharisees came out and began to question him, seeking from him a sign from heaven, and testing him. ⁸12 He sighed deeply in his spirit, and said, "Why does this generation[81] seek a sign? Most certainly I tell you, no sign will be given to this generation."

⁸13 He left them, and again entering into the boat, departed to the other side. ⁸14 They forgot to take bread; and they didn't have more than one loaf in the boat with them. ⁸15 He warned them, saying, "Take heed: beware of the yeast of the Pharisees and the yeast of Herod."

⁸16 They reasoned with one another, saying, "It's because we have no bread."

⁸17 Jesus, perceiving it, said to them, "Why do you reason that it's because you have no bread? Don't you perceive yet, neither understand? Is your heart still hardened? ⁸18 Having eyes, don't you see? Having ears, don't you hear? Don't you remember? ⁸19 When I broke the five loaves among the five thousand, how many baskets full of broken pieces did you take up?"

They told him, "Twelve."

⁸20 "When the seven loaves fed the four thousand, how many baskets full of broken pieces did you take up?"

They told him, "Seven."

⁸21 He asked them, "Don't you understand yet?"

⁸22 He came to Bethsaida. They brought a blind man to him, and begged him to touch him. ⁸23 He took hold of the blind man by the hand, and brought him out of the village. When he had spat on his eyes, and laid his hands on him, he asked him if he saw anything.

⁸24 He looked up, and said, "I see men; for I see them like trees walking."

⁸25 Then again he laid his hands on his eyes. He looked intently, and was restored, and saw everyone clearly. ⁸26 He sent him away to his house, saying, "Don't enter into the village, nor tell anyone in the village."

---

[81]8:12 8:12 The word translated "generation" here (genea) could also be translated "people", "race", or "family".

The American Book of Prayer

The Lord's Prayer

Our Father, who art in heaven,
Hallowed be thy name.
Thy Kingdom come.
Thy will be done on Earth, as it is in heaven.
Give us this day our daily bread.
And forgive us our trespasses,
As we forgive those that trespass against us.
And lead us not into temptation,
But deliver us from evil.
For thine is the kingdom,
The power, and the glory,
For ever and ever.
AMEN

Day Twenty-Four

Daily Prayer

Alone with none but thee, my God,
I journey on my way.
What need I fear when thou art near,
Oh king of night and day?
More safe am I within thy hand
Than if a host did round me stand.
-Columba of Scotland, (A.D. 521-597)[14]

Prayer of Confession

Almighty and most merciful Father; we have erred, and strayed from your ways like lost sheep. We have followed too much the devices and desires of our own hearts. We have offended against your holy laws. We have left undone those things which we ought to have done; and we have done those things which we ought not to have done; and there is no health in us. O Lord, have mercy upon us, miserable offenders. Spare those, O God, who confess their faults. Restore those who are penitent; according to your promises declared unto mankind in Christ Jesus our Lord. And grant, O most merciful Father,

for his sake; that we may hereafter live a godly, righteous, and sober life, to the glory of thy holy Name. Amen.
-Revised prayer from *The Book of Common Prayer*, 1662

Daily Wisdom

1 Doth not wisdom cry? and understanding put forth her voice?
2 She standeth in the top of high places, by the way in the places of the paths.
3 She crieth at the gates, at the entry of the city, at the coming in at the doors.
4 Unto you, O men, I call; and my voice *is* to the sons of man.
5 O ye simple, understand wisdom: and, ye fools, be ye of an understanding heart.
6 Hear; for I will speak of excellent things; and the opening of my lips *shall be* right things.
7 For my mouth shall speak truth; and wickedness *is* an abomination to my lips.
8 All the words of my mouth *are* in righteousness; *there is* nothing froward or perverse in them.
9 They *are* all plain to him that understandeth, and right to them that find knowledge.
10 Receive my instruction, and not silver; and knowledge rather than choice gold.
11 For wisdom *is* better than rubies; and all the things that may be desired are not to be compared to it.
-Proverbs 8:1-11, *The King James Bible*, 1769 edition of 1611 text

Day Twenty-Four

Readings from the Holy Bible

The Holy Gospel According to John (JOHN 8:1-59)

8

[8]1 but Jesus went to the Mount of Olives. [8]2 Now very early in the morning, he came again into the temple, and all the people came to him. He sat down and taught them. [8]3 The scribes and the Pharisees brought a woman taken in adultery. Having set her in the middle,
[8]4 they told him, "Teacher, we found this woman in adultery, in the very act. [8]5 Now in our law, Moses commanded us to stone such women. What then do you say about her?" [8]6 They said this testing him, that they might have something to accuse him of.
But Jesus stooped down and wrote on the ground with his finger.
[8]7 But when they continued asking him, he looked up and said to them, "He who is without sin among you, let him throw the first stone at her." [8]8 Again he stooped down and wrote on the ground with his finger.
[8]9 They, when they heard it, being convicted by their conscience, went out one by one, beginning from the oldest, even to the last. Jesus was left alone with the woman where she was, in the middle. [8]10 Jesus, standing up, saw her and said, "Woman, where are your accusers? Did no one condemn you?"
[8]11 She said, "No one, Lord."
Jesus said, "Neither do I condemn you. Go your way. From now on, sin no more."[82]
[8]12 Again, therefore, Jesus spoke to them, saying, "I am the light of the world. He who follows me will not walk in the darkness, but will have the light of life."
[8]13 The Pharisees therefore said to him, "You testify about yourself. Your testimony is not valid."
[8]14 Jesus answered them, "Even if I testify about myself, my testimony is true, for I know where I came from, and where I am going;

---

[82]8:11 8:11 NU includes John 7:53–John 8:11, but puts brackets around it to indicate that the textual critics had less confidence that this was original.

but you don't know where I came from, or where I am going. ⁸**15** You judge according to the flesh. I judge no one. ⁸**16** Even if I do judge, my judgment is true, for I am not alone, but I am with the Father who sent me. ⁸**17** It's also written in your law that the testimony of two people is valid. ⁸**18** I am one who testifies about myself, and the Father who sent me testifies about me."

⁸**19** They said therefore to him, "Where is your Father?"
Jesus answered, "You know neither me nor my Father. If you knew me, you would know my Father also." ⁸**20** Jesus spoke these words in the treasury, as he taught in the temple. Yet no one arrested him, because his hour had not yet come. ⁸**21** Jesus said therefore again to them, "I am going away, and you will seek me, and you will die in your sins. Where I go, you can't come."

⁸**22** The Jews therefore said, "Will he kill himself, because he says, 'Where I am going, you can't come'?"

⁸**23** He said to them, "You are from beneath. I am from above. You are of this world. I am not of this world. ⁸**24** I said therefore to you that you will die in your sins; for unless you believe that I am⁸³ he, you will die in your sins."

⁸**25** They said therefore to him, "Who are you?"
Jesus said to them, "Just what I have been saying to you from the beginning. ⁸**26** I have many things to speak and to judge concerning you. However he who sent me is true; and the things which I heard from him, these I say to the world."

⁸**27** They didn't understand that he spoke to them about the Father.
⁸**28** Jesus therefore said to them, "When you have lifted up the Son of Man, then you will know that I am he, and I do nothing of myself, but as my Father taught me, I say these things. ⁸**29** He who sent me is with me. The Father hasn't left me alone, for I always do the things that are pleasing to him."

⁸**30** As he spoke these things, many believed in him. ⁸**31** Jesus therefore said to those Jews who had believed him, "If you remain in my word, then you are truly my disciples. ⁸**32** You will know the truth, and the truth will make you free." #

---

⁸³8:24 8:24 or, I AM
#8:32 8:32 Psalm 119:45

Day Twenty-Four

⁸33 They answered him, "We are Abraham's offspring, and have never been in bondage to anyone. How do you say, 'You will be made free'?"

⁸34 Jesus answered them, "Most certainly I tell you, everyone who commits sin is the bondservant of sin. ⁸35 A bondservant doesn't live in the house forever. A son remains forever. ⁸36 If therefore the Son makes you free, you will be free indeed. ⁸37 I know that you are Abraham's offspring, yet you seek to kill me, because my word finds no place in you. ⁸38 I say the things which I have seen with my Father; and you also do the things which you have seen with your father."

⁸39 They answered him, "Our father is Abraham."

Jesus said to them, "If you were Abraham's children, you would do the works of Abraham. ⁸40 But now you seek to kill me, a man who has told you the truth which I heard from God. Abraham didn't do this. ⁸41 You do the works of your father."

They said to him, "We were not born of sexual immorality. We have one Father, God."

⁸42 Therefore Jesus said to them, "If God were your father, you would love me, for I came out and have come from God. For I haven't come of myself, but he sent me. ⁸43 Why don't you understand my speech? Because you can't hear my word. ⁸44 You are of your father, the devil, and you want to do the desires of your father. He was a murderer from the beginning, and doesn't stand in the truth, because there is no truth in him. When he speaks a lie, he speaks on his own; for he is a liar, and the father of lies.

⁸45 But because I tell the truth, you don't believe me. ⁸46 Which of you convicts me of sin? If I tell the truth, why do you not believe me? ⁸47 He who is of God hears the words of God. For this cause you don't hear, because you are not of God."

⁸48 Then the Jews answered him, "Don't we say well that you are a Samaritan, and have a demon?"

⁸49 Jesus answered, "I don't have a demon, but I honor my Father and you dishonor me.

⁸50 But I don't seek my own glory. There is one who seeks and judges. ⁸51 Most certainly, I tell you, if a person keeps my word, he will never see death."

⁸⁵²Then the Jews said to him, "Now we know that you have a demon. Abraham died, as did the prophets; and you say, 'If a man keeps my word, he will never taste of death.' ⁸⁵³Are you greater than our father, Abraham, who died? The prophets died. Who do you make yourself out to be?"

⁸⁵⁴Jesus answered, "If I glorify myself, my glory is nothing. It is my Father who glorifies me, of whom you say that he is our God. ⁸⁵⁵You have not known him, but I know him. If I said, 'I don't know him,' I would be like you, a liar. But I know him and keep his word. ⁸⁵⁶Your father Abraham rejoiced to see my day. He saw it, and was glad."

⁸⁵⁷The Jews therefore said to him, "You are not yet fifty years old! Have you seen Abraham?"

⁸⁵⁸Jesus said to them, "Most certainly, I tell you, before Abraham came into existence, I AM."

⁸⁵⁹Therefore they took up stones to throw at him, but Jesus was hidden, and went out of the temple, having gone through the middle of them, and so passed by.

The Lord's Prayer

Our Father, who art in heaven,
Hallowed be thy name.
Thy Kingdom come.
Thy will be done on Earth, as it is in heaven.
Give us this day our daily bread.
And forgive us our trespasses,
As we forgive those that trespass against us.
And lead us not into temptation,
But deliver us from evil.
For thine is the kingdom,
The power, and the glory,
For ever and ever.
AMEN

Day Twenty-Five

Daily Prayer

Lord Jesus, let me know myself and know Thee,
And desire nothing save only Thee.
Let me hate myself and love Thee.
Let me do everything for the sake of Thee.
Let me humble myself and exalt Thee.
Let me think nothing except Thee.
Let me die to myself and live in Thee.
Let me accept whatever happens as from Thee.
Let me banish self and follow Thee, and ever desire to follow Thee.
Let me fly from myself and take refuge in Thee,
that I may deserve to be defended by Thee.
Let me fear for myself, let me fear Thee,
and let me be among those who are chosen by Thee.
Let me distrust myself and put my trust in Thee.

> "Let me accept whatever happens as from Thee. Let me banish self and follow Thee, and ever desire to follow Thee."

Let me be willing to obey for the sake of Thee.
Let me cling to nothing save only to Thee,
and let me be poor because of Thee.
Look upon me, that I may love Thee.
Call me that I may see Thee,
And forever enjoy Thee.
-Augustine of Hippo, (A.D. 354-430)

Prayer of Confession

Almighty and most merciful Father; we have erred, and strayed from your ways like lost sheep. We have followed too much the devices and desires of our own hearts. We have offended against your holy laws. We have left undone those things which we ought to have done; and we have done those things which we ought not to have done; and there is no health in us. O Lord, have mercy upon us, miserable offenders. Spare those, O God, who confess their faults. Restore those who are penitent; according to your promises declared unto mankind in Christ Jesus our Lord. And grant, O most merciful Father, for his sake; that we may hereafter live a godly, righteous, and sober life, to the glory of thy holy Name. Amen.
-Revised prayer from *The Book of Common Prayer*, 1662

Daily Wisdom

13 The fear of the LORD *is* to hate evil: pride, and arrogancy, and the evil way, and the froward mouth, do I hate.
14 Counsel *is* mine, and sound wisdom: I *am* understanding; I have strength.
15 By me kings reign, and princes decree justice.
16 By me princes rule, and nobles, *even* all the judges of the earth.

Day Twenty-Five

17 I love them that love me; and those that seek me early shall find me.
18 Riches and honor *are* with me; *yea*, durable riches and righteousness.
19 My fruit *is* better than gold, yea, than fine gold; and my revenue than choice silver.
20 I lead in the way of righteousness, in the midst of the paths of judgment:
21 That I may cause those that love me to inherit substance; and I will fill their treasures.
22 The LORD possessed me in the beginning of his way, before his works of old.
-Proverbs 8:13-22, *The King James Bible*, 1769 edition of 1611 text

Readings from the Holy Bible

The Holy Gospel According to Matthew (MATTHEW 16:13-18:9)

MATTHEW 16:1-18:9, THE FOUNDING OF THE CHURCH

16

[16]**1** The Pharisees and Sadducees came, and testing him, asked him to show them a sign from heaven. [16]**2** But he answered them, "When it is evening, you say, 'It will be fair weather, for the sky is red.' [16]**3** In the morning, 'It will be foul weather today, for the sky is red and threatening.' Hypocrites! You know how to discern the appearance of the sky, but you can't discern the signs of the times! [16]**4** An evil and adulterous generation seeks after a sign, and there will be no sign given to it, except the sign of the prophet Jonah."
He left them, and departed. [16]**5** The disciples came to the other side and had forgotten to take bread. [16]**6** Jesus said to them, "Take heed and beware of the yeast of the Pharisees and Sadducees."
[16]**7** They reasoned among themselves, saying, "We brought no bread."

The American Book of Prayer

16:8 Jesus, perceiving it, said, "Why do you reason among yourselves, you of little faith, 'because you have brought no bread?' **16:9** Don't you yet perceive, neither remember the five loaves for the five thousand, and how many baskets you took up? **16:10** Nor the seven loaves for the four thousand, and how many baskets you took up? **16:11** How is it that you don't perceive that I didn't speak to you concerning bread? But beware of the yeast of the Pharisees and Sadducees."

16:12 Then they understood that he didn't tell them to beware of the yeast of bread, but of the teaching of the Pharisees and Sadducees.

16:13 Now when Jesus came into the parts of Caesarea Philippi, he asked his disciples, saying, "Who do men say that I, the Son of Man, am?"

16:14 They said, "Some say John the Baptizer, some, Elijah, and others, Jeremiah, or one of the prophets."

16:15 He said to them, "But who do you say that I am?"

16:16 Simon Peter answered, "You are the Christ, the Son of the living God."

16:17 Jesus answered him, "Blessed are you, Simon Bar Jonah, for flesh and blood has not revealed this to you, but my Father who is in heaven. **16:18** I also tell you that you are Peter,[84] and on this rock [85] I will build my assembly, and the gates of Hades[86] will not prevail against it. **16:19** I will give to you the keys of the Kingdom of Heaven, and whatever you bind on earth will have been bound in heaven; and whatever you release on earth will have been released in heaven."

16:20 Then he commanded the disciples that they should tell no one that he was Jesus the Christ. **16:21** From that time, Jesus began to show his disciples that he must go to Jerusalem and suffer many things from the elders, chief priests, and scribes, and be killed, and the third day be raised up.

16:22 Peter took him aside, and began to rebuke him, saying, "Far be it from you, Lord! This will never be done to you."

16:23 But he turned, and said to Peter, "Get behind me, Satan! You are a stumbling block to me, for you are not setting your mind on the

---

[84] 16:18 16:18 Peter's name, Petros in Greek, is the word for a specific rock or stone.
[85] 16:18 16:18 Greek, petra, a rock mass or bedrock.
[86] 16:18 16:18 or, Hell

Day Twenty-Five

things of God, but on the things of men." ¹⁶24 Then Jesus said to his disciples, "If anyone desires to come after me, let him deny himself, and take up his cross, and follow me. ¹⁶25 For whoever desires to save his life will lose it, and whoever will lose his life for my sake will find it. ¹⁶26 For what will it profit a man, if he gains the whole world, and forfeits his life? Or what will a man give in exchange for his life? ¹⁶27 For the Son of Man will come in the glory of his Father with his angels, and then he will render to everyone according to his deeds. ¹⁶28 ¹⁶Most certainly I tell you, there are some standing here who will in no way taste of death, until they see the Son of Man coming in his Kingdom."

17

¹⁷1 After six days, Jesus took with him Peter, James, and John his brother, and brought them up into a high mountain by themselves. ¹⁷2 He was transfigured before them. His face shone like the sun, and his garments became as white as the light. ¹⁷3 Behold, Moses and Elijah appeared to them talking with him.
¹⁷4 Peter answered, and said to Jesus, "Lord, it is good for us to be here. If you want, let's make three tents here: one for you, one for Moses, and one for Elijah."
¹⁷5 While he was still speaking, behold, a bright cloud overshadowed them. Behold, a voice came out of the cloud, saying, "This is my beloved Son, in whom I am well pleased. Listen to him."
¹⁷6 When the disciples heard it, they fell on their faces, and were very afraid. ¹⁷7 Jesus came and touched them and said, "Get up, and don't be afraid." ¹⁷8 Lifting up their eyes, they saw no one, except Jesus alone. ¹⁷9 As they were coming down from the mountain, Jesus commanded them, saying, "Don't tell anyone what you saw, until the Son of Man has risen from the dead."
¹⁷10 His disciples asked him, saying, "Then why do the scribes say that Elijah must come first?"
¹⁷11 Jesus answered them, "Elijah indeed comes first, and will restore all things, ¹⁷12 but I tell you that Elijah has come already, and they didn't recognize him, but did to him whatever they wanted to. Even so the Son of Man will also suffer by them." ¹⁷13 Then the disciples understood that he spoke to them of John the Baptizer.

¹⁷14 When they came to the multitude, a man came to him, kneeling down to him, and saying, ¹⁷15 "Lord, have mercy on my son, for he is epileptic, and suffers grievously; for he often falls into the fire, and often into the water. ¹⁷16 So I brought him to your disciples, and they could not cure him."

¹⁷17 Jesus answered, "Faithless and perverse generation! How long will I be with you? How long will I bear with you? Bring him here to me."

¹⁷18 Jesus rebuked him, the demon went out of him, and the boy was cured from that hour.

¹⁷19 Then the disciples came to Jesus privately, and said, "Why weren't we able to cast it out?"

¹⁷20 He said to them, "Because of your unbelief. For most certainly I tell you, if you have faith as a grain of mustard seed, you will tell this mountain, 'Move from here to there,' and it will move; and nothing will be impossible for you. ¹⁷21 But this kind doesn't go out except by prayer and fasting." [87]

¹⁷22 While they were staying in Galilee, Jesus said to them, "The Son of Man is about to be delivered up into the hands of men, ¹⁷23 and they will kill him, and the third day he will be raised up."

They were exceedingly sorry. ¹⁷24 When they had come to Capernaum, those who collected the didrachma coins[88] came to Peter, and said, "Doesn't your teacher pay the didrachma?" ¹⁷25 He said, "Yes."

When he came into the house, Jesus anticipated him, saying, "What do you think, Simon? From whom do the kings of the earth receive toll or tribute? From their children, or from strangers?"

¹⁷26 Peter said to him, "From strangers."

Jesus said to him, "Therefore the children are exempt. ¹⁷27 ¹⁷But, lest we cause them to stumble, go to the sea, cast a hook, and take up the first fish that comes up. When you have opened its mouth, you will find a stater coin.[89] Take that, and give it to them for me and you."

---

[87] 17:21 17:21 NU omits verse 21.
[88] 17:24 17:24 A didrachma is a Greek silver coin worth 2 drachmas, about as much as 2 Roman denarii, or about 2 days' wages. It was commonly used to pay the half-shekel temple tax, because 2 drachmas were worth one half shekel of silver. A shekel is about 10 grams or about 0.35 ounces.
[89] 17:27 17:27 A stater is a silver coin equivalent to four Attic or two Alexandrian drachmas, or a Jewish shekel: just exactly enough to cover the half-shekel temple tax

Day Twenty-Five

18

¹⁸¹ In that hour the disciples came to Jesus, saying, "Who then is greatest in the Kingdom of Heaven?"
¹⁸² Jesus called a little child to himself, and set him in the middle of them, ¹⁸³ and said, "Most certainly I tell you, unless you turn, and become as little children, you will in no way enter into the Kingdom of Heaven. ¹⁸⁴ Whoever therefore humbles himself as this little child is the greatest in the Kingdom of Heaven. ¹⁸⁵ Whoever receives one such little child in my name receives me, ¹⁸⁶ but whoever causes one of these little ones who believe in me to stumble, it would be better for him if a huge millstone were hung around his neck, and that he were sunk in the depths of the sea.
¹⁸⁷ "Woe to the world because of occasions of stumbling! For it must be that the occasions come, but woe to that person through whom the occasion comes! ¹⁸⁸ If your hand or your foot causes you to stumble, cut it off, and cast it from you. It is better for you to enter into life maimed or crippled, rather than having two hands or two feet to be cast into the eternal fire. ¹⁸⁹ If your eye causes you to stumble, pluck it out, and cast it from you. It is better for you to enter into life with one eye, rather than having two eyes to be cast into the Gehenna[90] of fire.

The Lord's Prayer

Our Father, who art in heaven,
Hallowed be thy name.
Thy Kingdom come.
Thy will be done on Earth, as it is in heaven.
Give us this day our daily bread.
And forgive us our trespasses,
As we forgive those that trespass against us.

---

for two people. A shekel is about 10 grams or about 0.35 ounces, usually in the form of a silver coin.
[90] 18:9 18:9 or, Hell

The American Book of Prayer

And lead us not into temptation,
But deliver us from evil.
For thine is the kingdom,
The power, and the glory,
For ever and ever.
AMEN

Day Twenty-Six

Daily Prayer

I bind to myself today
The strong virtue of the Invocation of the Trinity:
I believe the Trinity in the Unity
The Creator of the Universe.
I bind to myself today
The virtue of the Incarnation
of Christ with His Baptism,
The virtue of His crucifixion
with His burial,
The virtue of His Resurrection
with His Ascension,
The virtue of His coming on
the Judgement Day.
I bind to myself today
The virtue of the love of seraphim,
In the obedience of angels,
In the hope of resurrection unto reward,
In prayers of Patriarchs,
In predictions of Prophets,
In preaching of Apostles,
In faith of Confessors,
In purity of holy Virgins,
In deeds of righteous men.

> "I bind to myself today
> the virtue of the love of
> seraphim,
> in the obedience of angels,
> in the hope of resurrection
> unto reward ..."

I bind to myself today
The power of Heaven,
The light of the sun,
The brightness of the moon,
The splendour of fire,
The flashing of lightning,
The swiftness of wind,
The depth of sea,
The stability of earth,
The compactness of rocks.
I bind to myself today
God's Power to guide me,
God's Might to uphold me,
God's Wisdom to teach me,
God's Eye to watch over me,
God's Ear to hear me,
God's Word to give me speech,
God's Hand to guide me,
God's Way to lie before me,
God's Shield to shelter me,
God's Host to secure me,
Against the snares of demons,
Against the seductions of vices,
Against the lusts of nature,
Against everyone who meditates injury to me,
Whether far or near,
Whether few or with many.
- *From St. Patrick's Breast-plate, Patrick of Ireland, 5th Century Bishop of Ireland*[15]

Prayer of Confession

Almighty and most merciful Father; we have erred, and strayed from your ways like lost sheep. We have followed too much the devices and desires of our own hearts. We have offended against your holy laws. We have left undone

Day Twenty-Six

those things which we ought to have done; and we have done those things which we ought not to have done; and there is no health in us. O Lord, have mercy upon us, miserable offenders. Spare those, O God, who confess their faults. Restore those who are penitent; according to your promises declared unto mankind in Christ Jesus our Lord. And grant, O most merciful Father, for his sake; that we may hereafter live a godly, righteous, and sober life, to the glory of thy holy Name. Amen.
-Revised prayer from *The Book of Common Prayer*, 1662

Daily Wisdom

23 I was set up from everlasting, from the beginning, or ever the earth was.
24 When *there were* no depths, I was brought forth; when *there were* no fountains abounding with water.
25 Before the mountains were settled, before the hills was I brought forth:
26 While as yet he had not made the earth, nor the fields, nor the highest part of the dust of the world.
27 When he prepared the heavens, I *was* there: when he set a compass upon the face of the depth:
28 When he established the clouds above: when he strengthened the fountains of the deep:
29 When he gave to the sea his decree, that the waters should not pass his commandment: when he appointed the foundations of the earth:
30 Then I was by him, *as* one brought up *with him*: and I was daily *his* delight, rejoicing always before him;
31 Rejoicing in the habitable part of his earth; and my delights *were* with the sons of men.
32 Now therefore hearken unto me, O ye children: for blessed *are they that* keep my ways.
33 Hear instruction, and be wise, and refuse it not.

34 Blessed *is* the man that heareth me, watching daily at my gates, waiting at the posts of my doors.
35 For whoso findeth me findeth life, and shall obtain favour of the LORD.
36 But he that sinneth against me wrongeth his own soul: all they that hate me love death.
-Proverbs 8:23-36, *The King James Bible*, 1769 edition of 1611 text

Readings from the Holy Bible

The Holy Gospel According to Luke (LUKE 9:51-10:24; LUKE 15:1-32)

LUKE 9:51-10:24, THE SAMARITANS AND THE SEVENTY-TWO

9:51 It came to pass, when the days were near that he should be taken up, he intently set his face to go to Jerusalem **52** and sent messengers before his face. They went and entered into a village of the Samaritans, so as to prepare for him. **53** They didn't receive him, because he was traveling with his face set toward Jerusalem. **54** When his disciples, James and John, saw this, they said, "Lord, do you want us to command fire to come down from the sky, and destroy them, just as Elijah did?"
9:55 But he turned and rebuked them, "You don't know of what kind of spirit you are. **56** For the Son of Man didn't come to destroy men's lives, but to save them."
They went to another village. **9:57** As they went on the way, a certain man said to him, "I
want to follow you wherever you go, Lord."
9:58 Jesus said to him, "The foxes have holes, and the birds of the sky have nests, but the Son of Man has no place to lay his head."
9:59 He said to another, "Follow me!"
But he said, "Lord, allow me first to go and bury my father."
9:60 But Jesus said to him, "Leave the dead to bury their own dead, but you go and announce God's Kingdom."

Day Twenty-Six

⁹61 Another also said, "I want to follow you, Lord, but first allow me to say good-bye to those who are at my house."
⁹62 But Jesus said to him, ⁹"No one, having put his hand to the plow, and looking back, is fit for God's Kingdom."

10

¹⁰1 Now after these things, the Lord also appointed seventy others, and sent them two by two ahead of him⁹¹ into every city and place where he was about to come. ¹⁰2 Then he said to them, "The harvest is indeed plentiful, but the laborers are few. Pray therefore to the Lord of the harvest, that he may send out laborers into his harvest. ¹⁰3 Go your ways. Behold, I send you out as lambs among wolves. ¹⁰4 Carry no purse, nor wallet, nor sandals. Greet no one on the way. ¹⁰5 Into whatever house you enter, first say, 'Peace be to this house.' ¹⁰6 If a son of peace is there, your peace will rest on him; but if not, it will return to you. ¹⁰7 Remain in that same house, eating and drinking the things they give, for the laborer is worthy of his wages. Don't go from house to house. ¹⁰8 Into whatever city you enter, and they receive you, eat the things that are set before you. ¹⁰9 Heal the sick who are there, and tell them, 'God's Kingdom has come near to you.' ¹⁰10 But into whatever city you enter, and they don't receive you, go out into its streets and say, ¹⁰11 'Even the dust from your city that clings to us, we wipe off against you. Nevertheless know this, that God's Kingdom has come near to you.' ¹⁰12 I tell you, it will be more tolerable in that day for Sodom than for that city. ¹⁰13 "Woe to you, Chorazin! Woe to you, Bethsaida! For if the mighty works had been done in Tyre and Sidon which were done in you, they would have repented long ago, sitting in sackcloth and ashes. ¹⁰14 But it will be more tolerable for Tyre and Sidon in the judgment than for you. ¹⁰15 You, Capernaum, who are exalted to heaven, will be brought down to Hades. ⁹² ¹⁰16 Whoever listens to you listens to me, and whoever rejects you rejects me. Whoever rejects me rejects him who sent me."
¹⁰17 The seventy returned with joy, saying, "Lord, even the demons are subject to us in your name!"

---

⁹¹10:1 10:1 literally, "before his face"
⁹²10:15 10:15 Hades is the lower realm of the dead, or Hell.

¹⁰**18** He said to them, "I saw Satan having fallen like lightning from heaven. ¹⁰**19** Behold, I give you authority to tread on serpents and scorpions, and over all the power of the enemy. Nothing will in any way hurt you. ¹⁰**20** Nevertheless, don't rejoice in this, that the spirits are subject to you, but rejoice that your names are written in heaven."
¹⁰**21** In that same hour Jesus rejoiced in the Holy Spirit, and said, "I thank you, O Father, Lord of heaven and earth, that you have hidden these things from the wise and understanding, and revealed them to little children. Yes, Father, for so it was well-pleasing in your sight."
¹⁰**22** Turning to the disciples, he said, "All things have been delivered to me by my Father. No one knows who the Son is, except the Father, and who the Father is, except the Son, and he to whomever the Son desires to reveal him."
¹⁰**23** Turning to the disciples, he said privately, "Blessed are the eyes which see the things that you see, ¹⁰**24** for I tell you that many prophets and kings desired to see the things which you see, and didn't see them, and to hear the things which you hear, and didn't hear them."

LUKE 15:1-32, THE LOST SHEEP, COIN AND SON

15

¹⁵**1** Now all the tax collectors and sinners were coming close to him to hear him. ¹⁵**2** The Pharisees and the scribes murmured, saying, "This man welcomes sinners, and eats with them."
¹⁵**3** He told them this parable. ¹⁵**4** "Which of you men, if you had one hundred sheep, and lost one of them, wouldn't leave the ninety-nine in the wilderness, and go after the one that was lost, until he found it? ¹⁵**5** When he has found it, he carries it on his shoulders, rejoicing. ¹⁵**6** When he comes home, he calls together his friends and his neighbors, saying to them, 'Rejoice with me, for I have found my sheep which was lost!' ¹⁵**7** I tell you that even so there will be more joy in heaven over one sinner who repents, than over ninety-nine righteous people who need no repentance. ¹⁵**8** Or what woman, if she had ten drachma[93] coins, if she lost one drachma coin, wouldn't light a lamp, sweep the house, and seek diligently until she found it? ¹⁵**9** When she

---

[93]15:8 15:8 A drachma coin was worth about 2 days wages for an agricultural laborer.

Day Twenty-Six

has found it, she calls together her friends and neighbors, saying, 'Rejoice with me, for I have found the drachma which I had lost.' **15:10** Even so, I tell you, there is joy in the presence of the angels of God over one sinner repenting."

15:11 He said, "A certain man had two sons. **15:12** The younger of them said to his father, 'Father, give me my share of your property.' He divided his livelihood between them. **15:13** Not many days after, the younger son gathered all of this together and traveled into a far country. There he wasted his property with riotous living. **15:14** When he had spent all of it, there arose a severe famine in that country, and he began to be in need. **15:15** He went and joined himself to one of the citizens of that country, and he sent him into his fields to feed pigs. **15:16** He wanted to fill his belly with the husks that the pigs ate, but no one gave him any. **15:17** But when he came to himself he said, 'How many hired servants of my father's have bread enough to spare, and I'm dying with hunger! **15:18** I will get up and go to my father, and will tell him, "Father, I have sinned against heaven, and in your sight. **15:19** I am no more worthy to be called your son. Make me as one of your hired servants."'

15:20 "He arose, and came to his father. But while he was still far off, his father saw him, and was moved with compassion, and ran, and fell on his neck, and kissed him. **15:21** The son said to him, 'Father, I have sinned against heaven and in your sight. I am no longer worthy to be called your son.'

15:22 "But the father said to his servants, 'Bring out the best robe, and put it on him. Put a ring on his hand, and shoes on his feet. **15:23** Bring the fattened calf, kill it, and let's eat, and celebrate; **15:24** for this, my son, was dead, and is alive again. He was lost, and is found.' Then they began to celebrate.

15:25 "Now his elder son was in the field. As he came near to the house, he heard music and dancing. **15:26** He called one of the servants to him, and asked what was going on. **15:27** He said to him, 'Your brother has come, and your father has killed the fattened calf, because he has received him back safe and healthy.' **15:28** But he was angry, and would not go in. Therefore his father came out, and begged him. **15:29** But he answered his father, 'Behold, these many years I have served you, and I never disobeyed a commandment of yours, but you never gave me a goat, that I might celebrate with my friends. ¹⁵30 But when this your son came, who has devoured your living with prostitutes, you killed the fattened calf for him.'

¹⁵31 "He said to him, 'Son, you are always with me, and all that is mine is yours. ¹⁵32 ¹⁵But it was appropriate to celebrate and be glad, for this, your brother, was dead, and is alive again. He was lost, and is found.'"

The Lords Prayer

Our Father, who art in heaven,
Hallowed be thy name.
Thy Kingdom come.
Thy will be done on Earth, as it is in heaven.
Give us this day our daily bread.
And forgive us our trespasses,
As we forgive those that trespass against us.
And lead us not into temptation,
But deliver us from evil.
For thine is the kingdom,
The power, and the glory,
For ever and ever.
AMEN

Day Twenty-Seven

Daily Prayer

I invoke today all these virtues
Against every hostile merciless power
Which may assail my body and my soul,
Against the incantations of false prophets,
Against the black laws of heathenism,
Against the false laws of heresy,
Against the deceits of idolatry,
Against the spells of women, and smiths, and druids,
Against every knowledge that binds the soul of man.
Christ, protect me today
Against every poison, against burning,
Against drowning, against death-wound,
That I may receive abundant reward.
Christ with me, Christ before me,
Christ behind me, Christ within me,

> *"Christ, protect me today against every poison, against burning, against drowning, against death-wound. That I may receive abundant reward."*

Christ beneath me, Christ above me,
Christ at my right, Christ at my left,
Christ in the fort,
Christ in the chariot seat,
Christ in the ship,
Christ in the heart of everyone who thinks of me,
Christ in the mouth of everyone who speaks to me,
Christ in every eye that sees me,
Christ in every ear that hears me.
I bind to myself today
The strong virtue of an invocation of the Trinity,
I believe the Trinity in the Unity
The Creator of the Universe.
- *From St. Patrick's Breast-plate, Patrick of Ireland, 5th Century Bishop of Ireland*[16]

Prayer of Confession

Almighty and most merciful Father; we have erred, and strayed from your ways like lost sheep. We have followed too much the devices and desires of our own hearts. We have offended against your holy laws. We have left undone those things which we ought to have done; and we have done those things which we ought not to have done; and there is no health in us. O Lord, have mercy upon us, miserable offenders. Spare those, O God, who confess their faults. Restore those who are penitent; according to your promises declared unto mankind in Christ Jesus our Lord. And grant, O most merciful Father, for his sake; that we may hereafter live a godly, righteous, and sober life, to the glory of thy holy Name. Amen.
-Revised prayer from *The Book of Common Prayer*, 1662

Day Twenty-Seven

Daily Wisdom

1 Wisdom hath builded her house, she hath hewn out her seven pillars:
2 She hath killed her beasts; she hath mingled her wine; she hath also furnished her table.
3 She hath sent forth her maidens: she crieth upon the highest places of the city,
4 Whoso *is* simple, let him turn in hither: *as for* him that wanteth understanding, she saith to him,
5 Come, eat of my bread, and drink of the wine *which* I have mingled.
6 Forsake the foolish, and live; and go in the way of understanding.
7 He that reproveth a scorner getteth to himself shame: and he that rebuketh a wicked *man getteth* himself a blot.
8 Reprove not a scorner, lest he hate thee: rebuke a wise man, and he will love thee.
9 Give *instruction* to a wise *man*, and he will be yet wiser: teach a just *man*, and he will increase in learning.
10 The fear of the LORD *is* the beginning of wisdom: and the knowledge of the holy *is* understanding.
11 For by me thy days shall be multiplied, and the years of thy life shall be increased.
12 If thou be wise, thou shalt be wise for thyself: but *if* thou scornest, thou alone shalt bear *it*.
-Proverbs 9:1-12, *The King James Bible*, 1769 edition of 1611 text

The American Book of Prayer

Readings from the Holy Bible

The Holy Gospel According to Luke (LUKE 16:1-31; LUKE 17:1-19; LUKE 18:1-14)

LUKE 16:1-17:19, PARABLES AND HEALINGS

16

¹⁶**1** He also said to his disciples, "There was a certain rich man who had a manager. An accusation was made to him that this man was wasting his possessions. ¹⁶**2** He called him, and said to him, 'What is this that I hear about you? Give an accounting of your management, for you can no longer be manager.'

¹⁶**3** "The manager said within himself, 'What will I do, seeing that my lord is taking away the management position from me? I don't have strength to dig. I am ashamed to beg. ¹⁶**4** I know what I will do, so that when I am removed from management, they may receive me into their houses.' ¹⁶**5** Calling each one of his lord's debtors to him, he said to the first, 'How much do you owe to my lord?' ¹⁶**6** He said, 'A hundred batos[94] of oil.' He said to him, 'Take your bill, and sit down quickly and write fifty.' ¹⁶**7** Then he said to another, 'How much do you owe?' He said, 'A hundred cors[95] of wheat.' He said to him, 'Take your bill, and write eighty.'

¹⁶**8** "His lord commended the dishonest manager because he had done wisely, for the children of this world are, in their own generation, wiser than the children of the light. ¹⁶**9** I tell you, make for yourselves friends by means of unrighteous mammon, so that when you fail, they may receive you into the eternal tents. ¹⁶**10** He who is faithful in a very little is faithful also in much. He who is dishonest in a very little is also dishonest in much. ¹⁶**11** If therefore you have not been faithful in the unrighteous mammon, who will commit to your trust the true riches? ¹⁶**12** If you have not been faithful in that which is another's, who will give you that which is your own? ¹⁶**13** No servant can serve

---

[94]16:6 16:6 100 batos is about 395 liters or 104 U. S. gallons.
[95]16:7 16:7 100 cors = about 2,110 liters or 600 bushels.

Day Twenty-Seven

two masters, for either he will hate the one, and love the other; or else he will hold to one, and despise the other. You aren't
able to serve God and Mammon."[96]

16:14 The Pharisees, who were lovers of money, also heard all these things, and they scoffed at him. **16:15** He said to them, "You are those who justify yourselves in the sight of men, but God knows your hearts. For that which is exalted among men is an abomination in the sight of God. **16:16** The law and the prophets were until John. From that time the Good News of God's Kingdom is preached, and everyone is forcing his way into it. **16:17** But it is easier for heaven and earth to pass away, than for one tiny stroke of a pen in the law to fall. **16:18** Everyone who divorces his wife and marries another commits adultery. He who marries one who is divorced from a husband commits adultery.

16:19 "Now there was a certain rich man, and he was clothed in purple and fine linen, living in luxury every day. **16:20** A certain beggar, named Lazarus, was taken to his gate, full of sores, **16:21** and desiring to be fed with the crumbs that fell from the rich man's table. Yes, even the dogs came and licked his sores. **16:22** The beggar died, and he was carried away by the angels to Abraham's bosom. The rich man also died, and was buried. **16:23** In Hades,[97] he lifted up his eyes, being in torment, and saw Abraham far off, and Lazarus at his bosom. **16:24** He cried and said, 'Father Abraham, have mercy on me, and send Lazarus, that he may dip the tip of his finger in water, and cool my tongue! For I am in anguish in this flame.'

16:25 "But Abraham said, 'Son, remember that you, in your lifetime, received your good things, and Lazarus, in the same way, bad things. But here he is now comforted, and you are in anguish. **16:26** Besides all this, between us and you there is a great gulf fixed, that those who want to pass from here to you are not able, and that no one may cross over from there to us.'

16:27 "He said, 'I ask you therefore, father, that you would send him to my father's house; **16:28** for I have five brothers, that he may testify to them, so they won't also come into this place of torment.'

---

[96] 16:13 16:13 "Mammon" refers to riches or a false god of wealth.
[97] 16:23 16:23 or, Hell

¹⁶29 "But Abraham said to him, 'They have Moses and the prophets. Let them listen to them.'
¹⁶30 "He said, 'No, father Abraham, but if one goes to them from the dead, they will repent.'
¹⁶31 ¹⁶"He said to him, 'If they don't listen to Moses and the prophets, neither will they be persuaded if one rises from the dead.'"

17

¹⁷1 He said to the disciples, "It is impossible that no occasions of stumbling should come, but woe to him through whom they come! ¹⁷2 It would be better for him if a millstone were hung around his neck, and he were thrown into the sea, rather than that he should cause one of these little ones to stumble. ¹⁷3 Be careful. If your brother sins against you, rebuke him. If he repents, forgive him. ¹⁷4 If he sins against you seven times in the day, and seven times returns, saying, 'I repent,' you shall forgive him."
¹⁷5 The apostles said to the Lord, "Increase our faith."
¹⁷6 The Lord said, "If you had faith like a grain of mustard seed, you would tell this sycamore tree, 'Be uprooted, and be planted in the sea,' and it would obey you. ¹⁷7 But who is there among you, having a servant plowing or keeping sheep, that will say when he comes in from the field, 'Come immediately and sit down at the table,' ¹⁷8 and will not rather tell him, 'Prepare my supper, clothe yourself properly, and serve me, while I eat and drink. Afterward you shall eat and drink'? ¹⁷9 Does he thank that servant because he did the things that were commanded? I think not. ¹⁷10 Even so you also, when you have done all the things that are commanded you, say, 'We are unworthy servants. We have done our duty.'"
¹⁷11 As he was on his way to Jerusalem, he was passing along the borders of Samaria and Galilee. ¹⁷12 As he entered into a certain village, ten men who were lepers met him, who stood at a distance. ¹⁷13 They lifted up their
voices, saying, "Jesus, Master, have mercy on us!"
¹⁷14 When he saw them, he said to them, "Go and show yourselves to the priests." As they went, they were cleansed. ¹⁷15 One of them, when he saw that he was healed, turned back, glorifying God with a loud voice. ¹⁷16 He fell on his face at Jesus' feet, giving him thanks; and he

Day Twenty-Seven

was a Samaritan. ¹⁷17 Jesus answered, "Weren't the ten cleansed? But where are the nine? ¹⁷18 Were there none found who returned to give glory to God, except this foreigner?" ¹⁷19 Then he said to him, "Get up, and go your way. Your faith has healed you."

LUKE 18:1-14, THE WIDOW AND THE TAX COLLECTOR

18

¹⁸1 He also spoke a parable to them that they must always pray, and not give up, ¹⁸2 saying, "There was a judge in a certain city who didn't fear God, and didn't respect man. ¹⁸3 A widow was in that city, and she often came to him, saying, 'Defend me from my adversary!' ¹⁸4 He wouldn't for a while, but afterward he said to himself, 'Though I neither fear God, nor respect man, ¹⁸5 yet because this widow bothers me, I will defend her, or else she will wear me out by her continual coming.'"

¹⁸6 The Lord said, "Listen to what the unrighteous judge says. ¹⁸7 Won't God avenge his chosen ones who are crying out to him day and night, and yet he exercises patience with them? ¹⁸8 I tell you that he will avenge them quickly. Nevertheless, when the Son of Man comes, will he find faith on the earth?"

¹⁸9 He spoke also this parable to certain people who were convinced of their own righteousness, and who despised all others. ¹⁸10 "Two men went up into the temple to pray; one was a Pharisee, and the other was a tax collector. ¹⁸11 The Pharisee stood and prayed to himself like this: 'God, I thank you that I am not like the rest of men, extortionists, unrighteous, adulterers, or even like this tax collector. ¹⁸12 I fast twice a week. I give tithes of all that I get.' ¹⁸13 But the tax collector, standing far away, wouldn't even lift up his eyes to heaven, but beat his breast, saying, 'God, be merciful to me, a sinner!' ¹⁸14 I tell you, this man went down to his house justified rather than the other; for everyone who exalts himself will be humbled, but he who humbles himself will be exalted."

The Lord's Prayer

Our Father, who art in heaven,
Hallowed be thy name.
Thy Kingdom come.
Thy will be done on Earth, as it is in heaven.
Give us this day our daily bread.
And forgive us our trespasses,
As we forgive those that trespass against us.
And lead us not into temptation,
But deliver us from evil.
For thine is the kingdom,
The power, and the glory,
For ever and ever.
AMEN

Day Twenty-Eight

Daily Prayer

I thank you, my Heavenly Father, through Jesus Christ, Your dear Son, that You have kept me this night from all harm and danger, and I pray that You would also keep me today from sin and every evil, that all my doings and life may please You. For into Your hands I commend myself, my body and soul, and all things. Let Your holy angel be with me, that the evil foe may have no power over me.
– *Martin Luther, Protestant Reformer*

> "*I pray that You would also keep me today from sin and every evil, that all my doings and life may please You.*"

Prayer of Confession

Almighty and most merciful Father; we have erred, and strayed from your ways like lost sheep. We have followed

too much the devices and desires of our own hearts. We have offended against your holy laws. We have left undone those things which we ought to have done; and we have done those things which we ought not to have done; and there is no health in us. O Lord, have mercy upon us, miserable offenders. Spare those, O God, who confess their faults. Restore those who are penitent; according to your promises declared unto mankind in Christ Jesus our Lord. And grant, O most merciful Father, for his sake; that we may hereafter live a godly, righteous, and sober life, to the glory of thy holy Name. Amen.
-Revised prayer from *The Book of Common Prayer*, 1662

Daily Wisdom

1 The proverbs of Solomon. A wise son maketh a glad father: but a foolish son *is* the heaviness of his mother.
2 Treasures of wickedness profit nothing: but righteousness delivereth from death.
3 The LORD will not suffer the soul of the righteous to famish: but he casteth away the substance of the wicked.
4 He becometh poor that dealeth *with* a slack hand: but the hand of the diligent maketh rich.
5 He that gathereth in summer *is* a wise son: *but* he that sleepeth in harvest *is* a son that causeth shame.
6 Blessings *are* upon the head of the just: but violence covereth the mouth of the wicked.
7 The memory of the just *is* blessed: but the name of the wicked shall rot.
8 The wise in heart will receive commandments: but a prating fool shall fall.
9 He that walketh uprightly walketh surely: but he that perverteth his ways shall be known.
10 He that winketh with the eye causeth sorrow: but a prating fool shall fall.

Day Twenty-Eight

11 The mouth of a righteous *man is* a well of life: but violence covereth the mouth of the wicked.
12 Hatred stirreth up strifes: but love covereth all sins.
-Proverbs 10:1-12, *The King James Bible,* 1769 edition of 1611 text

Readings from the Holy Bible

The Holy Gospel According to John (JOHN 9:1-41; JOHN 10:1-42)

JOHN 9:1-10:42

9

⁹**1** As he passed by, he saw a man blind from birth. ⁹**2** His disciples asked him, "Rabbi, who sinned, this man or his parents, that he was born blind?"
⁹**3** Jesus answered, "This man didn't sin, nor did his parents; but, that the works of God might be revealed in him. ⁹**4** I must work the works of him who sent me while it is day. The night is coming, when no one can work. ⁹**5** While I am in the world, I am the light of the world." ⁹**6** When he had said this, he spat on the ground, made mud with the saliva, anointed the blind man's eyes with the mud, ⁹**7** and said to him, "Go, wash in the pool of Siloam" (which means "Sent"). So he went away, washed, and came back seeing. ⁹**8** The neighbors therefore, and those who saw that he was blind before, said, "Isn't this he who sat and begged?" ⁹**9** Others were saying, "It is he." Still others were saying, "He looks like him."
He said, "I am he." ⁹**10** They therefore were asking him, "How were your eyes opened?"
⁹**11** He answered, "A man called Jesus made mud, anointed my eyes, and said to me, 'Go to the pool of Siloam and wash.' So I went away and washed, and I received sight."
⁹**12** Then they asked him, "Where is he?"
He said, "I don't know."

⁹¹³ They brought him who had been blind to the Pharisees. ⁹¹⁴ It was a Sabbath when Jesus made the mud and opened his eyes. ⁹¹⁵ Again therefore the Pharisees also asked him how he received his sight. He said to them, "He put mud on my eyes, I washed, and I see."
⁹¹⁶ Some therefore of the Pharisees said, "This man is not from God, because he doesn't keep the Sabbath." Others said, "How can a man who is a sinner do such signs?" There was division among them.
⁹¹⁷ Therefore they asked the blind man again, "What do you say about him, because he opened your eyes?"
He said, "He is a prophet."
⁹¹⁸ The Jews therefore didn't believe concerning him, that he had been blind, and had received his sight, until they called the parents of him who had received his sight, ⁹¹⁹ and asked them, "Is this your son, whom you say was born blind? How then does he now see?"
⁹²⁰ His parents answered them, "We know that this is our son, and that he was born blind; ⁹²¹ but how he now sees, we don't know; or who opened his eyes, we don't know. He is of age. Ask him. He will speak for himself." ⁹²² His parents said these things because they feared the Jews; for the Jews had already agreed that if any man would confess him as Christ, he would be put out of the synagogue.
⁹²³ Therefore his parents said, "He is of age. Ask him."
⁹²⁴ So they called the man who was blind a second time, and said to him, "Give glory to God. We know that this man is a sinner."
⁹²⁵ He therefore answered, "I don't know if he is a sinner. One thing I do know: that though I was blind, now I see."
⁹²⁶ They said to him again, "What did he do to you? How did he open your eyes?"
⁹²⁷ He answered them, "I told you already, and you didn't listen. Why do you want to hear it again? You don't also want to become his disciples, do you?"
⁹²⁸ They insulted him and said, "You are his disciple, but we are disciples of Moses. ⁹²⁹ We know that God has spoken to Moses. But as for this man, we don't know where he comes from."
⁹³⁰ The man answered them, "How amazing! You don't know where he comes from, yet he opened my eyes. ⁹³¹ We know that God doesn't listen to sinners, but if anyone is a worshiper of God, and

Day Twenty-Eight

does his will, he listens to him.# ⁹32 Since the world began it has never been heard of that anyone opened the eyes of someone born blind. ⁹33 If this man were not from God, he could do nothing."
⁹34 They answered him, "You were altogether born in sins, and do you teach us?" Then they threw him out.
⁹35 Jesus heard that they had thrown him out, and finding him, he said, "Do you believe in the Son of God?"
⁹36 He answered, "Who is he, Lord, that I may believe in him?"
⁹37 Jesus said to him, "You have both seen him, and it is he who speaks with you."
⁹38 He said, "Lord, I believe!" and he worshiped him.
⁹39 Jesus said, "I came into this world for judgment, that those who don't see may see; and that those who see may become blind."
⁹40 Those of the Pharisees who were with him heard these things, and said to him, "Are we also blind?"
⁹41 Jesus said to them, ⁹"If you were blind, you would have no sin; but now you say, 'We see.' Therefore your sin remains.

10

¹⁰1 "Most certainly, I tell you, one who doesn't enter by the door into the sheep fold, but climbs up some other way, is a thief and a robber.
¹⁰2 But one who enters in by the door is the shepherd of the sheep.
¹⁰3 The gatekeeper opens the gate for him, and the sheep listen to his voice. He calls his own sheep by name, and leads them out. ¹⁰4 Whenever he brings out his own sheep, he goes before them, and the sheep follow him, for they know his voice. ¹⁰5 They will by no means follow a stranger, but will flee from him; for they don't know the voice of strangers." ¹⁰6 Jesus spoke this parable to them, but they didn't understand what he was telling them.
¹⁰7 Jesus therefore said to them again, "Most certainly, I tell you, I am the sheep's door. ¹⁰8 All who came before me are thieves and robbers, but the sheep didn't listen to them. ¹⁰9 I am the door. If anyone enters in by me, he will be saved, and will go in and go out, and will find pasture. ¹⁰10 The thief only comes to steal, kill, and destroy. I came that they may have life, and may have it abundantly.

#9:31 9:31 Psalm 66:18; Proverbs 15:29; 28:9

¹⁰11 I am the good shepherd.# The good shepherd lays down his life for the sheep. ¹⁰12 He who is a hired hand, and not a shepherd, who doesn't own the sheep, sees the wolf coming, leaves the sheep, and flees. The wolf snatches the sheep, and scatters them. ¹⁰13 The hired hand flees because he is a hired hand, and doesn't care for the sheep. ¹⁰14 I am the good shepherd. I know my own, and I'm known by my own; ¹⁰15 even as the Father knows me, and I know the Father. I lay down my life for the sheep. ¹⁰16 I have other sheep, which are not of this fold.# I must bring them also, and they will hear my voice. They will become one flock with one shepherd. ¹⁰17 Therefore the Father loves me, because I lay down my life, # that I may take it again. ¹⁰18 No one takes it away from me, but I lay it down by myself. I have power to lay it down, and I have power to take it again. I received this commandment from my Father."

¹⁰19 Therefore a division arose again among the Jews because of these words. ¹⁰20 Many of them said, "He has a demon, and is insane! Why do you listen to him?" ¹⁰21 Others said, "These are not the sayings of one possessed by a demon. It isn't possible for a demon to open the eyes of the blind, is it?"#

¹⁰22 It was the Feast of the Dedication⁹⁸ at Jerusalem. ¹⁰23 It was winter, and Jesus was walking in the temple, in Solomon's porch. ¹⁰24 The Jews therefore came around him and said to him, "How long will you hold us in suspense? If you are the Christ, tell us plainly." ¹⁰25 Jesus answered them, "I told you, and you don't believe. The works that I do in my Father's name, these testify about me. ¹⁰26 But you don't believe, because you are not of my sheep, as I told you. ¹⁰27 My sheep hear my voice, and I know them, and they follow me. ¹⁰28 I give eternal life to them. They will never perish, and no one will snatch them out of my hand. ¹⁰29 My Father who has given them to me is greater than all. No one is able to snatch them out of my Father's hand. ¹⁰30 I and the Father are one."

#10:11 10:11 Isaiah 40:11; Ezekiel 34:11-12,15,22
#10:16 10:16 Isaiah 56:8
#10:17 10:17 Isaiah 53:7-8
#10:21 10:21 Exodus 4:11
⁹⁸10:22 10:22 The "Feast of the Dedication" is the Greek name for "Hanukkah", a celebration of the rededication of the Temple.

Day Twenty-Eight

¹⁰³¹ Therefore Jews took up stones again to stone him. ¹⁰³² Jesus answered them, "I have shown you many good works from my Father. For which of those works do you stone me?"
¹⁰³³ The Jews answered him, "We don't stone you for a good work, but for blasphemy: because you, being a man, make yourself God."
¹⁰³⁴ Jesus answered them, "Isn't it written in your law, 'I said, you are gods?'# ¹⁰³⁵ If he called them gods, to whom the word of God came (and the Scripture can't be broken), ¹⁰³⁶ do you say of him whom the Father sanctified and sent into the world, 'You blaspheme,' because I said, 'I am the Son of God?' ¹⁰³⁷ If I don't do the works of my Father, don't believe me. ¹⁰³⁸ But if I do them, though you don't believe me, believe the works, that you may know and believe that the Father is in me, and I in the Father."
¹⁰³⁹ They sought again to seize him, and he went out of their hand.
¹⁰⁴⁰ He went away again beyond the Jordan into the place where John was baptizing at first, and he stayed there. ¹⁰⁴¹ Many came to him. They said, "John indeed did no sign, but everything that John said about this man is true." ¹⁰⁴² Many believed in him there.

The Lord's Prayer

Our Father, who art in heaven,
Hallowed be thy name.
Thy Kingdom come.
Thy will be done on Earth, as it is in heaven.
Give us this day our daily bread.
And forgive us our trespasses,
As we forgive those that trespass against us.
And lead us not into temptation,
But deliver us from evil.
For thine is the kingdom,

#10:34 10:34 Psalm 82:6

The American Book of Prayer

The power, and the glory,
For ever and ever.
AMEN

Day Twenty-Nine

Daily Prayer

Thou Eternal God, out of whose absolute power and infinite intelligence the whole universe has come into being, we humbly confess that we have not loved thee with our hearts, souls and minds, and we have not loved our neighbors as Christ loved us. We have all too often lived by our own selfish impulses rather than by the life of sacrificial love as revealed by Christ. We often give in order to receive. We love our friends and hate our enemies. We go the first mile but dare not travel the second. We forgive but dare not forget. And so as we look within ourselves, we are confronted with the appalling fact that the history of our lives is the history of an eternal revolt against you. But thou, O God, have mercy upon us. Forgive us for what we could have been but failed to be. Give us the intelligence to know your will. Give us the courage to do your will.

> "We have all too often lived by our own selfish impulses rather than by the life of sacrificial love as revealed by Christ."

Give us the devotion to love your will. In the name and spirit of Jesus, we pray. Amen.
- *Martin Luther King Jr.*[17]

Prayer of Confession

Almighty and most merciful Father; we have erred, and strayed from your ways like lost sheep. We have followed too much the devices and desires of our own hearts. We have offended against your holy laws. We have left undone those things which we ought to have done; and we have done those things which we ought not to have done; and there is no health in us. O Lord, have mercy upon us, miserable offenders. Spare those, O God, who confess their faults. Restore those who are penitent; according to your promises declared unto mankind in Christ Jesus our Lord. And grant, O most merciful Father, for his sake; that we may hereafter live a godly, righteous, and sober life, to the glory of thy holy Name. Amen.
-Revised prayer from *The Book of Common Prayer*, 1662

Daily Wisdom

16 A fool's wrath is presently known: but a prudent *man* covereth shame.
17 *He that* speaketh truth sheweth forth righteousness: but a false witness deceit.
18 There is that speaketh like the piercings of a sword: but the tongue of the wise *is* health.
19 The lip of truth shall be established for ever: but a lying tongue *is* but for a moment.
20 Deceit *is* in the heart of them that imagine evil: but to the counsellors of peace *is* joy.
21 There shall no evil happen to the just: but the wicked shall be filled with mischief.
22 Lying lips *are* abomination to the LORD: but they that deal truly *are* his delight.

Day Twenty-Nine

23 A prudent man concealeth knowledge: but the heart of fools proclaimeth foolishness.
24 The hand of the diligent shall bear rule: but the slothful shall be under tribute.
25 Heaviness in the heart of man maketh it stoop: but a good word maketh it glad.
26 The righteous *is* more excellent than his neighbour: but the way of the wicked seduceth them.
27 The slothful *man* roasteth not that which he took in hunting: but the substance of a diligent man *is* precious.
28 In the way of righteousness *is* life; and *in* the pathway *thereof there is* no death.
-Proverbs 12:16-28, *The King James Bible*, 1769 edition of 1611 text

Readings from the Holy Bible

The Holy Gospel According to Matthew, Mark, and Luke (MATTHEW 18:15-35; MARK 9:38-41; LUKE 12:13-21; LUKE 13 and 14)

MATTHEW 18:15-35, BROTHERS WHO SIN AGAINST YOU AND THE SERVANT

15 "If your brother sins against you, go, show him his fault between you and him alone. If he listens to you, you have gained back your brother. **16** But if he doesn't listen, take one or two more with you, that at the mouth of two or three witnesses every word may be established.# **17** If he refuses to listen to them, tell it to the assembly. If he refuses to hear the assembly also, let him be to you as a Gentile or a tax collector. **18** Most certainly I tell you, whatever things you bind on earth will have been bound in heaven, and whatever things you release on earth will have been released in heaven. **19** Again, assuredly I tell you, that if two of you will agree on earth concerning anything that they will ask, it will be done for them by my Father who

---

#18:16 18:16 Deuteronomy 19:15

is in heaven. ¹⁸20 For where two or three are gathered together in my name, there I am in the middle of them."

¹⁸21 Then Peter came and said to him, "Lord, how often shall my brother sin against me, and I forgive him? Until seven times?"

¹⁸22 Jesus said to him, "I don't tell you until seven times, but, until seventy times seven. ¹⁸23 Therefore the Kingdom of Heaven is like a certain king, who wanted to reconcile accounts with his servants. ¹⁸24 When he had begun to reconcile, one was brought to him who owed him ten thousand talents.⁹⁹ ¹⁸25 But because he couldn't pay, his lord commanded him to be sold, with his wife, his children, and all that he had, and payment to be made. ¹⁸26 The servant therefore fell down and knelt before him, saying, 'Lord, have patience with me, and I will repay you all!' ¹⁸27 The lord of that servant, being moved with compassion, released him, and forgave him the debt.

¹⁸28 "But that servant went out, and found one of his fellow servants, who owed him one hundred denarii,¹⁰⁰ and he grabbed him, and took him by the throat, saying, 'Pay me what you owe!'

¹⁸29 "So his fellow servant fell down at his feet and begged him, saying, 'Have patience with me, and I will repay you!' ¹⁸30 He would not, but went and cast him into prison, until he should pay back that which was due. ¹⁸31 So when his fellow servants saw what was done, they were exceedingly sorry, and came and told their lord all that was done. ¹⁸32 Then his lord called him in, and said to him, 'You wicked servant! I forgave you all that debt, because you begged me. ¹⁸33 Shouldn't you also have

had mercy on your fellow servant, even as I had mercy on you?' ¹⁸34 His lord was angry, and delivered him to the tormentors, until he should pay all that was due to him. ¹⁸35 ¹⁸So my heavenly Father will also do to you, if you don't each forgive your brother from your hearts for his misdeeds."

---

⁹⁹18:24 18:24 Ten thousand talents (about 300 metric tons of silver) represents an extremely large sum of money, equivalent to about 60,000,000 denarii, where one denarius was typical of one day's wages for agricultural labor.

¹⁰⁰18:28 18:28 100 denarii was about one sixtieth of a talent, or about 500 grams (1.1 pounds) of silver.

Day Twenty-Nine

MARK 9:38-41, THOSE WHO ARE "NOT WITH US"

⁹38 John said to him, "Teacher, we saw someone who doesn't follow us casting out demons in your name; and we forbade him, because he doesn't follow us."
⁹39 But Jesus said, "Don't forbid him, for there is no one who will do a mighty work in my name, and be able quickly to speak evil of me.
⁹40 For whoever is not against us is on our side. ⁹41 For whoever will give you a cup of water to drink in my name, because you are Christ's, most certainly I tell you, he will in no way lose his reward.

LUKE 12:13-21, THE RICH FOOL

¹²13 One of the multitude said to him, "Teacher, tell my brother to divide the inheritance with me."
¹²14 But he said to him, "Man, who made me a judge or an arbitrator over you?" ¹²15 He said to them, "Beware! Keep yourselves from covetousness, for a man's life doesn't consist of the abundance of the things which he possesses."
¹²16 He spoke a parable to them, saying, "The ground of a certain rich man produced abundantly. ¹²17 He reasoned within himself, saying, 'What will I do, because I don't have room to store my crops?' ¹²18 He said, 'This is what I will do. I will pull down my barns, build bigger ones, and there I will store all my grain and my goods. ¹²19 I will tell my soul, "Soul, you have many goods laid up for many years. Take your ease, eat, drink, and be merry."'
¹²20 "But God said to him, 'You foolish one, tonight your soul is required of you. The things which you have prepared—whose will they be?' ¹²21 So is he who lays up treasure for himself, and is not rich toward God."

LUKE 13 & 14

13

¹³1 Now there were some present at the same time who told him about the Galileans, whose blood Pilate had mixed with their sacrifices.
¹³2 Jesus answered them, "Do you think that these Galileans were worse sinners than all the other Galileans, because they suffered such

things? ¹³3 I tell you, no, but unless you repent, you will all perish in the same way. ¹³4 Or those eighteen, on whom the tower in Siloam fell and killed them; do you think that they were worse offenders than all the men who dwell in Jerusalem? ¹³5 I tell you, no, but, unless you repent, you will all perish in the same way."
¹³6 He spoke this parable. "A certain man had a fig tree planted in his vineyard, and he came seeking fruit on it, and found none. ¹³7 He said to the vine dresser, 'Behold, these three years I have come looking for fruit on this fig tree, and found none. Cut it down. Why does it waste the soil?' ¹³8 He answered, 'Lord, leave it alone this year also, until I dig around it and fertilize it. ¹³9 If it bears fruit, fine; but if not, after that, you can cut it down.'"
¹³10 He was teaching in one of the synagogues on the Sabbath day. ¹³11 Behold, there was a woman who had a spirit of infirmity eighteen years. She was bent over, and could in no way straighten herself up. ¹³12 When Jesus saw her, he called her, and said to her, "Woman, you are freed from your infirmity." ¹³13 He laid his hands on her, and immediately she stood up straight and glorified God.
¹³14 The ruler of the synagogue, being indignant because Jesus had healed on the Sabbath, said to the multitude, "There are six days in which men ought to work. Therefore come on those days and be healed, and not on the Sabbath day!"
¹³15 Therefore the Lord answered him, "You hypocrites! Doesn't each one of you free his ox or his donkey from the stall on the Sabbath, and lead him away to water? ¹³16 Ought not this woman, being a daughter of Abraham whom Satan had bound eighteen long years, be freed from this bondage on the Sabbath day?" ¹³17 As he said these things, all his adversaries were disappointed and all the multitude rejoiced for all the glorious things that were done by him.
¹³18 He said, "What is God's Kingdom like? To what shall I compare it? ¹³19 It is like a grain of mustard seed which a man took and put in his own garden. It grew and became a large tree, and the birds of the sky live in its branches."
¹³20 Again he said, "To what shall I compare God's Kingdom? ¹³21 It is like yeast, which a woman took and hid in three measures [101] of flour, until it was all leavened."

---

[101]13:21 13:21 literally, three sata. 3 sata is about 39 liters or a bit more than a bushel.

Day Twenty-Nine

¹³22 He went on his way through cities and villages, teaching, and traveling on to Jerusalem. ¹³23 One said to him, "Lord, are they few who are saved?"

He said to them, ¹³24 "Strive to enter in by the narrow door, for many, I tell you, will seek to enter in and will not be able. ¹³25 When once the master of the house has risen up, and has shut the door, and you begin to stand outside and to knock at the door, saying, 'Lord, Lord, open to us!' then he will answer and tell you, 'I don't know you or where you come from.' ¹³26 Then you will begin to say, 'We ate and drank in your presence, and you taught in our streets.' ¹³27 He will say, 'I tell you, I don't know where you come from. Depart from me, all you workers of iniquity.' ¹³28 There will be weeping and gnashing of teeth when you see Abraham, Isaac, Jacob, and all the prophets in God's Kingdom, and yourselves being thrown outside. ¹³29 They will come from the east, west, north, and south, and will sit down in God's Kingdom. ¹³30 Behold, there are some who are last who will be first, and there are some who are first who will be last."

¹³31 On that same day, some Pharisees came, saying to him, "Get out of here, and go away, for Herod wants to kill you."

¹³32 He said to them, "Go and tell that fox, 'Behold, I cast out demons and perform cures today and tomorrow, and the third day I complete my mission. ¹³33 Nevertheless I must go on my way today and tomorrow and the next day, for it can't be that a prophet would perish outside of Jerusalem.'

¹³34 "Jerusalem, Jerusalem, you who kills the prophets and stones those who are sent to her! How often I wanted to gather your children together, like a hen gathers her own brood under her wings, and you refused! ¹³35 ⁱ³Behold, your house is left to you desolate. I tell you, you will not see me until you say, 'Blessed is he who comes in the name of the Lord!'" #

14

¹⁴1 When he went into the house of one of the rulers of the Pharisees on a Sabbath to eat bread, they were watching him. ¹⁴2 Behold, a certain man who had dropsy was in front of him. ¹⁴3 Jesus, answering,

---

#13:35 13:35 Psalm 118:26

spoke to the lawyers and Pharisees, saying, "Is it lawful to heal on the Sabbath?"

¹⁴4 But they were silent.

He took him, and healed him, and let him go. ¹⁴5 He answered them, "Which of you, if your son[102] or an ox fell into a well, wouldn't immediately pull him out on a Sabbath day?"

¹⁴6 They couldn't answer him regarding these things.

¹⁴7 He spoke a parable to those who were invited, when he noticed how they chose the best seats, and said to them, ¹⁴8 "When you are invited by anyone to a wedding feast, don't sit in the best seat, since perhaps someone more honorable than you might be invited by him, ¹⁴9 and he who invited both of you would come and tell you, 'Make room for this person.' Then you would begin, with shame, to take the lowest place. ¹⁴10 But when you are invited, go and sit in the lowest place, so that when he who invited you comes, he may tell you, 'Friend, move up higher.' Then you will be honored in the presence of all who sit at the table with you. ¹⁴11 For everyone who exalts himself will be humbled, and whoever humbles himself will be exalted."

¹⁴12 He also said to the one who had invited him, "When you make a dinner or a supper, don't call your friends, nor your brothers, nor your kinsmen, nor rich neighbors, or perhaps they might also return the favor, and pay you back. ¹⁴13 But when you make a feast, ask the poor, the maimed, the lame, or the blind; ¹⁴14 and you will be blessed, because they don't have the resources to repay you. For you will be repaid in the resurrection of the righteous."

¹⁴15 When one of those who sat at the table with him heard these things, he said to him, "Blessed is he who will feast in God's Kingdom!"

¹⁴16 But he said to him, "A certain man made a great supper, and he invited many people. ¹⁴17 He sent out his servant at supper time to tell those who were invited, 'Come, for everything is ready now.' ¹⁴18 They all as one began to make excuses.

"The first said to him, 'I have bought a field, and I must go and see it. Please have me excused.'

¹⁴19 "Another said, 'I have bought five yoke of oxen, and I must go try them out. Please have me excused.'

---

[102]14:5 14:5 TR reads "donkey" instead of "son"

Day Twenty-Nine

14:20 "Another said, 'I have married a wife, and therefore I can't come.'

14:21 "That servant came, and told his lord these things. Then the master of the house, being angry, said to his servant, 'Go out quickly into the streets and lanes of the city, and bring in the poor, maimed, blind, and lame.'

14:22 "The servant said, 'Lord, it is done as you commanded, and there is still room.'

14:23 "The lord said to the servant, 'Go out into the highways and hedges, and compel them to come in, that my house may be filled.

14:24 For I tell you that none of those men who were invited will taste of my supper.'"

14:25 Now great multitudes were going with him. He turned and said to them, **14:26** "If anyone comes to me, and doesn't disregard[103] his own father, mother, wife, children, brothers, and sisters, yes, and his own life also, he can't be my disciple. **14:27** Whoever doesn't bear his own cross, and come after me, can't be my disciple. **14:28** For which of you, desiring to build a tower, doesn't first sit down and count the cost, to see if he has enough to complete it? **14:29** Or perhaps, when he has laid a foundation, and is not able to finish, everyone who sees begins to mock him, **14:30** saying, 'This man began to build, and wasn't able to finish.' **14:31** Or what king, as he goes to encounter another king in war, will not sit down first and consider whether he is able with ten thousand to meet him who comes against him with twenty thousand? **14:32** Or else, while the other is yet a great way off, he sends an envoy, and asks for conditions of peace. **14:33** So therefore whoever of you who doesn't renounce all that he has, he can't be my disciple. **14:34** Salt is good, but if the salt becomes flat and tasteless, with what do you season it? **14:35** [14]It is fit neither for the soil nor for the manure pile. It is thrown out. He who has ears to hear, let him hear."

---

[103] 14:26 14:26 or, hate

The American Book of Prayer

The Lord's Prayer

Our Father, who art in heaven,
Hallowed be thy name.
Thy Kingdom come.
Thy will be done on Earth, as it is in heaven.
Give us this day our daily bread.
And forgive us our trespasses,
As we forgive those that trespass against us.
And lead us not into temptation,
But deliver us from evil.
For thine is the kingdom,
The power, and the glory,
For ever and ever.
AMEN

Day Thirty

Daily Prayer

Thou Whose hand did lead Thy chosen people
Through the desert on their pilgrim way,
In Thy mercy grant us now Thy blessing,
Jesus help us all to watch and pray.
Father, Thou art pure and holy, holy,
May our hearts Thy temple be,
O, make us humble, meek and lowly,
Poor in spirit, Savior, more like Thee.
Give us water from the sacred fountain,
While we journey in a thirsty land;
Strong in Thee no earthly foe can harm us,
Thou our Rock on which we firmly stand.
Gentle Savior, Thou wilt never leave us,
Still from danger and from storm defend,
Sweet the promise to Thy faithful children,
Thou wilt guide and keep them to the end.
Though we pass the dark and rolling river,
Thou wilt bear us safely to the shore;
We shall praise Thee in the vales of Eden,
With the saints and angels evermore.
-"*Sacred Fountain,*" *a hymn by Fanny Crosby*

> "While we journey in a thirsty land; Strong in Thee no earthly foe can harm us, thou our Rock on which we firmly stand."

Prayer of Confession

Almighty and most merciful Father; we have erred, and strayed from your ways like lost sheep. We have followed too much the devices and desires of our own hearts. We have offended against your holy laws. We have left undone those things which we ought to have done; and we have done those things which we ought not to have done; and there is no health in us. O Lord, have mercy upon us, miserable offenders. Spare those, O God, who confess their faults. Restore those who are penitent; according to your promises declared unto mankind in Christ Jesus our Lord. And grant, O most merciful Father, for his sake; that we may hereafter live a godly, righteous, and sober life, to the glory of thy holy Name. Amen.
-Revised prayer from *The Book of Common Prayer*, 1662

Daily Wisdom

A Psalm of David.
1 The LORD *is* my shepherd; I shall not want.
2 He maketh me to lie down in green pastures: he leadeth me beside the still waters.
3 He restoreth my soul: he leadeth me in the paths of righteousness for his name's sake.
4 Yea, though I walk through the valley of the shadow of death, I will fear no evil: for thou *art* with me; thy rod and thy staff they comfort me.
5 Thou preparest a table before me in the presence of mine enemies: thou anointest my head with oil; my cup runneth over.
6 Surely goodness and mercy shall follow me all the days of my life: and I will dwell in the house of the LORD for ever.
-Psalm 23, *The King James Bible*, 1769 edition of 1611 text

Day Thirty

Readings from the Holy Bible

The Holy Gospel According to Mark, and Matthew (MARK 9:42-10:31; MATTHEW 20:1-34)

MARK 9:42-10:31, SIN, DIVORCE, CHILDREN, AND THE RICH MAN

⁹42 Whoever will cause one of these little ones who believe in me to stumble, it would be better for him if he were thrown into the sea with a millstone hung around his neck. ⁹43 If your hand causes you to stumble, cut it off. It is better for you to enter into life maimed, rather than having your two hands to go into Gehenna, [104] into the unquenchable fire, ⁹44 'where their worm doesn't die, and the fire is not quenched.' #[105] ⁹45 If your foot causes you to stumble, cut it off. It is better for you to enter into life lame, rather than having your two feet to be cast into Gehenna, [106] into the fire that will never be quenched— ⁹46 'where their worm doesn't die, and the fire is not quenched.' [107] ⁹47 If your eye causes you to stumble, cast it out. It is better for you to enter into God's Kingdom with one eye, rather than having two eyes to be cast into the Gehenna[108] of fire, ⁹48 'where their worm doesn't die, and the fire is not quenched.' # ⁹49 For everyone will be salted with fire, and every sacrifice will be seasoned with salt. ⁹50 ⁹Salt is good, but if the salt has lost its saltiness, with what will you season it? Have salt in yourselves, and be at peace with one another."

10

¹⁰1 He arose from there and came into the borders of Judea and beyond the Jordan. Multitudes came together to him again. As he usually did, he was again teaching them. ¹⁰2 Pharisees came to him

---

[104]9:43 9:43 or, Hell
#9:44 9:44 Isaiah 66:24
[105]9:44 9:44 NU omits verse 44.
[106]9:45 9:45 or, Hell
[107]9:46 9:46 NU omits verse 46.
[108]9:47 9:47 or, Hell
#9:48 9:48 Isaiah 66:24

testing him, and asked him, "Is it lawful for a man to divorce his wife?"

¹⁰3 He answered, "What did Moses command you?"

¹⁰4 They said, "Moses allowed a certificate of divorce to be written, and to divorce her."

¹⁰5 But Jesus said to them, "For your hardness of heart, he wrote you this commandment. ¹⁰6 But from the beginning of the creation, God made them male and female.# ¹⁰7 For this cause a man will leave his father and mother, and will join to his wife, ¹⁰8 and the two will become one flesh,# so that they are no longer two, but one flesh. ¹⁰9 What therefore God has joined together, let no man separate."

¹⁰10 In the house, his disciples asked him again about the same matter.

¹⁰11 He said to them, "Whoever divorces his wife, and marries another, commits adultery against her. ¹⁰12 If a woman herself divorces her husband, and marries another, she commits adultery."

¹⁰13 They were bringing to him little children, that he should touch them, but the disciples rebuked those who were bringing them.

¹⁰14 But when Jesus saw it, he was moved with indignation, and said to them, "Allow the little children to come to me! Don't forbid them, for God's Kingdom belongs to such as these. ¹⁰15 Most certainly I tell you, whoever will not receive God's Kingdom like a little child, he will in no way enter into it." ¹⁰16 He took them in his arms, and blessed them, laying his hands on them.

¹⁰17 As he was going out into the way, one ran to him, knelt before him, and asked him, "Good Teacher, what shall I do that I may inherit eternal life?"

¹⁰18 Jesus said to him, "Why do you call me good? No one is good except one—God. ¹⁰19 You know the commandments: 'Do not murder,' 'Do not commit adultery,' 'Do not steal,' 'Do not give false testimony,' 'Do not defraud,' 'Honor your father and mother.'"#

¹⁰20 He said to him, "Teacher, I have observed all these things from my youth."

#10:6 10:6 Genesis 1:27
#10:8 10:8 Genesis 2:24
#10:19 10:19 Exodus 20:12-16; Deuteronomy 5:16-20

Day Thirty

10:21 Jesus looking at him loved him, and said to him, "One thing you lack. Go, sell whatever you have, and give to the poor, and you will have treasure in heaven; and come, follow me, taking up the cross." **10:22** But his face fell at that saying, and he went away sorrowful, for he was one who had great possessions. **10:23** Jesus looked around, and said to his disciples, "How difficult it is for those who have riches to enter into God's Kingdom!"
10:24 The disciples were amazed at his words. But Jesus answered again, "Children, how hard it is for those who trust in riches to enter into God's Kingdom! **10:25** It is easier for a camel to go through a needle's eye than for a rich man to enter into God's Kingdom."
10:26 They were exceedingly astonished, saying to him, "Then who can be saved?"
10:27 Jesus, looking at them, said, "With men it is impossible, but not with God, for all things are possible with God."
10:28 Peter began to tell him, "Behold, we have left all, and have followed you."
10:29 Jesus said, "Most certainly I tell you, there is no one who has left house, or brothers, or sisters, or father, or mother, or wife, or children, or land, for my sake, and for the sake of the Good News, **10:30** but he will receive one hundred times more now in this time: houses, brothers, sisters, mothers, children, and land, with persecutions; and in the age to come eternal life. **10:31** But many who are first will be last; and the last first."

MATTHEW 20:1-34

20

1 "For the Kingdom of Heaven is like a man who was the master of a household, who went out early in the morning to hire laborers for his vineyard. **20:2** When he had agreed with the laborers for a denarius[109] a day, he sent them into his vineyard. **20:3** He went out about the third hour,[110] and saw others standing idle in the marketplace. **20:4** He said to them, 'You also go into the vineyard, and whatever is right I will

---

[109]20:2 20:2 A denarius is a silver Roman coin worth 1/25th of a Roman aureus. This was a common wage for a day of farm labor.
[110]20:3 20:3 Time was measured from sunrise to sunset, so the third hour would be about 9:00 a.m.

give you.' So they went their way. ²⁰5 Again he went out about the sixth and the ninth hour,[111] and did likewise. ²⁰6 About the eleventh hour[112] he went out, and found others standing idle. He said to them, 'Why do you stand here all day idle?'

²⁰7 "They said to him, 'Because no one has hired us.'
"He said to them, 'You also go into the vineyard, and you will receive whatever is right.' ²⁰8 When evening had come, the lord of the vineyard said to his manager, 'Call the laborers and pay them their wages, beginning from the last to the first.'

²⁰9 "When those who were hired at about the eleventh hour came, they each received a denarius. ²⁰10 When the first came, they supposed that they would receive more; and they likewise each received a denarius. ²⁰11 When they received it, they murmured against the master of the household, ²⁰12 saying, 'These last have spent one hour, and you have made them equal to us, who have borne the burden of the day and the scorching heat!'

²⁰13 "But he answered one of them, 'Friend, I am doing you no wrong. Didn't you agree with me for a denarius? ²⁰14 Take that which is yours, and go your way. It is my desire to give to this last just as much as to you. ²⁰15 Isn't it lawful for me to do what I want to with what I own? Or is your eye evil, because I am good?' ²⁰16 So the last will be first, and the first last. For many are called, but few are chosen."

²⁰17 As Jesus was going up to Jerusalem, he took the twelve disciples aside, and on the way he said to them, ²⁰18 "Behold, we are going up to Jerusalem, and the Son of Man will be delivered to the chief priests and scribes, and they will condemn him to death, ²⁰19 and will hand him over to the Gentiles to mock, to scourge, and to crucify; and the third day he will be raised up."

²⁰20 Then the mother of the sons of Zebedee came to him with her sons, kneeling and asking a certain thing of him. ²⁰21 He said to her, "What do you want?"
She said to him, "Command that these, my two sons, may sit, one on your right hand, and one on your left hand, in your Kingdom."

---

[111] 20:5 20:5 noon and 3:00 p.m.
[112] 20:6 20:6 5:00 p.m.

Day Thirty

²⁰22 But Jesus answered, "You don't know what you are asking. Are you able to drink the cup that I am about to drink, and be baptized with the baptism that I am baptized with?"
They said to him, "We are able."
²⁰23 He said to them, "You will indeed drink my cup, and be baptized with the baptism that I am baptized with, but to sit on my right hand and on my left hand is not mine to give; but it is for whom it has been prepared by my Father."
²⁰24 When the ten heard it, they were indignant with the two brothers.
²⁰25 But Jesus summoned them, and said, "You know that the rulers of the nations lord it over them, and their great ones exercise authority over them. ²⁰26 It shall not be so among you, but whoever desires to become great among you shall be[113] your servant. ²⁰27 Whoever desires to be first among you shall be your bondservant, ²⁰28 even as the Son of Man came not to be served, but to serve, and to give his life as a ransom for many."
²⁰29 As they went out from Jericho, a great multitude followed him.
²⁰30 Behold, two blind men sitting by the road, when they heard that Jesus was passing by, cried out, "Lord, have mercy on us, you son of David!" ²⁰31 The multitude rebuked them, telling them that they should be quiet, but they cried out even more, "Lord, have mercy on us, you son of David!"
²⁰32 Jesus stood still, and called them, and asked, "What do you want me to do for you?"
²⁰33 They told him, "Lord, that our eyes may be opened."
²⁰34 Jesus, being moved with compassion, touched their eyes; and immediately their eyes received their sight, and they followed him.

---

[113]20:26 20:26 TR reads "let him be" instead of "shall be"

The Lord's Prayer

Our Father, who art in heaven,
Hallowed be thy name.
Thy Kingdom come.
Thy will be done on Earth, as it is in heaven.
Give us this day our daily bread.
And forgive us our trespasses,
As we forgive those that trespass against us.
And lead us not into temptation,
But deliver us from evil.
For thine is the kingdom,
The power, and the glory,
For ever and ever.
AMEN

Day Thirty-One

Daily Prayer

O LORD, strengthen our faith; kindle it more in ferventness and love towards thee, and our neighbors, for thy sake. Suffer us not, most dear Father, to receive thy word any more in vain; but grant us always the assistance of thy grace and Holy Spirit, that in heart, word, and deed, we may sanctify and do worship to thy name. Help to amplify and increase thy kingdom; that whatsoever thou send, we may be heartily well content with thy good pleasure and will. Let us not lack the thing – O Father! – without the which we cannot serve thee; but bless thou so all the works of our hands, that we may have sufficient, and not be chargeable, but rather helpful unto others.

-*John Knox, Scottish Protestant Reformer*

> "Help to amplify and increase thy kingdom; that whatsoever thou send, we may be heartily well content with thy good pleasure and will."

Prayer of Confession

Almighty and most merciful Father; we have erred, and strayed from your ways like lost sheep. We have followed too much the devices and desires of our own hearts. We have offended against your holy laws. We have left undone those things which we ought to have done; and we have done those things which we ought not to have done; and there is no health in us. O Lord, have mercy upon us, miserable offenders. Spare those, O God, who confess their faults. Restore those who are penitent; according to your promises declared unto mankind in Christ Jesus our Lord. And grant, O most merciful Father, for his sake; that we may hereafter live a godly, righteous, and sober life, to the glory of thy holy Name. Amen.
-Revised prayer from *The Book of Common Prayer*, 1662

Daily Wisdom

A Psalm of David.
1 The earth *is* the LORD'S, and the fulness thereof; the world, and they that dwell therein.
2 For he hath founded it upon the seas, and established it upon the floods.
3 Who shall ascend into the hill of the LORD? or who shall stand in his holy place?
4 He that hath clean hands, and a pure heart; who hath not lifted up his soul unto vanity, nor sworn deceitfully.
5 He shall receive the blessing from the LORD, and righteousness from the God of his salvation.
6 This *is* the generation of them that seek him, that seek thy face, O Jacob. Selah.
7 Lift up your heads, O ye gates; and be ye lift up, ye everlasting doors; and the King of glory shall come in.

Day Thirty-One

8 Who *is* this King of glory? The LORD strong and mighty, the LORD mighty in battle.
9 Lift up your heads, O ye gates; even lift *them* up, ye everlasting doors; and the King of glory shall come in.
10 Who is this King of glory? The LORD of hosts, he *is* the King of glory. Selah.
-Psalm 24, *The King James Bible*, 1769 edition of 1611 text

Readings from the Holy Bible

The Holy Gospel According to Luke and Matthew (LUKE 18:35-19:10; MATTHEW 21:1-22:14)

LUKE 18:35-19:10, BARTIMAEUS AND ZACCHAEUS

¹⁸**35** As he came near Jericho, a certain blind man sat by the road, begging. ¹⁸**36** Hearing a multitude going by, he asked what this meant. ¹⁸**37** They told him that Jesus of Nazareth was passing by. ¹⁸**38** He cried out, "Jesus, you son of David, have mercy on me!" ¹⁸**39** Those who led the way rebuked him, that he should be quiet; but he cried out all the more, "You son of David, have mercy on me!"
¹⁸**40** Standing still, Jesus commanded him to be brought to him. When he had come near, he asked him, ¹⁸**41** "What do you want me to do?" He said, "Lord, that I may see again."
¹⁸**42** Jesus said to him, "Receive your sight. Your faith has healed you."
¹⁸**43** Immediately he received his sight and followed him, glorifying God. All the people, when they saw it, praised God. ¹⁸

19

¹⁹**1** He entered and was passing through Jericho. ¹⁹**2** There was a man named Zacchaeus. He was a chief tax collector, and he was rich. ¹⁹**3** He was trying to see who Jesus was, and couldn't because of the crowd, because he was short. ¹⁹**4** He ran on ahead, and climbed up into a sycamore tree to see him, for he was going to pass that way. ¹⁹**5** When Jesus came to the place, he looked up and saw him, and said to him, "Zacchaeus, hurry and come down, for today I must stay at

your house." **19:6** He hurried, came down, and received him joyfully. **19:7** When they saw it, they all murmured, saying, "He has gone in to lodge with a man who is a sinner."
19:8 Zacchaeus stood and said to the Lord, "Behold, Lord, half of my goods I give to the poor. If I have wrongfully exacted anything of anyone, I restore four times as much."
19:9 Jesus said to him, "Today, salvation has come to this house, because he also is a son of Abraham. **19:10** For the Son of Man came to seek and to save that which was lost."

MATTHEW 21:1-22:14

21

21:1 When they came near to Jerusalem, and came to Bethsphage,[114] to the Mount of Olives, then Jesus sent two disciples, **21:2** saying to them, "Go into the village that is opposite you, and immediately you will find a donkey tied, and a colt with her. Untie them, and bring them to me. **21:3** If anyone says anything to you, you shall say, 'The Lord needs them,' and immediately he will send them."
21:4 All this was done, that it might be fulfilled which was spoken through the prophet, saying,
21:5 "Tell the daughter of Zion,
behold, your King comes to you,
humble, and riding on a donkey,
on a colt, the foal of a donkey."#
21:6 The disciples went, and did just as Jesus commanded them, **21:7** and brought the donkey and the colt, and laid their clothes on them; and he sat on them. **21:8** A very great multitude spread their clothes on the road. Others cut branches from the trees, and spread them on the road. **21:9** The multitudes who went in front of him, and those who followed, kept shouting,
"Hosanna [115] to the son of David! Blessed is he who comes in the name of the Lord! Hosanna in the highest!" #

---

[114]21:1 21:1 TR & NU read "Bethphage" instead of "Bethsphage"
#21:5 21:5 Zechariah 9:9
[115]21:9 21:9 "Hosanna" means "save us" or "help us, we pray".
#21:9 21:9 Psalm 118:26

Day Thirty-One

²¹10 When he had come into Jerusalem, all the city was stirred up, saying, "Who is this?" ²¹11 The multitudes said, "This is the prophet, Jesus, from Nazareth of Galilee."
²¹12 Jesus entered into the temple of God, and drove out all of those who sold and bought in the temple, and overthrew the money changers' tables and the seats of those who sold the doves. ²¹13 He said to them, "It is written, 'My house shall be called a house of prayer,'# but you have made it a den of robbers!"
²¹14 The blind and the lame came to him in the temple, and he healed them. ²¹15 But when the chief priests and the scribes saw the wonderful things that he did, and the children who were crying in the temple and saying, "Hosanna to the son of David!" they were indignant, ²¹16 and said to him, "Do you hear what these are saying?" Jesus said to them, "Yes. Did you never read, 'Out of the mouth of babes and nursing babies you have perfected praise?'"
²¹17 He left them, and went out of the city to Bethany, and camped there. ²¹18 Now in the morning, as he returned to the city, he was hungry. ²¹19 Seeing a fig tree by the road, he came to it, and found nothing on it but leaves. He said to it, "Let there be no fruit from you forever!"

Immediately the fig tree withered away. ²¹20 When the disciples saw it, they marveled, saying, "How did the fig tree immediately wither away?"
²¹21 Jesus answered them, "Most certainly I tell you, if you have faith, and don't doubt, you will not only do what was done to the fig tree, but even if you told this mountain, 'Be taken up and cast into the sea,' it would be done. ²¹22 All things, whatever you ask in prayer, believing, you will receive."
²¹23 When he had come into the temple, the chief priests and the elders of the people came to him as he was teaching, and said, "By what authority do you do these things? Who gave you this authority?" ²¹24 Jesus answered them, "I also will ask you one question, which if you tell me, I likewise will tell you by what authority I do these things. ²¹25 The baptism of John, where was it from? From heaven or from men?"

#21:13 21:13 Isaiah 56:7

They reasoned with themselves, saying, "If we say, 'From heaven,' he will ask us, 'Why then did you not believe him?' ^{21}26 But if we say, 'From men,' we fear the multitude, for all hold John as a prophet." ^{21}27 They answered Jesus, and said, "We don't know."
He also said to them, "Neither will I tell you by what authority I do these things. ^{21}28 But what do you think? A man had two sons, and he came to the first, and said, 'Son, go work today in my vineyard.' ^{21}29 He answered, 'I will not,' but afterward he changed his mind, and went. ^{21}30 He came to the second, and said the same thing. He answered, 'I'm going, sir,' but he didn't go. ^{21}31 Which of the two did the will of his father?"
They said to him, "The first."
Jesus said to them, "Most certainly I tell you that the tax collectors and the prostitutes are entering into God's Kingdom before you. ^{21}32 For John came to you in the way of righteousness, and you didn't believe him, but the tax collectors and the prostitutes believed him. When you saw it, you didn't even repent afterward, that you might believe him. ^{21}33 "Hear another parable. There was a man who was a master of a household, who planted a vineyard, set a hedge about it, dug a wine press in it, built a tower, leased it out to farmers, and went into another country. ^{21}34 When the season for the fruit came near, he sent his servants to the farmers, to receive his fruit. ^{21}35 The farmers took his servants, beat one, killed another, and stoned another. ^{21}36 Again, he sent other servants more than the first: and they treated them the same way. ^{21}37 But afterward he sent to them his son, saying, 'They will respect my son.' ^{21}38 But the farmers, when they saw the son, said among themselves, 'This is the heir. Come, let's kill him, and seize his inheritance.' ^{21}39 So they took him, and threw him out of the vineyard, and killed him. ^{21}40 When therefore the lord of the vineyard comes, what will he do to those farmers?"
^{21}41 They told him, "He will miserably destroy those miserable men, and will lease out the vineyard to other farmers, who will give him the fruit in its season."
^{21}42 Jesus said to them, "Did you never read in the Scriptures,
'The stone which the builders rejected
was made the head of the corner.
This was from the Lord.
It is marvelous in our eyes?'

Day Thirty-One

²¹⁴³ "Therefore I tell you, God's Kingdom will be taken away from you, and will be given to a nation producing its fruit. ²¹⁴⁴ He who falls on this stone will be broken to pieces, but on whomever it will fall, it will scatter him as dust."
²¹⁴⁵ When the chief priests and the Pharisees heard his parables, they perceived that he spoke about them. ²¹⁴⁶ When they sought to seize him, they feared the multitudes, because they considered him to be a prophet. ²¹

22

²²1 Jesus answered and spoke to them again in parables, saying, ²²2 "The Kingdom of Heaven is like a certain king, who made a wedding feast for his son, ²²3 and sent out his servants to call those who were invited to the wedding feast, but they would not come. ²²4 Again he sent out other servants, saying, 'Tell those who are invited, "Behold, I have prepared my dinner. My cattle and my fatlings are killed, and all things are ready. Come to the wedding feast!"' ²²5 But they made light of it, and went their ways, one to his own farm, another to his merchandise, ²²6 and the rest grabbed his servants, and treated them shamefully, and killed them. ²²7 When the king heard that, he was angry, and sent his armies, destroyed those murderers, and burned their city.
²²8 "Then he said to his servants, 'The wedding is ready, but those who were invited weren't worthy. ²²9 Go therefore to the intersections of the highways, and as many as you may find, invite to the wedding feast.' ²²10 Those servants went out into the highways, and gathered together as many as they found, both bad and good. The wedding was filled with guests. ²²11 But when the king came in to see the guests, he saw there a man who didn't have on wedding clothing, ²²12 and he said to him, 'Friend, how did you come in here not wearing wedding clothing?' He was speechless. ²²13 Then the king said to the servants, 'Bind him hand and foot, take him away, and throw him into the outer darkness. That is where the weeping and grinding of teeth will be.' ²²14 For many are called, but few chosen."

The American Book of Prayer

The Lord's Prayer

Our Father, who art in heaven,
Hallowed be thy name.
Thy Kingdom come.
Thy will be done on Earth, as it is in heaven.
Give us this day our daily bread.
And forgive us our trespasses,
As we forgive those that trespass against us.
And lead us not into temptation,
But deliver us from evil.
For thine is the kingdom,
The power, and the glory,
For ever and ever.
AMEN

Day Thirty-Two

Daily Prayer

A mighty Fortress is our God,
A Bulwark never failing;
Our Helper He amid the flood
Of mortal ills prevailing:
For still our ancient foe
Doth seek to work us woe;
His craft and power are great,
And, armed with cruel hate,
On earth is not his equal.
Did we in our own strength confide,
Our striving would be losing;
Were not the right Man on our side,
The Man of God's own choosing:
Dost ask who that may be?
Christ Jesus, it is He;
Lord Sabaoth His Name,
From age to age the same,
And He must win the battle.
-"*A Mighty Fortress Is Our God,*" *a hymn by Martin Luther, Protestant Reformer*

> "*A mighty Fortress is our God, a Bulwark never failing, our Helper He amid the flood, of mortal ills prevailing ...*"

Prayer of Confession

Almighty and most merciful Father; we have erred, and strayed from your ways like lost sheep. We have followed too much the devices and desires of our own hearts. We have offended against your holy laws. We have left undone those things which we ought to have done; and we have done those things which we ought not to have done; and there is no health in us. O Lord, have mercy upon us, miserable offenders. Spare those, O God, who confess their faults. Restore those who are penitent; according to your promises declared unto mankind in Christ Jesus our Lord. And grant, O most merciful Father, for his sake; that we may hereafter live a godly, righteous, and sober life, to the glory of thy holy Name. Amen.
-Revised prayer from *The Book of Common Prayer*, 1662

Daily Wisdom

A Psalm of David.
1 The LORD *is* my light and my salvation; whom shall I fear? the LORD *is* the strength of my life; of whom shall I be afraid?
2 When the wicked, *even* mine enemies and my foes, came upon me to eat up my flesh, they stumbled and fell.
3 Though an host should encamp against me, my heart shall not fear: though war should rise against me, in this *will* I *be* confident.
4 One *thing* have I desired of the LORD, that will I seek after; that I may dwell in the house of the LORD all the days of my life, to behold the beauty of the LORD, and to enquire in his temple.
5 For in the time of trouble he shall hide me in his pavilion: in the secret of his tabernacle shall he hide me; he shall set me up upon a rock.

Day Thirty-Two

6 And now shall mine head be lifted up above mine enemies round about me: therefore will I offer in his tabernacle sacrifices of joy; I will sing, yea, I will sing praises unto the LORD.
-Psalm 27:1-6, *The King James Bible*, 1769 edition of 1611 text

Readings from the Holy Bible

The Holy Gospel According to Luke and Matthew (LUKE 10:29-42; LUKE 12:41-59; LUKE 17:20-37; MATTHEW 22:15-23:39)

LUKE 10:29-42, THE GOOD SAMARITAN

^{10}29 But he, desiring to justify himself, asked Jesus, "Who is my neighbor?"
^{10}30 Jesus answered, "A certain man was going down from Jerusalem to Jericho, and he fell among robbers, who both stripped him and beat him, and departed, leaving him half dead. ^{10}31 By chance a certain priest was going down that way. When he saw him, he passed by on the other side. ^{10}32 In the same way a Levite also, when he came to the place, and saw him, passed by on the other side. ^{10}33 But a certain Samaritan, as he traveled, came where he was. When he saw him, he was moved with compassion, ^{10}34 came to him, and bound up his wounds, pouring on oil and wine. He set him on his own animal, brought him to an inn, and took care of him. ^{10}35 On the next day, when he departed, he took out two denarii, gave them to the host, and said to him, 'Take care of him. Whatever you spend beyond that, I will repay you when I return.' ^{10}36 Now which of these three do you think seemed to be a neighbor to him who fell among the robbers?"
^{10}37 He said, "He who showed mercy on him."
Then Jesus said to him, "Go and do likewise."
^{10}38 As they went on their way, he entered into a certain village, and a certain woman named Martha received him into her house. ^{10}39 She had a sister called Mary, who also sat at Jesus' feet, and heard his word. ^{10}40 But Martha was distracted with much serving, and she

came up to him, and said, "Lord, don't you care that my sister left me to serve alone? Ask her therefore to help me."
¹⁰41 Jesus answered her, "Martha, Martha, you are anxious and troubled about many things, ¹⁰42 but one thing is needed. Mary has chosen the good part, which will not be taken away from her."

LUKE 12:41-59, THE WIDOW AND THE END OF THE WORLD

¹²41 Peter said to him, "Lord, are you telling this parable to us, or to everybody?"
¹²42 The Lord said, "Who then is the faithful and wise steward, whom his lord will set over his household, to give them their portion of food at the right times? ¹²43 Blessed is that servant whom his lord will find doing so when he comes. ¹²44 Truly I tell you, that he will set him over all that he has. ¹²45 But if that servant says in his heart, 'My lord delays his coming,' and begins to beat the menservants and the maidservants, and to eat and drink, and to be drunken, ¹²46 then the lord of that servant will come in a day when he isn't expecting him, and in an hour that he doesn't know, and will cut him in two, and place his portion with the unfaithful. ¹²47 That servant, who knew his lord's will, and didn't prepare, nor do what he wanted, will be beaten with many stripes, ¹²48 but he who didn't know, and did things worthy of stripes, will be beaten with few stripes. To whomever much is given, of him will much be required; and to whom much was entrusted, of him more will be asked.
¹²49 "I came to throw fire on the earth. I wish it were already kindled. ¹²50 But I have a baptism to be baptized with, and how distressed I am until it is accomplished! ¹²51 Do you think that I have come to give peace in the earth? I tell you, no, but rather division. ¹²52 For from now on, there will be five in one house divided, three against two, and two against three. ¹²53 They will be divided, father against son, and son against father; mother against daughter, and daughter against her mother; mother-in-law against her daughter-in-law, and daughter-in-law against her mother-in-law."
¹²54 He said to the multitudes also, "When you see a cloud rising from the west, immediately you say, 'A shower is coming,' and so it happens. ¹²55 When a south wind blows, you say, 'There will be a

Day Thirty-Two

scorching heat,' and it happens. **12:56** You hypocrites! You know how to interpret the appearance of the earth and the sky, but how is it that you don't interpret this time? **12:57** Why don't you judge for yourselves what is right? **12:58** For when you are going with your adversary before the magistrate, try diligently on the way to be released from him, lest perhaps he drag you to the judge, and the judge deliver you to the officer, and the officer throw you into prison. **12:59** [12]I tell you, you will by no means get out of there, until you have paid the very last penny.[116]"

LUKE 17:20-37, THE COMING KINGDOM OF THE LORD

17:20 Being asked by the Pharisees when God's Kingdom would come, he answered them, "God's Kingdom doesn't come with observation; **17:21** neither will they say, 'Look, here!' or, 'Look, there!' for behold, God's Kingdom is within you."
17:22 He said to the disciples, "The days will come when you will desire to see one of the days of the Son of Man, and you will not see it. **17:23** They will tell you, 'Look, here!' or 'Look, there!' Don't go away or follow after them, **17:24** for as the lightning, when it flashes out of one part under the sky, shines to another part under the sky; so will the Son of Man be in his day. **17:25** But first, he must suffer many things and be rejected by this generation. **17:26** As it was in the days of Noah, even so will it be also in the days of the Son of Man. **17:27** They ate, they drank, they married, and they were given in marriage until the day that Noah entered into the ship, and the flood came and destroyed them all. **17:28** Likewise, even as it was in the days of Lot: they ate, they drank, they bought, they sold, they planted, they built; **17:29** but in the day that Lot went out from Sodom, it rained fire and sulfur from the sky and destroyed them all. **17:30** It will be the same way in the day that the Son of Man is revealed. **17:31** In that day, he who will be on the housetop and his goods in the house, let him not go down to take them away. Let him who is in the field likewise not turn back. **17:32** Remember Lot's wife! **17:33** Whoever seeks to save his life loses

---

[116]12:59 12:59 literally, lepton. A lepton is a very small brass Jewish coin worth half a Roman quadrans each, which is worth a quarter of the copper assarion. Lepta are worth less than 1% of an agricultural worker's daily wages.

it, but whoever loses his life preserves it. ¹⁷³⁴ I tell you, in that night there will be two people in one bed. One will be taken and the other will be left. ¹⁷³⁵ There will be two grinding grain together. One will be taken and the other will be left." ¹⁷³⁶ ¹¹⁷ [See footnote.]

¹⁷³⁷ They, answering, asked him, "Where, Lord?"

He said to them, "Where the body is, there the vultures will also be gathered together."

MATTHEW 22:15-23:39

²²¹⁵ Then the Pharisees went and took counsel how they might entrap him in his talk. ²²¹⁶ They sent their disciples to him, along with the Herodians, saying, "Teacher, we know that you are honest, and teach the way of God in truth, no matter whom you teach, for you aren't partial to anyone. ²²¹⁷ Tell us therefore, what do you think? Is it lawful to pay taxes to Caesar, or not?"

²²¹⁸ But Jesus perceived their wickedness, and said, "Why do you test me, you hypocrites? ²²¹⁹ Show me the tax money."

They brought to him a denarius.

²²²⁰ He asked them, "Whose is this image and inscription?"

²²²¹ They said to him, "Caesar's."

Then he said to them, "Give therefore to Caesar the things that are Caesar's, and to God the things that are God's."

²²²² When they heard it, they marveled, and left him, and went away. ²²²³ On that day Sadducees (those who say that there is no resurrection) came to him. They asked him, ²²²⁴ saying, "Teacher, Moses said, 'If a man dies, having no children, his brother shall marry his wife, and raise up offspring¹¹⁸ for his brother.' ²²²⁵ Now there were with us seven brothers. The first married and died, and having no offspring left his wife to his brother. ²²²⁶ In the same way, the second also, and the third, to the seventh. ²²²⁷ After them all, the woman died. ²²²⁸ In the resurrection therefore, whose wife will she be of the seven? For they all had her."

---

¹¹⁷17:36 17:36 Some Greek manuscripts add: "Two will be in the field: the one taken, and the other left."
¹¹⁸22:24 22:24 or, seed

Day Thirty-Two

²²29 But Jesus answered them, "You are mistaken, not knowing the Scriptures, nor the power of God. ²²30 For in the resurrection they neither marry, nor are given in marriage, but are like God's angels in heaven. ²²31 But concerning the resurrection of the dead, haven't you read that which was spoken to you by God, saying, ²²32 'I am the God of Abraham, and the God of Isaac, and the God of Jacob?'# God is not the God of the dead, but of the living."

²²33 When the multitudes heard it, they were astonished at his teaching. ²²34 But the Pharisees, when they heard that he had silenced the Sadducees, gathered themselves together. ²²35 One of them, a lawyer, asked him a question, testing him. ²²36 "Teacher, which is the greatest commandment in the law?"

²²37 Jesus said to him, "'You shall love the Lord your God with all your heart, with all your soul, and with all your mind.'# ²²38 This is the first and great commandment. ²²39 A second likewise is this, 'You shall love your neighbor as yourself.'# ²²40 The whole law and the prophets depend on these two commandments."

²²41 Now while the Pharisees were gathered together, Jesus asked them a question, ²²42 saying, "What do you think of the Christ? Whose son is he?"

They said to him, "Of David."

²²43 He said to them, "How then does David in the Spirit call him Lord, saying,

²²44 'The Lord said to my Lord,
sit on my right hand,
until I make your enemies a footstool for your feet?'#

²²45 "If then David calls him Lord, how is he his son?"

²²46 No one was able to answer him a word, neither did any man dare ask him any more questions from that day forward. ²²

23

²³1 Then Jesus spoke to the multitudes and to his disciples, ²³2 saying, "The scribes and the Pharisees sat on Moses' seat. ²³3 All things

---

#22:32 22:32 Exodus 3:6
#22:37 22:37 Deuteronomy 6:5
#22:39 22:39 Leviticus 19:18
#22:44 22:44 Psalm 110:1

therefore whatever they tell you to observe, observe and do, but don't do their works; for they say, and don't do. **23:4** For they bind heavy burdens that are grievous to be borne, and lay them on men's shoulders; but they themselves will not lift a finger to help them. **23:5** But they do all their works to be seen by men. They make their phylacteries [119] broad, enlarge the fringes[120] of their garments, **23:6** and love the place of honor at feasts, the best seats in the synagogues, **23:7** the salutations in the marketplaces, and to be called 'Rabbi, Rabbi' by men.

23:8 But don't you be called 'Rabbi,' for one is your teacher, the Christ, and all of you are brothers. **23:9** Call no man on the earth your father, for one is your Father, he who is in heaven. **23:10** Neither be called masters, for one is your master, the Christ. **23:11** But he who is greatest among you will be your servant. **23:12** Whoever exalts himself will be humbled, and whoever humbles himself will be exalted.

23:13 "Woe to you, scribes and Pharisees, hypocrites! For you devour widows' houses, and as a pretense you make long prayers. Therefore you will receive greater condemnation. **23:14** "But woe to you, scribes and Pharisees, hypocrites! Because you shut up the Kingdom of Heaven against men; for you don't enter in yourselves, neither do you allow those who are entering in to enter.[121] **23:15** Woe to you, scribes and Pharisees, hypocrites! For you travel around by sea and land to make one proselyte; and when he becomes one, you make him twice as much a son of Gehenna[122] as yourselves.

23:16 "Woe to you, you blind guides, who say, 'Whoever swears by the temple, it is nothing; but whoever swears by the gold of the temple, he is obligated.' **23:17** You blind fools! For which is greater, the gold, or the temple that sanctifies the gold? **23:18** 'Whoever swears by the altar, it is nothing; but whoever swears by the gift that is on it, he is obligated?' **23:19** You blind fools! For which is greater, the gift, or the altar that sanctifies the gift? **23:20** He therefore who swears by the

---

[119]23:5 23:5 phylacteries (tefillin in Hebrew) are small leather pouches that some Jewish men wear on their forehead and arm in prayer. They are used to carry a small scroll with some Scripture in it. See Deuteronomy 6:8.
[120]23:5 23:5 or, tassels
[121]23:14 23:14 Some Greek texts reverse the order of verses 13 and 14, and some omit verse 13, numbering verse 14 as 13. NU omits verse 14.
[122]23:15 23:15 or, Hell

Day Thirty-Two

altar, swears by it, and by everything on it. **23:21** He who swears by the temple, swears by it, and by him who has been living[123] in it. **23:22** He who swears by heaven, swears by the throne of God, and by him who sits on it.

23:23 "Woe to you, scribes and Pharisees, hypocrites! For you tithe mint, dill, and cumin,[124] and have left undone the weightier matters of the law: justice, mercy, and faith. But you ought to have done these, and not to have left the other undone. **23:24** You blind guides, who strain out a gnat, and swallow a camel!

23:25 "Woe to you, scribes and Pharisees, hypocrites! For you clean the outside of the cup and of the platter, but within they are full of extortion and unrighteousness.[125] **23:26** You blind Pharisee, first clean the inside of the cup and of the platter, that its outside may become clean also.

23:27 "Woe to you, scribes and Pharisees, hypocrites! For you are like whitened tombs, which outwardly appear beautiful, but inwardly are full of dead men's bones, and of all uncleanness. **23:28** Even so you also outwardly appear righteous to men, but inwardly you are full of hypocrisy and iniquity.

23:29 "Woe to you, scribes and Pharisees, hypocrites! For you build the tombs of the prophets, and decorate the tombs of the righteous, **23:30** and say, 'If we had lived in the days of our fathers, we wouldn't have been partakers with them in the blood of the prophets.'

23:31 Therefore you testify to yourselves that you are children of those who killed the prophets.

23:32 Fill up, then, the measure of your fathers. **23:33** You serpents, you offspring of vipers, how will you escape the judgment of Gehenna?[126] **23:34** Therefore behold, I send to you prophets, wise men, and scribes. Some of them you will kill and crucify; and some of them you will scourge in your synagogues, and persecute from city to city; **23:35** that on you may come all the righteous blood shed on the earth, from the blood of righteous Abel to the blood of Zachariah son of Barachiah, whom you killed between the sanctuary and the altar.

---

[123] 23:21 23:21 NU reads "lives"
[124] 23:23 23:23 cumin is an aromatic seed from Cuminum cyminum, resembling caraway in flavor and appearance. It is used as a spice.
[125] 23:25 23:25 TR reads "self-indulgence" instead of "unrighteousness"
[126] 23:33 23:33 or, Hell

[2336] Most certainly I tell you, all these things will come upon this generation.
[2337] "Jerusalem, Jerusalem, who kills the prophets, and stones those who are sent to her! How often I would have gathered your children together, even as a hen gathers her chicks under her wings, and you would not! [2338] Behold, your house is left to you desolate.
[2339] [23]For I tell you, you will not see me from now on, until you say, 'Blessed is he who comes in the name of the Lord!'"

The Lord's Prayer

Our Father, who art in heaven,
Hallowed be thy name.
Thy Kingdom come.
Thy will be done on Earth, as it is in heaven.
Give us this day our daily bread.
And forgive us our trespasses,
As we forgive those that trespass against us.
And lead us not into temptation,
But deliver us from evil.
For thine is the kingdom,
The power, and the glory,
For ever and ever.
AMEN

Day Thirty-Three

Daily Prayer

Grant, Almighty God, that as we were from our beginning lost, when thou wert pleased to extend to us thy hand, and to restore us to salvation for the sake of thy Son; and that as we continue even daily to run headlong to our own ruin, O grant that we may not, by sinning so often, so provoke at length thy displeasure as to cause thee to take away from us the mercy which thou hast hitherto exercised towards us, and through which thou hast adopted us: but by thy Spirit destroy the wickedness of our heart, and restore us to a sound mind, that we may ever cleave to thee with a true and sincere heart, that being fortified by thy defense, we may continue safe even amidst all kinds of danger, until at length thou gathers us into that blessed rest, which has been prepared for us in heaven by our Lord Jesus Christ. Amen.

-John Calvin, Protestant Reformer

> *"... but by thy Spirit destroy the wickedness of our heart, and restore us to a sound mind ..."*

Prayer of Confession

Almighty and most merciful Father; we have erred, and strayed from your ways like lost sheep. We have followed too much the devices and desires of our own hearts. We have offended against your holy laws. We have left undone those things which we ought to have done; and we have done those things which we ought not to have done; and there is no health in us. O Lord, have mercy upon us, miserable offenders. Spare those, O God, who confess their faults. Restore those who are penitent; according to your promises declared unto mankind in Christ Jesus our Lord. And grant, O most merciful Father, for his sake; that we may hereafter live a godly, righteous, and sober life, to the glory of thy holy Name. Amen.
-Revised prayer from *The Book of Common Prayer*, 1662

Daily Wisdom

7 Hear, O LORD, *when* I cry with my voice: have mercy also upon me, and answer me.
8 *When thou saidst,* Seek ye my face; my heart said unto thee, Thy face, LORD, will I seek.
9 Hide not thy face *far* from me; put not thy servant away in anger: thou hast been my help; leave me not, neither forsake me, O God of my salvation.
10 When my father and my mother forsake me, then the LORD will take me up.
11 Teach me thy way, O LORD, and lead me in a plain path, because of mine enemies.
12 Deliver me not over unto the will of mine enemies: for false witnesses are risen up against me, and such as breathe out cruelty.
13 *I had fainted,* unless I had believed to see the goodness of the LORD in the land of the living.

Day Thirty-Three

14 Wait on the LORD: be of good courage, and he shall strengthen thine heart: wait, I say, on the LORD.
-Psalm 27:7-14, *The King James Bible*, 1769 edition of 1611 text

Readings from the Holy Bible

The Holy Gospel According to Matthew (MATTHEW 24 & 25)

MATTHEW 24 & 25

24

²⁴**1** Jesus went out from the temple, and was going on his way. His disciples came to him to show him the buildings of the temple. ²⁴**2** But he answered them, "You see all of these things, don't you? Most certainly I tell you, there will not be left here one stone on another, that will not be thrown down."
²⁴**3** As he sat on the Mount of Olives, the disciples came to him privately, saying, "Tell us, when will these things be? What is the sign of your coming, and of the end of the age?"
²⁴**4** Jesus answered them, "Be careful that no one leads you astray. ²⁴**5** For many will come in my name, saying, 'I am the Christ,' and will lead many astray. ²⁴**6** You will hear of wars and rumors of wars. See that you aren't troubled, for all this must happen, but the end is not yet. ²⁴**7** For nation will rise against nation, and kingdom against kingdom; and there will be famines, plagues, and earthquakes in various places. ²⁴**8** But all these things are the beginning of birth pains. ²⁴**9** Then they will deliver you up to oppression, and will kill you. You will be hated by all of the nations for my name's sake. ²⁴**10** Then many will stumble, and will deliver up one another, and will hate one another. ²⁴**11** Many false prophets will arise, and will lead many astray. ²⁴**12** Because iniquity will be multiplied, the love of many will grow cold. ²⁴**13** But he who endures to the end will be saved. ²⁴**14** This Good News of the Kingdom will be preached in the whole world for a testimony to all the nations, and then the end will come.

²⁴15 "When, therefore, you see the abomination of desolation, [#] which was spoken of through Daniel the prophet, standing in the holy place (let the reader understand), ²⁴16 then let those who are in Judea flee to the mountains. ²⁴17 Let him who is on the housetop not go down to take out the things that are in his house. ²⁴18 Let him who is in the field not return back to get his clothes. ²⁴19 But woe to those who are with child and to nursing mothers in those days! ²⁴20 Pray that your flight will not be in the winter, nor on a Sabbath, ²⁴21 for then there will be great suffering,[127] such as has not been from the beginning of the world until now, no, nor ever will be. ²⁴22 Unless those days had been shortened, no flesh would have been saved. But for the sake of the chosen ones, those days will be shortened.

²⁴23 "Then if any man tells you, 'Behold, here is the Christ,' or, 'There,' don't believe it. ²⁴24 For there will arise false christs, and false prophets, and they will show great signs and wonders, so as to lead astray, if possible, even the chosen ones.

²⁴25 "Behold, I have told you beforehand. ²⁴26 If therefore they tell you, 'Behold, he is in the wilderness,' don't go out; or 'Behold, he is in the inner rooms,' don't believe it. ²⁴27 For as the lightning flashes from the east, and is seen even to the west, so will the coming of the Son of Man be. ²⁴28 For wherever the carcass is, that is where the vultures [128] gather together. ²⁴29 But immediately after the suffering[129] of those days, the sun will be darkened, the moon will not give its light, the stars will fall from the sky, and the powers of the heavens will be shaken;[#] ²⁴30 and then the sign of the Son of Man will appear in the sky. Then all the tribes of the earth will mourn, and they will see the Son of Man coming on the clouds of the sky with power and great glory. ²⁴31 He will send out his angels with a great sound of a trumpet, and they will gather together his chosen ones from the four winds, from one end of the sky to the other.

²⁴32 "Now from the fig tree learn this parable. When its branch has now become tender, and produces its leaves, you know that the summer is near. ²⁴33 Even so you also, when you see all these things,

---

[#]24:15 24:15 Daniel 9:27; 11:31; 12:11
[127]24:21 24:21 or, oppression
[128]24:28 24:28 or, eagles
[129]24:29 24:29 or, oppression
[#]24:29 24:29 Isaiah 13:10; 34:4

Day Thirty-Three

know that it is near, even at the doors. ²⁴34 Most certainly I tell you, this generation[130] will not pass away, until all these things are accomplished. ²⁴35 Heaven and earth will pass away, but my words will not pass away. ²⁴36 But no one knows of that day and hour, not even the angels of heaven,[131] but my Father only.

²⁴37 "As the days of Noah were, so will the coming of the Son of Man be. ²⁴38 For as in those days which were before the flood they were eating and drinking, marrying and giving in marriage, until the day that Noah entered into the ship, ²⁴39 and they didn't know until the flood came, and took them all away, so will the coming of the Son of Man be. ²⁴40 Then two men will be in the field: one will be taken and one will be left. ²⁴41 Two women will be grinding at the mill: one will be taken and one will be left. ²⁴42 Watch therefore, for you don't know in what hour your Lord comes. ²⁴43 But know this, that if the master of the house had known in what watch of the night the thief was coming, he would have watched, and would not have allowed his house to be broken into. ²⁴44 Therefore also be ready, for in an hour that you don't expect, the Son of Man will come.

²⁴45 "Who then is the faithful and wise servant, whom his lord has set over his household, to give them their food in due season? ²⁴46 Blessed is that servant whom his lord finds doing so when he comes. ²⁴47 Most certainly I tell you that he will set him over all that he has. ²⁴48 But if that evil servant should say in his heart, 'My lord is delaying his coming,' ²⁴49 and begins to beat his fellow servants, and eat and drink with the drunkards, ²⁴50 the lord of that servant will come in a day when he doesn't expect it, and in an hour when he doesn't know it, ²⁴51 ²⁴and will cut him in pieces, and appoint his portion with the hypocrites. That is where the weeping and grinding of teeth will be.

25

²⁵1 "Then the Kingdom of Heaven will be like ten virgins, who took their lamps, and went out to meet the bridegroom. ²⁵2 Five of them were foolish, and five were wise. ²⁵3 Those who were foolish, when

---

[130]24:34 24:34 The word for "generation" (genea) can also be translated as "race."
[131]24:36 24:36 NU adds "nor the son"

they took their lamps, took no oil with them, ²⁵4 but the wise took oil in their vessels with their lamps. ²⁵5 Now while the bridegroom delayed, they all slumbered and slept. ²⁵6 But at midnight there was a cry, 'Behold! The bridegroom is coming! Come out to meet him!' ²⁵7 Then all those virgins arose, and trimmed their lamps.¹³² ²⁵8 The foolish said to the wise, 'Give us some of your oil, for our lamps are going out.' ²⁵9 But the wise answered, saying, 'What if there isn't enough for us and you? You go rather to those who sell, and buy for yourselves.' ²⁵10 While they went away to buy, the bridegroom came, and those who were ready went in with him to the wedding feast, and the door was shut. ²⁵11 Afterward the other virgins also came, saying, 'Lord, Lord, open to us.' ²⁵12 But he answered, 'Most certainly I tell you, I don't know you.' ²⁵13 Watch therefore, for you don't know the day nor the hour in which the Son of Man is coming.

²⁵14 "For it is like a man, going into another country, who called his own servants, and entrusted his goods to them. ²⁵15 To one he gave five talents,¹³³ to another two, to another one; to each according to his own ability. Then he went on his journey. ²⁵16 Immediately he who received the five talents went and traded with them, and made another five talents. ²⁵17 In the same way, he also who got the two gained another two. ²⁵18 But he who received the one talent went away and dug in the earth, and hid his lord's money.

²⁵19 "Now after a long time the lord of those servants came, and reconciled accounts with them. ²⁵20 He who received the five talents came and brought another five talents, saying, 'Lord, you delivered to me five talents. Behold, I have gained another five talents in addition to them.'

²⁵21 "His lord said to him, 'Well done, good and faithful servant. You have been faithful over a few things, I will set you over many things. Enter into the joy of your lord.'

²⁵22 "He also who got the two talents came and said, 'Lord, you delivered to me two talents. Behold, I have gained another two talents in addition to them.'

---

¹³²25:7 25:7 The end of the wick of an oil lamp needs to be cut off periodically to avoid having it become clogged with carbon deposits. The wick height is also adjusted so that the flame burns evenly and gives good light without producing a lot of smoke.
¹³³25:15 25:15 A talent is about 30 kilograms or 66 pounds (usually used to weigh silver unless otherwise specified)

Day Thirty-Three

²⁵23 "His lord said to him, 'Well done, good and faithful servant. You have been faithful over a few things, I will set you over many things. Enter into the joy of your lord.'

²⁵24 "He also who had received the one talent came and said, 'Lord, I knew you that you are a hard man, reaping where you didn't sow, and gathering where you didn't scatter. ²⁵25 I was afraid, and went away and hid your talent in the earth. Behold, you have what is yours.'

²⁵26 "But his lord answered him, 'You wicked and slothful servant. You knew that I reap where I didn't sow, and gather where I didn't scatter. ²⁵27 You ought therefore to have deposited my money with the bankers, and at my coming I should have received back my own with interest. ²⁵28 Take away therefore the talent from him, and give it to him who has the ten talents. ²⁵29 For to everyone who has will be given, and he will have abundance, but from him who doesn't have, even that which he has will be taken away. ²⁵30 Throw out the unprofitable servant into the outer darkness, where there will be weeping and gnashing of teeth.'

²⁵31 "But when the Son of Man comes in his glory, and all the holy angels with him, then he will sit on the throne of his glory. ²⁵32 Before him all the nations will be gathered, and he will separate them one from another, as a shepherd separates the sheep from the goats. ²⁵33 He will set the sheep on his right hand, but the goats on the left. ²⁵34 Then the King will tell those on his right hand, 'Come, blessed of my Father, inherit the Kingdom prepared for you from the foundation of the world; ²⁵35 for I was hungry, and you gave me food to eat. I was thirsty, and you gave me drink. I was a stranger, and you took me in. ²⁵36 I was naked, and you clothed me. I was sick, and you visited me. I was in prison, and you came to me.'

²⁵37 "Then the righteous will answer him, saying, 'Lord, when did we see you hungry, and feed you; or thirsty, and give you a drink? ²⁵38 When did we see you as a stranger, and take you in; or naked, and clothe you? ²⁵39 When did we see you sick, or in prison, and come to you?'

²⁵40 "The King will answer them, 'Most certainly I tell you, because you did it to one of the least of these my brothers,[134] you did it to

---

[134]25:40 25:40 The word for "brothers" here may be also correctly translated "brothers and sisters" or "siblings."

me.' ²⁵41 Then he will say also to those on the left hand, 'Depart from me, you cursed, into the eternal fire which is prepared for the devil and his angels; ²⁵42 for I was hungry, and you didn't give me food to eat; I was thirsty, and you gave me no drink; ²⁵43 I was a stranger, and you didn't take me in; naked, and you didn't clothe me; sick, and in prison, and you didn't visit me.'
²⁵44 "Then they will also answer, saying, 'Lord, when did we see you hungry, or thirsty, or a stranger, or naked, or sick, or in prison, and didn't help you?'
²⁵45 "Then he will answer them, saying, 'Most certainly I tell you, because you didn't do it to one of the least of these, you didn't do it to me.' ²⁵46 ²⁵These will go away into eternal punishment, but the righteous into eternal life."

The Lord's Prayer

Our Father, who art in heaven,
Hallowed be thy name.
Thy Kingdom come.
Thy will be done on Earth, as it is in heaven.
Give us this day our daily bread.
And forgive us our trespasses,
As we forgive those that trespass against us.
And lead us not into temptation,
But deliver us from evil.
For thine is the kingdom,
The power, and the glory,
For ever and ever.
AMEN

Day Thirty-Four

Daily Prayer

My friends, before I begin the expression of those thoughts that I deem appropriate to this moment, would you permit me the privilege of uttering a little private prayer of my own. And I ask that you bow your heads. Almighty God, as we stand here at this moment my future associates in the Executive branch of Government join me in beseeching that Thou will make full and complete our dedication to the service of the people in this throng, and their fellow citizens everywhere. Give us, we pray, the power to discern clearly right from wrong, and allow all our words and actions to be governed thereby, and by the laws of this land. Especially we pray that our concern shall be for all the people regardless of station, race or calling. May cooperation be permitted and be the mutual aim of those who, under the concepts of our Constitution, hold

> "Especially we pray that our concern shall be for all the people regardless of station, race or calling."

to differing political faiths; so that all may work for the good of our beloved country and Thy glory. Amen.
-*The 34th president of the United States, Dwight Eisenhower, in his 1953 inaugural address.*[18]

Prayer of Confession

Almighty and most merciful Father; we have erred, and strayed from your ways like lost sheep. We have followed too much the devices and desires of our own hearts. We have offended against your holy laws. We have left undone those things which we ought to have done; and we have done those things which we ought not to have done; and there is no health in us. O Lord, have mercy upon us, miserable offenders. Spare those, O God, who confess their faults. Restore those who are penitent; according to your promises declared unto mankind in Christ Jesus our Lord. And grant, O most merciful Father, for his sake; that we may hereafter live a godly, righteous, and sober life, to the glory of thy holy Name. Amen.
-Revised prayer from *The Book of Common Prayer*, 1662

Daily Wisdom

6 Blessed *be* the LORD, because he hath heard the voice of my supplications.
7 The LORD *is* my strength and my shield; my heart trusted in him, and I am helped: therefore my heart greatly rejoiceth; and with my song will I praise him.
8 The LORD *is* their strength, and he *is* the saving strength of his anointed.
9 Save thy people, and bless thine inheritance: feed them also, and lift them up for ever.
-Psalm 28:6-9, *The King James Bible*, 1769 edition of 1611 text

Day Thirty-Four

Readings from the Holy Bible

The Holy Gospel According to John (JOHN 11 & 12)

JOHN 11 & 12

11

¹¹1 Now a certain man was sick, Lazarus from Bethany, of the village of Mary and her sister, Martha. ¹¹2 It was that Mary who had anointed the Lord with ointment and wiped his feet with her hair, whose brother, Lazarus, was sick. ¹¹3 The sisters therefore sent to him, saying, "Lord, behold, he for whom you have great affection is sick." ¹¹4 But when Jesus heard it, he said, "This sickness is not to death, but for the glory of God, that God's Son may be glorified by it." ¹¹5 Now Jesus loved Martha, and her sister, and Lazarus. ¹¹6 When therefore he heard that he was sick, he stayed two days in the place where he was.
¹¹7 Then after this he said to the disciples, "Let's go into Judea again."
¹¹8 The disciples asked him, "Rabbi, the Jews were just trying to stone you. Are you going there again?"
¹¹9 Jesus answered, "Aren't there twelve hours of daylight? If a man walks in the day, he doesn't stumble, because he sees the light of this world. ¹¹10 But if a man walks in the night, he stumbles, because the light isn't in him." ¹¹11 He said these things, and after that, he said to them, "Our friend, Lazarus, has fallen asleep, but I am going so that I may awake him out of sleep."
¹¹12 The disciples therefore said, "Lord, if he has fallen asleep, he will recover."
¹¹13 Now Jesus had spoken of his death, but they thought that he spoke of taking rest in sleep. ¹¹14 So Jesus said to them plainly then, "Lazarus is dead. ¹¹15 I am glad for your sakes that I was not there, so that you may believe. Nevertheless, let's go to him."
¹¹16 Thomas therefore, who is called Didymus,[135] said to his fellow disciples, "Let's go also, that we may die with him."

---

[135] 11:16 11:16 "Didymus" means "Twin".

11:17 So when Jesus came, he found that he had been in the tomb four days already. **11:18** Now Bethany was near Jerusalem, about fifteen stadia[136] away. **11:19** Many of the Jews had joined the women around Martha and Mary, to console them concerning their brother. **11:20** Then when Martha heard that Jesus was coming, she went and met him, but Mary stayed in the house. **11:21** Therefore Martha said to Jesus, "Lord, if you would have been here, my brother wouldn't have died.
11:22 Even now I know that whatever you ask of God, God will give you." **11:23** Jesus said to her, "Your brother will rise again."
11:24 Martha said to him, "I know that he will rise again in the resurrection at the last day."
11:25 Jesus said to her, "I am the resurrection and the life. He who believes in me will still live, even if he dies. **11:26** Whoever lives and believes in me will never die. Do you believe this?"
11:27 She said to him, "Yes, Lord. I have come to believe that you are the Christ, God's Son, he who comes into the world."
11:28 When she had said this, she went away and called Mary, her sister, secretly, saying, "The Teacher is here and is calling you."
11:29 When she heard this, she arose quickly and went to him. **11:30** Now Jesus had not yet come into the village, but was in the place where Martha met him. **11:31** Then the Jews who were with her in the house and were consoling her, when they saw Mary, that she rose up quickly and went out, followed her, saying, "She is going to the tomb to weep there." **11:32** Therefore when Mary came to where Jesus was and saw him, she fell down at his feet, saying to him, "Lord, if you would have been here, my brother wouldn't have died."
11:33 When Jesus therefore saw her weeping, and the Jews weeping who came with her, he groaned in the spirit, and was troubled, **11:34** and said, "Where have you laid him?"
They told him, "Lord, come and see."
11:35 Jesus wept.
11:36 The Jews therefore said, "See how much affection he had for him!" **11:37** Some of them said, "Couldn't this man, who opened the eyes of him who was blind, have also kept this man from dying?"

---

[136]11:18 11:18 15 stadia is about 2.8 kilometers or 1.7 miles

Day Thirty-Four

¹¹38 Jesus therefore, again groaning in himself, came to the tomb. Now it was a cave, and a stone lay against it. ¹¹39 Jesus said, "Take away the stone."

Martha, the sister of him who was dead, said to him, "Lord, by this time there is a stench, for he has been dead four days."

¹¹40 Jesus said to her, "Didn't I tell you that if you believed, you would see God's glory?"

¹¹41 So they took away the stone from the place where the dead man was lying.¹³⁷ Jesus lifted up his eyes, and said, "Father, I thank you that you listened to me. ¹¹42 I know that you always listen to me, but because of the multitude standing around I said this, that they may believe that you sent me." ¹¹43 When he had said this, he cried with a loud voice, "Lazarus, come out!"

¹¹44 He who was dead came out, bound hand and foot with wrappings, and his face was wrapped around with a cloth.

Jesus said to them, "Free him, and let him go."

¹¹45 Therefore many of the Jews who came to Mary and saw what Jesus did believed in him. ¹¹46 But some of them went away to the Pharisees and told them the things which Jesus had done. ¹¹47 The chief priests therefore and the Pharisees gathered a council, and said, "What are we doing? For this man does many signs. ¹¹48 If we leave him alone like this, everyone will believe in him, and the Romans will come and take away both our place and our nation."

¹¹49 But a certain one of them, Caiaphas, being high priest that year, said to them, "You know nothing at all, ¹¹50 nor do you consider that it is advantageous for us that one man should die for the people, and that the whole nation not perish." ¹¹51 Now he didn't say this of himself, but being high priest that year, he prophesied that Jesus would die for the nation, ¹¹52 and not for the nation only, but that he might also gather together into one the children of God who are scattered abroad. ¹¹53 So from that day forward they took counsel that they might put him to death. ¹¹54 Jesus therefore walked no more openly among the Jews, but departed from there into the country near the wilderness, to a city called Ephraim. He stayed there with his disciples.

---

¹³⁷11:41 11:41 NU omits "from the place where the dead man was lying."

¹¹55 Now the Passover of the Jews was at hand. Many went up from the country to Jerusalem before the Passover, to purify themselves. ¹¹56 Then they sought for Jesus and spoke with one another as they stood in the temple, "What do you think—that he isn't coming to the feast at all?" ¹¹57 Now the chief priests and the Pharisees had commanded that if anyone knew where he was, he should report it, that they might seize him. ¹¹

12

¹²1 Then six days before the Passover, Jesus came to Bethany, where Lazarus was, who had been dead, whom he raised from the dead. ¹²2 So they made him a supper there. Martha served, but Lazarus was one of those who sat at the table with him. ¹²3 Therefore Mary took a pound[138] of ointment of pure nard, very precious, and anointed Jesus's feet and wiped his feet with her hair. The house was filled with the fragrance of the ointment. ¹²4 Then Judas Iscariot, Simon's son, one of his disciples, who would betray him, said, ¹²5 "Why wasn't this ointment sold for three hundred denarii,[139] and given to the poor?" ¹²6 Now he said this, not because he cared for the poor, but because he was a thief, and having the money box, used to steal what was put into it. ¹²7 But Jesus said, "Leave her alone. She has kept this for the day of my burial. ¹²8 For you always have the poor with you, but you don't always have me."
¹²9 A large crowd therefore of the Jews learned that he was there, and they came, not for
Jesus' sake only, but that they might see Lazarus also, whom he had raised from the dead. ¹²10 But the chief priests conspired to put Lazarus to death also, ¹²11 because on account of him many of the Jews went away and believed in Jesus.
¹²12 On the next day a great multitude had come to the feast. When they heard that Jesus was coming to Jerusalem, ¹²13 they took the branches of the palm trees and went out to meet him, and cried out,

---

[138]12:3 12:3 a Roman pound of 12 ounces, or about 340 grams
[139]12:5 12:5 300 denarii was about a year's wages for an agricultural laborer.

Day Thirty-Four

"Hosanna![140] Blessed is he who comes in the name of the Lord,[#] the King of Israel!"

[12:14] Jesus, having found a young donkey, sat on it. As it is written, [12:15] "Don't be afraid, daughter of Zion. Behold, your King comes, sitting on a donkey's colt."[#] [12:16] His disciples didn't understand these things at first, but when Jesus was glorified, then they remembered that these things were written about him, and that they had done these things to him. [12:17] The multitude therefore that was with him when he called Lazarus out of the tomb and raised him from the dead was testifying about it. [12:18] For this cause also the multitude went and met him, because they heard that he had done this sign. [12:19] The Pharisees therefore said among themselves, "See how you accomplish nothing. Behold, the world has gone after him."

[12:20] Now there were certain Greeks among those that went up to worship at the feast. [12:21] These, therefore, came to Philip, who was from Bethsaida of Galilee, and asked him, saying, "Sir, we want to see Jesus." [12:22] Philip came and told Andrew, and in turn, Andrew came with Philip, and they told Jesus. [12:23] Jesus answered them, "The time has come for the Son of Man to be glorified. [12:24] Most certainly I tell you, unless a grain of wheat falls into the earth and dies, it remains by itself alone. But if it dies, it bears much fruit. [12:25] He who loves his life will lose it. He who hates his life in this world will keep it to eternal life. [12:26] If anyone serves me, let him follow me. Where I am, there my servant will also be. If anyone serves me, the Father will honor him.

[12:27] "Now my soul is troubled. What shall I say? 'Father, save me from this time?' But I came to this time for this cause. [12:28] Father, glorify your name!"

Then a voice came out of the sky, saying, "I have both glorified it, and will glorify it again."

[12:29] Therefore the multitude who stood by and heard it said that it had thundered. Others said, "An angel has spoken to him."

[12:30] Jesus answered, "This voice hasn't come for my sake, but for your sakes. [12:31] Now is the judgment of this world. Now the prince of this

---

[140] 12:13 12:13 "Hosanna" means "save us" or "help us, we pray".
[#] 12:13 12:13 Psalm 118:25-26
[#] 12:15 12:15 Zechariah 9:9

world will be cast out. **1232** And I, if I am lifted up from the earth, will draw all people to myself." **1233** But he said this, signifying by what kind of death he should die. **1234** The multitude answered him, "We have heard out of the law that the Christ remains forever.# How do you say, 'The Son of Man must be lifted up?' Who is this Son of Man?"

1235 Jesus therefore said to them, "Yet a little while the light is with you. Walk while you have the light, that darkness doesn't overtake you. He who walks in the darkness doesn't know where he is going. **1236** While you have the light, believe in the light, that you may become children of light." Jesus said these things, and he departed and hid himself from them. **1237** But though he had done so many signs before them, yet they didn't believe in him, **1238** that the word of Isaiah the prophet might be fulfilled, which he spoke,
"Lord, who has believed our report?
To whom has the arm of the Lord been revealed?"#
1239 For this cause they couldn't believe, for Isaiah said again,
1240 "He has blinded their eyes and he hardened their heart,
lest they should see with their eyes,
and perceive with their heart,
and would turn,
and I would heal them."#
1241 Isaiah said these things when he saw his glory, and spoke of him.
1242 Nevertheless even many of the rulers believed in him, but because of the Pharisees they didn't confess it, so that they wouldn't be put out of the synagogue, **1243** for they loved men's praise more than God's praise.

1244 Jesus cried out and said, "Whoever believes in me, believes not in me, but in him who sent me. **1245** He who sees me sees him who sent me. **1246** I have come as a light into the world, that whoever believes in me may not remain in the darkness. **1247** If anyone listens to my sayings, and doesn't believe, I don't judge him. For I came not to judge the world, but to save the world. **1248** He who rejects me, and doesn't receive my sayings, has one who judges him. The word that I

#12:34 12:34 Isaiah 9:7; Daniel 2:44; See Isaiah 53:8
#12:38 12:38 Isaiah 53:1
#12:40 12:40 Isaiah 6:10
#12:41 12:41 Isaiah 6:1

Day Thirty-Four

spoke will judge him in the last day. ¹²⁴⁹ For I spoke not from myself, but the Father who sent me, he gave me a commandment, what I should say, and what I should speak. ¹²⁵⁰ ¹²I know that his commandment is eternal life. The things therefore which I speak, even as the Father has said to me, so I speak."

The Lord's Prayer

Our Father, who art in heaven,
Hallowed be thy name.
Thy Kingdom come.
Thy will be done on Earth, as it is in heaven.
Give us this day our daily bread.
And forgive us our trespasses,
As we forgive those that trespass against us.
And lead us not into temptation,
But deliver us from evil.
For thine is the kingdom,
The power, and the glory,
For ever and ever.
AMEN

Day Thirty-Five

Daily Prayer

Yeah that we shall see the great Head of the Church once more ... raise up unto Himself certain young men whom He may use in this glorious employ. And what manner of men will they be? Men mighty in the Scriptures, their lives dominated by a sense of the greatness, the majesty and holiness of God, and their minds and hearts aglow with the great truths of the doctrines of grace.

> "They will be men who will preach with broken hearts and tear-filled eyes, and upon whose ministries God will grant an extraordinary effusion of the Holy Spirit, and who will witness signs and wonders following in the transformation of multitudes of human lives."

They will be men who have learned what it is to die to self, to human aims and personal ambitions; men who are willing to be 'fools for Christ's sake,' who will bear

reproach and falsehood, who will labor and suffer, and whose supreme desire will be, not to gain earth's accolades, but to win the Master's approbation when they appear before His awesome judgment seat. They will be men who will preach with broken hearts and tear-filled eyes, and upon whose ministries God will grant an extraordinary effusion of the Holy Spirit, and who will witness 'signs and wonders following' in the transformation of multitudes of human lives."
- *George Whitefield, one of the most prominent pastors in American history.*

Prayer of Confession

Almighty and most merciful Father; we have erred, and strayed from your ways like lost sheep. We have followed too much the devices and desires of our own hearts. We have offended against your holy laws. We have left undone those things which we ought to have done; and we have done those things which we ought not to have done; and there is no health in us. O Lord, have mercy upon us, miserable offenders. Spare those, O God, who confess their faults. Restore those who are penitent; according to your promises declared unto mankind in Christ Jesus our Lord. And grant, O most merciful Father, for his sake; that we may hereafter live a godly, righteous, and sober life, to the glory of thy holy Name. Amen.
-Revised prayer from *The Book of Common Prayer*, 1662

Daily Wisdom

1 Give unto the LORD, O ye mighty, give unto the LORD glory and strength.
2 Give unto the LORD the glory due unto his name; worship the LORD in the beauty of holiness.

Day Thirty-Five

3 The voice of the LORD *is* upon the waters: the God of glory thundereth: the LORD *is* upon many waters.
4 The voice of the LORD *is* powerful; the voice of the LORD *is* full of majesty.
5 The voice of the LORD breaketh the cedars; yea, the LORD breaketh the cedars of Lebanon.
6 He maketh them also to skip like a calf; Lebanon and Sirion like a young unicorn.
7 The voice of the LORD divideth the flames of fire.
8 The voice of the LORD shaketh the wilderness; the LORD shaketh the wilderness of Kadesh.
9 The voice of the LORD maketh the hinds to calve, and discovereth the forests: and in his temple doth every one speak of *his* glory.
10 The LORD sitteth upon the flood; yea, the LORD sitteth King for ever.
11 The LORD will give strength unto his people; the LORD will bless his people with peace.
-Psalm 29, *The King James Bible*, 1769 edition of 1611 text

Readings from the Holy Bible

The Holy Gospel According to Matthew and John (MATTHEW 26:1-26:30; JOHN 13:1-30)

MATTHEW 26:1-26:30, JUDAS BETRAYS JESUS AND THE LORD'S SUPPER

26

[26]**1** When Jesus had finished all these words, he said to his disciples, [26]**2** "You know that after two days the Passover is coming, and the Son of Man will be delivered up to be crucified." [26]**3** Then the chief priests, the scribes, and the elders of the people were gathered together in the court of the high priest, who was called Caiaphas. [26]**4** They took counsel together that they might take Jesus by

deceit, and kill him. ²⁶5 But they said, "Not during the feast, lest a riot occur among the people."

²⁶6 Now when Jesus was in Bethany, in the house of Simon the leper, ²⁶7 a woman came to him having an alabaster jar of very expensive ointment, and she poured it on his head as he sat at the table. ²⁶8 But when his disciples saw this, they were indignant, saying, "Why this waste? ²⁶9 For this ointment might have been sold for much, and given to the poor."

²⁶10 However, knowing this, Jesus said to them, "Why do you trouble the woman? She has done a good work for me. ²⁶11 For you always have the poor with you; but you don't always have me. ²⁶12 For in pouring this ointment on my body, she did it to prepare me for burial. ²⁶13 Most certainly I tell you, wherever this Good News is preached in the whole world, what this woman has done will also be spoken of as a memorial of her."

²⁶14 Then one of the twelve, who was called Judas Iscariot, went to the chief priests, ²⁶15 and said, "What are you willing to give me, that I should deliver him to you?" They weighed out for him thirty pieces of silver. ²⁶16 From that time he sought opportunity to betray him.

²⁶17 Now on the first day of unleavened bread, the disciples came to Jesus, saying to him, "Where do you want us to prepare for you to eat the Passover?"

²⁶18 He said, "Go into the city to a certain person, and tell him, 'The Teacher says, "My time is at hand. I will keep the Passover at your house with my disciples."'"

²⁶19 The disciples did as Jesus commanded them, and they prepared the Passover. ²⁶20 Now when evening had come, he was reclining at the table with the twelve disciples. ²⁶21 As they were eating, he said, "Most certainly I tell you that one of you will betray me."

²⁶22 They were exceedingly sorrowful, and each began to ask him, "It isn't me, is it, Lord?"

²⁶23 He answered, "He who dipped his hand with me in the dish will betray me. ²⁶24 The Son of Man goes, even as it is written of him, but woe to that man through whom the Son of Man is betrayed! It would be better for that man if he had not been born."

²⁶25 Judas, who betrayed him, answered, "It isn't me, is it, Rabbi?" He said to him, "You said it."

Day Thirty-Five

²⁶**26** As they were eating, Jesus took bread, gave thanks for[141] it, and broke it. He gave to the disciples, and said, "Take, eat; this is my body." ²⁶**27** He took the cup, gave thanks, and gave to them, saying, "All of you drink it, ²⁶**28** for this is my blood of the new covenant, which is poured out for many for the remission of sins. ²⁶**29** But I tell you that I will not drink of this fruit of the vine from now on, until that day when I drink it anew with you in my Father's Kingdom." ²⁶**30** When they had sung a hymn, they went out to the Mount of Olives.

JOHN 13:1-30, JESUS WASHES THE DISCIPLES AND PREDICTS BETRAYAL

13

¹³**1** Now before the feast of the Passover, Jesus, knowing that his time had come that he would depart from this world to the Father, having loved his own who were in the world, he loved them to the end. ¹³**2** During supper, the devil having already put into the heart of Judas Iscariot, Simon's son, to betray him, ¹³**3** Jesus, knowing that the Father had given all things into his hands, and that he came from God, and was going to God, ¹³**4** arose from supper, and laid aside his outer garments. He took a towel and wrapped a towel around his waist. ¹³**5** Then he poured water into the basin, and began to wash the disciples' feet and to wipe them with the towel that was wrapped around him. ¹³**6** Then he came to Simon Peter. He said to him, "Lord, do you wash my feet?"
¹³**7** Jesus answered him, "You don't know what I am doing now, but you will understand later."
¹³**8** Peter said to him, "You will never wash my feet!"
Jesus answered him, "If I don't wash you, you have no part with me."
¹³**9** Simon Peter said to him, "Lord, not my feet only, but also my hands and my head!"
¹³**10** Jesus said to him, "Someone who has bathed only needs to have his feet washed, but is completely clean. You are clean, but not all of you." ¹³**11** For he knew him who would betray him, therefore he said, "You are not all clean." ¹³**12** So when he had washed their feet, put his

---

[141]26:26 26:26 TR reads "blessed" instead of "gave thanks for"

outer garment back on, and sat down again, he said to them, "Do you know what I have done to you? ¹³13 You call me, 'Teacher' and 'Lord.' You say so correctly, for so I am. ¹³14 If I then, the Lord and the Teacher, have washed your feet, you also ought to wash one another's feet. ¹³15 For I have given you an example, that you should also do as I have done to you. ¹³16 Most certainly I tell you, a servant is not greater than his lord, neither is one who is sent greater than he who sent him. ¹³17 If you know these things, blessed are you if you do them. ¹³18 I don't speak concerning all of you. I know whom I have chosen. But that the Scripture may be fulfilled, 'He who eats bread with me has lifted up his heel against me.'# ¹³19 From now on, I tell you before it happens, that when it happens, you may believe that I am he. ¹³20 Most certainly I tell you, he who receives whomever I send, receives me; and he who receives me, receives him who sent me."

¹³21 When Jesus had said this, he was troubled in spirit, and testified, "Most certainly I tell you that one of you will betray me."

¹³22 The disciples looked at one another, perplexed about whom he spoke. ¹³23 One of his disciples, whom Jesus loved, was at the table, leaning against Jesus' breast. ¹³24 Simon Peter therefore beckoned to him, and said to him, "Tell us who it is of whom he speaks." ¹³25 He, leaning back, as he was, on Jesus' breast, asked him, "Lord, who is it?" ¹³26 Jesus therefore answered, "It is he to whom I will give this piece of bread when I have dipped it." So when he had dipped the piece of bread, he gave it to Judas, the son of Simon Iscariot. ¹³27 After the piece of bread, then Satan entered into him.

Then Jesus said to him, "What you do, do quickly."

¹³28 Now nobody at the table knew why he said this to him. ¹³29 For some thought, because Judas had the money box, that Jesus said to him, "Buy what things we need for the feast," or that he should give something to the poor. ¹³30 Therefore having received that morsel, he went out immediately. It was night.

#13:18 13:18 Psalm 41:9

Day Thirty-Five

The Lord's Prayer

Our Father, who art in heaven,
Hallowed be thy name.
Thy Kingdom come.
Thy will be done on Earth, as it is in heaven.
Give us this day our daily bread.
And forgive us our trespasses,
As we forgive those that trespass against us.
And lead us not into temptation,
But deliver us from evil.
For thine is the kingdom,
The power, and the glory,
For ever and ever.
AMEN

Day Thirty-Six

Daily Prayer

FIRST PRAYER OF THE CONTINENTAL CONGRESS, 1774 (Partial)

With Thee there is mercy and plenteous redemption: in O Lord our Heavenly Father, high and mighty King of kings, and Lord of lords, who dost from thy throne behold all the dwellers on earth and reignest with power supreme and uncontrolled over all the Kingdoms, Empires and Governments; look down in mercy, we beseech Thee, on these our American States, who have fled to Thee from the rod of the oppressor and thrown themselves on Thy gracious protection, desiring to be henceforth dependent only on Thee. To Thee have they appealed for the righteousness of their cause; to Thee do

> "To Thee have they appealed for the righteousness of their cause; to Thee do they now look up for that countenance and support, which Thou alone canst give."

they now look up for that countenance and support, which Thou alone canst give. Take them, therefore, Heavenly Father, under Thy nurturing care; give them wisdom in Council and valor in the field; defeat the malicious designs of our cruel adversaries; convince them of the unrighteousness of their Cause and if they persist in their sanguinary purposes, of own unerring justice, sounding in their hearts, constrain them to drop the weapons of war from their unnerved hands in the day of battle!
-Reverend Jacob Duché, Rector of Christ Church of Philadelphia, Pennsylvania. Prayer delivered to the Continental Congress on September 7, 1774.

Prayer of Confession

Almighty and most merciful Father; we have erred, and strayed from your ways like lost sheep. We have followed too much the devices and desires of our own hearts. We have offended against your holy laws. We have left undone those things which we ought to have done; and we have done those things which we ought not to have done; and there is no health in us. O Lord, have mercy upon us, miserable offenders. Spare those, O God, who confess their faults. Restore those who are penitent; according to your promises declared unto mankind in Christ Jesus our Lord. And grant, O most merciful Father, for his sake; that we may hereafter live a godly, righteous, and sober life, to the glory of thy holy Name. Amen.
-Revised prayer from *The Book of Common Prayer*, 1662

Daily Wisdom

7 LORD, by thy favour thou hast made my mountain to stand strong: thou didst hide thy face, *and* I was troubled.

Day Thirty-Six

8 I cried to thee, O LORD; and unto the LORD I made supplication.
9 What profit *is there* in my blood, when I go down to the pit? Shall the dust praise thee? shall it declare thy truth?
10 Hear, O LORD, and have mercy upon me: LORD, be thou my helper.
11 Thou hast turned for me my mourning into dancing: thou hast put off my sackcloth, and girded me with gladness;
12 To the end that *my* glory may sing praise to thee, and not be silent. O LORD my God, I will give thanks unto thee for ever.
-Psalm 30:7-12, *The King James Bible*, 1769 edition of 1611 text

Readings from the Holy Bible

The Holy Gospel According to John (JOHN 13:31-16:33)

JOHN 13:31-16:33, JESUS' LAST TEACHINGS FOR THE DISCIPLES

¹³**31** When he had gone out, Jesus said, "Now the Son of Man has been glorified, and God has been glorified in him. ¹³**32** If God has been glorified in him, God will also glorify him in himself, and he will glorify him immediately. ¹³**33** Little children, I will be with you a little while longer. You will seek me, and as I said to the Jews, 'Where I am going, you can't come,' so now I tell you. ¹³**34** A new commandment I give to you, that you love one another. Just as I have loved you, you also love one another. ¹³**35** By this everyone will know that you are my disciples, if you have love for one another."
¹³**36** Simon Peter said to him, "Lord, where are you going?"
Jesus answered, "Where I am going, you can't follow now, but you will follow afterwards."
¹³**37** Peter said to him, "Lord, why can't I follow you now? I will lay down my life for you."

13:38 Jesus answered him, 13"Will you lay down your life for me? Most certainly I tell you, the rooster won't crow until you have denied me three times.

14

14:1 "Don't let your heart be troubled. Believe in God. Believe also in me. 14:2 In my Father's house are many homes. If it weren't so, I would have told you. I am going to prepare a place for you. 14:3 If I go and prepare a place for you, I will come again, and will receive you to myself; that where I am, you may be there also. 14:4 You know where I go, and you know the way."
14:5 Thomas said to him, "Lord, we don't know where you are going. How can we know the way?"
14:6 Jesus said to him, "I am the way, the truth, and the life. No one comes to the Father, except through me. 14:7 If you had known me, you would have known my Father also. From now on, you know him, and have seen him."
14:8 Philip said to him, "Lord, show us the Father, and that will be enough for us."
14:9 Jesus said to him, "Have I been with you such a long time, and do you not know me, Philip? He who has seen me has seen the Father. How do you say, 'Show us the Father?' 14:10 Don't you believe that I am in the Father, and the Father in me? The words that I tell you, I speak not from myself; but the Father who lives in me does his works. 14:11 Believe me that I am in the Father, and the Father in me; or else believe me for the very works' sake. 14:12 Most certainly I tell you, he who believes in me, the works that I do, he will do also; and he will do greater works than these, because I am going to my Father. 14:13 Whatever you will ask in my name, I will do it, that the Father may be glorified in the Son. 14:14 If you will ask anything in my name, I will do it. 14:15 If you love me, keep my commandments. 14:16 I will pray to the Father, and he
will give you another Counselor, 14:2 that he may be with you forever: 14:17 the Spirit of truth, whom the world can't receive; for it doesn't see him and doesn't know him. You know him, for he lives with you,

---

14:214:16 14:16 Greek παρακλητον: Counselor, Helper, Intercessor, Advocate, and Comforter.

Day Thirty-Six

and will be in you. ¹⁴18 I will not leave you orphans. I will come to you. ¹⁴19 Yet a little while, and the world will see me no more; but you will see me. Because I live, you will live also. ¹⁴20 In that day you will know that I am in my Father, and you in me, and I in you. ¹⁴21 One who has my commandments and keeps them, that person is one who loves me. One who loves me will be loved by my Father, and I will love him, and will reveal myself to him."

¹⁴22 Judas (not Iscariot) said to him, "Lord, what has happened that you are about to reveal yourself to us, and not to the world?"
¹⁴23 Jesus answered him, "If a man loves me, he will keep my word. My Father will love him, and we will come to him, and make our home with him. ¹⁴24 He who doesn't love me doesn't keep my words. The word which you hear isn't mine, but the Father's who sent me. ¹⁴25 I have said these things to you while still living with you. ¹⁴26 But the Counselor, the Holy Spirit, whom the Father will send in my name, will teach you all things, and will remind you of all that I said to you. ¹⁴27 Peace I leave with you. My peace I give to you; not as the world gives, I give to you. Don't let your heart be troubled, neither let it be fearful. ¹⁴28 You heard how I told you, 'I go away, and I come to you.' If you loved me, you would have rejoiced, because I said 'I am going to my Father;' for the Father is greater than I. ¹⁴29 Now I have told you before it happens so that when it happens, you may believe. ¹⁴30 I will no more speak much with you, for the prince of the world comes, and he has nothing in me. ¹⁴31 ¹⁴But that the world may know that I love the Father, and as the Father commanded me, even so I do. Arise, let's go from here.

15

¹⁵1 "I am the true vine, and my Father is the farmer. ¹⁵2 Every branch in me that doesn't bear fruit, he takes away. Every branch that bears fruit, he prunes, that it may bear more fruit. ¹⁵3 You are already pruned clean because of the word which I have spoken to you. ¹⁵4 Remain in me, and I in you. As the branch can't bear fruit by itself unless it remains in the vine, so neither can you, unless you remain in me. ¹⁵5 I am the vine. You are the branches. He who remains in me and I in him bears much fruit, for apart from me you can do nothing. ¹⁵6 If a man doesn't remain in me, he is thrown out as a branch and is

withered; and they gather them, throw them into the fire, and they are burned. ¹⁵7 If you remain in me, and my words remain in you, you will ask whatever you desire, and it will be done for you.

¹⁵8 "In this my Father is glorified, that you bear much fruit; and so you will be my disciples. ¹⁵9 Even as the Father has loved me, I also have loved you. Remain in my love. ¹⁵10 If you keep my commandments, you will remain in my love; even as I have kept my Father's commandments, and remain in his love. ¹⁵11 I have spoken these things to you, that my joy may remain in you, and that your joy may be made full.

¹⁵12 "This is my commandment, that you love one another, even as I have loved you. ¹⁵13 Greater love has no one than this, that someone lay down his life for his friends. ¹⁵14 You are my friends, if you do whatever I command you. ¹⁵15 No longer do I call you servants, for the servant doesn't know what his lord does. But I have called you friends, for everything that I heard from my Father, I have made known to you. ¹⁵16 You didn't choose me, but I chose you and appointed you, that you should go and bear fruit, and that your fruit should remain; that whatever you will ask of the Father in my name, he may give it to you.

¹⁵17 "I command these things to you, that you may love one another. ¹⁵18 If the world hates you, you know that it has hated me before it hated you. ¹⁵19 If you were of the world, the world would love its own. But because you are not of the world, since I chose you out of the world, therefore the world hates you. ¹⁵20 Remember the word that I said to you: 'A servant is not greater than his lord.'# If they persecuted me, they will also persecute you. If they kept my word, they will also keep yours. ¹⁵21 But they will do all these things to you for my name's sake, because they don't know him who sent me. ¹⁵22 If I had not come and spoken to them, they would not have had sin; but now they have no excuse for their sin. ¹⁵23 He who hates me, hates my Father also. ¹⁵24 If I hadn't done among them the works which no one else did, they wouldn't have had sin. But now they have seen and also hated both me and my Father. ¹⁵25 But this happened so that the

---

#15:20 15:20 John 13:16

Day Thirty-Six

word may be fulfilled which was written in their law, 'They hated me without a cause.'#

15:26 "When the Counselor[143] has come, whom I will send to you from the Father, the Spirit of truth, who proceeds from the Father, he will testify about me. **15:27** **15**You will also testify, because you have been with me from the beginning.

16

16:1 "I have said these things to you so that you wouldn't be caused to stumble. **16:2** They will put you out of the synagogues. Yes, the time comes that whoever kills you will think that he offers service to God. **16:3** They will do these things[144] because they have not known the Father, nor me. **16:4** But I have told you these things, so that when the time comes, you may remember that I told you about them. I didn't tell you these things from the beginning, because I was with you. **16:5** But now I am going to him who sent me, and none of you asks me, 'Where are you going?' **16:6** But because I have told you these things, sorrow has filled your heart. **16:7** Nevertheless I tell you the truth: It is to your advantage that I go away, for if I don't go away, the Counselor won't come to you. But if I go, I will send him to you. **16:8** When he has come, he will convict the world about sin, about righteousness, and about judgment; **16:9** about sin, because they don't believe in me; **16:10** about righteousness, because I am going to my Father, and you won't see me any more; **16:11** about judgment, because the prince of this world has been judged.

16:12 "I still have many things to tell you, but you can't bear them now. **16:13** However when he, the Spirit of truth, has come, he will guide you into all truth, for he will not speak from himself; but whatever he hears, he will speak. He will declare to you things that are coming. **16:14** He will glorify me, for he will take from what is mine, and will declare it to you. **16:15** All things that the Father has are mine; therefore I said that he takes[145] of mine and will declare it to you. **16:16**

#15:25   15:25 Psalm 35:19; 69:4
[143]15:26   15:26 Greek Parakletos: Counselor, Helper, Advocate, Intercessor, and Comforter.
[144]16:3   16:3 TR adds "to you"
[145]16:15   16:15 TR reads "will take" instead of "takes"

The American Book of Prayer

A little while, and you will not see me. Again a little while, and you will see me."

¹⁶17 Some of his disciples therefore said to one another, "What is this that he says to us, 'A little while, and you won't see me, and again a little while, and you will see me;' and, 'Because I go to the Father'?"
¹⁶18 They said therefore, "What is this that he says, 'A little while'? We don't know what he is saying."
¹⁶19 Therefore Jesus perceived that they wanted to ask him, and he said to them, "Do you inquire among yourselves concerning this, that I said, 'A little while, and you won't see me, and again a little while, and you will see me?' ¹⁶20 Most certainly I tell you that you will weep and lament, but the world will rejoice. You will be sorrowful, but your sorrow will be turned into joy. ¹⁶21 A woman, when she gives birth, has sorrow because her time has come. But when she has delivered the child, she doesn't remember the anguish any more, for the joy that a human being is born into the world. ¹⁶22 Therefore you now have sorrow, but I will see you again, and your heart
will rejoice, and no one will take your joy away from you.
¹⁶23 "In that day you will ask me no questions. Most certainly I tell you, whatever you may ask of the Father in my name, he will give it to you. ¹⁶24 Until now, you have asked nothing in my name. Ask, and you will receive, that your joy may be made full. ¹⁶25 I have spoken these things to you in figures of speech. But the time is coming when I will no more speak to you in figures of speech, but will tell you plainly about the Father. ¹⁶26 In that day you will ask in my name; and I don't say to you that I will pray to the Father for you, ¹⁶27 for the Father himself loves you, because you have loved me, and have believed that I came from God. ¹⁶28 I came from the Father, and have come into the world. Again, I leave the world, and go to the Father."
¹⁶29 His disciples said to him, "Behold, now you are speaking plainly, and using no figures of speech. ¹⁶30 Now we know that you know all things, and don't need for anyone to question you. By this we believe that you came from God."
¹⁶31 Jesus answered them, "Do you now believe? ¹⁶32 Behold, the time is coming, yes, and has now come, that you will be scattered, everyone to his own place, and you will leave me alone. Yet I am not alone, because the Father is with me. ¹⁶33 ¹⁶I have told you these

Day Thirty-Six

things, that in me you may have peace. In the world you have trouble; but cheer up! I have overcome the world."

The Lord's Prayer

Our Father, who art in heaven,
Hallowed be thy name.
Thy Kingdom come.
Thy will be done on Earth, as it is in heaven.
Give us this day our daily bread.
And forgive us our trespasses,
As we forgive those that trespass against us.
And lead us not into temptation,
But deliver us from evil.
For thine is the kingdom,
The power, and the glory,
For ever and ever.
AMEN

Day Thirty-Seven

Daily Prayer

FIRST PRAYER OF THE CONTINENTAL CONGRESS, 1774 (Partial)

Be Thou present, O God of wisdom, and direct the councils of this honorable assembly; enable them to settle things on the best and surest foundation. That the scene of blood may be speedily closed; that order, harmony and peace may be effectually restored, and truth and justice, religion and piety, prevail and flourish amongst the people. Preserve the health of their bodies and vigor of their minds; shower down on them and the millions they here represent, such temporal blessings as Thou seest expedient for them in this world and crown them with everlasting glory in the

> *"Preserve the health of their bodies and vigor of their minds; shower down on them and the millions they here represent, such temporal blessings as Thou seest expedient for them in this world and crown them with everlasting glory in the world to come."*

world to come. All this we ask in the name and through the merits of Jesus Christ, Thy Son and our Savior.
-*Reverend Jacob Duché, Rector of Christ Church of Philadelphia, Pennsylvania. Prayer delivered to the Continental Congress on September 7, 1774.*

Prayer of Confession

Almighty and most merciful Father; we have erred, and strayed from your ways like lost sheep. We have followed too much the devices and desires of our own hearts. We have offended against your holy laws. We have left undone those things which we ought to have done; and we have done those things which we ought not to have done; and there is no health in us. O Lord, have mercy upon us, miserable offenders. Spare those, O God, who confess their faults. Restore those who are penitent; according to your promises declared unto mankind in Christ Jesus our Lord. And grant, O most merciful Father, for his sake; that we may hereafter live a godly, righteous, and sober life, to the glory of thy holy Name. Amen.
-*Revised prayer from* The Book of Common Prayer, *1662*

Daily Wisdom

1 Blessed *is he whose* transgression *is* forgiven, *whose* sin *is* covered.
2 Blessed *is* the man unto whom the LORD imputeth not iniquity, and in whose spirit *there is* no guile.
3 When I kept silence, my bones waxed old through my roaring all the day long.
4 For day and night thy hand was heavy upon me: my moisture is turned into the drought of summer. Selah.
5 I acknowledged my sin unto thee, and mine iniquity have I not hid. I said, I will confess my transgressions unto the LORD; and thou forgavest the iniquity of my sin. Selah.

Day Thirty-Seven

6 For this shall every one that is godly pray unto thee in a time when thou mayest be found: surely in the floods of great waters they shall not come nigh unto him.
7 Thou *art* my hiding place; thou shalt preserve me from trouble; thou shalt compass me about with songs of deliverance. Selah.
8 I will instruct thee and teach thee in the way which thou shalt go: I will guide thee with mine eye.
9 Be ye not as the horse, *or* as the mule, *which* have no understanding: whose mouth must be held in with bit and bridle, lest they come near unto thee.
10 Many sorrows *shall be* to the wicked: but he that trusteth in the LORD, mercy shall compass him about.
11 Be glad in the LORD, and rejoice, ye righteous: and shout for joy, all *ye that are* upright in heart.
-Psalm 32, *The King James Bible*, 1769 edition of 1611 text

Readings from the Holy Bible

The Holy Gospel According to Matthew and John (MATTHEW 26:36-46; JOHN 17:1-18:24)

MATTHEW 26:36-46, THE GARDEN OF GETHSEMANE

^{26}**36** Then Jesus came with them to a place called Gethsemane, and said to his disciples, "Sit here, while I go there and pray." ^{26}**37** He took with him Peter and the two sons of Zebedee, and began to be sorrowful and severely troubled. ^{26}**38** Then he said to them, "My soul is exceedingly sorrowful, even to death. Stay here, and watch with me."
^{26}**39** He went forward a little, fell on his face, and prayed, saying, "My Father, if it is possible, let this cup pass away from me; nevertheless, not what I desire, but what you desire."
^{26}**40** He came to the disciples, and found them sleeping, and said to Peter, "What, couldn't you watch with me for one hour? ^{26}**41** Watch

and pray, that you don't enter into temptation. The spirit indeed is willing, but the flesh is weak."

²⁶42 Again, a second time he went away, and prayed, saying, "My Father, if this cup can't pass away from me unless I drink it, your desire be done." ²⁶43 He came again and found them sleeping, for their eyes were heavy. ²⁶44 He left them again, went away, and prayed a third time, saying the same words. ²⁶45 Then he came to his disciples, and said to them, "Sleep on now, and take your rest. Behold, the hour is at hand, and the Son of Man is betrayed into the hands of sinners. ²⁶46 Arise, let's be going. Behold, he who betrays me is at hand."

JOHN 17:1-18:24, JESUS IS ARRESTED

17

¹⁷1 Jesus said these things, then lifting up his eyes to heaven, he said, "Father, the time has come. Glorify your Son, that your Son may also glorify you; ¹⁷2 even as you gave him authority over all flesh, so he will give eternal life to all whom you have given him. ¹⁷3 This is eternal life, that they should know you, the only true God, and him whom you sent, Jesus Christ. ¹⁷4 I glorified you on the earth. I have accomplished the work which you have given me to do. ¹⁷5 Now, Father, glorify me with your own self with the glory which I had with you before the world existed. ¹⁷6 I revealed your name to the people whom you have given me out of the world. They were yours, and you have given them to me. They have kept your word. ¹⁷7 Now they have known that all things whatever you have given me are from you, ¹⁷8 for the words which you have given me I have given to them, and they received them, and knew for sure that I came from you. They have believed that you sent me. ¹⁷9 I pray for them.
I don't pray for the world, but for those whom you have given me, for they are yours. ¹⁷10 All things that are mine are yours, and yours are mine, and I am glorified in them. ¹⁷11 I am no more in the world, but these are in the world, and I am coming to you. Holy Father, keep them through your name which you have given me, that they may be one, even as we are. ¹⁷12 While I was with them in the world, I kept them in your name. I have kept those whom you have given me. None

Day Thirty-Seven

of them is lost except the son of destruction, that the Scripture might be fulfilled. ¹⁷13 But now I come to you, and I say these things in the world, that they may have my joy made full in themselves. ¹⁷14 I have given them your word. The world hated them, because they are not of the world, even as I am not of the world. ¹⁷15 I pray not that you would take them from the world, but that you would keep them from the evil one. ¹⁷16 They are not of the world even as I am not of the world. ¹⁷17 Sanctify them in your truth. Your word is truth.# ¹⁷18 As you sent me into the world, even so I have sent them into the world. ¹⁷19 For their sakes I sanctify myself, that they themselves also may be sanctified in truth. ¹⁷20 Not for these only do I pray, but for those also who will believe in me through their word, ¹⁷21 that they may all be one; even as you, Father, are in me, and I in you, that they also may be one in us; that the world may believe that you sent me. ¹⁷22 The glory which you have given me, I have given to them; that they may be one, even as we are one; ¹⁷23 I in them, and you in me, that they may be perfected into one; that the world may know that you sent me and loved them, even as you loved me. ¹⁷24 Father, I desire that they also whom you have given me be with me where I am, that they may see my glory, which you have given me, for you loved me before the foundation of the world. ¹⁷25 Righteous Father, the world hasn't known you, but I knew you; and these knew that you sent me. ¹⁷26 ¹⁷I made known to them your name, and will make it known; that the love with which you loved me may be in them, and I in them."

18

¹⁸1 When Jesus had spoken these words, he went out with his disciples over the brook Kidron, where there was a garden, into which he and his disciples entered. ¹⁸2 Now Judas, who betrayed him, also knew the place, for Jesus often met there with his disciples. ¹⁸3 Judas then, having taken a detachment of soldiers and officers from the chief priests and the Pharisees, came there with lanterns, torches, and weapons. ¹⁸4 Jesus therefore, knowing all the things that were happening to him, went out, and said to them, "Who are you looking for?"
¹⁸5 They answered him, "Jesus of Nazareth."

#17:17 17:17 Psalm 119:142

Jesus said to them, "I am he."
Judas also, who betrayed him, was standing with them. ¹⁸6 When therefore he said to them, "I am he," they went backward, and fell to the ground.
¹⁸7 Again therefore he asked them, "Who are you looking for?"
They said, "Jesus of Nazareth."
¹⁸8 Jesus answered, "I told you that I am he. If therefore you seek me, let these go their way," ¹⁸9 that the word might be fulfilled which he spoke, "Of those whom you have given me, I have lost none."#
¹⁸10 Simon Peter therefore, having a sword, drew it, struck the high priest's servant, and cut off his right ear. The servant's name was Malchus. ¹⁸11 Jesus therefore said to Peter, "Put the sword into its sheath. The cup which the Father has given me, shall I not surely drink it?"
¹⁸12 So the detachment, the commanding officer, and the officers of the Jews seized Jesus and bound him, ¹⁸13 and led him to Annas first, for he was father-in-law to Caiaphas, who was high priest that year.
¹⁸14 Now it was Caiaphas who advised the Jews that it was expedient that one man should perish for the people. ¹⁸15 Simon Peter followed Jesus, as did another disciple. Now that disciple was known to the high priest, and entered in with Jesus into the court of the high priest; ¹⁸16 but Peter was standing at the door outside. So the other disciple, who was known to the high priest, went out and spoke to her who kept the door, and brought in Peter. ¹⁸17 Then the maid who kept the door said to Peter, "Are you also one of this man's disciples?"
He said, "I am not."
¹⁸18 Now the servants and the officers were standing there, having made a fire of coals, for it was cold. They were warming themselves. Peter was with them, standing and warming himself. ¹⁸19 The high priest therefore asked Jesus about his disciples and about his teaching. ¹⁸20 Jesus answered him, "I spoke openly to the world. I always taught in synagogues, and in the temple, where the Jews always meet. I said nothing in secret. ¹⁸21 Why do you ask me? Ask those who have heard me what I said to them. Behold, they know the things which I said."

#18:9 18:9 John 6:39

Day Thirty-Seven

18:22 When he had said this, one of the officers standing by slapped Jesus with his hand, saying, "Do you answer the high priest like that?"
18:23 Jesus answered him, "If I have spoken evil, testify of the evil; but if well, why do you beat me?"
18:24 Annas sent him bound to Caiaphas, the high priest. **18:25** Now Simon Peter was standing and warming himself. They said therefore to him, "You aren't also one of his disciples, are you?"

The Lord's Prayer

Our Father, who art in heaven,
Hallowed be thy name.
Thy Kingdom come.
Thy will be done on Earth, as it is in heaven.
Give us this day our daily bread.
And forgive us our trespasses,
As we forgive those that trespass against us.
And lead us not into temptation,
But deliver us from evil.
For thine is the kingdom,
The power, and the glory,
For ever and ever.
AMEN

Day Thirty-Eight

Daily Prayer

Pray for me, that I may become fervent, as a flame of fire in my work, and may be abundantly succeeded, and that it would please God, however unworthy I am, to improve me as an instrument of His glory, and advancing the kingdom of Christ.
-Jonathan Edwards, 18th century American pastor

> *"Pray for me, that I may become fervent, as a flame of fire in my work ..."*

Prayer of Confession

Almighty and most merciful Father; we have erred, and strayed from your ways like lost sheep. We have followed too much the devices and desires of our own hearts. We have offended against your holy laws. We have left undone those things which we ought to have done; and we have done those things which we ought not to have done; and there is no health in us. O Lord, have mercy upon us,

miserable offenders. Spare those, O God, who confess their faults. Restore those who are penitent; according to your promises declared unto mankind in Christ Jesus our Lord. And grant, O most merciful Father, for his sake; that we may hereafter live a godly, righteous, and sober life, to the glory of thy holy Name. Amen.
-Revised prayer from *The Book of Common Prayer*, 1662

Daily Wisdom

1 As the hart panteth after the water brooks, so panteth my soul after thee, O God.
2 My soul thirsteth for God, for the living God: when shall I come and appear before God?
3 My tears have been my meat day and night, while they continually say unto me, Where *is* thy God?
4 When I remember these *things*, I pour out my soul in me: for I had gone with the multitude, I went with them to the house of God, with the voice of joy and praise, with a multitude that kept holyday.
5 Why art thou cast down, O my soul? and *why* art thou disquieted in me? hope thou in God: for I shall yet praise him *for* the help of his countenance.
6 O my God, my soul is cast down within me: therefore will I remember thee from the land of Jordan, and of the Hermonites, from the hill Mizar.
7 Deep calleth unto deep at the noise of thy waterspouts: all thy waves and thy billows are gone over me.
8 *Yet* the LORD will command his lovingkindness in the daytime, and in the night his song *shall be* with me, *and* my prayer unto the God of my life.
9 I will say unto God my rock, Why hast thou forgotten me? why go I mourning because of the oppression of the enemy?
10 *As* with a sword in my bones, mine enemies reproach me; while they say daily unto me, Where *is* thy God?

Day Thirty-Eight

11 Why art thou cast down, O my soul? and why art thou disquieted within me? hope thou in God: for I shall yet praise him, *who is* the health of my countenance, and my God.
-Psalm 42, *The King James Bible*, 1769 edition of 1611 text

Readings from the Holy Bible

The Holy Gospel According to Matthew, Luke, and John (MATTHEW 26:57-27:10; LUKE 23:1-23:25; JOHN 19:1-16)

MATTHEW 26:57-27:10, JESUS MOCKED AND PLACED ON TRIAL

26:57 Those who had taken Jesus led him away to Caiaphas the high priest, where the scribes and the elders were gathered together. **26:58** But Peter followed him from a distance, to the court of the high priest, and entered in and sat with the officers, to see the end. **26:59** Now the chief priests, the elders, and the whole council sought false testimony against Jesus, that they might put him to death; **26:60** and they found none. Even though many false witnesses came forward, they found none. But at last two false witnesses came forward, **26:61** and said, "This man said, 'I am able to destroy the temple of God, and to build it in three days.'" **26:62** The high priest stood up, and said to him, "Have you no answer? What is this that these testify against you?" **26:63** But Jesus held his peace. The high priest answered him, "I adjure you by the living God, that you tell us whether you are the Christ, the Son of God." **26:64** Jesus said to him, "You have said it. Nevertheless, I tell you, after this you will see the Son of Man sitting at the right hand of Power, and coming on the clouds of the sky." **26:65** Then the high priest tore his clothing, saying, "He has spoken blasphemy! Why do we need any more witnesses? Behold, now you have heard his blasphemy. **26:66** What do you think?"

They answered, "He is worthy of death!" ²⁶67 Then they spat in his face and beat him with their fists, and some slapped him, ²⁶68 saying, "Prophesy to us, you Christ! Who hit you?"
²⁶69 Now Peter was sitting outside in the court, and a maid came to him, saying, "You were also with Jesus, the Galilean!"
²⁶70 But he denied it before them all, saying, "I don't know what you are talking about."
²⁶71 When he had gone out onto the porch, someone else saw him, and said to those who were there, "This man also was with Jesus of Nazareth."
²⁶72 Again he denied it with an oath, "I don't know the man."
²⁶73 After a little while those who stood by came and said to Peter, "Surely you are also one of them, for your speech makes you known."
²⁶74 Then he began to curse and to swear, "I don't know the man!" Immediately the rooster crowed. ²⁶75 Peter remembered the word which Jesus had said to him, ²⁶"Before the rooster crows, you will deny me three times." Then he went out and wept bitterly.

27

²⁷1 Now when morning had come, all the chief priests and the elders of the people took counsel against Jesus to put him to death: ²⁷2 and they bound him, and led him away, and delivered him up to Pontius Pilate, the governor. ²⁷3 Then Judas, who betrayed him, when he saw that Jesus was condemned, felt remorse, and brought back the thirty pieces of silver to the chief priests and elders, ²⁷4 saying, "I have sinned in that I betrayed innocent blood."
But they said, "What is that to us? You see to it."
²⁷5 He threw down the pieces of silver in the sanctuary, and departed. He went away and hanged himself. ²⁷6 The chief priests took the pieces of silver, and said, "It's not
lawful to put them into the treasury, since it is the price of blood." ²⁷7 They took counsel, and bought the potter's field with them, to bury strangers in. ²⁷8 Therefore that field was called "The Field of Blood" to this day. ²⁷9 Then that which was spoken through Jeremiah[146] the prophet was fulfilled, saying,

---

[146]27:9 27:9 some manuscripts omit "Jeremiah"

Day Thirty-Eight

"They took the thirty pieces of silver,
the price of him upon whom a price had been set,
whom some of the children of Israel priced,
²⁷10 and they gave them for the potter's field,
as the Lord commanded me."#

LUKE 23:1-23:25, JESUS STANDS BEFORE HEROD AND PILATE

23

²³1 The whole company of them rose up and brought him before Pilate. ²³2 They began to accuse him, saying, "We found this man perverting the nation, forbidding paying taxes to Caesar, and saying that he himself is Christ, a king."
²³3 Pilate asked him, "Are you the King of the Jews?"
He answered him, "So you say."
²³4 Pilate said to the chief priests and the multitudes, "I find no basis for a charge against this man."
²³5 But they insisted, saying, "He stirs up the people, teaching throughout all Judea, beginning from Galilee even to this place."
²³6 But when Pilate heard Galilee mentioned, he asked if the man was a Galilean. ²³7 When he found out that he was in Herod's jurisdiction, he sent him to Herod, who was also in Jerusalem during those days. ²³8 Now when Herod saw Jesus, he was exceedingly glad, for he had wanted to see him for a long time, because he had heard many things about him. He hoped to see some miracle done by him. ²³9 He questioned him with many words, but he gave no answers. ²³10 The chief priests and the scribes stood, vehemently accusing him.
²³11 Herod with his soldiers humiliated him and mocked him. Dressing him in luxurious clothing, they sent him back to Pilate.
²³12 Herod and Pilate became friends with each other that very day, for before that they were enemies with each other.
²³13 Pilate called together the chief priests, the rulers, and the people, ²³14 and said to them, "You brought this man to me as one that perverts the people, and behold, having examined him before you, I found no basis for a charge against this man concerning those things

---

#27:10 27:10 Zechariah 11:12-13; Jeremiah 19:1-13; 32:6-9

of which you accuse him. ²³15 Neither has Herod, for I sent you to him, and see, nothing worthy of death has been done by him. ²³16 I will therefore chastise him and release him."

²³17 Now he had to release one prisoner to them at the feast.[147]

²³18 But they all cried out together, saying, "Away with this man! Release to us Barabbas!"— ²³19 one who was thrown into prison for a certain revolt in the city, and for murder.

²³20 Then Pilate spoke to them again, wanting to release Jesus, ²³21 but they shouted, saying, "Crucify! Crucify him!"

²³22 He said to them the third time, "Why? What evil has this man done? I have found no capital crime in him. I will therefore chastise him and release him." ²³23 But they were urgent with loud voices, asking that he might be crucified. Their voices and the voices of the chief priests prevailed. ²³24 Pilate decreed that what they asked for should be done. ²³25 He released him who had been thrown into prison for insurrection and murder, for whom they asked, but he delivered Jesus up to their will.

JOHN 19:1-16, JESUS SENTENCED TO BE CRUCIFIED

19

¹⁹1 So Pilate then took Jesus, and flogged him. ¹⁹2 The soldiers twisted thorns into a crown, and put it on his head, and dressed him in a purple garment. ¹⁹3 They kept saying, "Hail, King of the Jews!" and they kept slapping him.

¹⁹4 Then Pilate went out again, and said to them, "Behold, I bring him out to you, that you may know that I find no basis for a charge against him."

¹⁹5 Jesus therefore came out, wearing the crown of thorns and the purple garment. Pilate said to them, "Behold, the man!"

¹⁹6 When therefore the chief priests and the officers saw him, they shouted, saying, "Crucify! Crucify!"

Pilate said to them, "Take him yourselves, and crucify him, for I find no basis for a charge against him."

¹⁹7 The Jews answered him, "We have a law, and by our law he ought to die, because he made himself the Son of God."

---

[147]23:17 23:17 NU omits verse 17.

Day Thirty-Eight

[19]8 When therefore Pilate heard this saying, he was more afraid. [19]9 He entered into the Praetorium again, and said to Jesus, "Where are you from?" But Jesus gave him no answer. [19]10 Pilate therefore said to him, "Aren't you speaking to me? Don't you know that I have power to release you and have power to crucify you?"

[19]11 Jesus answered, "You would have no power at all against me, unless it were given to you from above. Therefore he who delivered me to you has greater sin."

[19]12 At this, Pilate was seeking to release him, but the Jews cried out, saying, "If you release this man, you aren't Caesar's friend! Everyone who makes himself a king speaks against Caesar!"

[19]13 When Pilate therefore heard these words, he brought Jesus out and sat down on the judgment seat at a place called "The Pavement", but in Hebrew, "Gabbatha." [19]14 Now it was the Preparation Day of the Passover, at about the sixth hour.[148] He said to the Jews, "Behold, your King!"

[19]15 They cried out, "Away with him! Away with him! Crucify him!" Pilate said to them, "Shall I crucify your King?"

The chief priests answered, "We have no king but Caesar!"

[19]16 So then he delivered him to them to be crucified. So they took Jesus and led him away.

The Lord's Prayer

Our Father, who art in heaven,
Hallowed be thy name.
Thy Kingdom come.
Thy will be done on Earth, as it is in heaven.
Give us this day our daily bread.
And forgive us our trespasses,
As we forgive those that trespass against us.
And lead us not into temptation,

---

[148]19:14 19:14 "the sixth hour" would have been 6:00 a.m. according to the Roman timekeeping system, or noon for the Jewish timekeeping system in use, then.

The American Book of Prayer

But deliver us from evil.
For thine is the kingdom,
The power, and the glory,
For ever and ever.
AMEN

Day Thirty-Nine

Daily Prayer

I am no longer my own, but thine.
Put me to what thou wilt, rank me with whom thou wilt.
Put me to doing, put me to suffering.
Let me be employed for thee or laid aside for thee,
exalted for thee or brought low for thee.
Let me be full, let me be empty.
Let me have all things, let me have nothing.
I freely and heartily yield all things to thy pleasure and disposal.
And now, O glorious and blessed God, Father, Son and Holy Spirit,
thou art mine, and I am thine. So be it.
And the covenant which I have made on earth,
let it be ratified in heaven.
Amen.

-John Wesley, "Wesley Covenant Prayer"[19]

> *"Let me be full, let me be empty. Let me have all things, let me have nothing. I freely and heartily yield all things to thy pleasure and disposal."*

The American Book of Prayer

Prayer of Confession

Almighty and most merciful Father; we have erred, and strayed from your ways like lost sheep. We have followed too much the devices and desires of our own hearts. We have offended against your holy laws. We have left undone those things which we ought to have done; and we have done those things which we ought not to have done; and there is no health in us. O Lord, have mercy upon us, miserable offenders. Spare those, O God, who confess their faults. Restore those who are penitent; according to your promises declared unto mankind in Christ Jesus our Lord. And grant, O most merciful Father, for his sake; that we may hereafter live a godly, righteous, and sober life, to the glory of thy holy Name. Amen.
-Revised prayer from *The Book of Common Prayer*, 1662

Daily Wisdom

2 My help *cometh* from the LORD, which made heaven and earth.
3 He will not suffer thy foot to be moved: he that keepeth thee will not slumber.
4 Behold, he that keepeth Israel shall neither slumber nor sleep.
5 The LORD *is* thy keeper: the LORD *is* thy shade upon thy right hand.
6 The sun shall not smite thee by day, nor the moon by night.
7 The LORD shall preserve thee from all evil: he shall preserve thy soul.
8 The LORD shall preserve thy going out and thy coming in from this time forth, and even for evermore.
-Psalm 121, *The King James Bible*, 1769 edition of 1611 text

Day Thirty-Nine

Readings from the Holy Bible

The Holy Gospel According to Matthew and John (MATTHEW 27:27-28:15; JOHN 20:10-18)

MATTHEW 27:27-28:15, THE DEATH AND RESURRECTION

27

²⁷1 Now when morning had come, all the chief priests and the elders of the people took counsel against Jesus to put him to death: ²⁷2 and they bound him, and led him away, and delivered him up to Pontius Pilate, the governor. ²⁷3 Then Judas, who betrayed him, when he saw that Jesus was condemned, felt remorse, and brought back the thirty pieces of silver to the chief priests and elders, ²⁷4 saying, "I have sinned in that I betrayed innocent blood."
But they said, "What is that to us? You see to it."
²⁷5 He threw down the pieces of silver in the sanctuary, and departed. He went away and hanged himself. ²⁷6 The chief priests took the pieces of silver, and said, "It's not lawful to put them into the treasury, since it is the price of blood." ²⁷7 They took counsel, and bought the potter's field with them, to bury strangers in. ²⁷8 Therefore that field was called "The Field of Blood" to this day. ²⁷9 Then that which was spoken through Jeremiah¹⁴⁹ the prophet was fulfilled, saying,
"They took the thirty pieces of silver,
the price of him upon whom a price had been set,
whom some of the children of Israel priced,
²⁷10 and they gave them for the potter's field,
as the Lord commanded me."#
²⁷11 Now Jesus stood before the governor: and the governor asked him, saying, "Are you the King of the Jews?"
Jesus said to him, "So you say."
²⁷12 When he was accused by the chief priests and elders, he answered nothing. ²⁷13 Then Pilate said to him, "Don't you hear how many things they testify against you?"

---

¹⁴⁹27:9 27:9 some manuscripts omit "Jeremiah"
#27:10 27:10 Zechariah 11:12-13; Jeremiah 19:1-13; 32:6-9

2714 He gave him no answer, not even one word, so that the governor marveled greatly. **2715** Now at the feast the governor was accustomed to release to the multitude one prisoner, whom they desired. **2716** They had then a notable prisoner, called Barabbas. **2717** When therefore they were gathered together, Pilate said to them, "Whom do you want me to release to you? Barabbas, or Jesus, who is called Christ?" **2718** For he knew that because of envy they had delivered him up.

2719 While he was sitting on the judgment seat, his wife sent to him, saying, "Have nothing to do with that righteous man, for I have suffered many things today in a dream because of him." **2720** Now the chief priests and the elders persuaded the multitudes to ask for Barabbas, and destroy Jesus. **2721** But the governor answered them, "Which of the two do you want me to release to you?"

They said, "Barabbas!"

2722 Pilate said to them, "What then shall I do to Jesus, who is called Christ?"

They all said to him, "Let him be crucified!"

2723 But the governor said, "Why? What evil has he done?"

But they cried out exceedingly, saying, "Let him be crucified!"

2724 So when Pilate saw that nothing was being gained, but rather that a disturbance was starting, he took water, and washed his hands before the multitude, saying, "I am innocent of the blood of this righteous person. You see to it." **2725** All the people answered, "May his blood be on us, and on our children!"

2726 Then he released to them Barabbas, but Jesus he flogged and delivered to be crucified. **2727** Then the governor's soldiers took Jesus into the Praetorium, and gathered the whole garrison together against him. **2728** They stripped him, and put a scarlet robe on him. **2729** They braided a crown of thorns and put it on his head, and a reed in his right hand; and they kneeled down before him, and mocked him, saying, "Hail, King of the Jews!" **2730** They spat on him, and took the reed and struck him on the head. **2731** When they had mocked him, they took the robe off him, and put his clothes on him, and led him away to crucify him.

2732 As they came out, they found a man of Cyrene, Simon by name, and they compelled him to go with them, that he might carry his cross. **2733** When they came to a place called "Golgotha", that is to say,

Day Thirty-Nine

"The place of a skull," ²⁷34 they gave him sour wine¹⁵⁰ to drink mixed with gall. When he had tasted it, he would not drink. ²⁷35 When they had crucified him, they divided his clothing among them, casting lots,¹⁵¹ ²⁷36 and they sat and watched him there. ²⁷37 They set up over his head the accusation against him written, "THIS IS JESUS, THE KING OF THE JEWS."

²⁷38 Then there were two robbers crucified with him, one on his right hand and one on the left. ²⁷39 Those who passed by blasphemed him, wagging their heads, ²⁷40 and saying, "You who destroy the temple, and build it in three days, save yourself! If you are the Son of God, come down from the cross!"

²⁷41 Likewise the chief priests also mocking, with the scribes, the Pharisees,¹⁵² and the elders, said, ²⁷42 "He saved others, but he can't save himself. If he is the King of Israel, let him come down from the cross now, and we will believe in him. ²⁷43 He trusts in God. Let God deliver him now, if he wants him; for he said, 'I am the Son of God.'"

²⁷44 The robbers also who were crucified with him cast on him the same reproach.

²⁷45 Now from the sixth hour¹⁵³ there was darkness over all the land until the ninth hour.¹⁵⁴ ²⁷46 About the ninth hour Jesus cried with a loud voice, saying, "Eli, Eli, lima¹⁵⁵ sabachthani?" That is, "My God, my God, why have you forsaken me?"#

²⁷47 Some of them who stood there, when they heard it, said, "This man is calling Elijah."

²⁷48 Immediately one of them ran, and took a sponge, and filled it with vinegar, and put it on a reed, and gave him a drink. ²⁷49 The rest said, "Let him be. Let's see whether Elijah comes to save him."

²⁷50 Jesus cried again with a loud voice, and yielded up his spirit.

²⁷51 Behold, the veil of the temple was torn in two from the top to the bottom. The earth quaked and the rocks were split. ²⁷52 The tombs

---

¹⁵⁰27:34 27:34 or, vinegar
¹⁵¹27:35 27:35 TR adds "that it might be fulfilled which was spoken by the prophet: 'They divided my garments among them, and for my clothing they cast lots;'" [see Psalm 22:18 and John 19:24]
¹⁵²27:41 27:41 TR omits "the Pharisees"
¹⁵³27:45 27:45 noon
¹⁵⁴27:45 27:45 3:00 p.m.
¹⁵⁵27:46 27:46 TR reads "lama" instead of "lima"
#27:46 27:46 Psalm 22:1

were opened, and many bodies of the saints who had fallen asleep were raised; **2753** and coming out of the tombs after his resurrection, they entered into the holy city and appeared to many. **2754** Now the centurion, and those who were with him watching Jesus, when they saw the earthquake, and the things that were done, feared exceedingly, saying, "Truly this was the Son of God."
2755 Many women were there watching from afar, who had followed Jesus from Galilee, serving him. **2756** Among them were Mary Magdalene, Mary the mother of James and Joses, and the mother of the sons of Zebedee. **2757** When evening had come, a rich man from Arimathaea, named Joseph, who himself was also Jesus' disciple came. **2758** This man went to Pilate, and asked for Jesus' body. Then Pilate commanded the body to be given up. **2759** Joseph took the body, and wrapped it in a clean linen cloth, **2760** and laid it in his own new tomb, which he had cut out in the rock, and he rolled a great stone against the door of the tomb, and departed. **2761** Mary Magdalene was there, and the other Mary, sitting opposite the tomb. **2762** Now on the next day, which was the day after the Preparation Day, the chief priests and the Pharisees were gathered together to Pilate, **2763** saying, "Sir, we remember what that deceiver said while he was still alive: 'After three days I will rise again.' **2764** Command therefore that the tomb be made secure until the third day, lest perhaps his disciples come at night and steal him away, and tell the people, 'He is risen from the dead;' and the last deception will be worse than the first."
2765 Pilate said to them, "You have a guard. Go, make it as secure as you can." **2766** So they went with the guard and made the tomb secure, sealing the stone. 27

28

281 Now after the Sabbath, as it began to dawn on the first day of the week, Mary Magdalene and the other Mary came to see the tomb. **282** Behold, there was a great earthquake, for an angel of the Lord descended from the sky, and came and rolled away the stone from the door, and sat on it. **283** His appearance was like lightning, and his clothing white as snow. **284** For fear of him, the guards shook, and became like dead men. **285** The angel answered the women, "Don't be afraid, for I know that you seek Jesus, who has been crucified. **286** He

Day Thirty-Nine

is not here, for he has risen, just like he said. Come, see the place where the Lord was lying. ²⁸7 Go quickly and tell his disciples, 'He has risen from the dead, and behold, he goes before you into Galilee; there you will see him.' Behold, I have told you."
²⁸8 They departed quickly from the tomb with fear and great joy, and ran to bring his disciples word. ²⁸9 As they went to tell his disciples, behold, Jesus met them, saying, "Rejoice!"
They came and took hold of his feet, and worshiped him.
²⁸10 Then Jesus said to them, "Don't be afraid. Go tell my brothers [156] that they should go into Galilee, and there they will see me."
²⁸11 Now while they were going, behold, some of the guards came into the city, and told the chief priests all the things that had happened.
²⁸12 When they were assembled with the elders, and had taken counsel, they gave a large amount of silver to the soldiers, ²⁸13 saying, "Say that his disciples came by night, and stole him away while we slept. ²⁸14 If this comes to the governor's ears, we will persuade him and make you free of worry." ²⁸15 So they took the money and did as they were told. This saying was spread abroad among the Jews, and continues until today.

JOHN 20:10-18, JESUS APPEARS TO MARY MAGDALENE

²⁰10 So the disciples went away again to their own homes.
²⁰11 But Mary was standing outside at the tomb weeping. So as she wept, she stooped and looked into the tomb, ²⁰12 and she saw two angels in white sitting, one at the head, and one at the feet, where the body of Jesus had lain. ²⁰13 They asked her, "Woman, why are you weeping?"
She said to them, "Because they have taken away my Lord, and I don't know where they have laid him." ²⁰14 When she had said this, she turned around and saw Jesus standing, and didn't know that it was Jesus.
²⁰15 Jesus said to her, "Woman, why are you weeping? Who are you looking for?"

---

[156]28:10 28:10 The word for "brothers" here may be also correctly translated "brothers and sisters" or "siblings."

She, supposing him to be the gardener, said to him, "Sir, if you have carried him away, tell me where you have laid him, and I will take him away."

[20]16 Jesus said to her, "Mary."

She turned and said to him, "Rabboni!"[157] which is to say, "Teacher!"[158]

[20]17 Jesus said to her, "Don't hold me, for I haven't yet ascended to my Father; but go to my brothers and tell them, 'I am ascending to my Father and your Father, to my God and your God.'"

[20]18 Mary Magdalene came and told the disciples that she had seen the Lord, and that he had said these things to her.

The Lord's Prayer

Our Father, who art in heaven,
Hallowed be thy name.
Thy Kingdom come.
Thy will be done on Earth, as it is in heaven.
Give us this day our daily bread.
And forgive us our trespasses,
As we forgive those that trespass against us.
And lead us not into temptation,
But deliver us from evil.
For thine is the kingdom,
The power, and the glory,
For ever and ever.
AMEN

---

[157]20:16 20:16 Rabboni is a transliteration of the Hebrew word for "great teacher."
[158]20:16 20:16 or, Master

Day Forty

On Evangelism

You have nothing to do but to save souls. Therefore, spend and be spent in this work. And go not only to those that need you, but to those that need you most. It is not your business to preach so many times, and to take care of this or that society; but to save as many souls as you can; to bring as many sinners as you possibly can to repentance.
-*John Wesley*[20]

> "You have nothing to do but to save souls. Therefore, spend and be spent in this work."

Prayer of Confession

Almighty and most merciful Father; we have erred, and strayed from your ways like lost sheep. We have followed too much the devices and desires of our own hearts. We have offended against your holy laws. We have left undone those things which we ought to have done; and we have done those things which we ought not to have done; and there is no health in us. O Lord, have mercy upon us, miserable offenders. Spare those, O God, who

confess their faults. Restore those who are penitent; according to your promises declared unto mankind in Christ Jesus our Lord. And grant, O most merciful Father, for his sake; that we may hereafter live a godly, righteous, and sober life, to the glory of thy holy Name. Amen.
-Revised prayer from *The Book of Common Prayer*, 1662

Daily Wisdom

1 Out of the depths have I cried unto thee, O LORD.
2 Lord, hear my voice: let thine ears be attentive to the voice of my supplications.
3 If thou, LORD, shouldest mark iniquities, O Lord, who shall stand?
4 But *there is* forgiveness with thee, that thou mayest be feared.
5 I wait for the LORD, my soul doth wait, and in his word do I hope.
6 My soul *waiteth* for the Lord more than they that watch for the morning: *I say, more than* they that watch for the morning.
7 Let Israel hope in the LORD: for with the LORD *there is* mercy, and with him *is* plenteous redemption.
8 And he shall redeem Israel from all his iniquities.
-Psalm 130, *The King James Bible*, 1769 edition of 1611 text

Day Forty

Readings from the Holy Bible

The Holy Gospel According to Luke, John, and Matthew (LUKE 24:13-24:49; JOHN 20:24-21:25; MATTHEW 28:16-20; LUKE 24:50-53)

LUKE 24:13-24:49, THE ROAD TO EMMAUS

²⁴13 Behold, two of them were going that very day to a village named Emmaus, which was sixty stadia[159] from Jerusalem. ²⁴14 They talked with each other about all of these things which had happened. ²⁴15 While they talked and questioned together, Jesus himself came near, and went with them. ²⁴16 But their eyes were kept from recognizing him. ²⁴17 He said to them, "What are you talking about as you walk, and are sad?"

²⁴18 One of them, named Cleopas, answered him, "Are you the only stranger in Jerusalem who doesn't know the things which have happened there in these days?"

²⁴19 He said to them, "What things?" They said to him, "The things concerning Jesus, the Nazarene, who was a prophet mighty in deed and word before God and all the people; ²⁴20 and how the chief priests and our rulers delivered him up to be condemned to death, and crucified him. ²⁴21 But we were hoping that it was he who would redeem Israel. Yes, and besides all this, it is now the third day since these things happened. ²⁴22 Also, certain women of our company amazed us, having arrived early at the tomb; ²⁴23 and when they didn't find his body, they came saying that they had also seen a vision of angels, who said that he was alive. ²⁴24 Some of us went to the tomb, and found it just like the women had said, but they didn't see him."

²⁴25 He said to them, "Foolish men, and slow of heart to believe in all that the prophets have spoken! ²⁴26 Didn't the Christ have to suffer these things and to enter into his glory?" ²⁴27 Beginning from Moses and from all the prophets, he explained to them in all the Scriptures the things concerning himself. ²⁴28 They came near to the village where they were going, and he acted like he would go further.

---

[159]24:13 24:13 60 stadia = about 11 kilometers or about 7 miles.

²⁴29 They urged him, saying, "Stay with us, for it is almost evening, and the day is almost over."
He went in to stay with them. ²⁴30 When he had sat down at the table with them, he took the bread and gave thanks. Breaking it, he gave it to them. ²⁴31 Their eyes were opened and they recognized him, then he vanished out of their sight. ²⁴32 They said to one another, "Weren't our hearts burning within us, while he spoke to us along the way, and while he opened the Scriptures to us?" ²⁴33 They rose up that very hour, returned to Jerusalem, and found the eleven gathered together, and those who were with them, ²⁴34 saying, "The Lord is risen indeed, and has appeared to Simon!" ²⁴35 They related the things that happened along the way, and how he was recognized by them in the breaking of the bread.

²⁴36 As they said these things, Jesus himself stood among them, and said to them, "Peace be to you."

²⁴37 But they were terrified and filled with fear, and supposed that they had seen a spirit.

²⁴38 He said to them, "Why are you troubled? Why do doubts arise in your hearts? ²⁴39 See my hands and my feet, that it is truly me. Touch me and see, for a spirit doesn't have flesh and bones, as you see that I have." ²⁴40 When he had said this, he showed them his hands and his feet. ²⁴41 While they still didn't believe for joy, and wondered, he said to them, "Do you have anything here to eat?"

²⁴42 They gave him a piece of a broiled fish and some honeycomb. ²⁴43 He took them, and ate in front of them. ²⁴44 He said to them, "This is what I told you, while I was still with you, that all things which are written in the law of Moses, the prophets, and the psalms, concerning me must be fulfilled."

²⁴45 Then he opened their minds, that they might understand the Scriptures. ²⁴46 He said to them, "Thus it is written, and thus it was necessary for the Christ to suffer and to rise from the dead the third day, ²⁴47 and that repentance and remission of sins should be preached in his name to all the nations, beginning at Jerusalem. ²⁴48 You are witnesses of these things. ²⁴49 Behold, I send out the promise of my Father on you. But wait in the city of Jerusalem until you are clothed with power from on high."

Day Forty

JOHN 20:24-21:25, THOMAS, MIRACULOUS FISHING, AND PETER

²⁰24 But Thomas, one of the twelve, called Didymus, wasn't with them when Jesus came. ²⁰25 The other disciples therefore said to him, "We have seen the Lord!"
But he said to them, "Unless I see in his hands the print of the nails, put my finger into the print of the nails, and put my hand into his side, I will not believe."
²⁰26 After eight days again his disciples were inside and Thomas was with them. Jesus came, the doors being locked, and stood in the middle, and said, "Peace be to you." ²⁰27 Then he said to Thomas, "Reach here your finger, and see my hands. Reach here your hand, and put it into my side. Don't be unbelieving, but believing."
²⁰28 Thomas answered him, "My Lord and my God!"
²⁰29 Jesus said to him, "Because you have seen me,[160] you have believed. Blessed are those who have not seen, and have believed."
²⁰30 Therefore Jesus did many other signs in the presence of his disciples, which are not written in this book; ²⁰31 but these are written, that you may believe that Jesus is the Christ, the Son of God, and that believing you may have life in his name. ²⁰

21

²¹1 After these things, Jesus revealed himself again to the disciples at the sea of Tiberias. He revealed himself this way. ²¹2 Simon Peter, Thomas called Didymus, Nathanael of Cana in Galilee, and the sons of Zebedee, and two others of his disciples were together. ²¹3 Simon Peter said to them, "I'm going fishing."
They told him, "We are also coming with you." They immediately went out, and entered into the boat. That night, they caught nothing.
²¹4 But when day had already come, Jesus stood on the beach, yet the disciples didn't know that it was Jesus. ²¹5 Jesus therefore said to them, "Children, have you anything to eat?"
They answered him, "No."
²¹6 He said to them, "Cast the net on the right side of the boat, and you will find some."

---

[160]20:29 20:29 TR adds "Thomas,"

They cast it therefore, and now they weren't able to draw it in for the multitude of fish. ²¹7 That disciple therefore whom Jesus loved said to Peter, "It's the Lord!"
So when Simon Peter heard that it was the Lord, he wrapped his coat around himself (for he was naked), and threw himself into the sea.
²¹8 But the other disciples came in the little boat (for they were not far from the land, but about two hundred cubits[161] away), dragging the net full of fish. ²¹9 So when they got out on the land, they saw a fire of coals there, with fish and bread laid on it. ²¹10 Jesus said to them, "Bring some of the fish which you have just caught."
²¹11 Simon Peter went up, and drew the net to land, full of one hundred fifty-three great fish. Even though there were so many, the net wasn't torn.
²¹12 Jesus said to them, "Come and eat breakfast!"
None of the disciples dared inquire of him, "Who are you?" knowing that it was the Lord.
²¹13 Then Jesus came and took the bread, gave it to them, and the fish likewise. ²¹14 This is now the third time that Jesus was revealed to his disciples after he had risen from the dead. ²¹15 So when they had eaten their breakfast, Jesus said to Simon Peter, "Simon, son of Jonah, do you love me more than these?"
He said to him, "Yes, Lord; you know that I have affection for you."
He said to him, "Feed my lambs." ²¹16 He said to him again a second time, "Simon, son of Jonah, do you love me?"
He said to him, "Yes, Lord; you know that I have affection for you."
He said to him, "Tend my sheep." ²¹17 He said to him the third time, "Simon, son of Jonah, do you have affection for me?" Peter was grieved because he asked him the third time, "Do you have affection for me?" He said to him, "Lord, you know everything. You know that I have affection for you."
Jesus said to him, "Feed my sheep. ²¹18 Most certainly I tell you, when you were young, you dressed yourself and walked where you wanted to. But when you are old, you will stretch out your hands, and another will dress you and carry you where you don't want to go."
²¹19 Now he said this, signifying by what kind of death he would glorify God. When he had said this, he said to him, "Follow me."

---

[161] 21:8 21:8 200 cubits is about 100 yards or about 91 meters

Day Forty

²¹20 Then Peter, turning around, saw a disciple following. This was the disciple whom Jesus loved, the one who had also leaned on Jesus' breast at the supper and asked, "Lord, who is going to betray you?" ²¹21 Peter seeing him, said to Jesus, "Lord, what about this man?" ²¹22 Jesus said to him, "If I desire that he stay until I come, what is that to you? You follow me." ²¹23 This saying therefore went out among the brothers,[162] that this disciple wouldn't die. Yet Jesus didn't say to him that he wouldn't die, but, "If I desire that he stay until I come, what is that to you?" ²¹24 This is the disciple who testifies about these things, and wrote these things. We know that his witness is true. ²¹25 There are also many other things which Jesus did, which if they would all be written, I suppose that even the world itself wouldn't have room for the books that would be written.

MATTHEW 28:16-20, THE GREAT COMMISSION

²⁸16 But the eleven disciples went into Galilee, to the mountain where Jesus had sent them. ²⁸17 When they saw him, they bowed down to him, but some doubted. ²⁸18 Jesus came to them and spoke to them, saying, "All authority has been given to me in heaven and on earth. ²⁸19 Go[163] and make disciples of all nations, baptizing them in the name of the Father and of the Son and of the Holy Spirit, ²⁸20 ²⁸teaching them to observe all things that I commanded you. Behold, I am with you always, even to the end of the age." Amen. LUKE 24:50-53, THE GLORIOUS ASCENSION
²⁴50 He led them out as far as Bethany, and he lifted up his hands, and blessed them. ²⁴51 While he blessed them, he withdrew from them, and was carried up into heaven. ²⁴52 They worshiped him, and returned to Jerusalem with great joy, ²⁴53 and were continually in the temple, praising and blessing God. Amen. ²⁴

---

[162]21:23 21:23 The word for "brothers" here may be also correctly translated "brothers and sisters" or "siblings."
[163]28:19 28:19 TR and NU add "therefore"

The American Book of Prayer

The Lord's Prayer

Our Father, who art in heaven,
Hallowed be thy name.
Thy Kingdom come.
Thy will be done on Earth, as it is in heaven.
Give us this day our daily bread.
And forgive us our trespasses,
As we forgive those that trespass against us.
And lead us not into temptation,
But deliver us from evil.
For thine is the kingdom,
The power, and the glory,
For ever and ever.
AMEN

The Book of Acts

Readings from the Holy Bible

The Acts of the Apostles

1

1 The first book I wrote, Theophilus, concerned all that Jesus began both to do and to teach, **2** until the day in which he was received up, after he had given commandment through the Holy Spirit to the apostles whom he had chosen. **3** To these he also showed himself alive after he suffered, by many proofs, appearing to them over a period of forty days, and speaking about God's Kingdom. **4** Being assembled together with them, he commanded them, "Don't depart from Jerusalem, but wait for the promise of the Father, which you heard from me. **5** For John indeed baptized in water, but you will be baptized in the Holy Spirit not many days from now."

6 Therefore when they had come together, they asked him, "Lord, are you now restoring the kingdom to Israel?"

7 He said to them, "It isn't for you to know times or seasons which the Father has set within his own authority. **8** But you will receive power when the Holy Spirit has come upon you. You will be witnesses to me in Jerusalem, in all Judea and Samaria, and to the uttermost parts of the earth."

9 When he had said these things, as they were looking, he was taken up, and a cloud received him out of their sight. **10** While they were looking steadfastly into the sky as he went, behold,[164] two men stood by them in white clothing, **11** who also said, "You men of Galilee, why do you stand looking into the sky? This Jesus, who was received up from you into the sky, will come back in the same way as you saw him going into the sky."

12 Then they returned to Jerusalem from the mountain called Olivet, which is near Jerusalem, a Sabbath day's journey away. **13** When they had come in, they went up into the upper room where they were staying; that is Peter, John, James, Andrew, Philip, Thomas, Bartholomew, Matthew, James the son of Alphaeus, Simon the

---

[164]**1:10** *1:10* "Behold", from "ἰδού", means look at, take notice, observe, see, or gaze at. It is often used as an interjection.

Zealot, and Judas the son of James. ¹⁴ All these with one accord continued steadfastly in prayer and supplication, along with the women, and Mary the mother of Jesus, and with his brothers.
¹⁵ In these days, Peter stood up in the middle of the disciples (and the number of names was about one hundred twenty), and said,
¹⁶ "Brothers, it was necessary that this Scripture should be fulfilled, which the Holy Spirit spoke before by the mouth of David concerning Judas, who was guide to those who took Jesus. ¹⁷ For he was counted with us, and received his portion in this ministry. ¹⁸ Now this man obtained a field with the reward for his wickedness, and falling headlong, his body burst open, and all his intestines gushed out. ¹⁹ It became known to everyone who lived in Jerusalem that in their language that field was called 'Akeldama,' that is, 'The field of blood.'
¹²⁰ For it is written in the book of Psalms,
'Let his habitation be made desolate.
Let no one dwell in it;'#
and, 'Let another take his office.'#
¹²¹ "Of the men therefore who have accompanied us all the time that the Lord Jesus went in and out among us, ²² beginning from the baptism of John, to the day that he was received up from us, of these one must become a witness with us of his resurrection."
²³ They put forward two, Joseph called Barsabbas, who was also called Justus, and Matthias. ²⁴ They prayed and said, "You, Lord, who know the hearts of all men, show which one of these two you have chosen ²⁵ to take part in this ministry and apostleship from which Judas fell away, that he might go to his own place." ²⁶ They drew lots for them, and the lot fell on Matthias, and he was counted with the eleven apostles.

2

²1 Now when the day of Pentecost had come, they were all with one accord in one place. ²2 Suddenly there came from the sky a sound like the rushing of a mighty wind, and it filled all the house where they were sitting. ²3 Tongues like fire appeared and were distributed to them, and one sat on each of them. ²4 They were all filled with the

---

#1:20 1:20 Psalm 69:25
#1:20 1:20 Psalm 109:8

The Acts of the Apostles

Holy Spirit, and began to speak with other languages, as the Spirit gave them the ability to speak. ²5 Now there were dwelling in Jerusalem Jews, devout men, from every nation under the sky. ²6 When this sound was heard, the multitude came together and were bewildered, because everyone heard them speaking in his own language. ²7 They were all amazed and marveled, saying to one another, "Behold, aren't all these who speak Galileans? ²8 How do we hear, everyone in our own native language? ²9 Parthians, Medes, Elamites, and people from Mesopotamia, Judea, Cappadocia, Pontus, Asia, ²10 Phrygia, Pamphylia, Egypt, the parts of Libya around Cyrene, visitors from Rome, both Jews and proselytes, ²11 Cretans and Arabians: we hear them speaking in our languages the mighty works of God!" ²12 They were all amazed, and were perplexed, saying to one another, "What does this mean?" ²13 Others, mocking, said, "They are filled with new wine."

²14 But Peter, standing up with the eleven, lifted up his voice, and spoke out to them, "You men of Judea, and all you who dwell at Jerusalem, let this be known to you, and listen to my words. ²15 For these aren't drunken, as you suppose, seeing it is only the third hour of the day.[165] ²16 But this is what has been spoken through the prophet Joel:

²17 'It will be in the last days, says God,
that I will pour out my Spirit on all flesh.
Your sons and your daughters will prophesy.
Your young men will see visions.
Your old men will dream dreams.
²18 Yes, and on my servants and on my handmaidens in those days,
I will pour out my Spirit, and they will prophesy.
²19 I will show wonders in the sky above,
and signs on the earth beneath:
blood, and fire, and billows of smoke.
²20 The sun will be turned into darkness,
and the moon into blood,
before the great and glorious day of the Lord comes.

---

[165]2:15 *2:15* about 9:00 a.m.

²21 It will be that whoever will call on the name of the Lord will be saved.'#

²22 "Men of Israel, hear these words! Jesus of Nazareth, a man approved by God to you by mighty works and wonders and signs which God did by him among you, even as you yourselves know, ²23 him, being delivered up by the determined counsel and foreknowledge of God, you have taken by the hand of lawless men, crucified and killed; ²24 whom God raised up, having freed him from the agony of death, because it was not possible that he should be held by it. ²25 For David says concerning him,

'I saw the Lord always before my face,

for he is on my right hand, that I should not be moved.

²26 Therefore my heart was glad, and my tongue rejoiced.

Moreover my flesh also will dwell in hope;

²27 because you will not leave my soul in Hades,¹⁶⁶

neither will you allow your Holy One to see decay.

²28 You made known to me the ways of life.

You will make me full of gladness with your presence.'#

²29 "Brothers, I may tell you freely of the patriarch David, that he both died and was buried, and his tomb is with us to this day. ²30 Therefore, being a prophet, and knowing that God had sworn with an oath to him that of the fruit of his body, according to the flesh, he would raise up the Christ to sit on his throne, ²31 he foreseeing this spoke about the resurrection of the Christ, that his soul wasn't left in Hades,¹⁶⁷ and his flesh didn't see decay. ²32 This Jesus God raised up, to which we all are witnesses. ²33 Being therefore exalted by the right hand of God, and having received from the Father the promise of the Holy Spirit, he has poured out this, which you now see and hear. ²34 For David didn't ascend into the heavens, but he says himself,

'The Lord said to my Lord, "Sit by my right hand

²35 until I make your enemies a footstool for your feet."'#

#2:21 2:21 Joel 2:28-32
¹⁶⁶2:27 *2:27* or, Hell
#2:28 2:28 Psalm 16:8-11
¹⁶⁷2:31 *2:31* or, Hell
#2:35 2:35 Psalm 110:1

The Acts of the Apostles

²36 "Let all the house of Israel therefore know certainly that God has made him both Lord and Christ, this Jesus whom you crucified."
²37 Now when they heard this, they were cut to the heart, and said to Peter and the rest of the apostles, "Brothers, what shall we do?"
²38 Peter said to them, "Repent, and be baptized, every one of you, in the name of Jesus Christ for the forgiveness of sins, and you will receive the gift of the Holy Spirit. ²39 For the promise is to you, and to your children, and to all who are far off, even as many as the Lord our God will call to himself." ²40 With many other words he testified, and exhorted them, saying, "Save yourselves from this crooked generation!"
²41 Then those who gladly received his word were baptized. There were added that day about three thousand souls. ²42 They continued steadfastly in the apostles' teaching and fellowship, in the breaking of bread, and prayer. ²43 Fear came on every soul, and many wonders and signs were done through the apostles. ²44 All who believed were together, and had all things in common. ²45 They sold their possessions and goods, and distributed them to all, according as anyone had need. ²46 Day by day, continuing steadfastly with one accord in the temple, and breaking bread at home, they took their food with gladness and singleness of heart, ²47 praising God, and having favor with all the people. The Lord added to the assembly day by day those who were being saved. ²

3

³1 Peter and John were going up into the temple at the hour of prayer, the ninth hour.[168] ³2 A certain man who was lame from his mother's womb was being carried, whom they laid daily at the door of the temple which is called Beautiful, to ask gifts for the needy of those who entered into the temple. ³3 Seeing Peter and John about to go into the temple, he asked to receive gifts for the needy. ³4 Peter, fastening his eyes on him, with John, said, "Look at us." ³5 He listened to them, expecting to receive something from them. ³6 But Peter said, "I have no silver or gold, but what I have, that I give you. In the name of Jesus Christ of Nazareth, get up and walk!" ³7 He took him by the

---

[168]**3:1** *3:1* 3:00 p.m.

right hand and raised him up. Immediately his feet and his ankle bones received strength. ³8 Leaping up, he stood and began to walk. He entered with them into the temple, walking, leaping, and praising God. ³9 All the people saw him walking and praising God. ³10 They recognized him, that it was he who used to sit begging for gifts for the needy at the Beautiful Gate of the temple. They were filled with wonder and amazement at what had happened to him. ³11 As the lame man who was healed held on to Peter and John, all the people ran together to them in the porch that is called Solomon's, greatly wondering.

³12 When Peter saw it, he responded to the people, "You men of Israel, why do you marvel at this man? Why do you fasten your eyes on us, as though by our own power or godliness we had made him walk? ³13 The God of Abraham, Isaac, and Jacob, the God of our fathers, has glorified his Servant Jesus, whom you delivered up, and denied in the presence of Pilate, when he had determined to release him. ³14 But you denied the Holy and Righteous One and asked for a murderer to be granted to you, ³15 and killed the Prince of life, whom God raised from the dead, to which we are witnesses. ³16 By faith in his name, his name has made this man strong, whom you see and know. Yes, the faith which is through him has given him this perfect soundness in the presence of you all.

³17 "Now, brothers,[169] I know that you did this in ignorance, as did also your rulers. ³18 But the things which God announced by the mouth of all his prophets, that Christ should suffer, he thus fulfilled. ³19 "Repent therefore, and turn again, that your sins may be blotted out, so that there may come times of refreshing from the presence of the Lord, ³20 and that he may send Christ Jesus, who was ordained for you before, ³21 whom heaven must receive until the times of restoration of all things, which God spoke long ago by the mouth of his holy prophets. ³22 For Moses indeed said to the fathers, 'The Lord God will raise up a prophet for you from among your brothers, like me. You shall listen to him in all things whatever he says to you. ³23 It will be that every soul that will not listen to that prophet will be utterly

---

[169]3:17 *3:17* The word for "brothers" here may be also correctly translated "brothers and sisters" or "siblings."

The Acts of the Apostles

destroyed from among the people.'# ³24 Yes, and all the prophets from Samuel and those who followed after, as many as have spoken, they also told of these days. ³25 You are the children of the prophets, and of the covenant which God made with our fathers, saying to Abraham, 'All the families of the earth will be blessed through your offspring.'¹⁷⁰# ³26 God, having raised up his servant Jesus, sent him to you first to bless you, in turning away every one of you from your wickedness." ³

4

⁴1 As they spoke to the people, the priests and the captain of the temple and the Sadducees came to them, ⁴2 being upset because they taught the people and proclaimed in Jesus the resurrection from the dead. ⁴3 They laid hands on them, and put them in custody until the next day, for it was now evening. ⁴4 But many of those who heard the word believed, and the number of the men came to be about five thousand.

⁴5 In the morning, their rulers, elders, and scribes were gathered together in Jerusalem. ⁴6 Annas the high priest was there, with Caiaphas, John, Alexander, and as many as were relatives of the high priest. ⁴7 When they had stood Peter and John in the middle of them, they inquired, "By what power, or in what name, have you done this?" ⁴8 Then Peter, filled with the Holy Spirit, said to them, "You rulers of the people, and elders of Israel, ⁴9 if we are examined today concerning a good deed done to a crippled man, by what means this man has been healed, ⁴10 may it be known to you all, and to all the people of Israel, that in the name of Jesus Christ of Nazareth, whom you crucified, whom God raised from the dead, this man stands here before you whole in him. ⁴11 He is 'the stone which was regarded as worthless by you, the builders, which has become the head of the corner.'# ⁴12 There is salvation in no one else, for there is no other name under heaven that is given among men, by which we must be saved!"

#3:23 3:23 Deuteronomy 18:15,18-19
¹⁷⁰3:25 *3:25* or, seed
#3:25 3:25 Genesis 22:18; 26:4
#4:11 4:11 Psalm 118:22

The American Book of Prayer

⁴13 Now when they saw the boldness of Peter and John, and had perceived that they were unlearned and ignorant men, they marveled. They recognized that they had been with Jesus. ⁴14 Seeing the man who was healed standing with them, they could say nothing against it. ⁴15 But when they had commanded them to go aside out of the council, they conferred among themselves, ⁴16 saying, "What shall we do to these men? Because indeed a notable miracle has been done through them, as can be plainly seen by all who dwell in Jerusalem, and we can't deny it. ⁴17 But so that this spreads no further among the people, let's threaten them, that from now on they don't speak to anyone in this name." ⁴18 They called them, and commanded them not to speak at all nor teach in the name of Jesus.

⁴19 But Peter and John answered them, "Whether it is right in the sight of God to listen to you rather than to God, judge for yourselves, ⁴20 for we can't help telling the things which we saw and heard."

⁴21 When they had further threatened them, they let them go, finding no way to punish them, because of the people; for everyone glorified God for that which was done. ⁴22 For the man on whom this miracle of healing was performed was more than forty years old.

⁴23 Being let go, they came to their own company and reported all that the chief priests and the elders had said to them. ⁴24 When they heard it, they lifted up their voice to God with one accord, and said, "O Lord, you are God, who made the heaven, the earth, the sea, and all that is in them; ⁴25 who by the mouth of your servant, David, said,
'Why do the nations rage,
and the peoples plot a vain thing?

⁴26 The kings of the earth take a stand,
and the rulers take council together,
against the Lord, and against his Christ.'[171][#]

⁴27 "For truly, in this city against your holy servant, Jesus, whom you anointed, both Herod and Pontius Pilate, with the Gentiles and the people of Israel, were gathered together ⁴28 to do whatever your hand and your council foreordained to happen. ⁴29 Now, Lord, look at their threats, and grant to your servants to speak your word with all boldness, ⁴30 while you stretch out your hand to heal; and that signs

---

[171]4:26 *4:26* Christ (Greek) and Messiah (Hebrew) both mean Anointed One.
[#]4:26 4:26 Psalm 2:1-2

The Acts of the Apostles

and wonders may be done through the name of your holy Servant Jesus."
4:31 When they had prayed, the place was shaken where they were gathered together. They were all filled with the Holy Spirit, and they spoke the word of God with boldness. **4:32** The multitude of those who believed were of one heart and soul. Not one of them claimed that anything of the things which he possessed was his own, but they had all things in common. **4:33** With great power, the apostles gave their testimony of the resurrection of the Lord Jesus. Great grace was on them all. **4:34** For neither was there among them any who lacked, for as many as were owners of lands or houses sold them, and brought the proceeds of the things that were sold, **4:35** and laid them at the apostles' feet, and distribution was made to each, according as anyone had need. **4:36** Joses, who by the apostles was also called Barnabas (which is, being interpreted, Son of Encouragement), a Levite, a man of Cyprus by race, **4:37** having a field, sold it and brought the money and laid it at the apostles' feet. **4**

5

5:1 But a certain man named Ananias, with Sapphira, his wife, sold a possession, **5:2** and kept back part of the price, his wife also being aware of it, then brought a certain part and laid it at the apostles' feet. **5:3** But Peter said, "Ananias, why has Satan filled your heart to lie to the Holy Spirit and to keep back part of the price of the land? **5:4** While you kept it, didn't it remain your own? After it was sold, wasn't it in your power? How is it that you have conceived this thing in your heart? You haven't lied to men, but to God."
5:5 Ananias, hearing these words, fell down and died. Great fear came on all who heard these things. **5:6** The young men arose and wrapped him up, and they carried him out and buried him. **5:7** About three hours later, his wife, not knowing what had happened, came in.
5:8 Peter answered her, "Tell me whether you sold the land for so much."

She said, "Yes, for so much."
5:9 But Peter asked her, "How is it that you have agreed together to tempt the Spirit of the Lord? Behold, the feet of those who have buried your husband are at the door, and they will carry you out."

⁵¹⁰ She fell down immediately at his feet and died. The young men came in and found her dead, and they carried her out and buried her by her husband. ⁵¹¹ Great fear came on the whole assembly, and on all who heard these things. ⁵¹² By the hands of the apostles many signs and wonders were done among the people. They were all with one accord in Solomon's porch. ⁵¹³ None of the rest dared to join them, however the people honored them. ⁵¹⁴ More believers were added to the Lord, multitudes of both men and women. ⁵¹⁵ They even carried out the sick into the streets, and laid them on cots and mattresses, so that as Peter came by, at the least his shadow might overshadow some of them. ⁵¹⁶ The multitude also came together from the cities around Jerusalem, bringing sick people and those who were tormented by unclean spirits: and they were all healed.

⁵¹⁷ But the high priest rose up, and all those who were with him (which is the sect of the Sadducees), and they were filled with jealousy ⁵¹⁸ and laid hands on the apostles, then put them in public custody. ⁵¹⁹ But an angel of the Lord opened the prison doors by night, and brought them out and said, ⁵²⁰ "Go stand and speak in the temple to the people all the words of this life."

⁵²¹ When they heard this, they entered into the temple about daybreak and taught. But the high priest came, and those who were with him, and called the council together, and all the senate of the children of Israel, and sent to the prison to have them brought. ⁵²² But the officers who came didn't find them in the prison. They returned and reported, ⁵²³ "We found the prison shut and locked, and the guards standing before the doors, but when we opened them, we found no one inside!"

⁵²⁴ Now when the high priest, the captain of the temple, and the chief priests heard these words, they were very perplexed about them and what might become of this. ⁵²⁵ One came and told them, "Behold, the men whom you put in prison are in the temple, standing and teaching the people." ⁵²⁶ Then the captain went with the officers, and brought them without violence, for they were afraid that the people might stone them.

⁵²⁷ When they had brought them, they set them before the council. The high priest questioned them, ⁵²⁸ saying, "Didn't we strictly command you not to teach in this name? Behold, you have filled

The Acts of the Apostles

Jerusalem with your teaching, and intend to bring this man's blood on us."

⁵29 But Peter and the apostles answered, "We must obey God rather than men. ⁵30 The God of our fathers raised up Jesus, whom you killed, hanging him on a tree. ⁵31 God exalted him with his right hand to be a Prince and a Savior, to give repentance to Israel, and remission of sins. ⁵32 We are his witnesses of these things; and so also is the Holy Spirit, whom God has given to those who obey him."

⁵33 But they, when they heard this, were cut to the heart, and were determined to kill them. ⁵34 But one stood up in the council, a Pharisee named Gamaliel, a teacher of the law, honored by all the people, and commanded to put the apostles out for a little while.

⁵35 He said to them, "You men of Israel, be careful concerning these men, what you are about to do. ⁵36 For before these days Theudas rose up, making himself out to be somebody; to whom a number of men, about four hundred, joined themselves. He was slain; and all, as many as obeyed him, were dispersed, and came to nothing. ⁵37 After this man, Judas of Galilee rose up in the days of the enrollment, and drew away some people after him. He also perished, and all, as many as obeyed him, were scattered abroad. ⁵38 Now I tell you, withdraw from these men, and leave them alone. For if this counsel or this work is of men, it will be overthrown. ⁵39 But if it is of God, you will not be able to overthrow it, and you would be found even to be fighting against God!"

⁵40 They agreed with him. Summoning the apostles, they beat them and commanded them not to speak in the name of Jesus, and let them go. ⁵41 They therefore departed from the presence of the council, rejoicing that they were counted worthy to suffer dishonor for Jesus' name.

⁵42 Every day, in the temple and at home, they never stopped teaching and preaching Jesus, the Christ. ⁵

6

⁶1 Now in those days, when the number of the disciples was multiplying, a complaint arose from the Hellenists[172] against the

---

[172]6:1 *6:1* The Hellenists used Greek language and culture, even though they were also of Hebrew descent.

Hebrews, because their widows were neglected in the daily service.
⁶2 The twelve summoned the multitude of the disciples and said, "It is not appropriate for us to forsake the word of God and serve tables.
⁶3 Therefore select from among you, brothers, seven men of good report, full of the Holy Spirit and of wisdom, whom we may appoint over this business. ⁶4 But we will continue steadfastly in prayer and in the ministry of the word."
⁶5 These words pleased the whole multitude. They chose Stephen, a man full of faith and of the Holy Spirit, Philip, Prochorus, Nicanor, Timon, Parmenas, and Nicolaus, a proselyte of Antioch; ⁶6 whom they set before the apostles. When they had prayed, they laid their hands on them. ⁶7 The word of God increased and the number of the disciples multiplied in Jerusalem exceedingly. A great company of the priests were obedient to the faith.
⁶8 Stephen, full of faith and power, performed great wonders and signs among the people. ⁶9 But some of those who were of the synagogue called "The Libertines", and of the Cyrenians, of the Alexandrians, and of those of Cilicia and Asia arose, disputing with Stephen. ⁶10 They weren't able to withstand the wisdom and the Spirit by which he spoke. ⁶11 Then they secretly induced men to say, "We have heard him speak blasphemous words against Moses and God."
⁶12 They stirred up the people, the elders, and the scribes, and came against him and seized him, then brought him in to the council,
⁶13 and set up false witnesses who said, "This man never stops speaking blasphemous words against this holy place and the law.
⁶14 For we have heard him say that this Jesus of Nazareth will destroy this place, and will change the customs which Moses delivered to us."
⁶15 All who sat in the council, fastening their eyes on him, saw his face like it was the face of an angel.

7

⁷1 The high priest said, "Are these things so?"
⁷2 He said, "Brothers and fathers, listen. The God of glory appeared to our father Abraham when he was in Mesopotamia, before he lived in Haran, ⁷3 and said to him, 'Get out of your land and away from your

The Acts of the Apostles

relatives, and come into a land which I will show you.'# ⁷4 Then he came out of the land of the Chaldaeans and lived in Haran. From there, when his father was dead, God moved him into this land, where you are now living. ⁷5 He gave him no inheritance in it, no, not so much as to set his foot on. He promised that he would give it to him for a possession, and to his offspring after him, when he still had no child. ⁷6 God spoke in this way: that his offspring would live as aliens in a strange land, and that they would be enslaved and mistreated for four hundred years. ⁷7 'I will judge the nation to which they will be in bondage,' said God, 'and after that they will come out, and serve me in this place.'# ⁷8 He gave him the covenant of circumcision. So Abraham became the father of Isaac, and circumcised him the eighth day. Isaac became the father of Jacob, and Jacob became the father of the twelve patriarchs.

⁷9 "The patriarchs, moved with jealousy against Joseph, sold him into Egypt. God was with him, ⁷10 and delivered him out of all his afflictions, and gave him favor and wisdom before Pharaoh, king of Egypt. He made him governor over Egypt and all his house. ⁷11 Now a famine came over all the land of Egypt and Canaan, and great affliction. Our fathers found no food. ⁷12 But when Jacob heard that there was grain in Egypt, he sent out our fathers the first time. ⁷13 On the second time Joseph was made known to his brothers, and Joseph's race was revealed to Pharaoh. ⁷14 Joseph sent and summoned Jacob, his father, and all his relatives, seventy-five souls. ⁷15 Jacob went down into Egypt and he died, himself and our fathers, ⁷16 and they were brought back to Shechem, and laid in the tomb that Abraham bought for a price in silver from the children of Hamor of Shechem.

⁷17 "But as the time of the promise came close which God had sworn to Abraham, the people grew and multiplied in Egypt, ⁷18 until there arose a different king, who didn't know Joseph. ⁷19 The same took advantage of our race, and mistreated our fathers, and forced them to throw out their babies, so that they wouldn't stay alive. ⁷20 At that time Moses was born, and was exceedingly handsome. He was nourished three months in his father's house. ⁷21 When he was thrown out, Pharaoh's daughter took him up and reared him as her

---

#7:3 7:3 Genesis 12:1
#7:7 7:7 Genesis 15:13-14

own son. ⁷22 Moses was instructed in all the wisdom of the Egyptians. He was mighty in his words and works. ⁷23 But when he was forty years old, it came into his heart to visit his brothers,¹⁷³ the children of Israel. ⁷24 Seeing one of them suffer wrong, he defended him, and avenged him who was oppressed, striking the Egyptian. ⁷25 He supposed that his brothers understood that God, by his hand, was giving them deliverance; but they didn't understand.

⁷26 "The day following, he appeared to them as they fought, and urged them to be at peace again, saying, 'Sirs, you are brothers. Why do you wrong one another?' ⁷27 But he who did his neighbor wrong pushed him away, saying, 'Who made you a ruler and a judge over us? ⁷28 Do you want to kill me, as you killed the Egyptian yesterday?'# ⁷29 Moses fled at this saying, and became a stranger in the land of Midian, where he became the father of two sons.

⁷30 "When forty years were fulfilled, an angel of the Lord appeared to him in the wilderness of Mount Sinai, in a flame of fire in a bush. ⁷31 When Moses saw it, he wondered at the sight. As he came close to see, a voice of the Lord came to him, ⁷32 'I am the God of your fathers, the God of Abraham, the God of Isaac, and the God of Jacob.'# Moses trembled, and dared not look. ⁷33 The Lord said to him, 'Take off your sandals, for the place where you stand is holy ground. ⁷34 I have surely seen the affliction of my people that is in Egypt, and have heard their groaning. I have come down to deliver them. Now come, I will send you into Egypt.'#

⁷35 "This Moses, whom they refused, saying, 'Who made you a ruler and a judge?'—God has sent him as both a ruler and a deliverer by the hand of the angel who appeared to him in the bush. ⁷36 This man led them out, having worked wonders and signs in Egypt, in the Red Sea, and in the wilderness for forty years. ⁷37 This is that Moses, who said to the children of Israel, 'The Lord our God will raise up a prophet for you from among your brothers, like me.'¹⁷⁴# ⁷38 This is he who

---

¹⁷³**7:23** *7:23* The word for "brothers" here and where the context allows may be also correctly translated "brothers and sisters" or "siblings."
#**7:28** 7:28 Exodus 2:14
#**7:32** 7:32 Exodus 3:6
#**7:34** 7:34 Exodus 3:5,7-8,10
¹⁷⁴**7:37** *7:37* TR adds "You shall listen to him."
#**7:37** 7:37 Deuteronomy 18:15

was in the assembly in the wilderness with the angel that spoke to him on Mount Sinai, and with our fathers, who received living revelations to give to us, **739** to whom our fathers wouldn't be obedient, but rejected him, and turned back in their hearts to Egypt, **740** saying to Aaron, 'Make us gods that will go before us, for as for this Moses, who led us out of the land of Egypt, we don't know what has become of him.'# **741** They made a calf in those days, and brought a sacrifice to the idol, and rejoiced in the works of their hands. **742** But God turned, and gave them up to serve the army of the sky,[175] as it is written in the book of the prophets,

'Did you offer to me slain animals and sacrifices
forty years in the wilderness, O house of Israel?
743 You took up the tabernacle of Moloch,
the star of your god Rephan,
the figures which you made to worship.
I will carry you away# beyond Babylon.'

744 "Our fathers had the tabernacle of the testimony in the wilderness, even as he who spoke to Moses commanded him to make it according to the pattern that he had seen; **745** which also our fathers, in their turn, brought in with Joshua when they entered into the possession of the nations, whom God drove out before the face of our fathers, to the days of David, **746** who found favor in the sight of God, and asked to find a habitation for the God of Jacob. **747** But Solomon built him a house. **748** However, the Most High doesn't dwell in temples made with hands, as the prophet says,

749 'heaven is my throne,
and the earth a footstool for my feet.
What kind of house will you build me?' says the Lord.
'Or what is the place of my rest?
750 Didn't my hand make all these things?'#

751 "You stiff-necked and uncircumcised in heart and ears, you always resist the Holy Spirit! As your fathers did, so you do. **752** Which of the prophets didn't your fathers persecute? They killed those who foretold

---

#**7:40** 7:40 Exodus 32:1
[175]**7:42** *7:42* This idiom could also be translated "host of heaven", or "angelic beings", or "heavenly bodies."
#**7:43** 7:43 Amos 5:25-27
#**7:50** 7:50 Isaiah 66:1-2

the coming of the Righteous One, of whom you have now become betrayers and murderers. ⁷53 You received the law as it was ordained by angels, and didn't keep it!"
⁷54 Now when they heard these things, they were cut to the heart, and they gnashed at him with their teeth. ⁷55 But he, being full of the Holy Spirit, looked up steadfastly into heaven and saw the glory of God, and Jesus standing on the right hand of God, ⁷56 and said, "Behold, I see the heavens opened, and the Son of Man standing at the right hand of God!"
⁷57 But they cried out with a loud voice and stopped their ears, then rushed at him with one accord. ⁷58 They threw him out of the city and stoned him. The witnesses placed their garments at the feet of a young man named Saul. ⁷59 They stoned Stephen as he called out, saying, "Lord Jesus, receive my spirit!" ⁷60 He kneeled down, and cried with a loud voice, "Lord, don't hold this sin against them!" When he had said this, he fell asleep. ⁷

8

⁸1 Saul was consenting to his death. A great persecution arose against the assembly which was in Jerusalem in that day. They were all scattered abroad throughout the regions of Judea and Samaria, except for the apostles. ⁸2 Devout men buried Stephen and lamented greatly over him. ⁸3 But Saul ravaged the assembly, entering into every house and dragged both men and women off to prison. ⁸4 Therefore those who were scattered abroad went around preaching the word. ⁸5 Philip went down to the city of Samaria, and proclaimed to them the Christ. ⁸6 The multitudes listened with one accord to the things that were spoken by Philip when they heard and saw the signs which he did. ⁸7 For unclean spirits came out of many of those who had them. They came out, crying with a loud voice. Many who had been paralyzed and lame were healed. ⁸8 There was great joy in that city.
⁸9 But there was a certain man, Simon by name, who used to practice sorcery in the city and amazed the people of Samaria, making himself out to be some great one, ⁸10 to whom they all listened, from the least to the greatest, saying, "This man is that great power of God."
⁸11 They listened to him, because for a long time he had amazed them with his sorceries. ⁸12 But when they believed Philip preaching good

The Acts of the Apostles

news concerning God's Kingdom and the name of Jesus Christ, they were baptized, both men and women. ⁸13 Simon himself also believed. Being baptized, he continued with Philip. Seeing signs and great miracles occurring, he was amazed.

⁸14 Now when the apostles who were at Jerusalem heard that Samaria had received the word of God, they sent Peter and John to them, ⁸15 who, when they had come down, prayed for them, that they might receive the Holy Spirit; ⁸16 for as yet he had fallen on none of them. They had only been baptized in the name of Christ Jesus. ⁸17 Then they laid their hands on them, and they received the Holy Spirit.

⁸18 Now when Simon saw that the Holy Spirit was given through the laying on of the apostles' hands, he offered them money, ⁸19 saying, "Give me also this power, that whomever I lay my hands on may receive the Holy Spirit." ⁸20 But Peter said to him, "May your silver perish with you, because you thought you could obtain the gift of God with money! ⁸21 You have neither part nor lot in this matter, for your heart isn't right before God. ⁸22 Repent therefore of this, your wickedness, and ask God if perhaps the thought of your heart may be forgiven you. ⁸23 For I see that you are in the poison of bitterness and in the bondage of iniquity."

⁸24 Simon answered, "Pray for me to the Lord, that none of the things which you have spoken happen to me."

⁸25 They therefore, when they had testified and spoken the word of the Lord, returned to Jerusalem, and preached the Good News to many villages of the Samaritans. ⁸26 But an angel of the Lord spoke to Philip, saying, "Arise, and go toward the south to the way that goes down from Jerusalem to Gaza. This is a desert."

⁸27 He arose and went; and behold, there was a man of Ethiopia, a eunuch of great authority under Candace, queen of the Ethiopians, who was over all her treasure, who had come to Jerusalem to worship.

⁸28 He was returning and sitting in his chariot, and was reading the prophet Isaiah.

⁸29 The Spirit said to Philip, "Go near, and join yourself to this chariot."

⁸30 Philip ran to him, and heard him reading Isaiah the prophet, and said, "Do you understand what you are reading?"

⁸31 He said, "How can I, unless someone explains it to me?" He begged Philip to come up and sit with him. ⁸32 Now the passage of the Scripture which he was reading was this,
"He was led as a sheep to the slaughter.
As a lamb before his shearer is silent,
so he doesn't open his mouth.
⁸33 In his humiliation, his judgment was taken away.
Who will declare His generation?
For his life is taken from the earth."#
⁸34 The eunuch answered Philip, "Who is the prophet talking about? About himself, or about someone else?"
⁸35 Philip opened his mouth, and beginning from this Scripture, preached to him about Jesus. ⁸36 As they went on the way, they came to some water, and the eunuch said, "Behold, here is water. What is keeping me from being baptized?"
⁸37 ¹⁷⁶ ⁸38 He commanded the chariot to stand still, and they both went down into the water, both Philip and the eunuch, and he baptized him.
⁸39 When they came up out of the water, the Spirit of the Lord caught Philip away, and the eunuch didn't see him any more, for he went on his way rejoicing. ⁸40 But Philip was found at Azotus. Passing through, he preached the Good News to all the cities, until he came to Caesarea. ⁸

9

⁹1 But Saul, still breathing threats and slaughter against the disciples of the Lord, went to the high priest ⁹2 and asked for letters from him to the synagogues of Damascus, that if he found any who were of the Way, whether men or women, he might bring them bound to Jerusalem. ⁹3 As he traveled, he got close to Damascus, and suddenly a light from the sky shone around him. ⁹4 He fell on the earth, and heard a voice saying to him, "Saul, Saul, why do you persecute me?" ⁹5 He said, "Who are you, Lord?"

#8:33 8:33 Isaiah 53:7,8
¹⁷⁶8:37 *8:37* TR adds Philip said, "If you believe with all your heart, you may." He answered, "I believe that Jesus Christ is the Son of God."

The Acts of the Apostles

The Lord said, "I am Jesus, whom you are persecuting.[177] ⁹6 But[178] rise up and enter into the city, then you will be told what you must do."

⁹7 The men who traveled with him stood speechless, hearing the sound, but seeing no one. ⁹8 Saul arose from the ground, and when his eyes were opened, he saw no one. They led him by the hand, and brought him into Damascus. ⁹9 He was without sight for three days, and neither ate nor drank.

⁹10 Now there was a certain disciple at Damascus named Ananias. The Lord said to him in a vision, "Ananias!"
He said, "Behold, it's me, Lord."

⁹11 The Lord said to him, "Arise, and go to the street which is called Straight, and inquire in the house of Judah[179] for one named Saul, a man of Tarsus. For behold, he is praying, ⁹12 and in a vision he has seen a man named Ananias coming in and laying his hands on him, that he might receive his sight."

⁹13 But Ananias answered, "Lord, I have heard from many about this man, how much evil he did to your saints at Jerusalem. ⁹14 Here he has authority from the chief priests to bind all who call on your name."

⁹15 But the Lord said to him, "Go your way, for he is my chosen vessel to bear my name before the nations and kings, and the children of Israel. ⁹16 For I will show him how many things he must suffer for my name's sake."

⁹17 Ananias departed and entered into the house. Laying his hands on him, he said, "Brother Saul, the Lord, who appeared to you on the road by which you came, has sent me that you may receive your sight and be filled with the Holy Spirit." ⁹18 Immediately something like scales fell from his eyes, and he received his sight. He arose and was baptized. ⁹19 He took food and was strengthened. Saul stayed several days with the disciples who were at Damascus. ⁹20 Immediately in the synagogues he proclaimed the Christ, that he is the Son of God. ⁹21 All who heard him were amazed, and said, "Isn't this he who in

---

[177]**9:5** *9:5* TR adds "It's hard for you to kick against the cattle prods."
[178]**9:6** *9:6* TR omits "But"
[179]**9:11** *9:11* or, Judas

Jerusalem made havoc of those who called on this name? And he had come here intending to bring them bound before the chief priests!" ⁹22 But Saul increased more in strength, and confounded the Jews who lived at Damascus, proving that this is the Christ. ⁹23 When many days were fulfilled, the Jews conspired together to kill him, ⁹24 but their plot became known to Saul. They watched the gates both day and night that they might kill him, ⁹25 but his disciples took him by night and let him down through the wall, lowering him in a basket. ⁹26 When Saul had come to Jerusalem, he tried to join himself to the disciples; but they were all afraid of him, not believing that he was a disciple. ⁹27 But Barnabas took him and brought him to the apostles, and declared to them how he had seen the Lord on the way, and that he had spoken to him, and how at Damascus he had preached boldly in the name of Jesus. ⁹28 He was with them entering into[180] Jerusalem, ⁹29 preaching boldly in the name of the Lord Jesus.[181] He spoke and disputed against the Hellenists,[182] but they were seeking to kill him. ⁹30 When the brothers[183] knew it, they brought him down to Caesarea, and sent him off to Tarsus. ⁹31 So the assemblies throughout all Judea, Galilee, and Samaria had peace, and were built up. They were multiplied, walking in the fear of the Lord and in the comfort of the Holy Spirit.

⁹32 As Peter went throughout all those parts, he came down also to the saints who lived at Lydda. ⁹33 There he found a certain man named Aeneas, who had been bedridden for eight years, because he was paralyzed. ⁹34 Peter said to him, "Aeneas, Jesus Christ heals you. Get up and make your bed!" Immediately he arose. ⁹35 All who lived at Lydda and in Sharon saw him, and they turned to the Lord.

⁹36 Now there was at Joppa a certain disciple named Tabitha, which when translated, means Dorcas.[184] This woman was full of good works and acts of mercy which she did. ⁹37 In those days, she became sick, and died. When they had washed her, they laid her in an upper room. ⁹38 As Lydda was near Joppa, the disciples, hearing that Peter

---

[180] 9:28 *9:28* TR and NU add "and going out"
[181] 9:29 *9:29* TR and NU omit "Jesus" and reverse the order of verses 28 & 29.
[182] 9:29 *9:29* The Hellenists were Hebrews who used Greek language and culture.
[183] 9:30 *9:30* The word for "brothers" here and where the context allows may also be correctly translated "brothers and sisters" or "siblings."
[184] 9:36 *9:36* "Dorcas" is Greek for "Gazelle."

The Acts of the Apostles

was there, sent two men[185] to him, imploring him not to delay in coming to them. **9:39** Peter got up and went with them. When he had come, they brought him into the upper room. All the widows stood by him weeping, and showing the coats and garments which Dorcas had made while she was with them. **9:40** Peter sent them all out, and knelt down and prayed. Turning to the body, he said, "Tabitha, get up!" She opened her eyes, and when she saw Peter, she sat up. **9:41** He gave her his hand, and raised her up. Calling the saints and widows, he presented her alive. **9:42** This became known throughout all Joppa, and many believed in the Lord. **9:43** He stayed many days in Joppa with a tanner named Simon. **9**

10

10:1 Now there was a certain man in Caesarea, Cornelius by name, a centurion of what was called the Italian Regiment, **10:2** a devout man, and one who feared God with all his house, who gave gifts for the needy generously to the people, and always prayed to God. **10:3** At about the ninth hour of the day,[186] he clearly saw in a vision an angel of God coming to him, and saying to him, "Cornelius!"
10:4 He, fastening his eyes on him, and being frightened, said, "What is it, Lord?"
He said to him, "Your prayers and your gifts to the needy have gone up for a memorial before God. **10:5** Now send men to Joppa, and get Simon, who is also called Peter. **10:6** He is staying with a tanner named Simon, whose house is by the seaside. [187]
10:7 When the angel who spoke to him had departed, Cornelius called two of his household servants and a devout soldier of those who waited on him continually. **10:8** Having explained everything to them, he sent them to Joppa. **10:9** Now on the next day as they were on their journey, and got close to the city, Peter went up on the housetop to pray at about noon. **10:10** He became hungry and desired to eat, but while they were preparing, he fell into a trance. **10:11** He saw heaven opened and a certain container descending to him, like a great sheet let down by four corners on the earth, **10:12** in which were all kinds of

---

[185]**9:38** *9:38* Reading from NU, TR; MT omits "two men"
[186]**10:3** *10:3* 3:00 p.m.
[187]**10:6** *10:6* TR adds "This one will tell you what it is necessary for you to do."

four-footed animals of the earth, wild animals, reptiles, and birds of the sky. ¹⁰13 A voice came to him, "Rise, Peter, kill and eat!"
¹⁰14 But Peter said, "Not so, Lord; for I have never eaten anything that is common or unclean."
¹⁰15 A voice came to him again the second time, "What God has cleansed, you must not call unclean." ¹⁰16 This was done three times, and immediately the vessel was received up into heaven. ¹⁰17 Now while Peter was very perplexed in himself what the vision which he had seen might mean, behold, the men who were sent by Cornelius, having made inquiry for Simon's house, stood before the gate, ¹⁰18 and called and asked whether Simon, who was also called Peter, was lodging there. ¹⁰19 While Peter was pondering the vision, the Spirit said to him, "Behold, three [188] men seek you. ¹⁰20 But arise, get down, and go with them, doubting nothing; for I have sent them."
¹⁰21 Peter went down to the men, and said, "Behold, I am he whom you seek. Why have you come?"
¹⁰22 They said, "Cornelius, a centurion, a righteous man and one who fears God, and well spoken of by all the nation of the Jews, was directed by a holy angel to invite you to his house, and to listen to what you say." ¹⁰23 So he called them in and provided a place to stay. On the next day Peter arose and went out with them, and some of the brothers from Joppa accompanied him. ¹⁰24 On the next day they entered into Caesarea. Cornelius was waiting for them, having called together his relatives and his near friends. ¹⁰25 When Peter entered, Cornelius met him, fell down at his feet, and worshiped him. ¹⁰26 But Peter raised him up, saying, "Stand up! I myself am also a man."
¹⁰27 As he talked with him, he went in and found many gathered together. ¹⁰28 He said to them, "You yourselves know how it is an unlawful thing for a man who is a Jew to join himself or come to one of another nation, but God has shown me that I shouldn't call any man unholy or unclean. ¹⁰29 Therefore I also came without complaint when I was sent for. I ask therefore, why did you send for me?"
¹⁰30 Cornelius said, "Four days ago, I was fasting until this hour, and at the ninth hour,[189] I prayed in my house, and behold, a man stood before me in bright clothing, ¹⁰31 and said, 'Cornelius, your prayer is

---

[188] 10:19 *10:19* Reading from TR and NU. MT omits "three"
[189] 10:30 *10:30* 3:00 p.m.

The Acts of the Apostles

heard, and your gifts to the needy are remembered in the sight of God. ¹⁰³²Send therefore to Joppa, and summon Simon, who is also called Peter. He is staying in the house of a tanner named Simon, by the seaside. When he comes, he will speak to you.' ¹⁰³³Therefore I sent to you at once, and it was good of you to come. Now therefore we are all here present in the sight of God to hear all things that have been commanded you by God."

¹⁰³⁴Peter opened his mouth and said, "Truly I perceive that God doesn't show favoritism; ¹⁰³⁵but in every nation he who fears him and works righteousness is acceptable to him. ¹⁰³⁶The word which he sent to the children of Israel, preaching good news of peace by Jesus Christ—he is Lord of all— ¹⁰³⁷you yourselves know what happened, which was proclaimed throughout all Judea, beginning from Galilee, after the baptism which John preached; ¹⁰³⁸even Jesus of Nazareth, how God anointed him with the Holy Spirit and with power, who went about doing good and healing all who were oppressed by the devil, for God was with him. ¹⁰³⁹We are witnesses of everything he did both in the country of the Jews, and in Jerusalem; whom they also[190] killed, hanging him on a tree. ¹⁰⁴⁰God raised him up the third day, and gave him to be revealed, ¹⁰⁴¹not to all the people, but to witnesses who were chosen before by God, to us, who ate and drank with him after he rose from the dead. ¹⁰⁴²He commanded us to preach to the people and to testify that this is he who is appointed by God as the Judge of the living and the dead. ¹⁰⁴³All the prophets testify about him, that through his name everyone who believes in him will receive remission of sins."

¹⁰⁴⁴While Peter was still speaking these words, the Holy Spirit fell on all those who heard the word. ¹⁰⁴⁵They of the circumcision who believed were amazed, as many as came with Peter, because the gift of the Holy Spirit was also poured out on the Gentiles. ¹⁰⁴⁶For they heard them speaking in other languages and magnifying God.

Then Peter answered, ¹⁰⁴⁷"Can anyone forbid these people from being baptized with water? They have received the Holy Spirit just like us." ¹⁰⁴⁸He commanded them to be baptized in the name of Jesus Christ. Then they asked him to stay some days. 10

---

[190]10:39 *10:39* TR omits "also"

11

¹¹1 Now the apostles and the brothers[191] who were in Judea heard that the Gentiles had also received the word of God. ¹¹2 When Peter had come up to Jerusalem, those who were of the circumcision contended with him, ¹¹3 saying, "You went in to uncircumcised men, and ate with them!"

¹¹4 But Peter began, and explained to them in order, saying, ¹¹5 "I was in the city of Joppa praying, and in a trance I saw a vision: a certain container descending, like it was a great sheet let down from heaven by four corners. It came as far as me. ¹¹6 When I had looked intently at it, I considered, and saw the four-footed animals of the earth, wild animals, creeping things, and birds of the sky. ¹¹7 I also heard a voice saying to me, 'Rise, Peter, kill and eat!' ¹¹8 But I said, 'Not so, Lord, for nothing unholy or unclean has ever entered into my mouth.'

¹¹9 But a voice answered me the second time out of heaven, 'What God has cleansed, don't you call unclean.' ¹¹10 This was done three times, and all were drawn up again into heaven. ¹¹11 Behold, immediately three men stood before the house where I was, having been sent from Caesarea to me. ¹¹12 The Spirit told me to go with them, without discriminating. These six brothers also accompanied me, and we entered into the man's house. ¹¹13 He told us how he had seen the angel standing in his house, and saying to him, 'Send to Joppa, and get Simon, who is called Peter, ¹¹14 who will speak to you words by which you will be saved, you and all your house.' ¹¹15 As I began to speak, the Holy Spirit fell on them, even as on us at the beginning. ¹¹16 I remembered the word of the Lord, how he said, 'John indeed baptized in water, but you will be baptized in the Holy Spirit.' ¹¹17 If then God gave to them the same gift as us, when we believed in the Lord Jesus Christ, who was I, that I could withstand God?"

¹¹18 When they heard these things, they held their peace, and glorified God, saying, "Then God has also granted to the Gentiles repentance to life!"

¹¹19 They therefore who were scattered abroad by the oppression that arose about Stephen traveled as far as Phoenicia, Cyprus, and Antioch,

---

[191]11:1 *11:1* The word for "brothers" here and where context allows may also be correctly translated "brothers and sisters" or "siblings."

The Acts of the Apostles

speaking the word to no one except to Jews only. ¹¹20 But there were some of them, men of Cyprus and Cyrene, who, when they had come to Antioch, spoke to the Hellenists,¹⁹² preaching the Lord Jesus. ¹¹21 The hand of the Lord was with them, and a great number believed and turned to the Lord. ¹¹22 The report concerning them came to the ears of the assembly which was in Jerusalem. They sent out Barnabas to go as far as Antioch, ¹¹23 who, when he had come, and had seen the grace of God, was glad. He exhorted them all, that with purpose of heart they should remain near to the Lord. ¹¹24 For he was a good man, and full of the Holy Spirit and of faith, and many people were added to the Lord.

¹¹25 Barnabas went out to Tarsus to look for Saul. ¹¹26 When he had found him, he brought him to Antioch. For a whole year they were gathered together with the assembly, and taught many people. The disciples were first called Christians in Antioch.

¹¹27 Now in these days, prophets came down from Jerusalem to Antioch. ¹¹28 One of them named Agabus stood up, and indicated by the Spirit that there should be a great famine all over the world, which also happened in the days of Claudius. ¹¹29 As any of the disciples had plenty, each determined to send relief to the brothers who lived in Judea; ¹¹30 which they also did, sending it to the elders by the hands of Barnabas and Saul. ¹¹

12

¹²1 Now about that time, King Herod stretched out his hands to oppress some of the assembly. ¹²2 He killed James, the brother of John, with the sword. ¹²3 When he saw that it pleased the Jews, he proceeded to seize Peter also. This was during the days of unleavened bread. ¹²4 When he had arrested him, he put him in prison, and delivered him to four squads of four soldiers each to guard him, intending to bring him out to the people after the Passover. ¹²5 Peter therefore was kept in the prison, but constant prayer was made by the assembly to God for him. ¹²6 The same night when Herod was about to bring him out, Peter was sleeping between two soldiers, bound with two chains. Guards in front of the door kept the prison.

---

[192]11:20 *11:20* A Hellenist is someone who keeps Greek customs and culture.

¹²7 And behold, an angel of the Lord stood by him, and a light shone in the cell. He struck Peter on the side, and woke him up, saying, "Stand up quickly!" His chains fell off his hands. ¹²8 The angel said to him, "Get dressed and put on your sandals." He did so. He said to him, "Put on your cloak and follow me." ¹²9 And he went out and followed him. He didn't know that what was being done by the angel was real, but thought he saw a vision. ¹²10 When they were past the first and the second guard, they came to the iron gate that leads into the city, which opened to them by itself. They went out, and went down one street, and immediately the angel departed from him.

¹²11 When Peter had come to himself, he said, "Now I truly know that the Lord has sent out his angel and delivered me out of the hand of Herod, and from everything the Jewish people were expecting."

¹²12 Thinking about that, he came to the house of Mary, the mother of John who was called Mark, where many were gathered together and were praying. ¹²13 When Peter knocked at the door of the gate, a servant girl named Rhoda came to answer. ¹²14 When she recognized Peter's voice, she didn't open the gate for joy, but ran in, and reported that Peter was standing in front of the gate.

¹²15 They said to her, "You are crazy!" But she insisted that it was so. They said, "It is his angel." ¹²16 But Peter continued knocking. When they had opened, they saw him, and were amazed. ¹²17 But he, beckoning to them with his hand to be silent, declared to them how the Lord had brought him out of the prison. He said, "Tell these things to James and to the brothers." Then he departed and went to another place.

¹²18 Now as soon as it was day, there was no small stir among the soldiers about what had become of Peter. ¹²19 When Herod had sought for him, and didn't find him, he examined the guards, then commanded that they should be put to death. He went down from Judea to Caesarea, and stayed there. ¹²20 Now Herod was very angry with the people of Tyre and Sidon. They came with one accord to him, and, having made Blastus, the king's personal aide, their friend, they asked for peace, because their country depended on the king's country for food. ¹²21 On an appointed day, Herod dressed himself in royal clothing, sat on the throne, and gave a speech to them. ¹²22 The people shouted, "The voice of a god, and not of a man!"

The Acts of the Apostles

¹²23 Immediately an angel of the Lord struck him, because he didn't give God the glory. Then he was eaten by worms and died. ¹²24 But the word of God grew and multiplied. ¹²25 Barnabas and Saul returned to[12193] Jerusalem when they had fulfilled their service, also taking with them John who was called Mark.

13

¹³1 Now in the assembly that was at Antioch there were some prophets and teachers: Barnabas, Simeon who was called Niger, Lucius of Cyrene, Manaen the foster brother of Herod the tetrarch, and Saul. ¹³2 As they served the Lord and fasted, the Holy Spirit said, "Separate Barnabas and Saul for me, for the work to which I have called them."

¹³3 Then, when they had fasted and prayed and laid their hands on them, they sent them away. ¹³4 So, being sent out by the Holy Spirit, they went down to Seleucia. From there they sailed to Cyprus.

¹³5 When they were at Salamis, they proclaimed God's word in the Jewish synagogues. They also had John as their attendant. ¹³6 When they had gone through the island to Paphos, they found a certain sorcerer, a false prophet, a Jew, whose name was Bar Jesus, ¹³7 who was with the proconsul, Sergius Paulus, a man of understanding. This man summoned Barnabas and Saul, and sought to hear the word of God. ¹³8 But Elymas the sorcerer (for so is his name by interpretation) withstood them, seeking to turn the proconsul away from the faith.

¹³9 But Saul, who is also called Paul, filled with the Holy Spirit, fastened his eyes on him, ¹³10 and said, "You son of the devil, full of all deceit and all cunning, you enemy of all righteousness, will you not cease to pervert the right ways of the Lord? ¹³11 Now, behold, the hand of the Lord is on you, and you will be blind, not seeing the sun for a season!"

Immediately a mist and darkness fell on him. He went around seeking someone to lead him by the hand. ¹³12 Then the proconsul, when he saw what was done, believed, being astonished at the teaching of the Lord.

---

[193]**12:25** *12:25* TR reads "from" instead of "to"

13 Now Paul and his company set sail from Paphos, and came to Perga in Pamphylia. John departed from them and returned to Jerusalem. **14** But they, passing on from Perga, came to Antioch of Pisidia. They went into the synagogue on the Sabbath day, and sat down. **15** After the reading of the law and the prophets, the rulers of the synagogue sent to them, saying, "Brothers, if you have any word of exhortation for the people, speak."

16 Paul stood up, and beckoning with his hand said, "Men of Israel, and you who fear God, listen. **17** The God of this people[194] chose our fathers, and exalted the people when they stayed as aliens in the land of Egypt, and with an uplifted arm, he led them out of it. **18** For a period of about forty years he put up with them in the wilderness. **19** When he had destroyed seven nations in the land of Canaan, he gave them their land for an inheritance for about four hundred fifty years. **20** After these things, he gave them judges until Samuel the prophet. **21** Afterward they asked for a king, and God gave to them Saul the son of Kish, a man of the tribe of Benjamin, for forty years. **22** When he had removed him, he raised up David to be their king, to whom he also testified, 'I have found David the son of Jesse, a man after my heart, who will do all my will.' **23** From this man's offspring, God has brought salvation[195] to Israel according to his promise, **24** before his coming, when John had first preached the baptism of repentance to Israel.[196] **25** As John was fulfilling his course, he said, 'What do you suppose that I am? I am not he. But behold, one comes after me, the sandals of whose feet I am not worthy to untie.'

26 Brothers, children of the stock of Abraham, and those among you who fear God, the word of this salvation is sent out to you. **27** For those who dwell in Jerusalem, and their rulers, because they didn't know him, nor the voices of the prophets which are read every Sabbath, fulfilled them by condemning him. **28** Though they found no cause for death, they still asked Pilate to have him killed. **29** When they had fulfilled all things that were written about him, they took him down from the tree, and laid him in a tomb. **30** But God raised him from the dead, **31** and he was seen for many days by those who came

---

[194]**13:17** *13:17* TR, NU add "Israel"
[195]**13:23** *13:23* TR, NU read "a Savior, Jesus" instead of "salvation"
[196]**13:24** *13:24* TR, NU read "to all the people of Israel" instead of "to Israel"

The Acts of the Apostles

up with him from Galilee to Jerusalem, who are his witnesses to the people. **13:32** We bring you good news of the promise made to the fathers, **13:33** that God has fulfilled this to us, their children, in that he raised up Jesus. As it is also written in the second psalm,
'You are my Son.
Today I have become your father.'#
13:34 "Concerning that he raised him up from the dead, now no more to return to corruption, he has spoken thus: 'I will give you the holy and sure blessings of David.'# **13:35** Therefore he says also in another psalm, 'You will not allow your Holy One to see decay.'# **13:36** For David, after he had in his own generation served the counsel of God, fell asleep, was laid with his fathers, and saw decay. **13:37** But he whom God raised up saw no decay. **13:38** Be it known to you therefore, brothers,[197] that through this man is proclaimed to you remission of sins, **13:39** and by him everyone who believes is justified from all things, from which you could not be justified by the law of Moses.
13:40 Beware therefore, lest that come on you which is spoken in the prophets:
13:41 'Behold, you scoffers, and wonder, and perish;
for I work a work in your days,
a work which you will in no way believe, if one declares it to you.'" #
13:42 So when the Jews went out of the synagogue, the Gentiles begged that these words might be preached to them the next Sabbath.
13:43 Now when the synagogue broke up, many of the Jews and of the devout proselytes followed Paul and Barnabas; who, speaking to them, urged them to continue in the grace of God. **13:44** The next Sabbath, almost the whole city was gathered together to hear the word of God.
13:45 But when the Jews saw the multitudes, they were filled with jealousy, and contradicted the things which were spoken by Paul, and blasphemed.
13:46 Paul and Barnabas spoke out boldly, and said, "It was necessary that God's word should be spoken to you first. Since indeed you

---

#**13:33** 13:33 Psalm 2:7
#**13:34** 13:34 Isaiah 55:3
#**13:35** 13:35 Psalm 16:10
[197]**13:38** *13:38* The word for "brothers" here and where the context allows may also be correctly translated "brothers and sisters" or "siblings."
#**13:41** 13:41 Habakkuk 1:5

thrust it from yourselves, and judge yourselves unworthy of eternal life, behold, we turn to the Gentiles. ¹³47 For so has the Lord commanded us, saying,
'I have set you as a light for the Gentiles,
that you should bring salvation to the uttermost parts of the earth.'" #
¹³48 As the Gentiles heard this, they were glad, and glorified the word of God. As many as were appointed to eternal life believed. ¹³49 The Lord's word was spread abroad throughout all the region. ¹³50 But the Jews stirred up the devout and prominent women and the chief men of the city, and stirred up a persecution against Paul and Barnabas, and threw them out of their borders. ¹³51 But they shook off the dust of their feet against them, and came to Iconium. ¹³52 The disciples were filled with joy and with the Holy Spirit. ¹³

14

¹⁴1 In Iconium, they entered together into the synagogue of the Jews, and so spoke that a great multitude both of Jews and of Greeks believed. ¹⁴2 But the disbelieving¹⁹⁸ Jews stirred up and embittered the souls of the Gentiles against the brothers. ¹⁴3 Therefore they stayed there a long time, speaking boldly in the Lord, who testified to the word of his grace, granting signs and wonders to be done by their hands. ¹⁴4 But the multitude of the city was divided. Part sided with the Jews, and part with the apostles. ¹⁴5 When some of both the Gentiles and the Jews, with their rulers, made a violent attempt to mistreat and stone them, ¹⁴6 they became aware of it and fled to the cities of Lycaonia, Lystra, Derbe, and the surrounding region. ¹⁴7 There they preached the Good News.
¹⁴8 At Lystra a certain man sat, impotent in his feet, a cripple from his mother's womb, who never had walked. ¹⁴9 He was listening to Paul speaking, who, fastening eyes on him, and seeing that he had faith to be made whole, ¹⁴10 said with a loud voice, "Stand upright on your feet!" He leaped up and walked. ¹⁴11 When the multitude saw what Paul had done, they lifted up their voice, saying in the language of Lycaonia, "The gods have come down to us in the likeness of men!" ¹⁴12 They called Barnabas "Jupiter", and Paul "Mercury", because he

---

#**13:47** 13:47 Isaiah 49:6
¹⁹⁸**14:2** *14:2* or, disobedient

The Acts of the Apostles

was the chief speaker. ¹⁴13 The priest of Jupiter, whose temple was in front of their city, brought oxen and garlands to the gates, and would have made a sacrifice along with the multitudes. ¹⁴14 But when the apostles, Barnabas and Paul, heard of it, they tore their clothes, and sprang into the multitude, crying out, ¹⁴15 "Men, why are you doing these things? We also are men of like passions with you, and bring you good news, that you should turn from these vain things to the living God, who made the sky, the earth, the sea, and all that is in them; ¹⁴16 who in the generations gone by allowed all the nations to walk in their own ways. ¹⁴17 Yet he didn't leave himself without witness, in that he did good and gave you[199] rains from the sky and fruitful seasons, filling our hearts with food and gladness."

¹⁴18 Even saying these things, they hardly stopped the multitudes from making a sacrifice to them. ¹⁴19 But some Jews from Antioch and Iconium came there, and having persuaded the multitudes, they stoned Paul, and dragged him out of the city, supposing that he was dead.

¹⁴20 But as the disciples stood around him, he rose up, and entered into the city. On the next day he went out with Barnabas to Derbe. ¹⁴21 When they had preached the Good News to that city, and had made many disciples, they returned to Lystra, Iconium, and Antioch, ¹⁴22 strengthening the souls of the disciples, exhorting them to continue in the faith, and that through many afflictions we must enter into God's Kingdom. ¹⁴23 When they had appointed elders for them in every assembly, and had prayed with fasting, they commended them to the Lord, on whom they had believed.

¹⁴24 They passed through Pisidia, and came to Pamphylia. ¹⁴25 When they had spoken the word in Perga, they went down to Attalia. ¹⁴26 From there they sailed to Antioch, from where they had been committed to the grace of God for the work which they had fulfilled. ¹⁴27 When they had arrived, and had gathered the assembly together, they reported all the things that God had done with them, and that he had opened a door of faith to the nations. ¹⁴28 They stayed there with the disciples for a long time. ¹⁴

---

[199]**14:17** *14:17* TR reads "us" instead of "you"

15

15:1 Some men came down from Judea and taught the brothers,[200] "Unless you are circumcised after the custom of Moses, you can't be saved." **15:2** Therefore when Paul and Barnabas had no small discord and discussion with them, they appointed Paul and Barnabas, and some others of them, to go up to Jerusalem to the apostles and elders about this question. **15:3** They, being sent on their way by the assembly, passed through both Phoenicia and Samaria, declaring the conversion of the Gentiles. They caused great joy to all the brothers. **15:4** When they had come to Jerusalem, they were received by the assembly and the apostles and the elders, and they reported everything that God had done with them.

15:5 But some of the sect of the Pharisees who believed rose up, saying, "It is necessary to circumcise them, and to command them to keep the law of Moses."

15:6 The apostles and the elders were gathered together to see about this matter. **15:7** When there had been much discussion, Peter rose up and said to them, "Brothers, you know that a good while ago God made a choice among you that by my mouth the nations should hear the word of the Good News and believe. **15:8** God, who knows the heart, testified about them, giving them the Holy Spirit, just like he did to us. **15:9** He made no distinction between us and them, cleansing their hearts by faith. **15:10** Now therefore why do you tempt God, that you should put a yoke on the neck of the disciples which neither our fathers nor we were able to bear? **15:11** But we believe that we are saved through the grace of the Lord Jesus, [201] just as they are."

15:12 All the multitude kept silence, and they listened to Barnabas and Paul reporting what signs and wonders God had done among the nations through them. **15:13** After they were silent, James answered, "Brothers, listen to me. **15:14** Simeon has reported how God first visited the nations to take out of them a people for his name. **15:15** This agrees with the words of the prophets. As it is written,
15:16 'After these things I will return.
I will again build the tabernacle of David, which has fallen.

---

[200]**15:1** *15:1* The word for "brothers" here and where the context allows may also be correctly translated "brothers and sisters" or "siblings."
[201]**15:11** *15:11* TR adds "Christ"

The Acts of the Apostles

I will again build its ruins.
I will set it up ¹⁵17 that the rest of men may seek after the Lord;
all the Gentiles who are called by my name,
says the Lord, who does all these things.'#
¹⁵18 "All of God's works are known to him from eternity.
¹⁵19 Therefore my judgment is that we don't trouble those from among the Gentiles who turn to God, ¹⁵20 but that we write to them that they abstain from the pollution of idols, from sexual immorality, from what is strangled, and from blood. ¹⁵21 For Moses from generations of old has in every city those who preach him, being read in the synagogues every Sabbath."
¹⁵22 Then it seemed good to the apostles and the elders, with the whole assembly, to choose men out of their company, and send them to Antioch with Paul and Barnabas: Judas called Barsabbas, and Silas, chief men among the brothers. ²⁰² ¹⁵23 They wrote these things by their hand:
"The apostles, the elders, and the brothers, to the brothers who are of the Gentiles in Antioch, Syria, and Cilicia: greetings. ¹⁵24 Because we have heard that some who went out from us have troubled you with words, unsettling your souls, saying, 'You must be circumcised and keep the law,' to whom we gave no commandment; ¹⁵25 it seemed good to us, having come to one accord, to choose out men and send them to you with our beloved Barnabas and Paul, ¹⁵26 men who have risked their lives for the name of our Lord Jesus Christ. ¹⁵27 We have sent therefore Judas and Silas, who themselves will also tell you the same things by word of mouth. ¹⁵28 For it seemed good to the Holy Spirit, and to us, to lay no greater burden on you than these necessary things: ¹⁵29 that you abstain from things sacrificed to idols, from blood, from things strangled, and from sexual immorality, from which if you keep yourselves, it will be well with you. Farewell."
¹⁵30 So, when they were sent off, they came to Antioch. Having gathered the multitude together, they delivered the letter. ¹⁵31 When they had read it, they rejoiced over the encouragement. ¹⁵32 Judas and Silas, also being prophets themselves, encouraged the brothers with

---

#**15:17** 15:17 Amos 9:11-12
²⁰²**15:22** *15:22* The word for "brothers" here and where the context allows may also be correctly translated "brothers and sisters" or "siblings."

many words and strengthened them. **15:33** After they had spent some time there, they were sent back with greetings from the brothers to the apostles. **15:34** [203] **15:35** But Paul and Barnabas stayed in Antioch, teaching and preaching the word of the Lord, with many others also. **15:36** After some days Paul said to Barnabas, "Let's return now and visit our brothers in every city in which we proclaimed the word of the Lord, to see how they are doing." **15:37** Barnabas planned to take John, who was called Mark, with them also. **15:38** But Paul didn't think that it was a good idea to take with them someone who had withdrawn from them in Pamphylia, and didn't go with them to do the work. **15:39** Then the contention grew so sharp that they separated from each other. Barnabas took Mark with him and sailed away to Cyprus, **15:40** but Paul chose Silas and went out, being commended by the brothers to the grace of God. **15:41** He went through Syria and Cilicia, strengthening the assemblies.

16

16:1 He came to Derbe and Lystra: and behold, a certain disciple was there, named Timothy, the son of a Jewess who believed; but his father was a Greek. **16:2** The brothers who were at Lystra and Iconium gave a good testimony about him. **16:3** Paul wanted to have him go out with him, and he took and circumcised him because of the Jews who were in those parts; for they all knew that his father was a Greek.
16:4 As they went on their way through the cities, they delivered the decrees to them to keep which had been ordained by the apostles and elders who were at Jerusalem. **16:5** So the assemblies were strengthened in the faith, and increased in number daily.
16:6 When they had gone through the region of Phrygia and Galatia, they were forbidden by the Holy Spirit to speak the word in Asia.
16:7 When they had come opposite Mysia, they tried to go into Bithynia, but the Spirit didn't allow them. **16:8** Passing by Mysia, they came down to Troas. **16:9** A vision appeared to Paul in the night. There was a man of Macedonia standing, begging him, and saying, "Come over into Macedonia and help us." **16:10** When he had seen the vision, immediately we sought to go out to Macedonia, concluding that the

---

[203] **15:34** *15:34* Some manuscripts add: But it seemed good to Silas to stay there.

The Acts of the Apostles

Lord had called us to preach the Good News to them. ¹⁶11 Setting sail therefore from Troas, we made a straight course to Samothrace, and the day following to Neapolis; ¹⁶12 and from there to Philippi, which is a city of Macedonia, the foremost of the district, a Roman colony. We were staying some days in this city.

¹⁶13 On the Sabbath day we went outside of the city by a riverside, where we supposed there was a place of prayer, and we sat down and spoke to the women who had come together. ¹⁶14 A certain woman named Lydia, a seller of purple, of the city of Thyatira, one who worshiped God, heard us. The Lord opened her heart to listen to the things which were spoken by Paul. ¹⁶15 When she and her household were baptized, she begged us, saying, "If you have judged me to be faithful to the Lord, come into my house and stay." So she persuaded us.

¹⁶16 As we were going to prayer, a certain girl having a spirit of divination met us, who brought her masters much gain by fortune telling. ¹⁶17 Following Paul and us, she cried out, "These men are servants of the Most High God, who proclaim to us a way of salvation!" ¹⁶18 She was doing this for many days.

But Paul, becoming greatly annoyed, turned and said to the spirit, "I command you in the name of Jesus Christ to come out of her!" It came out that very hour. ¹⁶19 But when her masters saw that the hope of their gain was gone, they seized Paul and Silas, and dragged them into the marketplace before the rulers. ¹⁶20 When they had brought them to the magistrates, they said, "These men, being Jews, are agitating our city ¹⁶21 and advocate customs which it is not lawful for us to accept or to observe, being Romans."

¹⁶22 The multitude rose up together against them and the magistrates tore their clothes from them, then commanded them to be beaten with rods. ¹⁶23 When they had laid many stripes on them, they threw them into prison, charging the jailer to keep them safely, ¹⁶24 who, having received such a command, threw them into the inner prison, and secured their feet in the stocks.

¹⁶25 But about midnight Paul and Silas were praying and singing hymns to God, and the prisoners were listening to them.

¹⁶26 Suddenly there was a great earthquake, so that the foundations of the prison were shaken; and immediately all the doors were opened, and everyone's bonds were loosened. ¹⁶27 The jailer, being roused out

of sleep and seeing the prison doors open, drew his sword and was about to kill himself, supposing that the prisoners had escaped. ¹⁶28 But Paul cried with a loud voice, saying, "Don't harm yourself, for we are all here!"

¹⁶29 He called for lights, sprang in, fell down trembling before Paul and Silas, ¹⁶30 brought them out, and said, "Sirs, what must I do to be saved?"

¹⁶31 They said, "Believe in the Lord Jesus Christ, and you will be saved, you and your household." ¹⁶32 They spoke the word of the Lord to him, and to all who were in his house.

¹⁶33 He took them the same hour of the night and washed their stripes, and was immediately baptized, he and all his household.

¹⁶34 He brought them up into his house, and set food before them, and rejoiced greatly, with all his household, having believed in God.

¹⁶35 But when it was day, the magistrates sent the sergeants, saying, "Let those men go."

¹⁶36 The jailer reported these words to Paul, saying, "The magistrates have sent to let you go; now therefore come out and go in peace."

¹⁶37 But Paul said to them, "They have beaten us publicly without a trial, men who are Romans, and have cast us into prison! Do they now release us secretly? No, most certainly, but let them come themselves and bring us out!"

¹⁶38 The sergeants reported these words to the magistrates, and they were afraid when they heard that they were Romans, ¹⁶39 and they came and begged them. When they had brought them out, they asked them to depart from the city. ¹⁶40 They went out of the prison, and entered into Lydia's house. When they had seen the brothers, they encouraged them, then departed. ¹⁶

17

¹⁷1 Now when they had passed through Amphipolis and Apollonia, they came to Thessalonica, where there was a Jewish synagogue.

¹⁷2 Paul, as was his custom, went in to them, and for three Sabbath days reasoned with them from the Scriptures, ¹⁷3 explaining and demonstrating that the Christ had to suffer and rise again from the dead, and saying, "This Jesus, whom I proclaim to you, is the Christ."

The Acts of the Apostles

¹⁷4 Some of them were persuaded, and joined Paul and Silas, of the devout Greeks a great multitude, and not a few of the chief women. ¹⁷5 But the unpersuaded Jews took along[204] some wicked men from the marketplace, and gathering a crowd, set the city in an uproar. Assaulting the house of Jason, they sought to bring them out to the people. ¹⁷6 When they didn't find them, they dragged Jason and certain brothers [205] before the rulers of the city, crying, "These who have turned the world upside down have come here also, ¹⁷7 whom Jason has received. These all act contrary to the decrees of Caesar, saying that there is another king, Jesus!" ¹⁷8 The multitude and the rulers of the city were troubled when they heard these things. ¹⁷9 When they had taken security from Jason and the rest, they let them go. ¹⁷10 The brothers immediately sent Paul and Silas away by night to Beroea. When they arrived, they went into the Jewish synagogue.

¹⁷11 Now these were more noble than those in Thessalonica, in that they received the word with all readiness of mind, examining the Scriptures daily to see whether these things were so. ¹⁷12 Many of them therefore believed; also of the prominent Greek women, and not a few men. ¹⁷13 But when the Jews of Thessalonica had knowledge that the word of God was proclaimed by Paul at Beroea also, they came there likewise, agitating the multitudes. ¹⁷14 Then the brothers immediately sent out Paul to go as far as to the sea, and Silas and Timothy still stayed there. ¹⁷15 But those who escorted Paul brought him as far as Athens. Receiving a commandment to Silas and Timothy that they should come to him very quickly, they departed.

¹⁷16 Now while Paul waited for them at Athens, his spirit was provoked within him as he saw the city full of idols. ¹⁷17 So he reasoned in the synagogue with the Jews and the devout persons, and in the marketplace every day with those who met him. ¹⁷18 Some of the Epicurean and Stoic philosophers also[206] were conversing with him. Some said, "What does this babbler want to say?"

Others said, "He seems to be advocating foreign deities," because he preached Jesus and the resurrection.

---

[204]17:5 *17:5* TR reads "And the Jews who were unpersuaded, becoming envious and taking along" instead of "But the unpersuaded Jews took along"

[205]17:6 *17:6* The word for "brothers" here and where the context allows may be also correctly translated "brothers and sisters" or "siblings."

[206]17:18 *17:18* TR omits "also"

17:19 They took hold of him and brought him to the Areopagus, saying, "May we know what this new teaching is, which you are speaking about? **17:20** For you bring certain strange things to our ears. We want to know therefore what these things mean." **17:21** Now all the Athenians and the strangers living there spent their time in nothing else, but either to tell or to hear some new thing.

17:22 Paul stood in the middle of the Areopagus, and said, "You men of Athens, I perceive that you are very religious in all things. **17:23** For as I passed along and observed the objects of your worship, I also found an altar with this inscription: 'TO AN UNKNOWN GOD.' What therefore you worship in ignorance, I announce to you. **17:24** The God who made the world and all things in it, he, being Lord of heaven and earth, doesn't dwell in temples made with hands. **17:25** He isn't served by men's hands, as though he needed anything, seeing he himself gives to all life and breath, and all things. **17:26** He made from one blood every nation of men to dwell on all the surface of the earth, having determined appointed seasons, and the boundaries of their dwellings, **17:27** that they should seek the Lord, if perhaps they might reach out for him and find him, though he is not far from each one of us. **17:28** 'For in him we live, move, and have our being.' As some of your own poets have said, 'For we are also his offspring.' **17:29** Being then the offspring of God, we ought not to think that the Divine Nature is like gold, or silver, or stone, engraved by art and design of man. **17:30** The times of ignorance therefore God overlooked. But now he commands that all people everywhere should repent, **17:31** because he has appointed a day in which he will judge the world in righteousness by the man whom he has ordained; of which he has given assurance to all men, in that he has raised him from the dead."

17:32 Now when they heard of the resurrection of the dead, some mocked; but others said, "We want to hear you again concerning this." **17:33** Thus Paul went out from among them. **17:34** But certain men joined with him and believed, among whom also was Dionysius the Areopagite, and a woman named Damaris, and others with them. 17

18

18:1 After these things Paul departed from Athens, and came to Corinth. **18:2** He found a certain Jew named Aquila, a man of Pontus by

The Acts of the Apostles

race, who had recently come from Italy, with his wife Priscilla, because Claudius had commanded all the Jews to depart from Rome. He came to them, ¹⁸3 and because he practiced the same trade, he lived with them and worked, for by trade they were tent makers. ¹⁸4 He reasoned in the synagogue every Sabbath and persuaded Jews and Greeks.

¹⁸5 But when Silas and Timothy came down from Macedonia, Paul was compelled by the Spirit, testifying to the Jews that Jesus was the Christ. ¹⁸6 When they opposed him and blasphemed, he shook out his clothing and said to them, "Your blood be on your own heads! I am clean. From now on, I will go to the Gentiles!"

¹⁸7 He departed there, and went into the house of a certain man named Justus, one who worshiped God, whose house was next door to the synagogue. ¹⁸8 Crispus, the ruler of the synagogue, believed in the Lord with all his house. Many of the Corinthians, when they heard, believed and were baptized. ¹⁸9 The Lord said to Paul in the night by a vision, "Don't be afraid, but speak and don't be silent; ¹⁸10 for I am with you, and no one will attack you to harm you, for I have many people in this city."

¹⁸11 He lived there a year and six months, teaching the word of God among them. ¹⁸12 But when Gallio was proconsul of Achaia, the Jews with one accord rose up against Paul and brought him before the judgment seat, ¹⁸13 saying, "This man persuades men to worship God contrary to the law."

¹⁸14 But when Paul was about to open his mouth, Gallio said to the Jews, "If indeed it were a matter of wrong or of wicked crime, you Jews, it would be reasonable that I should bear with you; ¹⁸15 but if they are questions about words and names and your own law, look to it yourselves. For I don't want to be a judge of these matters." ¹⁸16 So he drove them from the judgment seat.

¹⁸17 Then all the Greeks seized Sosthenes, the ruler of the synagogue, and beat him before the judgment seat. Gallio didn't care about any of these things.

¹⁸18 Paul, having stayed after this many more days, took his leave of the brothers, [20]7 and sailed from there for Syria, together with Priscilla and Aquila. He shaved his head in Cenchreae, for he had a vow.

---

[20]**18:18** *18:18* The word for "brothers" here and where the context allows may also be correctly translated "brothers and sisters" or "siblings."

[18]19 He came to Ephesus, and he left them there; but he himself entered into the synagogue, and reasoned with the Jews. [18]20 When they asked him to stay with them a longer time, he declined; [18]21 but taking his leave of them, he said, "I must by all means keep this coming feast in Jerusalem, but I will return again to you if God wills." Then he set sail from Ephesus.
[18]22 When he had landed at Caesarea, he went up and greeted the assembly, and went down to Antioch. [18]23 Having spent some time there, he departed, and went through the region of Galatia, and Phrygia, in order, establishing all the disciples. [18]24 Now a certain Jew named Apollos, an Alexandrian by race, an eloquent man, came to Ephesus. He was mighty in the Scriptures. [18]25 This man had been instructed in the way of the Lord; and being fervent in spirit, he spoke and taught accurately the things concerning Jesus, although he knew only the baptism of John. [18]26 He began to speak boldly in the synagogue. But when Priscilla and Aquila heard him, they took him aside, and explained to him the way of God more accurately.
[18]27 When he had determined to pass over into Achaia, the brothers encouraged him, and wrote to the disciples to receive him. When he had come, he greatly helped those who had believed through grace; [18]28 for he powerfully refuted the Jews, publicly showing by the Scriptures that Jesus was the Christ. [18]

19

[19]1 While Apollos was at Corinth, Paul, having passed through the upper country, came to Ephesus and found certain disciples. [19]2 He said to them, "Did you receive the Holy Spirit when you believed?"
They said to him, "No, we haven't even heard that there is a Holy Spirit."
[19]3 He said, "Into what then were you baptized?"
They said, "Into John's baptism."
[19]4 Paul said, "John indeed baptized with the baptism of repentance, saying to the people that they should believe in the one who would come after him, that is, in Jesus."
[19]5 When they heard this, they were baptized in the name of the Lord Jesus. [19]6 When Paul had laid his hands on them, the Holy Spirit came on them and they spoke with other languages and prophesied.

The Acts of the Apostles

¹⁹7 They were about twelve men in all. ¹⁹8 He entered into the synagogue and spoke boldly for a period of three months, reasoning and persuading about the things concerning God's Kingdom.
¹⁹9 But when some were hardened and disobedient, speaking evil of the Way before the multitude, he departed from them, and separated the disciples, reasoning daily in the school of Tyrannus. ¹⁹10 This continued for two years, so that all those who lived in Asia heard the word of the Lord Jesus, both Jews and Greeks.
¹⁹11 God worked special miracles by the hands of Paul, ¹⁹12 so that even handkerchiefs or aprons were carried away from his body to the sick, and the diseases departed from them, and the evil spirits went out. ¹⁹13 But some of the itinerant Jews, exorcists, took on themselves to invoke over those who had the evil spirits the name of the Lord Jesus, saying, "We adjure you by Jesus whom Paul preaches."
¹⁹14 There were seven sons of one Sceva, a Jewish chief priest, who did this.
¹⁹15 The evil spirit answered, "Jesus I know, and Paul I know, but who are you?" ¹⁹16 The man in whom the evil spirit was leaped on them, overpowered them, and prevailed against them, so that they fled out of that house naked and wounded. ¹⁹17 This became known to all, both Jews and Greeks, who lived at Ephesus. Fear fell on them all, and the name of the Lord Jesus was magnified. ¹⁹18 Many also of those who had believed came, confessing, and declaring their deeds.
¹⁹19 Many of those who practiced magical arts brought their books together and burned them in the sight of all. They counted their price, and found it to be fifty thousand pieces of silver.[208] ¹⁹20 So the word of the Lord was growing and becoming mighty.
¹⁹21 Now after these things had ended, Paul determined in the Spirit, when he had passed through Macedonia and Achaia, to go to Jerusalem, saying, "After I have been there, I must also see Rome."
¹⁹22 Having sent into Macedonia two of those who served him, Timothy and Erastus, he himself stayed in Asia for a while. ¹⁹23 About that time there arose no small disturbance concerning the Way.
¹⁹24 For a certain man named Demetrius, a silversmith who made

---

[208]**19:19** *19:19* The 50,000 pieces of silver here probably referred to 50,000 drachmas. If so, the value of the burned books was equivalent to about 160 man-years of wages for agricultural laborers

silver shrines of Artemis, brought no little business to the craftsmen, ¹⁹²⁵ whom he gathered together, with the workmen of like occupation, and said, "Sirs, you know that by this business we have our wealth. ¹⁹²⁶ You see and hear that not at Ephesus alone, but almost throughout all Asia, this Paul has persuaded and turned away many people, saying that they are no gods that are made with hands. ¹⁹²⁷ Not only is there danger that this our trade come into disrepute, but also that the temple of the great goddess Artemis will be counted as nothing and her majesty destroyed, whom all Asia and the world worships."

¹⁹²⁸ When they heard this they were filled with anger, and cried out, saying, "Great is Artemis of the Ephesians!" ¹⁹²⁹ The whole city was filled with confusion, and they rushed with one accord into the theater, having seized Gaius and Aristarchus, men of Macedonia, Paul's companions in travel. ¹⁹³⁰ When Paul wanted to enter in to the people, the disciples didn't allow him. ¹⁹³¹ Certain also of the Asiarchs, being his friends, sent to him and begged him not to venture into the theater. ¹⁹³² Some therefore cried one thing, and some another, for the assembly was in confusion. Most of them didn't know why they had come together. ¹⁹³³ They brought Alexander out of the multitude, the Jews putting him forward. Alexander beckoned with his hand, and would have made a defense to the people. ¹⁹³⁴ But when they perceived that he was a Jew, all with one voice for a time of about two hours cried out, "Great is Artemis of the Ephesians!"

¹⁹³⁵ When the town clerk had quieted the multitude, he said, "You men of Ephesus, what man is there who doesn't know that the city of the Ephesians is temple keeper of the great goddess Artemis, and of the image which fell down from Zeus? ¹⁹³⁶ Seeing then that these things can't be denied, you ought to be quiet and to do nothing rash. ¹⁹³⁷ For you have brought these men here, who are neither robbers of temples nor blasphemers of your goddess. ¹⁹³⁸ If therefore Demetrius and the craftsmen who are with him have a matter against anyone, the courts are open, and there are proconsuls. Let them press charges against one another. ¹⁹³⁹ But if you seek anything about other matters, it will be settled in the regular assembly. ¹⁹⁴⁰ For indeed we are in danger of being accused concerning today's riot, there being no cause. Concerning it, we wouldn't be able to give an account of this

The Acts of the Apostles

commotion." ¹⁹41 When he had thus spoken, he dismissed the assembly. ¹⁹

20

²⁰1 After the uproar had ceased, Paul sent for the disciples, took leave of them, and departed to go into Macedonia. ²⁰2 When he had gone through those parts, and had encouraged them with many words, he came into Greece. ²⁰3 When he had spent three months there, and a plot was made against him by Jews as he was about to set sail for Syria, he determined to return through Macedonia. ²⁰4 These accompanied him as far as Asia: Sopater of Beroea; Aristarchus and Secundus of the Thessalonians; Gaius of Derbe; Timothy; and Tychicus and Trophimus of Asia. ²⁰5 But these had gone ahead, and were waiting for us at Troas. ²⁰6 We sailed away from Philippi after the days of Unleavened Bread, and came to them at Troas in five days, where we stayed seven days.

²⁰7 On the first day of the week, when the disciples were gathered together to break bread, Paul talked with them, intending to depart on the next day, and continued his speech until midnight. ²⁰8 There were many lights in the upper room where we[209] were gathered together.

²⁰9 A certain young man named Eutychus sat in the window, weighed down with deep sleep. As Paul spoke still longer, being weighed down by his sleep, he fell down from the third floor and was taken up dead.

²⁰10 Paul went down and fell upon him, and embracing him said, "Don't be troubled, for his life is in him."

²⁰11 When he had gone up, and had broken bread and eaten, and had talked with them a long while, even until break of day, he departed.

²⁰12 They brought the boy in alive, and were greatly comforted.

²⁰13 But we, going ahead to the ship, set sail for Assos, intending to take Paul aboard there; for he had so arranged, intending himself to go by land. ²⁰14 When he met us at Assos, we took him aboard, and came to Mitylene. ²⁰15 Sailing from there, we came the following day opposite Chios. The next day we touched at Samos and stayed at Trogyllium, and the day after we came to Miletus. ²⁰16 For Paul had determined to sail past Ephesus, that he might not have to spend time

---

[209]**20:8** *20:8* TR reads "they" instead of "we"

in Asia; for he was hastening, if it were possible for him, to be in Jerusalem on the day of Pentecost.

[20]17 From Miletus he sent to Ephesus, and called to himself the elders of the assembly. [20]18 When they had come to him, he said to them, "You yourselves know, from the first day that I set foot in Asia, how I was with you all the time, [20]19 serving the Lord with all humility, with many tears, and with trials which happened to me by the plots of the Jews; [20]20 how I didn't shrink from declaring to you anything that was profitable, teaching you publicly and from house to house,

[20]21 testifying both to Jews and to Greeks repentance toward God, and faith toward our Lord Jesus.[210] [20]22 Now, behold, I go bound by the Spirit to Jerusalem, not knowing what will happen to me there; [20]23 except that the Holy Spirit testifies in every city, saying that bonds and afflictions wait for me. [20]24 But these things don't count; nor do I hold my life dear to myself, so that I may finish my race with joy, and the ministry which I received from the Lord Jesus, to fully testify to the Good News of the grace of God.

[20]25 "Now, behold, I know that you all, among whom I went about preaching God's Kingdom, will see my face no more. [20]26 Therefore I testify to you today that I am clean from the blood of all men, [20]27 for I didn't shrink from declaring to you the whole counsel of God.

[20]28 Take heed, therefore, to yourselves, and to all the flock, in which the Holy Spirit has made you overseers, to shepherd the assembly of the Lord and [211] God which he purchased with his own blood.

[20]29 For I know that after my departure, vicious wolves will enter in among you, not sparing the flock. [20]30 Men will arise from among your own selves, speaking perverse things, to draw away the disciples after them. [20]31 Therefore watch, remembering that for a period of three years I didn't cease to admonish everyone night and day with tears. [20]32 Now, brothers,[212] I entrust you to God and to the word of his grace, which is able to build up, and to give you the inheritance among all those who are sanctified. [20]33 I coveted no one's silver, gold, or clothing. [20]34 You yourselves know that these hands served

---

[210]**20:21** *20:21* TR adds "Christ"
[211]**20:28** *20:28* TR, NU omit "the Lord and"
[212]**20:32** *20:32* The word for "brothers" here and where the context allows may also be correctly translated "brothers and sisters" or "siblings."

The Acts of the Apostles

my necessities, and those who were with me. ²⁰35 In all things I gave you an example, that so laboring you ought to help the weak, and to remember the words of the Lord Jesus, that he himself said, 'It is more blessed to give than to receive.'"
²⁰36 When he had spoken these things, he knelt down and prayed with them all. ²⁰37 They all wept freely, and fell on Paul's neck and kissed him, ²⁰38 sorrowing most of all because of the word which he had spoken, that they should see his face no more. Then they accompanied him to the ship. ²⁰

21

²¹1 When we had departed from them and had set sail, we came with a straight course to Cos, and the next day to Rhodes, and from there to Patara. ²¹2 Having found a ship crossing over to Phoenicia, we went aboard, and set sail. ²¹3 When we had come in sight of Cyprus, leaving it on the left hand, we sailed to Syria and landed at Tyre, for the ship was there to unload her cargo. ²¹4 Having found disciples, we stayed there seven days. These said to Paul through the Spirit that he should not go up to Jerusalem. ²¹5 When those days were over, we departed and went on our journey. They all, with wives and children, brought us on our way until we were out of the city. Kneeling down on the beach, we prayed. ²¹6 After saying goodbye to each other, we went on board the ship, and they returned home again.
²¹7 When we had finished the voyage from Tyre, we arrived at Ptolemais. We greeted the brothers and stayed with them one day.
²¹8 On the next day, we who were Paul's companions departed, and came to Caesarea.
We entered into the house of Philip the evangelist, who was one of the seven, and stayed with him. ²¹9 Now this man had four virgin daughters who prophesied. ²¹10 As we stayed there some days, a certain prophet named Agabus came down from Judea. ²¹11 Coming to us and taking Paul's belt, he bound his own feet and hands, and said, "Thus says the Holy Spirit: 'So the Jews at Jerusalem will bind the man who owns this belt, and will deliver him into the hands of the Gentiles.'"
²¹12 When we heard these things, both we and they of that place begged him not to go up to Jerusalem. ²¹13 Then Paul answered,

"What are you doing, weeping and breaking my heart? For I am ready not only to be bound, but also to die at Jerusalem for the name of the Lord Jesus."

²¹14 When he would not be persuaded, we ceased, saying, "The Lord's will be done."

²¹15 After these days we took up our baggage and went up to Jerusalem. ²¹16 Some of the disciples from Caesarea also went with us, bringing one Mnason of Cyprus, an early disciple, with whom we would stay.

²¹17 When we had come to Jerusalem, the brothers received us gladly. ²¹18 The day following, Paul went in with us to James; and all the elders were present. ²¹19 When he had greeted them, he reported one by one the things which God had worked among the Gentiles through his ministry. ²¹20 They, when they heard it, glorified God. They said to him, "You see, brother, how many thousands there are among the Jews of those who have believed, and they are all zealous for the law. ²¹21 They have been informed about you, that you teach all the Jews who are among the Gentiles to forsake Moses, telling them not to circumcise their children and not to walk after the customs. ²¹22 What then? The assembly must certainly meet, for they will hear that you have come. ²¹23 Therefore do what we tell you. We have four men who have taken a vow. ²¹24 Take them and purify yourself with them, and pay their expenses for them, that they may shave their heads. Then all will know that there is no truth in the things that they have been informed about you, but that you yourself also walk keeping the law. ²¹25 But concerning the Gentiles who believe, we have written our decision that they should observe no such thing, except that they should keep themselves from food offered to idols, from blood, from strangled things, and from sexual immorality."

²¹26 Then Paul took the men, and the next day purified himself and went with them into the temple, declaring the fulfillment of the days of purification, until the offering was offered for every one of them. ²¹27 When the seven days were almost completed, the Jews from Asia, when they saw him in the temple, stirred up all the multitude and laid hands on him, ²¹28 crying out, "Men of Israel, help! This is the man who teaches all men everywhere against the people, and the law, and this place. Moreover, he also brought Greeks into the temple, and has defiled this holy place!" ²¹29 For they had seen Trophimus, the

The Acts of the Apostles

Ephesian, with him in the city, and they supposed that Paul had brought him into the temple. ²¹30 All the city was moved and the people ran together. They seized Paul and dragged him out of the temple. Immediately the doors were shut. ²¹31 As they were trying to kill him, news came up to the commanding officer of the regiment that all Jerusalem was in an uproar. ²¹32 Immediately he took soldiers and centurions and ran down to them. They, when they saw the chief captain and the soldiers, stopped beating Paul. ²¹33 Then the commanding officer came near, arrested him, commanded him to be bound with two chains, and inquired who he was and what he had done. ²¹34 Some shouted one thing, and some another, among the crowd. When he couldn't find out the truth because of the noise, he commanded him to be brought into the barracks.

²¹35 When he came to the stairs, he was carried by the soldiers because of the violence of the crowd; ²¹36 for the multitude of the people followed after, crying out, "Away with him!" ²¹37 As Paul was about to be brought into the barracks, he asked the commanding officer, "May I speak to you?"

He said, "Do you know Greek? ²¹38 Aren't you then the Egyptian, who before these days stirred up to sedition and led out into the wilderness the four thousand men of the Assassins?"

²¹39 But Paul said, "I am a Jew, from Tarsus in Cilicia, a citizen of no insignificant city. I beg you, allow me to speak to the people."

²¹40 When he had given him permission, Paul, standing on the stairs, beckoned with his hand to the people. When there was a great silence, he spoke to them in the Hebrew language, saying, ²¹

22

²²1 "Brothers and fathers, listen to the defense which I now make to you."

²²2 When they heard that he spoke to them in the Hebrew language, they were even more quiet. He said, ²²3 "I am indeed a Jew, born in Tarsus of Cilicia, but brought up in this city at the feet of Gamaliel, instructed according to the strict tradition of the law of our fathers, being zealous for God, even as you all are today. ²²4 I persecuted this Way to the death, binding and delivering into prisons both men and

women. ²²5 As also the high priest and all the council of the elders testify, from whom also I received letters to the brothers, and traveled to Damascus to bring them also who were there to Jerusalem in bonds to be punished. ²²6 As I made my journey, and came close to Damascus, about noon, suddenly a great light shone around me from the sky. ²²7 I fell to the ground, and heard a voice saying to me, 'Saul, Saul, why are you persecuting me?' ²²8 I answered, 'Who are you, Lord?' He said to me, 'I am Jesus of Nazareth, whom you persecute.' ²²9 "Those who were with me indeed saw the light and were afraid, but they didn't understand the voice of him who spoke to me. ²²10 I said, 'What shall I do, Lord?' The Lord said to me, 'Arise, and go into Damascus. There you will be told about all things which are appointed for you to do.' ²²11 When I couldn't see for the glory of that light, being led by the hand of those who were with me, I came into Damascus. ²²12 One Ananias, a devout man according to the law, well reported of by all the Jews who lived in Damascus, ²²13 came to me, and standing by me said to me, 'Brother Saul, receive your sight!' In that very hour I looked up at him. ²²14 He said, 'The God of our fathers has appointed you to know his will, and to see the Righteous One, and to hear a voice from his mouth. ²²15 For you will be a witness for him to all men of what you have seen and heard. ²²16 Now why do you wait? Arise, be baptized, and wash away your sins, calling on the name of the Lord.'

²²17 "When I had returned to Jerusalem, and while I prayed in the temple, I fell into a trance, ²²18 and saw him saying to me, 'Hurry and get out of Jerusalem quickly, because they will not receive testimony concerning me from you.' ²²19 I said, 'Lord, they themselves know that I imprisoned and beat in every synagogue those who believed in you. ²²20 When the blood of Stephen, your witness, was shed, I also was standing by, consenting to his death, and guarding the cloaks of those who killed him.'

²²21 "He said to me, 'Depart, for I will send you out far from here to the Gentiles.'"

²²22 They listened to him until he said that; then they lifted up their voice and said, "Rid the earth of this fellow, for he isn't fit to live!" ²²23 As they cried out, threw off their cloaks, and threw dust into the air, ²²24 the commanding officer commanded him to be brought into

The Acts of the Apostles

the barracks, ordering him to be examined by scourging, that he might know for what crime they shouted against him like that. ²²25 When they had tied him up with thongs, Paul asked the centurion who stood by, "Is it lawful for you to scourge a man who is a Roman, and not found guilty?"

²²26 When the centurion heard it, he went to the commanding officer and told him, "Watch what you are about to do, for this man is a Roman!"

²²27 The commanding officer came and asked him, "Tell me, are you a Roman?"

He said, "Yes."

²²28 The commanding officer answered, "I bought my citizenship for a great price."

Paul said, "But I was born a Roman."

²²29 Immediately those who were about to examine him departed from him, and the commanding officer also was afraid when he realized that he was a Roman, because he had bound him. ²²30 But on the next day, desiring to know the truth about why he was accused by the Jews, he freed him from the bonds, and commanded the chief priests and all the council to come together, and brought Paul down and set him before them. ²²

23

²³1 Paul, looking steadfastly at the council, said, "Brothers, I have lived before God in all good conscience until today."

²³2 The high priest, Ananias, commanded those who stood by him to strike him on the mouth.

²³3 Then Paul said to him, "God will strike you, you whitewashed wall! Do you sit to judge me according to the law, and command me to be struck contrary to the law?"

²³4 Those who stood by said, "Do you malign God's high priest?"

²³5 Paul said, "I didn't know, brothers, that he was high priest. For it is written, 'You shall not speak evil of a ruler of your people.'"# ²³6 But when Paul perceived that the one part were Sadducees and the other Pharisees, he cried out in the council, "Men and brothers, I am a

---

#**23:5** 23:5 Exodus 22:28

Pharisee, a son of Pharisees. Concerning the hope and resurrection of the dead I am being judged!"

²³7 When he had said this, an argument arose between the Pharisees and Sadducees, and the crowd was divided. ²³8 For the Sadducees say that there is no resurrection, nor angel, nor spirit; but the Pharisees confess all of these. ²³9 A great clamor arose, and some of the scribes of the Pharisees' part stood up, and contended, saying, "We find no evil in this man. But if a spirit or angel has spoken to him, let's not fight against God!"

²³10 When a great argument arose, the commanding officer, fearing that Paul would be torn in pieces by them, commanded the soldiers to go down and take him by force from among them, and bring him into the barracks.

²³11 The following night, the Lord stood by him and said, "Cheer up, Paul, for as you have testified about me at Jerusalem, so you must testify also at Rome."

²³12 When it was day, some of the Jews banded together, and bound themselves under a curse, saying that they would neither eat nor drink until they had killed Paul. ²³13 There were more than forty people who had made this conspiracy. ²³14 They came to the chief priests and the elders, and said, "We have bound ourselves under a great curse to taste nothing until we have killed Paul. ²³15 Now therefore, you with the council inform the commanding officer that he should bring him down to you tomorrow, as though you were going to judge his case more exactly. We are ready to kill him before he comes near."

²³16 But Paul's sister's son heard they were lying in wait, and he came and entered into the barracks and told Paul. ²³17 Paul summoned one of the centurions, and said, "Bring this young man to the commanding officer, for he has something to tell him."

²³18 So he took him, and brought him to the commanding officer, and said, "Paul, the prisoner, summoned me and asked me to bring this young man to you. He has something to tell you."

²³19 The commanding officer took him by the hand, and going aside, asked him privately, "What is it that you have to tell me?"

²³20 He said, "The Jews have agreed to ask you to bring Paul down to the council tomorrow, as though intending to inquire somewhat more accurately concerning him. ²³21 Therefore don't yield to them, for more than forty men lie in wait for him, who have bound themselves

under a curse to neither eat nor drink until they have killed him. Now they are ready, looking for the promise from you."

²³22 So the commanding officer let the young man go, charging him, "Tell no one that you have revealed these things to me." ²³23 He called to himself two of the centurions, and said, "Prepare two hundred soldiers to go as far as Caesarea, with seventy horsemen, and two hundred men armed with spears, at the third hour of the night."²¹³

²³24 He asked them to provide animals, that they might set Paul on one, and bring him safely to Felix the governor. ²³25 He wrote a letter like this:

²³26 "Claudius Lysias to the most excellent governor Felix: Greetings.
²³27 "This man was seized by the Jews, and was about to be killed by them, when I came with the soldiers and rescued him, having learned that he was a Roman. ²³28 Desiring to know the cause why they accused him, I brought him down to their council. ²³29 I found him to be accused about questions of their law, but not to be charged with anything worthy of death or of imprisonment. ²³30 When I was told that the Jews lay in wait for the man, I sent him to you immediately, charging his accusers also to bring their accusations against him before you. Farewell."

²³31 So the soldiers, carrying out their orders, took Paul and brought him by night to Antipatris. ²³32 But on the next day they left the horsemen to go with him, and returned to the barracks. ²³33 When they came to Caesarea and delivered the letter to the governor, they also presented Paul to him. ²³34 When the governor had read it, he asked what province he was from. When he understood that he was from Cilicia, he said, ²³35 "I will hear you fully when your accusers also arrive." He commanded that he be kept in Herod's palace. ²³

24

²⁴1 After five days, the high priest, Ananias, came down with certain elders and an orator, one Tertullus. They informed the governor against Paul. ²⁴2 When he was called, Tertullus began to accuse him, saying, "Seeing that by you we enjoy much peace, and that prosperity is coming to this nation by your foresight, ²⁴3 we accept it in all ways

---

²¹³**23:23** *23:23* about 9:00 p.m.

and in all places, most excellent Felix, with all thankfulness. **24:4** But that I don't delay you, I entreat you to bear with us and hear a few words. **24:5** For we have found this man to be a plague, an instigator of insurrections among all the Jews throughout the world, and a ringleader of the sect of the Nazarenes. **24:6** He even tried to profane the temple, and we arrested him.[214] **24:7** [215] **24:8** [216]By examining him yourself you may ascertain all these things of which we accuse him." **24:9** The Jews also joined in the attack, affirming that these things were so. **24:10** When the governor had beckoned to him to speak, Paul answered, "Because I know that you have been a judge of this nation for many years, I cheerfully make my defense, **24:11** seeing that you can verify that it is not more than twelve days since I went up to worship at Jerusalem. **24:12** In the temple they didn't find me disputing with anyone or stirring up a crowd, either in the synagogues, or in the city. **24:13** Nor can they prove to you the things of which they now accuse me. **24:14** But this I confess to you, that after the Way, which they call a sect, so I serve the God of our fathers, believing all things which are according to the law, and which are written in the prophets; **24:15** having hope toward God, which these also themselves look for, that there will be a resurrection of the dead, both of the just and unjust. **24:16** In this I also practice always having a conscience void of offense toward God and men. **24:17** Now after some years, I came to bring gifts for the needy to my nation, and offerings; **24:18** amid which certain Jews from Asia found me purified in the temple, not with a mob, nor with turmoil. **24:19** They ought to have been here before you, and to make accusation, if they had anything against me. **24:20** Or else let these men themselves say what injustice they found in me when I stood before the council, **24:21** unless it is for this one thing that I cried standing among them, 'Concerning the resurrection of the dead I am being judged before you today!'"
24:22 But Felix, having more exact knowledge concerning the Way, deferred them, saying, "When Lysias, the commanding officer, comes down, I will decide your case." **24:23** He ordered the centurion that

---

[214]**24:6** *24:6* TR adds "We wanted to judge him according to our law,"
[215]**24:7** *24:7* TR adds "but the commanding officer, Lysias, came by and with great violence took him out of our hands,"
[216]**24:8** *24:8* TR adds "commanding his accusers to come to you."

The Acts of the Apostles

Paul should be kept in custody, and should have some privileges, and not to forbid any of his friends to serve him or to visit him. ²⁴24 But after some days, Felix came with Drusilla, his wife, who was a Jewess, and sent for Paul, and heard him concerning the faith in Christ Jesus. ²⁴25 As he reasoned about righteousness, self-control, and the judgment to come, Felix was terrified, and answered, "Go your way for this time, and when it is convenient for me, I will summon you." ²⁴26 Meanwhile, he also hoped that money would be given to him by Paul, that he might release him. Therefore also he sent for him more often and talked with him. ²⁴27 But when two years were fulfilled, Felix was succeeded by Porcius Festus, and desiring to gain favor with the Jews, Felix left Paul in bonds. 24

25

²⁵1 Festus therefore, having come into the province, after three days went up to Jerusalem from Caesarea. ²⁵2 Then the high priest and the principal men of the Jews informed him against Paul, and they begged him, ²⁵3 asking a favor against him, that he would summon him to Jerusalem; plotting to kill him on the way. ²⁵4 However Festus answered that Paul should be kept in custody at Caesarea, and that he himself was about to depart shortly. ²⁵5 "Let them therefore", he said, "that are in power among you go down with me, and if there is anything wrong in the man, let them accuse him."
²⁵6 When he had stayed among them more than ten days, he went down to Caesarea, and on the next day he sat on the judgment seat, and commanded Paul to be brought. ²⁵7 When he had come, the Jews who had come down from Jerusalem stood around him, bringing against him many and grievous charges which they could not prove, ²⁵8 while he said in his defense, "Neither against the law of the Jews, nor against the temple, nor against Caesar, have I sinned at all."
²⁵9 But Festus, desiring to gain favor with the Jews, answered Paul and said, "Are you willing to go up to Jerusalem, and be judged by me there concerning these things?"
²⁵10 But Paul said, "I am standing before Caesar's judgment seat, where I ought to be tried. I have done no wrong to the Jews, as you also know very well. ²⁵11 For if I have done wrong and have committed anything worthy of death, I don't refuse to die; but if none

of those things is true that they accuse me of, no one can give me up to them. I appeal to Caesar!"

²⁵12 Then Festus, when he had conferred with the council, answered, "You have appealed to Caesar. To Caesar you shall go."

²⁵13 Now when some days had passed, King Agrippa and Bernice arrived at Caesarea, and greeted Festus. ²⁵14 As he stayed there many days, Festus laid Paul's case before the king, saying, "There is a certain man left a prisoner by Felix; ²⁵15 about whom, when I was at Jerusalem, the chief priests and the elders of the Jews informed me, asking for a sentence against him. ²⁵16 I answered them that it is not the custom of the Romans to give up any man to destruction before the accused has met the accusers face to face and has had opportunity to make his defense concerning the matter laid against him. ²⁵17 When therefore they had come together here, I didn't delay, but on the next day sat on the judgment seat and commanded the man to be brought. ²⁵18 When the accusers stood up, they brought no charges against him of such things as I supposed; ²⁵19 but had certain questions against him about their own religion, and about one Jesus, who was dead, whom Paul affirmed to be alive. ²⁵20 Being perplexed how to inquire concerning these things, I asked whether he was willing to go to Jerusalem and there be judged concerning these matters. ²⁵21 But when Paul had appealed to be kept for the decision of the emperor, I commanded him to be kept until I could send him to Caesar."

²⁵22 Agrippa said to Festus, "I also would like to hear the man myself."

"Tomorrow," he said, "you shall hear him."

²⁵23 So on the next day, when Agrippa and Bernice had come with great pomp, and they had entered into the place of hearing with the commanding officers and the principal men of the city, at the command of Festus, Paul was brought in. ²⁵24 Festus said, "King Agrippa, and all men who are here present with us, you see this man about whom all the multitude of the Jews petitioned me, both at Jerusalem and here, crying that he ought not to live any longer. ²⁵25 But when I found that he had committed nothing worthy of death, and as he himself appealed to the emperor I determined to send him, ²⁵26 of whom I have no certain thing to write to my lord. Therefore I have brought him out before you, and especially before you, King Agrippa, that, after examination, I may have something to

The Acts of the Apostles

write. ²⁵27 For it seems to me unreasonable, in sending a prisoner, not to also specify the charges against him." ²⁵

26

²⁶1 Agrippa said to Paul, "You may speak for yourself."
Then Paul stretched out his hand, and made his defense. ²⁶2 "I think myself happy, King Agrippa, that I am to make my defense before you today concerning all the things that I am accused by the Jews,
²⁶3 especially because you are expert in all customs and questions which are among the Jews. Therefore I beg you to hear me patiently.
²⁶4 "Indeed, all the Jews know my way of life from my youth up, which was from the beginning among my own nation and at Jerusalem; ²⁶5 having known me from the first, if they are willing to testify, that after the strictest sect of our religion I lived a Pharisee.
²⁶6 Now I stand here to be judged for the hope of the promise made by God to our fathers, ²⁶7 which our twelve tribes, earnestly serving night and day, hope to attain. Concerning this hope I am accused by the Jews, King Agrippa! ²⁶8 Why is it judged incredible with you, if God does raise the dead?
²⁶9 "I myself most certainly thought that I ought to do many things contrary to the name of Jesus of Nazareth. ²⁶10 I also did this in Jerusalem. I both shut up many of the saints in prisons, having received authority from the chief priests, and when they were put to death I gave my vote against them. ²⁶11 Punishing them often in all the synagogues, I tried to make them blaspheme. Being exceedingly enraged against them, I persecuted them even to foreign cities.
²⁶12 "Whereupon as I traveled to Damascus with the authority and commission from the chief priests, ²⁶13 at noon, O king, I saw on the way a light from the sky, brighter than the sun, shining around me and those who traveled with me. ²⁶14 When we had all fallen to the earth, I heard a voice saying to me in the Hebrew language, 'Saul, Saul, why are you persecuting me? It is hard for you to kick against the goads.'
²⁶15 "I said, 'Who are you, Lord?'
"He said, 'I am Jesus, whom you are persecuting. ²⁶16 But arise, and stand on your feet, for I have appeared to you for this purpose: to appoint you a servant and a witness both of the things which you have seen, and of the things which I will reveal to you; ²⁶17 delivering you

from the people, and from the Gentiles, to whom I send you, ²⁶18 to open their eyes, that they may turn from darkness to light and from the power of Satan to God, that they may receive remission of sins and an inheritance among those who are sanctified by faith in me.'
²⁶19 "Therefore, King Agrippa, I was not disobedient to the heavenly vision, ²⁶20 but declared first to them of Damascus, at Jerusalem, and throughout all the country of Judea, and also to the Gentiles, that they should repent and turn to God, doing works worthy of repentance. ²⁶21 For this reason the Jews seized me in the temple and tried to kill me. ²⁶22 Having therefore obtained the help that is from God, I stand to this day testifying both to small and great, saying nothing but what the prophets and Moses said would happen, ²⁶23 how the Christ must suffer, and how, by the resurrection of the dead, he would be first to proclaim light both to these people and to the Gentiles."
²⁶24 As he thus made his defense, Festus said with a loud voice, "Paul, you are crazy! Your great learning is driving you insane!"
²⁶25 But he said, "I am not crazy, most excellent Festus, but boldly declare words of truth and reasonableness. ²⁶26 For the king knows of these things, to whom also I speak freely. For I am persuaded that none of these things is hidden from him, for this has not been done in a corner. ²⁶27 King Agrippa, do you believe the prophets? I know that you believe."
²⁶28 Agrippa said to Paul, "With a little persuasion are you trying to make me a Christian?"
²⁶29 Paul said, "I pray to God, that whether with little or with much, not only you, but also all that hear me today, might become such as I am, except for these bonds."
²⁶30 The king rose up with the governor, and Bernice, and those who sat with them. ²⁶31 When they had withdrawn, they spoke to one another, saying, "This man does nothing worthy of death or of bonds." ²⁶32 Agrippa said to Festus, "This man might have been set free if he had not appealed to Caesar." ²⁶

27

²⁷1 When it was determined that we should sail for Italy, they delivered Paul and certain other prisoners to a centurion named Julius, of the Augustan band. ²⁷2 Embarking in a ship of Adramyttium, which was

The Acts of the Apostles

about to sail to places on the coast of Asia, we put to sea, Aristarchus, a Macedonian of Thessalonica, being with us. ²⁷3 The next day, we touched at Sidon. Julius treated Paul kindly, and gave him permission to go to his friends and refresh himself. ²⁷4 Putting to sea from there, we sailed under the lee of Cyprus, because the winds were contrary. ²⁷5 When we had sailed across the sea which is off Cilicia and Pamphylia, we came to Myra, a city of Lycia. ²⁷6 There the centurion found a ship of Alexandria sailing for Italy, and he put us on board. ²⁷7 When we had sailed slowly many days, and had come with difficulty opposite Cnidus, the wind not allowing us further, we sailed under the lee of Crete, opposite Salmone. ²⁷8 With difficulty sailing along it we came to a certain place called Fair Havens, near the city of Lasea.

²⁷9 When much time had passed and the voyage was now dangerous, because the Fast had now already gone by, Paul admonished them ²⁷10 and said to them, "Sirs, I perceive that the voyage will be with injury and much loss, not only of the cargo and the ship, but also of our lives." ²⁷11 But the centurion gave more heed to the master and to the owner of the ship than to those things which were spoken by Paul. ²⁷12 Because the haven was not suitable to winter in, the majority advised going to sea from there, if by any means they could reach Phoenix, and winter there, which is a port of Crete, looking southwest and northwest.

²⁷13 When the south wind blew softly, supposing that they had obtained their purpose, they weighed anchor and sailed along Crete, close to shore. ²⁷14 But before long, a stormy wind beat down from shore, which is called Euroclydon. [217] ²⁷15 When the ship was caught and couldn't face the wind, we gave way to it and were driven along. ²⁷16 Running under the lee of a small island called Clauda, we were able, with difficulty, to secure the boat. ²⁷17 After they had hoisted it up, they used cables to help reinforce the ship. Fearing that they would run aground on the Syrtis sand bars, they lowered the sea anchor, and so were driven along. ²⁷18 As we labored exceedingly with the storm, the next day they began to throw things overboard. ²⁷19 On the third day, they threw out the ship's tackle with their own hands. ²⁷20 When neither sun nor stars shone on us for many days, and no

---

[217]27:14 *27:14* Or, "a northeaster".

small storm pressed on us, all hope that we would be saved was now taken away.

[27]21 When they had been long without food, Paul stood up in the middle of them, and said, "Sirs, you should have listened to me, and not have set sail from Crete and have gotten this injury and loss.
[27]22 Now I exhort you to cheer up, for there will be no loss of life among you, but only of the ship. [27]23 For there stood by me this night an angel, belonging to the God whose I am and whom I serve,
[27]24 saying, 'Don't be afraid, Paul. You must stand before Caesar. Behold, God has granted you all those who sail with you.'
[27]25 Therefore, sirs, cheer up! For I believe God, that it will be just as it has been spoken to me. [27]26 But we must run aground on a certain island."

[27]27 But when the fourteenth night had come, as we were driven back and forth in the Adriatic Sea, about midnight the sailors surmised that they were drawing near to some land. [27]28 They took soundings, and found twenty fathoms.[218] After a little while, they took soundings again, and found fifteen fathoms.[219] [27]29 Fearing that we would run aground on rocky ground, they let go four anchors from the stern, and wished for daylight. [27]30 As the sailors were trying to flee out of the ship, and had lowered the boat into the sea, pretending that they would lay out anchors from the bow, [27]31 Paul said to the centurion and to the soldiers, "Unless these stay in the ship, you can't be saved." [27]32 Then the soldiers cut away the ropes of the boat, and let it fall off. [27]33 While the day was coming on, Paul begged them all to take some food, saying, "Today is the fourteenth day that you wait and continue fasting, having taken nothing. [27]34 Therefore I beg you to take some food; for this is for your safety; for not a hair will perish from any of your heads." [27]35 When he had said this, and had taken bread, he gave thanks to God in the presence of all, then he broke it and began to eat. [27]36 Then they all cheered up, and they also took food. [27]37 In all, we were two hundred seventy-six souls on the ship. [27]38 When they had eaten enough, they lightened the ship, throwing out the wheat into the sea. [27]39 When it was day, they didn't recognize the land, but they noticed a certain bay with a beach, and they decided to try to

---

[218]27:28 *27:28* 20 fathoms = 120 feet = 36.6 meters
[219]27:28 *27:28* 15 fathoms = 90 feet = 27.4 meters

drive the ship onto it. ²⁷40 Casting off the anchors, they left them in the sea, at the same time untying the rudder ropes. Hoisting up the foresail to the wind, they made for the beach. ²⁷41 But coming to a place where two seas met, they ran the vessel aground. The bow struck and remained immovable, but the stern began to break up by the violence of the waves.

²⁷42 The soldiers' counsel was to kill the prisoners, so that none of them would swim out and escape. ²⁷43 But the centurion, desiring to save Paul, stopped them from their purpose, and commanded that those who could swim should throw themselves overboard first to go toward the land; ²⁷44 and the rest should follow, some on planks, and some on other things from the ship. So they all escaped safely to the land. ²⁷

28

²⁸1 When we had escaped, then they[220] learned that the island was called Malta. ²⁸2 The natives showed us uncommon kindness; for they kindled a fire and received us all, because of the present rain and because of the cold. ²⁸3 But when Paul had gathered a bundle of sticks and laid them on the fire, a viper came out because of the heat, and fastened on his hand. ²⁸4 When the natives saw the creature hanging from his hand, they said to one another, "No doubt this man is a murderer, whom, though he has escaped from the sea, yet Justice has not allowed to live." ²⁸5 However he shook off the creature into the fire, and wasn't harmed. ²⁸6 But they expected that he would have swollen or fallen down dead suddenly, but when they watched for a long time and saw nothing bad happen to him, they changed their minds, and said that he was a god.

²⁸7 Now in the neighborhood of that place were lands belonging to the chief man of the island, named Publius, who received us, and courteously entertained us for three days. ²⁸8 The father of Publius lay sick of fever and dysentery. Paul entered in to him, prayed, and laying his hands on him, healed him. ²⁸9 Then when this was done, the rest also who had diseases in the island came and were cured. ²⁸10 They also honored us with many honors, and when we sailed, they put on board the things that we needed.

---

[220]**28:1** *28:1* NU reads "we"

²⁸11 After three months, we set sail in a ship of Alexandria which had wintered in the island, whose sign was "The Twin Brothers." ²⁸12 Touching at Syracuse, we stayed there three days. ²⁸13 From there we circled around and arrived at Rhegium. After one day, a south wind sprang up, and on the second day we came to Puteoli, ²⁸14 where we found brothers,²²¹ and were entreated to stay with them for seven days. So we came to Rome. ²⁸15 From there the brothers, when they heard of us, came to meet us as far as The Market of Appius and The Three Taverns. When Paul saw them, he thanked God and took courage. ²⁸16 When we entered into Rome, the centurion delivered the prisoners to the captain of the guard, but Paul was allowed to stay by himself with the soldier who guarded him.

²⁸17 After three days Paul called together those who were the leaders of the Jews. When they had come together, he said to them, "I, brothers, though I had done nothing against the people or the customs of our fathers, still was delivered prisoner from Jerusalem into the hands of the Romans, ²⁸18 who, when they had examined me, desired to set me free, because there was no cause of death in me. ²⁸19 But when the Jews spoke against it, I was constrained to appeal to Caesar, not that I had anything about which to accuse my nation. ²⁸20 For this cause therefore I asked to see you and to speak with you. For because of the hope of Israel I am bound with this chain."

²⁸21 They said to him, "We neither received letters from Judea concerning you, nor did any of the brothers come here and report or speak any evil of you. ²⁸22 But we desire to hear from you what you think. For, as concerning this sect, it is known to us that everywhere it is spoken against."

²⁸23 When they had appointed him a day, many people came to him at his lodging. He explained to them, testifying about God's Kingdom, and persuading them concerning Jesus, both from the law of Moses and from the prophets, from morning until evening. ²⁸24 Some believed the things which were spoken, and some disbelieved. ²⁸25 When they didn't agree among themselves, they departed after Paul had spoken one word, "The Holy Spirit spoke rightly through Isaiah the prophet to our fathers, ²⁸26 saying,

---

²²¹28:14 *28:14* The word for "brothers" here and where context allows may also be correctly translated "brothers and sisters" or "siblings."

The Acts of the Apostles

'Go to this people and say,
in hearing, you will hear,
but will in no way understand.
In seeing, you will see,
but will in no way perceive.
28:27 For this people's heart has grown callous.
Their ears are dull of hearing.
Their eyes they have closed.
Lest they should see with their eyes,
hear with their ears,
understand with their heart,
and would turn again,
then I would heal them.'#
28:28 "Be it known therefore to you, that the salvation of God is sent to the nations, and they will listen."
28:29 When he had said these words, the Jews departed, having a great dispute among themselves.²²²
28:30 Paul stayed two whole years in his own rented house and received all who were coming to him, **28:31** preaching God's Kingdom, and teaching the things concerning the Lord Jesus Christ with all boldness, without hindrance.

#**28:27** 28:27 Isaiah 6:9-10
²²²**28:29** *28:29* NU omits verse 29.

Holy Week

Palm Sunday

Prayer [21]

Holy Father from whom all blessings and love flow, I stand before you today in remembrance of your precious love and the sacrifice of your only Son. On this special day of the Christian year, I recall Jesus' entry into Jerusalem in fulfillment of ancient prophecy and I remain in awe of His love for all of humanity. I am, like all people, a sinner of the worst kind, and it is only through the love of Christ that I may be saved from this wretched state that I find myself in. Thank you Heavenly Father for your love and kindness toward me and for all of the blessings I have received. Amen.

Prayer of Confession

Almighty and most merciful Father; we have erred, and strayed from your ways like lost sheep. We have followed too much the devices and desires of our own hearts. We have offended against your holy laws. We have left undone those things which we ought to have done; and we have done those things which we ought not to have done; and there is no health in us. O Lord, have mercy upon us, miserable offenders. Spare those, O God, who confess their faults. Restore those who are penitent; according to your

promises declared unto mankind in Christ Jesus our Lord. And grant, O most merciful Father, for his sake; that we may hereafter live a godly, righteous, and sober life, to the glory of thy holy Name. Amen.
-Revised prayer from *The Book of Common Prayer*, 1662

Daily Wisdom

17 I shall not die, but live, and declare the works of the LORD.
18 The LORD hath chastened me sore: but he hath not given me over unto death.
19 Open to me the gates of righteousness: I will go into them, and I will praise the LORD:
20 This gate of the LORD, into which the righteous shall enter.
21 I will praise thee: for thou hast heard me, and art become my salvation.
22 The stone which the builders refused is become the head stone of the corner.
23 This is the LORD'S doing; it is marvellous in our eyes.
24 This is the day which the LORD hath made; we will rejoice and be glad in it.
25 Save now, I beseech thee, O LORD: O LORD, I beseech thee, send now prosperity.
26 Blessed be he that cometh in the name of the LORD: we have blessed you out of the house of the LORD.
27 God is the LORD, which hath shewed us light: bind the sacrifice with cords, even unto the horns of the altar.
28 Thou art my God, and I will praise thee: thou art my God, I will exalt thee.
29 O give thanks unto the LORD; for he is good: for his mercy endureth for ever.
-Psalm 118:17-29, *The King James Bible*, 1769 edition of 1611 text.

Palm Sunday

Readings from the Holy Bible

The Holy Gospel According to Matthew (MATTHEW 21:1-11)

MATTHEW 21:1-11

21

²¹1 When they came near to Jerusalem, and came to Bethsphage,²²³ to the Mount of Olives, then Jesus sent two disciples, ²¹2 saying to them, "Go into the village that is opposite you, and immediately you will find a donkey tied, and a colt with her. Untie them, and bring them to me. ²¹3 If anyone says anything to you, you shall say, 'The Lord needs them,' and immediately he will send them."

²¹4 All this was done, that it might be fulfilled which was spoken through the prophet, saying,

²¹5 "Tell the daughter of Zion,
behold, your King comes to you,
humble, and riding on a donkey,
on a colt, the foal of a donkey."#

²¹6 The disciples went, and did just as Jesus commanded them, ²¹7 and brought the donkey and the colt, and laid their clothes on them; and he sat on them. ²¹8 A very great multitude spread their clothes on the road. Others cut branches from the trees, and spread them on the road. ²¹9 The multitudes who went in front of him, and those who followed, kept shouting, "Hosanna ²²4 to the son of David! Blessed is he who comes in the name of the Lord! Hosanna in the highest!" #

²¹10 When he had come into Jerusalem, all the city was stirred up, saying, "Who is this?" ²¹11 The multitudes said, "This is the prophet, Jesus, from Nazareth of Galilee."

---

²²³21:1 21:1 TR & NU read "Bethphage" instead of "Bethsphage"
#21:5 21:5 Zechariah 9:9
²²⁴21:9 21:9 "Hosanna" means "save us" or "help us, we pray".
#21:9 21:9 Psalm 118:26

The American Book of Prayer

The Lord's Prayer

Our Father, who art in heaven,
Hallowed be thy name.
Thy Kingdom come.
Thy will be done on Earth, as it is in heaven.
Give us this day our daily bread.
And forgive us our trespasses,
As we forgive those that trespass against us.
And lead us not into temptation,
But deliver us from evil.
For thine is the kingdom,
The power, and the glory,
For ever and ever.
AMEN

Holy Monday

Prayer

All-knowing and everlasting God, help to prepare my soul for this Holy Week, as I, your humble servant, seek to better understand the truly incomprehensible love of Jesus' holy sacrifice. As his blood poured over the wood of His torturous and glorious cross, my sins were absolutely washed away. It is not through any merit of my own that I seek righteousness, but only because of your grace. Please help me grow in wisdom this week, and open my heart to the truth of your holy cross and its meaning in my life. Amen.

Prayer of Confession

Almighty and most merciful Father; we have erred, and strayed from your ways like lost sheep. We have followed too much the devices and desires of our own hearts. We have offended against your holy laws. We have left undone those things which we ought to have done; and we have done those things which we ought not to have done; and there is no health in us. O Lord, have mercy upon us, miserable offenders. Spare those, O God, who confess their faults. Restore those who are penitent; according to your

promises declared unto mankind in Christ Jesus our Lord. And grant, O most merciful Father, for his sake; that we may hereafter live a godly, righteous, and sober life, to the glory of thy holy Name. Amen.
-Revised prayer from *The Book of Common Prayer*, 1662

Daily Wisdom

1 The transgression of the wicked saith within my heart, that there is no fear of God before his eyes.
2 For he flattereth himself in his own eyes, until his iniquity be found to be hateful.
3 The words of his mouth are iniquity and deceit: he hath left off to be wise, and to do good.
4 He deviseth mischief upon his bed; he setteth himself in a way that is not good; he abhorreth not evil.
5 Thy mercy, O LORD, is in the heavens; and thy faithfulness reacheth unto the clouds.
6 Thy righteousness is like the great mountains; thy judgments are a great deep: O LORD, thou preservest man and beast.
7 How excellent is thy lovingkindness, O God! therefore the children of men put their trust under the shadow of thy wings.
8 They shall be abundantly satisfied with the fatness of thy house; and thou shalt make them drink of the river of thy pleasures.
9 For with thee is the fountain of life: in thy light shall we see light.
10 O continue thy lovingkindness unto them that know thee; and thy righteousness to the upright in heart.
11 Let not the foot of pride come against me, and let not the hand of the wicked remove me.
12 There are the workers of iniquity fallen: they are cast down, and shall not be able to rise.
-Psalm 36, *The King James Bible*, 1769 edition of 1611 text

Holy Monday

Readings from the Holy Bible

The Holy Gospel According to John (John 12:1-11)

JOHN 12:1-11

12

1 Then six days before the Passover, Jesus came to Bethany, where Lazarus was, who had been dead, whom he raised from the dead. **2** So they made him a supper there. Martha served, but Lazarus was one of those who sat at the table with him. **3** Therefore Mary took a pound[225] of ointment of pure nard, very precious, and anointed Jesus's feet and wiped his feet with her hair. The house was filled with the fragrance of the ointment. **4** Then Judas Iscariot, Simon's son, one of his disciples, who would betray him, said, **5** "Why wasn't this ointment sold for three hundred denarii,[226] and given to the poor?" **6** Now he said this, not because he cared for the poor, but because he was a thief, and having the money box, used to steal what was put into it. **7** But Jesus said, "Leave her alone. She has kept this for the day of my burial. **8** For you always have the poor with you, but you don't always have me."
9 A large crowd therefore of the Jews learned that he was there, and they came, not for Jesus' sake only, but that they might see Lazarus also, whom he had raised from the dead. **10** But the chief priests conspired to put Lazarus to death also, **11** because on account of him many of the Jews went away and believed in Jesus.

---

[225]12:3 12:3 a Roman pound of 12 ounces, or about 340 grams
[226]12:5 12:5 300 denarii was about a year's wages for an agricultural laborer.

The Lord's Prayer

Our Father, who art in heaven,
Hallowed be thy name.
Thy Kingdom come.
Thy will be done on Earth, as it is in heaven.
Give us this day our daily bread.
And forgive us our trespasses,
As we forgive those that trespass against us.
And lead us not into temptation,
But deliver us from evil.
For thine is the kingdom,
The power, and the glory,
For ever and ever.
AMEN

Holy Tuesday

Prayer

Holy Father, as the Christian world comes closer to the celebration of your only Son's perfect sacrifice, I pray for guidance and knowledge so that I may better know your will. I accept and understand that I am a sinner and that I am in desperate need of a savior, which you have graciously provided to the world. I struggle to understand the meaning of Christ's life God, and so much of what Jesus accomplished has been lost to history. Please renew my heart and mind Lord, and provide me with the understanding I need to live a Godly life. Amen.

Prayer of Confession

Almighty and most merciful Father; we have erred, and strayed from your ways like lost sheep. We have followed too much the devices and desires of our own hearts. We have offended against your holy laws. We have left undone those things which we ought to have done; and we have done those things which we ought not to have done; and there is no health in us. O Lord, have mercy upon us, miserable offenders. Spare those, O God, who confess their faults. Restore those who are penitent; according to your

promises declared unto mankind in Christ Jesus our Lord. And grant, O most merciful Father, for his sake; that we may hereafter live a godly, righteous, and sober life, to the glory of thy holy Name. Amen.
-Revised prayer from *The Book of Common Prayer*, 1662

Daily Wisdom

1 In thee, O LORD, do I put my trust: let me never be put to confusion.
2 Deliver me in thy righteousness, and cause me to escape: incline thine ear unto me, and save me.
3 Be thou my strong habitation, whereunto I may continually resort: thou hast given commandment to save me; for thou *art* my rock and my fortress.
4 Deliver me, O my God, out of the hand of the wicked, out of the hand of the unrighteous and cruel man.
5 For thou *art* my hope, O Lord GOD: *thou art* my trust from my youth.
6 By thee have I been holden up from the womb: thou art he that took me out of my mother's bowels: my praise *shall be* continually of thee.
7 I am as a wonder unto many; but thou *art* my strong refuge.
8 Let my mouth be filled *with* thy praise *and with* thy honor all the day.
9 Cast me not off in the time of old age; forsake me not when my strength faileth.
10 For mine enemies speak against me; and they that lay wait for my soul take counsel together,
11 Saying, God hath forsaken him: persecute and take him; for *there is* none to deliver *him*.
12 O God, be not far from me: O my God, make haste for my help.

Holy Tuesday

13 Let them be confounded *and* consumed that are adversaries to my soul; let them be covered *with* reproach and dishonor that seek my hurt.
14 But I will hope continually, and will yet praise thee more and more.
-Psalm 71:1-14, *The King James Bible*, 1769 edition of 1611 text

Readings from the Holy Bible

The Holy Gospel According to John (John 12:20-36)

JOHN 12:20-43
^{12}**20** Now there were certain Greeks among those that went up to worship at the feast. ^{12}**21** These, therefore, came to Philip, who was from Bethsaida of Galilee, and asked him, saying, "Sir, we want to see Jesus." ^{12}**22** Philip came and told Andrew, and in turn, Andrew came with Philip, and they told Jesus. ^{12}**23** Jesus answered them, "The time has come for the Son of Man to be glorified. ^{12}**24** Most certainly I tell you, unless a grain of wheat falls into the earth and dies, it remains by itself alone. But if it dies, it bears much fruit. ^{12}**25** He who loves his life will lose it. He who hates his life in this world will keep it to eternal life. ^{12}**26** If anyone serves me, let him follow me. Where I am, there my servant will also be. If anyone serves me, the Father will honor him.
^{12}**27** "Now my soul is troubled. What shall I say? 'Father, save me from this time?' But I came to this time for this cause. ^{12}**28** Father, glorify your name!"
Then a voice came out of the sky, saying, "I have both glorified it, and will glorify it again."
^{12}**29** Therefore the multitude who stood by and heard it said that it had thundered. Others said, "An angel has spoken to him."
^{12}**30** Jesus answered, "This voice hasn't come for my sake, but for your sakes. ^{12}**31** Now is the judgment of this world. Now the prince of this world will be cast out. ^{12}**32** And I, if I am lifted up from the earth, will draw all people to myself." ^{12}**33** But he said this, signifying by what

kind of death he should die. **¹234** The multitude answered him, "We have heard out of the law that the Christ remains forever.# How do you say, 'The Son of Man must be lifted up?' Who is this Son of Man?"

¹235 Jesus therefore said to them, "Yet a little while the light is with you. Walk while you have the light, that darkness doesn't overtake you. He who walks in the darkness doesn't know where he is going. **¹236** While you have the light, believe in the light, that you may become children of light." Jesus said these things, and he departed and hid himself from them. **¹237** But though he had done so many signs before them, yet they didn't believe in him, **¹238** that the word of Isaiah the prophet might be fulfilled, which he spoke,

"Lord, who has believed our report?
To whom has the arm of the Lord been revealed?"#

¹239 For this cause they couldn't believe, for Isaiah said again,
¹240 "He has blinded their eyes and he hardened their heart,
lest they should see with their eyes,
and perceive with their heart,
and would turn,
and I would heal them."#

¹241 Isaiah said these things when he saw his glory, and spoke of him. # **¹242** Nevertheless even many of the rulers believed in him, but because of the Pharisees they didn't confess it, so that they wouldn't be put out of the synagogue, **¹243** for they loved men's praise more than God's praise.

The Lord's Prayer

Our Father, who art in heaven,
Hallowed be thy name.
Thy Kingdom come.

#12:34 12:34 Isaiah 9:7; Daniel 2:44; See Isaiah 53:8
#12:38 12:38 Isaiah 53:1
#12:40 12:40 Isaiah 6:10
#12:41 12:41 Isaiah 6:1

Holy Tuesday

Thy will be done on Earth, as it is in heaven.
Give us this day our daily bread.
And forgive us our trespasses,
As we forgive those that trespass against us.
And lead us not into temptation,
But deliver us from evil.
For thine is the kingdom,
The power, and the glory,
For ever and ever.
AMEN

Holy Wednesday

Prayer

On this Holy Wednesday, grant peace, love, and faith to my family and friends. Oh merciful and holy God, please remember all those in my life who do not fully know, trust, or have faith in you, and know that I have absolute faith in your wisdom and sovereignty over the world. Help me to be a beacon of light to the world around me and a city on a hill for the world around me to see. Do not allow me to fall into spiritual complacency, and please continue to make me your loving servant. Amen.

Prayer of Confession

Almighty and most merciful Father; we have erred, and strayed from your ways like lost sheep. We have followed too much the devices and desires of our own hearts. We have offended against your holy laws. We have left undone those things which we ought to have done; and we have done those things which we ought not to have done; and there is no health in us. O Lord, have mercy upon us, miserable offenders. Spare those, O God, who confess their faults. Restore those who are penitent; according to your promises declared unto mankind in Christ Jesus our Lord. And grant, O most merciful Father, for his sake; that we

may hereafter live a godly, righteous, and sober life, to the glory of thy holy Name. Amen.
-Revised prayer from *The Book of Common Prayer*, 1662

Daily Wisdom

1 *Make haste*, O God, to deliver me; make haste to help me, O LORD.
2 Let them be ashamed and confounded that seek after my soul: let them be turned backward, and put to confusion, that desire my hurt.
3 Let them be turned back for a reward of their shame that say, Aha, aha.
4 Let all those that seek thee rejoice and be glad in thee: and let such as love thy salvation say continually, Let God be magnified.
5 But I *am* poor and needy: make haste unto me, O God: thou *art* my help and my deliverer; O LORD, make no tarrying.
-Psalm 70, *The King James Bible*, 1769 edition of 1611 text

Readings from the Holy Bible

The Holy Gospel According to John (John 13:21-30)

13:21 When Jesus had said this, he was troubled in spirit, and testified, "Most certainly I tell you that one of you will betray me."
13:22 The disciples looked at one another, perplexed about whom he spoke. **13:23** One of his disciples, whom Jesus loved, was at the table, leaning against Jesus' breast. **13:24** Simon Peter therefore beckoned to him, and said to him, "Tell us who it is of whom he speaks."
13:25 He, leaning back, as he was, on Jesus' breast, asked him, "Lord, who is it?"
13:26 Jesus therefore answered, "It is he to whom I will give this piece of bread when I have dipped it." So when he had dipped the piece of

Holy Wednesday

bread, he gave it to Judas, the son of Simon Iscariot. **¹³27** After the piece of bread, then Satan entered into him.
Then Jesus said to him, "What you do, do quickly."
¹³28 Now nobody at the table knew why he said this to him. **¹³29** For some thought, because Judas had the money box, that Jesus said to him, "Buy what things we need for the feast," or that he should give something to the poor. **¹³30** Therefore having received that morsel, he went out immediately. It was night.

The Lord's Prayer

Our Father, who art in heaven,
Hallowed be thy name.
Thy Kingdom come.
Thy will be done on Earth, as it is in heaven.
Give us this day our daily bread.
And forgive us our trespasses,
As we forgive those that trespass against us.
And lead us not into temptation,
But deliver us from evil.
For thine is the kingdom,
The power, and the glory,
For ever and ever.
AMEN

Maundy Thursday

Prayer

Lord God, on this Maundy Thursday during Holy Week, I come before you seeking humility. Christ, the King of kings, humbly washed the feet of His disciples despite being God Himself. How then can I continue on in my arrogant and prideful ways? Keep me far from my natural pride and allow me to kneel in humility as Christ did, living as a servant and placing no person before myself. Help me grow in compassion and stand firm against those who would harm others. Allow me to be a light unto the world and to be an example of the true Christian life. In Christ's name, Amen.

Prayer of Confession

Almighty and most merciful Father; we have erred, and strayed from your ways like lost sheep. We have followed too much the devices and desires of our own hearts. We have offended against your holy laws. We have left undone those things which we ought to have done; and we have done those things which we ought not to have done; and there is no health in us. O Lord, have mercy upon us, miserable offenders. Spare those, O God, who
confess their faults. Restore those who are penitent; according to your promises declared unto mankind in

Christ Jesus our Lord. And grant, O most merciful Father, for his sake; that we may hereafter live a godly, righteous, and sober life, to the glory of thy holy Name. Amen.
-Revised prayer from *The Book of Common Prayer*, 1662

Daily Wisdom

1 I love the LORD, because he hath heard my voice *and* my supplications.
2 Because he hath inclined his ear unto me, therefore will I call upon *him* as long as I live.
3 The sorrows of death compassed me, and the pains of hell gat hold upon me: I found trouble and sorrow.
4 Then called I upon the name of the LORD; O LORD, I beseech thee, deliver my soul.
5 Gracious *is* the LORD, and righteous; yea, our God *is* merciful.
6 The LORD preserveth the simple: I was brought low, and he helped me.
7 Return unto thy rest, O my soul; for the LORD hath dealt bountifully with thee.
8 For thou hast delivered my soul from death, mine eyes from tears, *and* my feet from falling.
9 I will walk before the LORD in the land of the living.
10 I believed, therefore have I spoken: I was greatly afflicted:
11 I said in my haste, All men *are* liars.
12 What shall I render unto the LORD *for* all his benefits toward me?
13 I will take the cup of salvation, and call upon the name of the LORD.
14 I will pay my vows unto the LORD now in the presence of all his people.
15 Precious in the sight of the LORD *is* the death of his saints.

Maundy Thursday

16 O LORD, truly I *am* thy servant; I *am* thy servant, *and* the son of thine handmaid: thou hast loosed my bonds.
17 I will offer to thee the sacrifice of thanksgiving, and will call upon the name of the LORD.
18 I will pay my vows unto the LORD now in the presence of all his people,
19 In the courts of the LORD'S house, in the midst of thee, O Jerusalem. Praise ye the LORD.
-Psalm 116, *The King James Bible*, 1769 edition of 1611 text

Readings from the Holy Bible

The Holy Gospel According to John (John 13:1-17; 13:31-35)

JOHN 13:1-17

13

13:1 Now before the feast of the Passover, Jesus, knowing that his time had come that he would depart from this world to the Father, having loved his own who were in the world, he loved them to the end. **13:2** During supper, the devil having already put into the heart of Judas Iscariot, Simon's son, to betray him, **13:3** Jesus, knowing that the Father had given all things into his hands, and that he came from God, and was going to God, **13:4** arose from supper, and laid aside his outer garments. He took a towel and wrapped a towel around his waist. **13:5** Then he poured water into the basin, and began to wash the disciples' feet and to wipe them with the towel that was wrapped around him. **13:6** Then he came to Simon Peter. He said to him, "Lord, do you wash my feet?"
13:7 Jesus answered him, "You don't know what I am doing now, but you will understand later." **13:8** Peter said to him, "You will never wash my feet!"
Jesus answered him, "If I don't wash you, you have no part with me."
13:9 Simon Peter said to him, "Lord, not my feet only, but also my hands and my head!"

13:10 Jesus said to him, "Someone who has bathed only needs to have his feet washed, but is completely clean. You are clean, but not all of you." **13:11** For he knew him who would betray him, therefore he said, "You are not all clean." **13:12** So when he had washed their feet, put his outer garment back on, and sat down again, he said to them, "Do you know what I have done to you? **13:13** You call me, 'Teacher' and 'Lord.' You say so correctly, for so I am. **13:14** If I then, the Lord and the Teacher, have washed your feet, you also ought to wash one another's feet. **13:15** For I have given you an example, that you should also do as I have done to you. **13:16** Most certainly I tell you, a servant is not greater than his lord, neither is one who is sent greater than he who sent him. **13:17** If you know these things, blessed are you if you do them.

JOHN 13:31-35

13:31 When he had gone out, Jesus said, "Now the Son of Man has been glorified, and God has been glorified in him. **13:32** If God has been glorified in him, God will also glorify him in himself, and he will glorify him immediately. **13:33** Little children, I will be with you a little while longer. You will seek me, and as I said to the Jews, 'Where I am going, you can't come,' so now I tell you. **13:34** A new commandment I give to you, that you love one another. Just as I have loved you, you also love one another. **13:35** By this everyone will know that you are my disciples, if you have love for one another."

Maundy Thursday

The Lord's Prayer

Our Father, who art in heaven,
Hallowed be thy name.
Thy Kingdom come.
Thy will be done on Earth, as it is in heaven.
Give us this day our daily bread.
And forgive us our trespasses,
As we forgive those that trespass against us.
And lead us not into temptation,
But deliver us from evil.
For thine is the kingdom,
The power, and the glory,
For ever and ever.
AMEN

Good Friday

Prayer

Father of all creation, today the world remembers the death of your only son, the Lord Jesus Christ, who died to save the earth from its sins. No matter how many years pass, it's truly impossible for the human mind to grasp the significance of one man's death. Jesus, acting as both the Lion and the Lamb of the world, sacrificed and conquered for the sake of all humanity. His bloody death on the cross stands forever as the defining act of love, mercy, and God's grace. We mourn Christ's suffering and death, because his sacrifice was only made necessary by our sinful and selfish ways. Christ paid a debt we could never ourselves pay or return, and the world is forever grateful for that reality. Amen.

Prayer of Confession

Almighty and most merciful Father; we have erred, and strayed from your ways like lost sheep. We have followed too much the devices and desires of our own hearts. We have offended against your holy laws. We have left undone those things which we ought to have done; and we have done those things which we ought not to have done; and there is no health in us. O Lord, have mercy upon us, miserable offenders. Spare those, O God, who confess their faults. Restore those who are penitent; according to your promises declared unto mankind in Christ Jesus our Lord. And grant, O most merciful Father,

for his sake; that we may hereafter live a godly, righteous, and sober life, to the glory of thy holy Name. Amen.
-Revised prayer from *The Book of Common Prayer*, 1662

Daily Wisdom

1 My God, my God, why hast thou forsaken me? *why art thou so* far from helping me, *and from* the words of my roaring?
2 O my God, I cry in the daytime, but thou hearest not; and in the night season, and am not silent.
3 But thou *art* holy, O *thou* that inhabitest the praises of Israel.
4 Our fathers trusted in thee: they trusted, and thou didst deliver them.
5 They cried unto thee, and were delivered: they trusted in thee, and were not confounded.
6 But I *am* a worm, and no man; a reproach of men, and despised of the people.
7 All they that see me laugh me to scorn: they shoot out the lip, they shake the head, *saying,*
8 He trusted on the LORD *that* he would deliver him: let him deliver him, seeing he delighted in him.
9 But thou *art* he that took me out of the womb: thou didst make me hope *when I was* upon my mother's breasts.
10 I was cast upon thee from the womb: thou *art* my God from my mother's belly.
11 Be not far from me; for trouble *is* near; for *there is* none to help.
12 Many bulls have compassed me: strong *bulls* of Bashan have beset me round.
13 They gaped upon me *with* their mouths, *as* a ravening and a roaring lion.
14 I am poured out like water, and all my bones are out of joint: my heart is like wax; it is melted in the midst of my bowels.

Good Friday

15 My strength is dried up like a potsherd; and my tongue cleaveth to my jaws; and thou hast brought me into the dust of death.

16 For dogs have compassed me: the assembly of the wicked have inclosed me: they pierced my hands and my feet.

17 I may tell all my bones: they look *and* stare upon me.

18 They part my garments among them, and cast lots upon my vesture.

19 But be not thou far from me, O LORD: O my strength, haste thee to help me.

20 Deliver my soul from the sword; my darling from the power of the dog.

21 Save me from the lion's mouth: for thou hast heard me from the horns of the unicorns.

22 I will declare thy name unto my brethren: in the midst of the congregation will I praise thee.

23 Ye that fear the LORD, praise him; all ye the seed of Jacob, glorify him; and fear him, all ye the seed of Israel.

24 For he hath not despised nor abhorred the affliction of the afflicted; neither hath he hid his face from him; but when he cried unto him, he heard.

25 My praise *shall be* of thee in the great congregation: I will pay my vows before them that fear him.

26 The meek shall eat and be satisfied: they shall praise the LORD that seek him: your heart shall live for ever.

27 All the ends of the world shall remember and turn unto the LORD: and all the kindreds of the nations shall worship before thee.

28 For the kingdom *is* the LORD'S: and he *is* the governor among the nations.

29 All *they that be* fat upon earth shall eat and worship: all they that go down to the dust shall bow before him: and none can keep alive his own soul.

30 A seed shall serve him; it shall be accounted to the Lord for a generation.

31 They shall come, and shall declare his righteousness unto a people that shall be born, that he hath done *this*.
-Psalm 22, *The King James Bible*, 1769 edition of 1611 text

Readings from the Holy Bible

The Holy Gospel According to John (John 18:1-19:42)

18

18:1 When Jesus had spoken these words, he went out with his disciples over the brook Kidron, where there was a garden, into which he and his disciples entered. **18:2** Now Judas, who betrayed him, also knew the place, for Jesus often met there with his disciples. **18:3** Judas then, having taken a detachment of soldiers and officers from the chief priests and the Pharisees, came there with lanterns, torches, and weapons. **18:4** Jesus therefore, knowing all the things that were happening to him, went out, and said to them, "Who are you looking for?"
18:5 They answered him, "Jesus of Nazareth."
Jesus said to them, "I am he."
Judas also, who betrayed him, was standing with them. **18:6** When therefore he said to them, "I am he," they went backward, and fell to the ground.
18:7 Again therefore he asked them, "Who are you looking for?"
They said, "Jesus of Nazareth."
18:8 Jesus answered, "I told you that I am he. If therefore you seek me, let these go their way," **18:9** that the word might be fulfilled which he spoke, "Of those whom you have given me, I have lost none."#
18:10 Simon Peter therefore, having a sword, drew it, struck the high priest's servant, and cut off his right ear. The servant's name was Malchus. **18:11** Jesus therefore said to Peter, "Put the sword into its sheath. The cup which the Father has given me, shall I not surely drink it?"
18:12 So the detachment, the commanding officer, and the

#18:9 18:9 John 6:39

Good Friday

officers of the Jews seized Jesus and bound him, ¹⁸13 and led him to Annas first, for he was father-in-law to Caiaphas, who was high priest that year. ¹⁸14 Now it was Caiaphas who advised the Jews that it was expedient that one man should perish for the people. ¹⁸15 Simon Peter followed Jesus, as did another disciple. Now that disciple was known to the high priest, and entered in with Jesus into the court of the high priest; ¹⁸16 but Peter was standing at the door outside. So the other disciple, who was known to the high priest, went out and spoke to her who kept the door, and brought in Peter. ¹⁸17 Then the maid who kept the door said to Peter, "Are you also one of this man's disciples?" He said, "I am not."

¹⁸18 Now the servants and the officers were standing there, having made a fire of coals, for it was cold. They were warming themselves. Peter was with them, standing and warming himself. ¹⁸19 The high priest therefore asked Jesus about his disciples and about his teaching. ¹⁸20 Jesus answered him, "I spoke openly to the world. I always taught in synagogues, and in the temple, where the Jews always meet. I said nothing in secret. ¹⁸21 Why do you ask me? Ask those who have heard me what I said to them. Behold, they know the things which I said."

¹⁸22 When he had said this, one of the officers standing by slapped Jesus with his hand, saying, "Do you answer the high priest like that?" ¹⁸23 Jesus answered him, "If I have spoken evil, testify of the evil; but if well, why do you beat me?"

¹⁸24 Annas sent him bound to Caiaphas, the high priest. ¹⁸25 Now Simon Peter was standing and warming himself. They said therefore to him, "You aren't also one of his disciples, are you?"
He denied it and said, "I am not."

¹⁸26 One of the servants of the high priest, being a relative of him whose ear Peter had cut off, said, "Didn't I see you in the garden with him?"

¹⁸27 Peter therefore denied it again, and immediately the rooster crowed.

¹⁸28 They led Jesus therefore from Caiaphas into the Praetorium. It was early, and they themselves didn't enter into the Praetorium, that they might not be defiled, but might eat the Passover. ¹⁸29 Pilate therefore went out to them, and said, "What accusation do you bring against this man?"

¹⁸30 They answered him, "If this man weren't an evildoer, we wouldn't have delivered him up to you."
¹⁸31 Pilate therefore said to them, "Take him yourselves, and judge him according to your law."
Therefore the Jews said to him, "It is illegal for us to put anyone to death," ¹⁸32 that the word of Jesus might be fulfilled, which he spoke, signifying by what kind of death he should die.
¹⁸33 Pilate therefore entered again into the Praetorium, called Jesus, and said to him, "Are you the King of the Jews?"
¹⁸34 Jesus answered him, "Do you say this by yourself, or did others tell you about me?"
¹⁸35 Pilate answered, "I'm not a Jew, am I? Your own nation and the chief priests delivered you to me. What have you done?"
¹⁸36 Jesus answered, "My Kingdom is not of this world. If my Kingdom were of this world, then my servants would fight, that I wouldn't be delivered to the Jews. But now my Kingdom is not from here."
¹⁸37 Pilate therefore said to him, "Are you a king then?"
Jesus answered, "You say that I am a king. For this reason I have been born, and for this reason I have come into the world, that I should testify to the truth. Everyone who is of the truth listens to my voice."
¹⁸38 Pilate said to him, "What is truth?"
When he had said this, he went out again to the Jews, and said to them, "I find no basis for a charge against him. ¹⁸39 But you have a custom, that I should release someone to you at the Passover. Therefore, do you want me to release to you the King of the Jews?"
¹⁸40 Then they all shouted again, saying, "Not this man, but Barabbas!" Now Barabbas was a robber. ¹⁸

19

¹⁹1 So Pilate then took Jesus, and flogged him. ¹⁹2 The soldiers twisted thorns into a crown, and put it on his head, and dressed him in a purple garment. ¹⁹3 They kept saying,
"Hail, King of the Jews!" and they kept slapping him.
¹⁹4 Then Pilate went out again, and said to them, "Behold, I bring him out to you, that you may know that I find no basis for a charge against him."

Good Friday

¹⁹5 Jesus therefore came out, wearing the crown of thorns and the purple garment. Pilate said to them, "Behold, the man!"
¹⁹6 When therefore the chief priests and the officers saw him, they shouted, saying, "Crucify! Crucify!"
Pilate said to them, "Take him yourselves, and crucify him, for I find no basis for a charge against him."
¹⁹7 The Jews answered him, "We have a law, and by our law he ought to die, because he made himself the Son of God."
¹⁹8 When therefore Pilate heard this saying, he was more afraid. ¹⁹9 He entered into the Praetorium again, and said to Jesus, "Where are you from?" But Jesus gave him no answer. ¹⁹10 Pilate therefore said to him, "Aren't you speaking to me? Don't you know that I have power to release you and have power to crucify you?"
¹⁹11 Jesus answered, "You would have no power at all against me, unless it were given to you from above. Therefore he who delivered me to you has greater sin."
¹⁹12 At this, Pilate was seeking to release him, but the Jews cried out, saying, "If you release this man, you aren't Caesar's friend! Everyone who makes himself a king speaks against Caesar!"
¹⁹13 When Pilate therefore heard these words, he brought Jesus out and sat down on the judgment seat at a place called "The Pavement", but in Hebrew, "Gabbatha." ¹⁹14 Now it was the Preparation Day of the Passover, at about the sixth hour.²²7 He said to the Jews, "Behold, your King!"
¹⁹15 They cried out, "Away with him! Away with him! Crucify him!" Pilate said to them, "Shall I crucify your King?" The chief priests answered, "We have no king but Caesar!"
¹⁹16 So then he delivered him to them to be crucified. So they took Jesus and led him
away. ¹⁹17 He went out, bearing his cross, to the place called "The Place of a Skull", which is called in Hebrew, "Golgotha", ¹⁹18 where they crucified him, and with him two others, on either side one, and Jesus in the middle. ¹⁹19 Pilate wrote a title also, and put it on the cross. There was written, "JESUS OF NAZARETH, THE KING OF THE JEWS." ¹⁹20 Therefore many of the Jews read this title, for the

---

²²719:14 19:14 "the sixth hour" would have been 6:00 a.m. according to the Roman timekeeping system, or noon for the Jewish timekeeping system in use, then.

place where Jesus was crucified was near the city; and it was written in Hebrew, in Latin, and in Greek. ¹⁹21 The chief priests of the Jews therefore said to Pilate, "Don't write, 'The King of the Jews,' but, 'he said, "I am King of the Jews."'"

¹⁹22 Pilate answered, "What I have written, I have written."

¹⁹23 Then the soldiers, when they had crucified Jesus, took his garments and made four parts, to every soldier a part; and also the coat. Now the coat was without seam, woven from the top throughout. ¹⁹24 Then they said to one another, "Let's not tear it, but cast lots for it to decide whose it will be," that the Scripture might be fulfilled, which says,

"They parted my garments among them.
For my cloak they cast lots."#

Therefore the soldiers did these things. ¹⁹25 But standing by Jesus' cross were his mother, his mother's sister, Mary the wife of Clopas, and Mary Magdalene. ¹⁹26 Therefore when Jesus saw his mother, and the disciple whom he loved standing there, he said to his mother, "Woman, behold, your son!" ¹⁹27 Then he said to the disciple, "Behold, your mother!" From that hour, the disciple took her to his own home.

¹⁹28 After this, Jesus, seeing[228] that all things were now finished, that the Scripture might be fulfilled, said, "I am thirsty." ¹⁹29 Now a vessel full of vinegar was set there; so they put a sponge full of the vinegar on hyssop, and held it at his mouth. ¹⁹30 When Jesus therefore had received the vinegar, he said, "It is finished." He bowed his head, and gave up his spirit.

¹⁹31 Therefore the Jews, because it was the Preparation Day, so that the bodies wouldn't remain on the cross on the Sabbath (for that Sabbath was a special one), asked of Pilate that their legs might be broken, and that they might be taken away. ¹⁹32 Therefore the soldiers came, and broke the legs of the first, and of the other who was crucified with him; ¹⁹33 but when they came to Jesus, and saw that he was already dead, they didn't break his legs. ¹⁹34 However one of the soldiers pierced his side with a spear, and immediately blood and water came out. ¹⁹35 He who has seen has testified, and his testimony

---

#19:24 19:24 Psalm 22:18
[228]19:28 19:28 NU, TR read "knowing" instead of "seeing"

Good Friday

is true. He knows that he tells the truth, that you may believe. **¹⁹³⁶** For these things happened that the Scripture might be fulfilled, "A bone of him will not be broken."# **¹⁹³⁷** Again another Scripture says, "They will look on him whom they pierced."#

¹⁹³⁸ After these things, Joseph of Arimathaea, being a disciple of Jesus, but secretly for fear of the Jews, asked of Pilate that he might take away Jesus' body. Pilate gave him permission. He came therefore and took away his body. **¹⁹³⁹** Nicodemus, who at first came to Jesus by night, also came bringing a mixture of myrrh and aloes, about a hundred Roman pounds.²²⁹ **¹⁹⁴⁰** So they took Jesus' body, and bound it in linen cloths with the spices, as the custom of the Jews is to bury. **¹⁹⁴¹** Now in the place where he was crucified there was a garden. In the garden was a new tomb in which no man had ever yet been laid. **¹⁹⁴²** Then because of the Jews' Preparation Day (for the tomb was near at hand) they laid Jesus there.

The Lord's Prayer

Our Father, who art in heaven,
Hallowed be thy name.
Thy Kingdom come.
Thy will be done on Earth, as it is in heaven.
Give us this day our daily bread.
And forgive us our trespasses,
As we forgive those that trespass against us.
And lead us not into temptation,
But deliver us from evil.
For thine is the kingdom,
The power, and the glory,
For ever and ever.
AMEN

#19:36 19:36 Exodus 12:46; Numbers 9:12; Psalm 34:20
#19:37 19:37 Zechariah 12:10
²²⁹19:39 19:39 100 Roman pounds of 12 ounces each, or about 72 pounds, or 33 Kilograms.

Holy Saturday

A Note on Holy Saturday

Holy Saturday has traditionally been one of the few days on the Christian calendar when services are often not celebrated. Rather, it is a time of reflection and preparation for the Lord's return on Easter Sunday. In line with that thinking, I offer only a brief prayer on Holy Saturday and encourage all Christians to spend the day in prayerful contemplation.

Prayer

Heavenly Father, you have blessed the world by sacrificing your only Son for the sake of sinners and we now eagerly await Easter, the day the world commemorates Christ's miraculous return.

Prayer of Confession

Almighty and most merciful Father; we have erred, and strayed from your ways like lost sheep. We have followed too much the devices and desires of our own hearts. We have offended against your holy laws. We have left undone those things which we ought to have done; and

we have done those things which we ought not to have done; and there is no health in us. O Lord, have mercy upon us, miserable offenders. Spare those, O God, who confess their faults. Restore those who are penitent; according to your promises declared unto mankind in Christ Jesus our Lord. And grant, O most merciful Father, for his sake; that we may hereafter live a godly, righteous, and sober life, to the glory of thy holy Name. Amen.
-Revised prayer from *The Book of Common Prayer*, 1662

The Lord's Prayer

Our Father, who art in heaven,
Hallowed be thy name.
Thy Kingdom come.
Thy will be done on Earth, as it is in heaven.
Give us this day our daily bread.
And forgive us our trespasses,
As we forgive those that trespass against us.
And lead us not into temptation,
But deliver us from evil.
For thine is the kingdom,
The power, and the glory,
For ever and ever.
AMEN

Easter

Prayer

Rejoice! Christ is risen, he is risen indeed!
Holy Father, I stand before you today in humility and thankfulness. Christ, through His death on the bloody cross and His resurrection, has clothed me in His righteousness and has delivered me from everlasting death. In baptism, I have died with Christ and have risen with Him, and it is only through the grace of God and the miracle of this holy day that I was blessed to be born again, not by a washing of the flesh but by a cleansing of the soul. Although I can never repay you for saving me from my naturally abhorrent and wretched state, I pledge to live my life as Christ commanded, knowing that I will fall short of His glory. Thank you, Father, for all that you have given to me and for all that you ever will give me. Whatever I have been given, I have been blessed and I am thankful for your supreme love. In Christ's holy, sacred, and blessed name, Amen.

Prayer of Confession

Almighty and most merciful Father; we have erred, and strayed from your ways like lost sheep. We have followed too much the devices and desires of our own hearts. We have offended against your holy laws. We have left undone those things which we ought to have done; and we have done those things which we ought not to have done; and there is no health in us. O Lord, have mercy upon us,

miserable offenders. Spare those, O God, who confess their faults. Restore those who are penitent; according to your promises declared unto mankind in Christ Jesus our Lord. And grant, O most merciful Father, for his sake; that we may hereafter live a godly, righteous, and sober life, to the glory of thy holy Name. Amen.
-Revised prayer from *The Book of Common Prayer*, 1662

Daily Wisdom

1 O give thanks unto the LORD; for *he is* good: because his mercy *endureth* for ever.
2 Let Israel now say, that his mercy *endureth* for ever.
3 Let the house of Aaron now say, that his mercy *endureth* for ever.
4 Let them now that fear the LORD say, that his mercy *endureth* for ever.
5 I called upon the LORD in distress: the LORD answered me, *and set me* in a large place.
6 The LORD *is* on my side; I will not fear: what can man do unto me?
7 The LORD taketh my part with them that help me: therefore shall I see *my desire* upon them that hate me.
8 *It is* better to trust in the LORD than to put confidence in man.
9 *It is* better to trust in the LORD than to put confidence in princes.
10 All nations compassed me about: but in the name of the LORD will I destroy them.
11 They compassed me about; yea, they compassed me about: but in the name of the LORD I will destroy them.
12 They compassed me about like bees; they are quenched as the fire of thorns: for in the name of the LORD I will destroy them.
13 Thou hast thrust sore at me that I might fall: but the LORD helped me.

Easter

14 The LORD *is* my strength and song, and is become my salvation.
15 The voice of rejoicing and salvation *is* in the tabernacles of the righteous: the right hand of the LORD doeth valiantly.
16 The right hand of the LORD is exalted: the right hand of the LORD doeth valiantly.
17 I shall not die, but live, and declare the works of the LORD.
18 The LORD hath chastened me sore: but he hath not given me over unto death.
19 Open to me the gates of righteousness: I will go into them, *and* I will praise the LORD:
20 This gate of the LORD, into which the righteous shall enter.
21 I will praise thee: for thou hast heard me, and art become my salvation.
22 The stone *which* the builders refused is become the head *stone* of the corner.
23 This is the LORD'S doing; it *is* marvellous in our eyes.
24 This *is* the day *which* the LORD hath made; we will rejoice and be glad in it.
25 Save now, I beseech thee, O LORD: O LORD, I beseech thee, send now prosperity.
26 Blessed *be* he that cometh in the name of the LORD: we have blessed you out of the house of the LORD.
27 God *is* the LORD, which hath shewed us light: bind the sacrifice with cords, *even* unto the horns of the altar.
28 Thou *art* my God, and I will praise thee: *thou art* my God, I will exalt thee.
29 O give thanks unto the LORD; for *he is* good: for his mercy *endureth* for ever.
-Psalm 22, *The King James Bible*, 1769 edition of 1611 text

The American Book of Prayer

Readings from the Holy Bible

The Holy Gospel According to John (John 20 & 21)

JOHN 20 & 21

20

20:1 Now on the first day of the week, Mary Magdalene went early, while it was still dark, to the tomb, and saw the stone taken away from the tomb. **20:2** Therefore she ran and came to Simon Peter and to the other disciple whom Jesus loved, and said to them, "They have taken away the Lord out of the tomb, and we don't know where they have laid him!"

20:3 Therefore Peter and the other disciple went out, and they went toward the tomb. **20:4** They both ran together. The other disciple outran Peter, and came to the tomb first. **20:5** Stooping and looking in, he saw the linen cloths lying, yet he didn't enter in. **20:6** Then Simon Peter came, following him, and entered into the tomb. He saw the linen cloths lying, **20:7** and the cloth that had been on his head, not lying with the linen cloths, but rolled up in a place by itself. **20:8** So then the other disciple who came first to the tomb also entered in, and he saw and believed. **20:9** For as yet they didn't know the Scripture, that he must rise from the dead. **20:10** So the disciples went away again to their own homes.

20:11 But Mary was standing outside at the tomb weeping. So as she wept, she stooped and looked into the tomb, **20:12** and she saw two angels in white sitting, one at the head, and one at the feet, where the body of Jesus had lain. **20:13** They asked her, "Woman, why are you weeping?"

She said to them, "Because they have taken away my Lord, and I don't know where they have laid him." **20:14** When she had said this, she turned around and saw Jesus standing, and didn't know that it was Jesus.

20:15 Jesus said to her, "Woman, why are you weeping? Who are you looking for?"

She, supposing him to be the gardener, said to him, "Sir, if

Easter

you have carried him away, tell me where you have laid him, and I will take him away."

²⁰16 Jesus said to her, "Mary."

She turned and said to him, "Rabboni!"[230] which is to say, "Teacher!"[231]

²⁰17 Jesus said to her, "Don't hold me, for I haven't yet ascended to my Father; but go to my brothers and tell them, 'I am ascending to my Father and your Father, to my God and your God.'"

²⁰18 Mary Magdalene came and told the disciples that she had seen the Lord, and that he had said these things to her. ²⁰19 When therefore it was evening on that day, the first day of the week, and when the doors were locked where the disciples were assembled, for fear of the Jews, Jesus came and stood in the middle, and said to them, "Peace be to you."

²⁰20 When he had said this, he showed them his hands and his side. The disciples therefore were glad when they saw the Lord. ²⁰21 Jesus therefore said to them again, "Peace be to you. As the Father has sent me, even so I send you." ²⁰22 When he had said this, he breathed on them, and said to them, "Receive the Holy Spirit! ²⁰23 If you forgive anyone's sins, they have been forgiven them. If you retain anyone's sins, they have been retained."

²⁰24 But Thomas, one of the twelve, called Didymus, wasn't with them when Jesus came. ²⁰25 The other disciples therefore said to him, "We have seen the Lord!"

But he said to them, "Unless I see in his hands the print of the nails, put my finger into the print of the nails, and put my hand into his side, I will not believe."

²⁰26 After eight days again his disciples were inside and Thomas was with them. Jesus came, the doors being locked, and stood in the middle, and said, "Peace be to you." ²⁰27 Then he said to Thomas, "Reach here your finger, and see my hands. Reach here your hand, and put it into my side. Don't be unbelieving, but believing."

²⁰28 Thomas answered him, "My Lord and my God!"

---

[230]20:16 20:16 Rabboni is a transliteration of the Hebrew word for "great teacher."
[231]20:16 20:16 or, Master

The American Book of Prayer

²⁰29 Jesus said to him, "Because you have seen me,[232] you have believed. Blessed are those who have not seen, and have believed." ²⁰30 Therefore Jesus did many other signs in the presence of his disciples, which are not written in this book; ²⁰31 but these are written, that you may believe that Jesus is the Christ, the Son of God, and that believing you may have life in his name. 20

21

²¹1 After these things, Jesus revealed himself again to the disciples at the sea of Tiberias. He revealed himself this way. ²¹2 Simon Peter, Thomas called Didymus, Nathanael of Cana in Galilee, and the sons of Zebedee, and two others of his disciples were together. ²¹3 Simon Peter said to them, "I'm going fishing."
They told him, "We are also coming with you." They immediately went out, and entered into the boat. That night, they caught nothing.
²¹4 But when day had already come, Jesus stood on the beach, yet the disciples didn't know that it was Jesus. ²¹5 Jesus therefore said to them, "Children, have you anything to eat?"
They answered him, "No."
²¹6 He said to them, "Cast the net on the right side of the boat, and you will find some."
They cast it therefore, and now they weren't able to draw it in for the multitude of fish. ²¹7 That disciple therefore whom Jesus loved said to Peter, "It's the Lord!"
So when Simon Peter heard that it was the Lord, he wrapped his coat around himself (for he was naked), and threw himself into the sea.
²¹8 But the other disciples came in the little boat (for they were not far from the land, but about two hundred cubits[233] away), dragging the net full of fish. ²¹9 So when they got out on the land, they saw a fire of coals there, with fish and bread laid on it. ²¹10 Jesus said to them, "Bring some of the fish which you have just caught."
²¹11 Simon Peter went up, and drew the net to land, full of one hundred fifty-three great fish. Even though there were so many, the net wasn't torn.
²¹12 Jesus said to them, "Come and eat breakfast!"

---

[232]20:29 20:29 TR adds "Thomas,"
[233]21:8 21:8 200 cubits is about 100 yards or about 91 meters

Easter

None of the disciples dared inquire of him, "Who are you?" knowing that it was the Lord.

21:13 Then Jesus came and took the bread, gave it to them, and the fish likewise. **21:14** This is now the third time that Jesus was revealed to his disciples after he had risen from the dead. **21:15** So when they had eaten their breakfast, Jesus said to Simon Peter, "Simon, son of Jonah, do you love me more than these?"

He said to him, "Yes, Lord; you know that I have affection for you."

He said to him, "Feed my lambs." **21:16** He said to him again a second time, "Simon, son of Jonah, do you love me?"

He said to him, "Yes, Lord; you know that I have affection for you."

He said to him, "Tend my sheep." **21:17** He said to him the third time, "Simon, son of Jonah, do you have affection for me?"

Peter was grieved because he asked him the third time, "Do you have affection for me?" He said to him, "Lord, you know everything. You know that I have affection for you."

Jesus said to him, "Feed my sheep. **21:18** Most certainly I tell you, when you were young, you dressed yourself and walked where you wanted to. But when you are old, you will stretch out your hands, and another will dress you and carry you where you don't want to go."

21:19 Now he said this, signifying by what kind of death he would glorify God. When he had said this, he said to him, "Follow me."

21:20 Then Peter, turning around, saw a disciple following. This was the disciple whom Jesus loved, the one who had also leaned on Jesus' breast at the supper and asked, "Lord, who is going to betray you?" **21:21** Peter seeing him, said to Jesus, "Lord, what about this man?" **21:22** Jesus said to him, "If I desire that he stay until I come, what is that to you? You follow me." **21:23** This saying therefore went out among the brothers,[234] that this disciple wouldn't die. Yet Jesus didn't say to him that he wouldn't die, but, "If I desire that he stay until I come, what is that to you?" **21:24** This is the disciple who testifies about these things, and wrote these things. We know that his witness is true. **21:25** There are also many other things which Jesus did, which if they would all be written, I suppose that even the world itself wouldn't have room for the books that would be written.

---

[234] 21:23 21:23 The word for "brothers" here may be also correctly translated "brothers and sisters" or "siblings."

The American Book of Prayer

The Lord's Prayer

Our Father, who art in heaven,
Hallowed be thy name.
Thy Kingdom come.
Thy will be done on Earth, as it is in heaven.
Give us this day our daily bread.
And forgive us our trespasses,
As we forgive those that trespass against us.
And lead us not into temptation,
But deliver us from evil.
For thine is the kingdom,
The power, and the glory,
For ever and ever.
AMEN

Christmas

Prayers and Readings for the Christmas Season

A Christmas Prayer

Give us, O God, the vision which can see Your love in the world in spite of human failure.
 Give us the faith to trust Your goodness in spite of our ignorance and weakness.
 Give us the knowledge that we may continue to pray with understanding hearts.
 And show us what each one of us can do to set forward the coming of the day of universal peace.
-Astronaut Frank Borman, 1968 Apollo 8 Christmas Prayer[22]

A Second Christmas Prayer

Loving God, Help us remember the birth of Jesus,
that we may share in the song of the angels, the gladness of the shepherds, and worship of the wise men.
Close the door of hate and open the door of love all over the world. Let kindness come with every gift and good desires with every greeting. Deliver us from evil by the blessing which Christ brings, and teach us to be merry with clear hearts.

May the Christmas morning make us happy to be thy children, and Christmas evening bring us to our beds with grateful thoughts, forgiving and forgiven, for Jesus' sake. Amen.
-*Robert Louis Stevenson (1850-1894)*[23]

Twas the Night Before Christmas

Twas the Night Before Christmas is one of the most famous poems in the world, but very few Americans know about its influential author, Clement Clarke Moore. Moore was born in 1779 to Episcopal Church (Anglican) leader Benjamin Moore, the bishop of the Episcopal Diocese of New York and former president of Columbia College who famously took part in George Washington's inauguration as president. The Moore family was very influential in New York City, and Clement Moore was an avid patriot who was involved in politics and religion from a very early age. In fact, one of the first well-known writings published by Moore was a pamphlet in support of the Federalist Party in 1804 that attacked Thomas Jefferson's rather liberal (even by today's standards) religious views. Moore was also very involved with Trinity Church in New York City, one of the most influential parishes of the Episcopal Church and still famous today.

Moore was a very well-educated man and very religious. He was a bible professor at the General Theological Seminary until 1850, and he used his advanced knowledge of German and Scandinavian folklores to create his now-famous vision of St. Nicholas, a real Christian saint.

Ironically, the imagined version of Moore's Santa Claus was in fact not anything like the previous stories involving St. Nicholas, but perhaps even more surprising is that the widely-held view of Santa Claus today doesn't even match the description or imagination of Moore himself. A careful reading of the story shows with near-certainty that St. Nicholas was meant to be viewed as a small "elf," not a large man. Note that St. Nick rides a "miniature sleigh" led by "tiny reindeer" and is referred to as being "lively and quick." Moore also describes St. Nicholas as small on several occasions.

Although this famous poem has been greatly criticized in recent years by religious evangelicals from all denominations as a contributing factor toward the demise of the true meaning of Christmas, I think this view is completely unfounded for a variety of reasons. First, the poem was first published near Christmas of 1823, and America didn't start changing its attitude toward Christmas until well into the 20th century, despite the poem's popularity. Second, the author was, by nearly all accounts, a very devout supporter of the church and was well-known for criticizing other famous Americans of the period for not being evangelical. To say he somehow wanted to make Christmas a shallow go-to-the-mall holiday is immensely unfair to the author. Third, if read in context, the poem is about Christian giving in the context of German and Scandinavian folklore, nothing close to what the holiday has transformed into today. To say the focus was shifted away from Christ is quite unfair given that the main character is an actual Christian bishop of the early church who was said to have done a great deal to advance the Christian faith and is known as the patron saint of children.

This is not to say that Christmas in the West doesn't need to change so that its focus is on Christ and not materialism; it obviously does. But eliminating an important part of American Christian tradition is simply not the answer. In fact, I think this poem should be part of the American Christian's future in relation to Christmas ... so long as it's told properly.

Twas the Night Before Christmas

By Clement Clarke Moore

Twas the night before Christmas, when all through the house,
Not a creature was stirring, not even a mouse.
The stockings were hung by the chimney with care,
In hopes that St Nicholas soon would be there.

The children were nestled all snug in their beds,
While visions of sugar-plums danced in their heads.
And mamma in her 'kerchief, and I in my cap,
Had just settled our brains for a long winter's nap.

When out on the lawn there arose such a clatter,
I sprang from the bed to see what was the matter.
Away to the window I flew like a flash,
Tore open the shutters and threw up the sash.

The moon on the breast of the new-fallen snow
Gave the lustre of mid-day to objects below.
When, what to my wondering eyes should appear,
But a miniature sleigh, and eight tinny reindeer.

With a little old driver, so lively and quick,
I knew in a moment it must be St Nick.
More rapid than eagles his coursers they came,
And he whistled, and shouted, and called them by name!

The American Book of Prayer

"Now Dasher! now, Dancer! now, Prancer and Vixen!
On, Comet! On, Cupid! on, on Donner and Blitzen!
To the top of the porch! to the top of the wall!
Now dash away! Dash away! Dash away all!"

As dry leaves that before the wild hurricane fly,
When they meet with an obstacle, mount to the sky.
So up to the house-top the coursers they flew,
With the sleigh full of Toys, and St Nicholas too.

And then, in a twinkling, I heard on the roof
The prancing and pawing of each little hoof.
As I drew in my head, and was turning around,
Down the chimney St Nicholas came with a bound.

He was dressed all in fur, from his head to his foot,
And his clothes were all tarnished with ashes and soot.
A bundle of Toys he had flung on his back,
And he looked like a peddler, just opening his pack.

His eyes-how they twinkled! his dimples how merry!
His cheeks were like roses, his nose like a cherry!
His droll little mouth was drawn up like a bow,
And the beard of his chin was as white as the snow.

The stump of a pipe he held tight in his teeth,
And the smoke it encircled his head like a wreath.
He had a broad face and a little round belly,
That shook when he laughed, like a bowlful of jelly!

He was chubby and plump, a right jolly old elf,
And I laughed when I saw him, in spite of myself!
A wink of his eye and a twist of his head,
Soon gave me to know I had nothing to dread.

He spoke not a word, but went straight to his work,
And filled all the stockings, then turned with a jerk.

And laying his finger aside of his nose,
And giving a nod, up the chimney he rose!

He sprang to his sleigh, to his team gave a whistle,
And away they all flew like the down of a thistle.
But I heard him exclaim, 'ere he drove out of sight,
"Happy Christmas to all, and to all a good-night!"

Prayer of Confession for Christmas

Almighty and most merciful Father; In this Christmas season, we remember the birth of your only son and our savior Jesus of Nazareth, and we humbly repent for not living our lives as well as we have been called to. The incredible story of His arrival on Earth is our focus this Christmas, and we pray that you will keep our hearts focused on the love of Christ, not on the materialism that has gripped our fallen world. With that in mind, we pray:

We have erred, and strayed from thy ways like lost sheep. We have followed too much the devices and desires of our own hearts. We have offended against your holy laws. We have left undone those things which we ought to have done; And we have done those things which we ought not to have done; And there is no health in us. But thou, O Lord, have mercy upon us, miserable offenders. Spare those, O God, who confess their faults. Restore those who are penitent; According to thy promises declared unto mankind in Christ Jesus our Lord. And grant, O most merciful Father, for his sake; That we may hereafter live a godly, righteous, and sober life, To the glory of thy holy Name. Amen.
–A revised version of the prayer contained in *The Book of Common Prayer*, 1662

Psalms for Christmas

PSALM 96

1 O sing unto the LORD a new song: sing unto the LORD, all the earth.
2 Sing unto the LORD, bless his name; shew forth his salvation from day to day.
3 Declare his glory among the heathen, his wonders among all people.
4 For the LORD *is* great, and greatly to be praised: he *is* to be feared above all gods.
5 For all the gods of the nations *are* idols: but the LORD made the heavens.
6 Honor and majesty *are* before him: strength and beauty *are* in his sanctuary.
7 Give unto the LORD, O ye kindreds of the people, give unto the LORD glory and strength.
8 Give unto the LORD the glory *due unto* his name: bring an offering, and come into his courts.
9 O worship the LORD in the beauty of holiness: fear before him, all the earth.
10 Say among the heathen *that* the LORD reigneth: the world also shall be established that it shall not be moved: he shall judge the people righteously.
11 Let the heavens rejoice, and let the earth be glad; let the sea roar, and the fulness thereof.
12 Let the field be joyful, and all that *is* therein: then shall all the trees of the wood rejoice
13 Before the LORD: for he cometh, for he cometh to judge the earth: he shall judge the world with righteousness, and the people with his truth.

PSALM 97

1 The LORD reigneth; let the earth rejoice; let the multitude of isles be glad *thereof.*

Prayers and Readings for the Christmas Season

2 Clouds and darkness *are* round about him: righteousness and judgment *are* the habitation of his throne.
3 A fire goeth before him, and burneth up his enemies round about.
4 His lightnings enlightened the world: the earth saw, and trembled.
5 The hills melted like wax at the presence of the LORD, at the presence of the Lord of the whole earth.
6 The heavens declare his righteousness, and all the people see his glory.
7 Confounded be all they that serve graven images, that boast themselves of idols: worship him, all *ye* gods.
8 Zion heard, and was glad; and the daughters of Judah rejoiced because of thy judgments, O LORD.
9 For thou, LORD, *art* high above all the earth: thou art exalted far above all gods.
10 Ye that love the LORD, hate evil: he preserveth the souls of his saints; he delivereth them out of the hand of the wicked.
11 Light is sown for the righteous, and gladness for the upright in heart.
12 Rejoice in the LORD, ye righteous; and give thanks at the remembrance of his holiness.

PSALM 98
1 O sing unto the LORD a new song; for he hath done marvellous things: his right hand, and his holy arm, hath gotten him the victory.
2 The LORD hath made known his salvation: his righteousness hath he openly shewed in the sight of the heathen.
3 He hath remembered his mercy and his truth toward the house of Israel: all the ends of the earth have seen the salvation of our God.
4 Make a joyful noise unto the LORD, all the earth: make a loud noise, and rejoice, and sing praise.

5 Sing unto the LORD with the harp; with the harp, and the voice of a psalm.
6 With trumpets and sound of cornet make a joyful noise before the LORD, the King.
7 Let the sea roar, and the fulness thereof; the world, and they that dwell therein.
8 Let the floods clap *their* hands: let the hills be joyful together
9 Before the LORD; for he cometh to judge the earth: with righteousness shall he judge the world, and the people with equity.
-Psalms 96, 97, and 98, *The King James Bible*, 1769 edition of 1611 text[24]

Readings from the Holy Bible

The Holy Gospel According to Luke and Matthew (LUKE 2:1-21; MATTHEW 1:18-2:23)

LUKE 2:1-21

2

2¹ Now in those days, a decree went out from Caesar Augustus that all the world should be enrolled. **²2** This was the first enrollment made when Quirinius was governor of Syria. **²3** All went to enroll themselves, everyone to his own city. **²4** Joseph also went up from Galilee, out of the city of Nazareth, into Judea, to David's city, which is called Bethlehem, because he was of the house and family of David; **²5** to enroll himself with Mary, who was pledged to be married to him as wife, being pregnant.
²6 While they were there, the day had come for her to give birth.
²7 She gave birth to her firstborn son. She wrapped him in bands of cloth, and laid him in a feeding trough, because there was no room for them in the inn. **²8** There were shepherds in the same country staying in the field, and keeping watch by night over their flock. **²9** Behold, an angel of the Lord stood by them, and the glory of the Lord shone around them, and they were terrified. **²10** The angel said to them,

Prayers and Readings for the Christmas Season

"Don't be afraid, for behold, I bring you good news of great joy which will be to all the people. ^{2}11 For there is born to you today, in David's city, a Savior, who is Christ the Lord. ^{2}12 This is the sign to you: you will find a baby wrapped in strips of cloth, lying in a feeding trough."
^{2}13 Suddenly, there was with the angel a multitude of the heavenly army praising God, and saying,
^{2}14 "Glory to God in the highest,
on earth peace, good will toward men."
^{2}15 When the angels went away from them into the sky, the shepherds said to one another, "Let's go to Bethlehem, now, and see this thing that has happened, which the Lord has made known to us." ^{2}16 They came with haste, and found both Mary and Joseph, and the baby was lying in the feeding trough. ^{2}17 When they saw it, they publicized widely the saying which was spoken to them about this child. ^{2}18 All who heard it wondered at the things which were spoken to them by the shepherds. ^{2}19 But Mary kept all these sayings, pondering them in her heart. ^{2}20 The shepherds returned, glorifying and praising God for all the things that they had heard and seen, just as it was told them. ^{2}21 When eight days were fulfilled for the circumcision of the child, his name was called Jesus, which was given by the angel before he was conceived in the womb.

MATT 1:18-2:23, A KING IS BORN

^{1}18 Now the birth of Jesus Christ was like this: After his mother, Mary, was engaged to Joseph, before they came together, she was found pregnant by the Holy Spirit. ^{1}19 Joseph, her husband, being a righteous man, and not willing to make her a public example, intended to put her away secretly. ^{1}20 But when he thought about these things, behold,[235] an angel of the Lord appeared to him in a dream, saying, "Joseph, son of David, don't be afraid to take to yourself Mary, your wife, for that which is conceived in her is of the Holy Spirit. ^{1}21 She shall give birth to a son. You shall call his name Jesus,[236] for it is he who shall save his people from their sins."

---

[235] 1:20 1:20 "Behold", from "ἰδοὺ", means look at, take notice, observe, see, or gaze at. It is often used as an interjection.
[236] 1:21 1:21 "Jesus" means "Salvation".

The American Book of Prayer

¹22 Now all this has happened that it might be fulfilled which was spoken by the Lord through the prophet, saying,
¹23 "Behold, the virgin shall be with child,
and shall give birth to a son.
They shall call his name Immanuel;"
which is, being interpreted, "God with us."#
¹24 Joseph arose from his sleep, and did as the angel of the Lord commanded him, and took his wife to himself; ¹25 and didn't know her sexually until she had given birth to her firstborn son. He named him Jesus.

2

²1 Now when Jesus was born in Bethlehem of Judea in the days of King Herod, behold, wise men²37 from the east came to Jerusalem, saying, ²2 "Where is he who is born King of the Jews? For we saw his star in the east, and have come to worship him." ²3 When King Herod heard it, he was troubled, and all Jerusalem with him. ²4 Gathering together all the chief priests and scribes of the people, he asked them where the Christ would be born. ²5 They said to him, "In Bethlehem of Judea, for this is written through the prophet,
²6 'You Bethlehem, land of Judah,
are in no way least among the princes of Judah:
for out of you shall come a governor,
who shall shepherd my people, Israel.'"#
²7 Then Herod secretly called the wise men, and learned from them exactly what time the star appeared. ²8 He sent them to Bethlehem, and said, "Go and search diligently for the young child. When you have found him, bring me word, so that I also may come and worship him."
²9 They, having heard the king, went their way; and behold, the star, which they saw in the east, went before them, until it came and stood over where the young child was. ²10 When they saw the star, they rejoiced with exceedingly great joy. ²11 They came into the house and

---

#1:23 1:23 Isaiah 7:14
²³⁷2:1 2:1 The word for "wise men" (magoi) can also mean teachers, scientists, physicians, astrologers, seers, interpreters of dreams, or sorcerers.
#2:6 2:6 Micah 5:2

Prayers and Readings for the Christmas Season

saw the young child with Mary, his mother, and they fell down and worshiped him. Opening their treasures, they offered to him gifts: gold, frankincense, and myrrh. **2:12** Being warned in a dream not to return to Herod, they went back to their own country another way.
2:13 Now when they had departed, behold, an angel of the Lord appeared to Joseph in a dream, saying, "Arise and take the young child and his mother, and flee into Egypt, and stay there until I tell you, for Herod will seek the young child to destroy him."
2:14 He arose and took the young child and his mother by night, and departed into Egypt, **2:15** and was there until the death of Herod; that it might be fulfilled which was spoken by the Lord through the prophet, saying, "Out of Egypt I called my son."#
2:16 Then Herod, when he saw that he was mocked by the wise men, was exceedingly angry, and sent out, and killed all the male children who were in Bethlehem and in all the surrounding countryside, from two years old and under, according to the exact time which he had learned from the wise men. **2:17** Then that which was spoken by Jeremiah the prophet was fulfilled, saying,
2:18 "A voice was heard in Ramah, lamentation, weeping and great mourning,
Rachel weeping for her children;
she wouldn't be comforted, because they are no more."#
2:19 But when Herod was dead, behold, an angel of the Lord appeared in a dream to Joseph in Egypt, saying, **2:20** "Arise and take the young child and his mother, and go into the land of Israel, for those who sought the young child's life are dead."
2:21 He arose and took the young child and his mother, and came into the land of Israel. **2:22** But when he heard that Archelaus was reigning over Judea in the place of his father, Herod, he was afraid to go there. Being warned in a dream, he withdrew into the region of Galilee, **2:23** and came and lived in a city called Nazareth; that it might be fulfilled which was spoken through the prophets: "He will be called a Nazarene."

#2:15 2:15 Hosea 11:1
#2:18 2:18 Jeremiah 31:15

The American Book of Prayer

The Lord's Prayer

Our Father, who art in heaven,
Hallowed be thy name.
Thy Kingdom come.
Thy will be done on Earth, as it is in heaven.
Give us this day our daily bread.
And forgive us our trespasses,
As we forgive those that trespass against us.
And lead us not into temptation,
But deliver us from evil.
For thine is the kingdom,
The power, and the glory,
For ever and ever.
AMEN

Prayers for Daily Life

A Prayer for the Final Abolition of Slavery

Heavenly Father, we humbly call upon you to send your Holy Spirit out into the world for the purpose of eliminating slavery once and for all. Much of the Western world lives in ignorance regarding the current slavery crisis. Guide the world toward peace and help us all see the full weight of modern slavery and serve you Lord by helping in its demise. For all those in the world suffering as slaves, bless them God with strength and peace. We beg you to lead them to lifelong freedom and faith. In Jesus' name we pray, Amen.

A Prayer for the End of War

Everlasting God, since the time of Cain and Abel, humanity has been at war with itself, giving in to sin for the sake of pride, greed, and power. Reform our souls, loving God, and transform our hearts so that we hate one another no longer. Keep all human life free from harm, and protect the world from the tragedy of war. In Christ's name, Amen.

A Prayer for Soldiers

Father, in a fallen world, soldiers are necessary to stand firm against evil and protect the world from being overcome by destructive forces. Keep those soldiers who stand for liberty, freedom, peace, and love free from harm. Help them in their time of need, and allow them, oh gracious God, to return home to family and friends who eagerly await their arrival. Lead them not toward suffering and destruction, and keep their hearts and minds focused on the glory of God. Amen.

A Prayer for the Families of Soldiers

Gracious God, assist those families of soldiers who must endure tremendous hardship for the sake of freedom, faith, love, and peace. In charity and love, save their sons and daughters, mothers and fathers, brothers and sisters, husbands and wives, and friends from harm. Bring peace into the lives of all those who have already given so much and never allow the world to forget the sacrifices so many make for the lives of strangers. May we all be filled with pride for the love they show the world. Amen.

A Prayer for Those Seeking Employment

Father, so many men and women seek employment in this fallen world in order to improve their own lives and the lives of their loved ones. Help all those currently looking for employment and provide them with happiness and financial peace. Amen

A Prayer for the End of Sin

Lord God, this fallen world is far from what it ought to be should humanity overcome its sinfulness and attain the life you so desperately want for us. We pray that you will soon return to the earth to bring a final end to the sin that captivates us all. Without your love and the grace provided by Christ's ultimate sacrifice, we remain absolute slaves to sin. Rid us of our sinful natures and bring our souls to a state of purity. Amen.

A Prayer for the Protection of God's Creation

God, you are the ultimate provider of the world, the creator of all things. When you formed the universe, you made all of your creation "good" in your sight. We then have a responsibility to treat the world and all of your creation with respect and love so that generations after us may witness the beauty of your created wonders. Help protect the world from destruction and assist humanity in balancing protecting nature, including animal life, with creating a modern world that is safe, clean, and productive for human life. Amen.

A Prayer for the Impoverished of the World

Heavenly Father, billions on this earth are suffering in poverty, living daily in conditions unfit for the modern world. Help us Lord to provide for these people and keep us from forgetting their struggles. Make our hearts charitable so that we may freely give what we can to aid in the end of poverty. Do not allow our hearts to be hard and let us not forget that "the meek shall inherit the earth." In Christ's name, Amen.

A Prayer for the Homeless

All-knowing and merciful Lord, protect all those people across the world who are living without a safe home. May you keep them dry, warm, and safe from all harm. Help them to find good homes, medical care, compassionate communities of faith, and generous neighbors. Amen.

A Prayer for Doctors, Nurses, and Other Medical Staff

Everlasting God, by your sovereign power and might, you have provided the world with talented and gifted minds who have the ability to heal the sick and save lives from seemingly certain death. Bless these men and women and help them continue to grow in wisdom, knowledge, faith, love, and compassion so that they may use their talents toward the healing of humanity. Wherever the sick stand in need of care, send the healers of the world, and never allow our doctors, nurses, and other medical staff members to forget the purpose of their training or that love is their chief obligation. Give them courage and strength, Lord, for without them, the world would surely be full of suffering. Amen.

A Prayer for Police Officers, Firefighters, Teachers, and Public Servants

Almighty Father, bless those public servants, the teachers, firefighters, police officers, and other public servants. Each day they are asked to make our communities stronger and more secure, a hopeless endeavor without your Divine assistance, Lord. Please bring strength, knowledge, wisdom, and compassion to these servants so that they may make the earth a better place for your creation to live in. Do not let them fall into laziness, apathy, or disinterest. In Jesus' holy and righteousness name, Amen.

A Prayer for Good Government

Most holy and righteous Father, bless our governing officials, politicians, and other public servants so that they may serve you and your creation with intelligence, wisdom, and compassion. Keep them from corruption and guide them to truth. Do not allow them to stunt the growth of liberty and assist them in spreading freedom to even the darkest parts of the world. Amen.

A Prayer in Preparation for Baptism

Everlasting Holy Father, as I prepare for my holy baptism, I am thankful for all that has been given to me, especially my faith, the source of all goodness in this world. I am eager at the opportunity to express my faith to the world and to have the waters of Christ wash over me, so, as the Word of God states, I may be made clean through faith. In Christ's name, Amen.

A Prayer for the Baptized

Heavenly Father, on this day, _____ has been baptized into your holy church. In baptism, (he/she) has both died and risen with Christ. Bless (his/her) soul and keep (him/her) safe from harm. Allow (him/her) not to fall from faith, and send the Holy Spirit into (his/her) life until (he/she) is united with you in heaven. In the name of the Father, the Son, and the Holy Ghost, Amen.

A Prayer in Preparation for the Lord's Supper

Holy Father, on the night Christ was betrayed, he broke bread and drank wine with His disciples, instructing them to repeat this act in memory of Him. I am so blessed to share in this truly holy meal with other saints in your church and long to partake of what Ignatius called, "the medicine of immortality." In preparation of this meal, I humbly repent of my sins and ask for forgiveness before you just as the apostle Paul taught in his own day. May this meal be worthy in your eyes, Lord. Amen.

A Prayer for the Clergy

My God, without dedicated servants and preachers of your Word and sacraments, the Christian church would not exist. Bless all those who have the courage to preach your sacred Word and who promote the Gospel. Give your ministers all they need to bring the world to faith. In Jesus' name we pray, Amen.

A Prayer in Preparation of a Wedding

Holy Father, as I prepare for my wedding, prepare my heart for the challenges ahead. Marriage is surely one of your greatest gifts to mankind, but it's not without its difficulties. Grant me patience and fill my heart with endless unconditional love so that I may fulfill all of my duties as a worthy, kind, loving, and gentile spouse. In your holy name, Amen.

A Prayer for a Married Couple

Lord God, bless _____ and _____ in their future life together as one flesh. Grant them peace and fill their marriage with unconditional love that never fails and weathers all storms. May their love be patient, kind, and focused on the grace of God. In Christ's name, Amen.

A Prayer in the Hope of Children

All-knowing and all-powerful God, it is my great and passionate desire to be a parent. Bless me and my spouse with the gift of life and love. Allow us to grow our family, always keeping your sovereign will as the focus of our lives. Provide us with the strength and patience to be wise parents and to teach our future children the truth of your love. In Christ's name, Amen.

A Prayer for Your Children
Heavenly Father, you have blessed me and my spouse with the incredible gift of life. We are so thankful for the love having a growing family has provided us. Please protect our children from harm and help us teach them the way of the Lord. Help them to overcome their sinful natures and bless them with long and fruitful lives. Assist me and my spouse so that our children may become faithful servants of God and compassionate members of this nation. May they always stand firm for freedom, liberty, love, and faith. In Christ's name, Amen.

A Prayer for the Faithless
Gracious God, faith is the greatest gift any person can receive, and yet billions of people live today without it. Send your Holy Spirit upon all those who do not believe in you, God. Soften their hearts and fill their souls with your Spirit. Make the faithful stronger and more willing evangelists, so that the Word may properly be spread throughout all of creation. Make your church a shining city on a hill for the world to see and be drawn to. In Jesus' name, Amen.

A Prayer for the Departed
Almighty God, with whom do live the spirits of
them that depart hence in the Lord, and with whom
the souls of the faithful, after they are delivered from the burden of the flesh, are in joy and felicity: We give thee hearty thanks, for that it hath pleased thee to deliver this

our brother out of the miseries of this sinful world; beseeching thee that it may please thee, of thy gracious goodness, shortly to accomplish the number of thine elect, and to hasten thy kingdom; that we, with all those that are departed in the true faith of thy holy Name, may have our perfect consummation and bliss, both in body and soul, in thy eternal and everlasting glory; through Jesus Christ our Lord. Amen.
-From the *Book of Common Prayer*, 1662[25]

A Treatise on the State of Man and God

Introduction

Since the very first humans glanced into the night sky and viewed the vast universe in its seemingly infinite wonder, mankind has searched for answers to life's most difficult and enduring questions.

In pursuit of these answers, man has surely created a number of imaginative religions, each proclaiming over time to be *the* true understanding of the relationship between the heavens and Earth. Nearly all of these contrived belief systems proclaim all others to be false, and some have claimed that such anthropological evidence is proof of the nonexistence of God. "Many cultures have their own version of 'god,'" skeptics say. "What makes you think *your* God is better than all the others? Why should I even believe at all?"

This sort of logic is understandable from the position of the skeptic, who must disprove a foundational part of the human experience for thousands of years to be false. But what is clearly lacking in such an approach is this: The existence of many wrong answers is not proof against another unevaluated answer. By this same philosophy, man would never have flown in the air, traveled to the moon, or developed an understanding of virtually anything that exists in the modern world, because he would have surely said a long time ago, "Man has tried to answer these questions and has failed over and over again, thus, there must not be an answer."

"All scientific answers are measurable," a skeptic may reply. "Therefore, all scientific answers can be verified. Questions of religion, however, cannot."

Assuming that we ought to throw out all of the miraculous experiences men have underwent throughout history that tend to point in the direction of the existence of an all-powerful supernatural Spirit and the fact that virtually every independent culture ever to roam Earth, even those who have operated independently of one another, have some tradition of God, the existence of God remains a more reasonable explanation than any other for the primary philosophical questions regarding the existence of man. In fact, I believe it requires far more blind faith to reject God's existence than it does to simply believe.

Proof in the Stars

There are only two conceptions of the universe — either God exists and the entirety of creation can be attributed to Him or everything that has ever happened and ever will happen is purely by chance, a fortunate roll of the preverbal dice. No other possibility is reasonable, and in that sense, this question, as difficult as it is, is quite straight forward. Either God exists or God does not exist; there is no middle ground.

If God does not exist, as an increasing number of individuals in the world today claim, then the creation of the world was a spontaneous event from which nonliving, unintelligent space, which is to say pure emptiness, produced *something* akin to energy or matter, which then, over a great period, eventually was able to reproduce more energy or matter until the random replication of inanimate objects, by pure happenchance, produced a living cell. This living cell then itself reproduced trillions of times, all the while evolving into more complicated living matter, until you end up with the world we have today — a world teeming with life at every turn that owes the entirety of its existence to an undefined force acting upon absolutely no matter at all, just empty space.

Assuming for a moment that such a hypothesis excludes the possibility that the initial "force" upon which the entire universe owes its existence was not an act of God or God Himself, the most obvious flaw in this "more-scientific-than-religion" hypothesis is that it isn't scientific at all. One can hypothesize all he or she wants, but without the ability to reproduce a universe with absolutely nothing in it, including energy and matter of any kind, and the ability to measure and replicate results of experimentation, the scientific method has been abandoned in favor of a quasi-form of religion in and of itself. To say one rejects the notion of God in favor of a purely natural view of creation is to say one embraces a philosophical construct with even less evidence and explanatory power than the most outrageous of religions.

At least the gods of ancient Greece, for instance, offered an explanation for the existence of the universe that was internally consistent if true. Suggesting the world was created from nothing, with nothing, by nothing, with only gravity and other inanimate forces (which themselves cannot be explained), is completely illogical and unscientific — so much so in fact that the only explanation for such a hypothesis is that any theory, regardless of plausibility, is better in the minds of some than a hypothesis which embraces God.

A Skeptic's God
Most reasonable skeptics acknowledge the difficulty of the position outlined above and choose to counter with a

hypothesis which imagines some kind of supernatural and unexplainable creative force that *could* be considered God but isn't really anything like the God promoted by religions. God, for these skeptics, is quite like gravity — yes It, whatever *It* is, exists, but there is no purpose, plan, or love in God, just directionless and meaningless forces that, by absolutely complete chance, created the entirety of the universe.

This again, however, is a completely unscientific hypothesis. If we are to imagine the existence of God playing out in a courtroom drama, skeptics of God could offer absolutely no evidence in favor of a vision of God that sees Him as a meaningless, brainless, blunt force. The best the skeptic can do is disprove certain beliefs held by various other religions. In other words, a skeptic could argue that the founder of Islam, Muhammad, was not a real prophet, that Jesus didn't really exist, or that the Jewish Torah was manmade. But even if a skeptic could completely disprove every facet of every religion, an impossible task, he or she would still have offered absolutely no evidence in favor of the position that God is a simple force. Skeptics would prefer to see believers abandon faith in favor of a completely disprovable position which makes no attempt at all to explain itself.

The Meaning of Creation

Once one admits that creation must be the result of a supernatural force of some kind, only two possibilities exist: Either that supernatural force created the universe with purpose or without purpose. The skeptic must argue the universe was created without purpose, because if the universe was created with purpose, religion would suddenly become all too probable. Again, however, the skeptic cannot make his or her case. It's impossible to prove that whatever supernatural force created the universe did so without any purpose at all. The skeptic can offer absolutely no evidence to suggest a meaningless creation. In fact, all of the evidence that does exist suggests a purpose.

By observing the universe — the movement of the planets, the rhythm of life on earth, the symbiosis of all of creation — it's impossible to deny that order exists. Surely one can point to chaos or seemingly random acts, but it's impossible to ignore the simplistic complexity of the ordered universe. Even if one is to argue that order is poor evidence of a meaningful creation, it's impossible to argue that it is not evidence at all. As such, the believer looking at the order in the universe has more evidence to his claim than the skeptic does to his assertion, which contains no evidence at all. If one chooses to deny a meaningful, purposeful creation, he does so by ignoring the only evidence that exists.

Not only is the skeptic incapable of proving a meaningless creation, he is utterly incapable of disproving a theory of meaningful creation. Further, the skeptic must admit that a supernatural force capable of creating the universe from absolutely nothing is, at the very least, capable of creating the universe with purpose.

God's Dartboard

The only claim a skeptic can make is that God's creation was random, despite all of the evidence to the contrary. This, of course, would require that God exists within ordinary time, is bound to its laws, and is unaware of what will occur in the future. Without appealing to a religious text, the believer cannot prove God exits apart from ordinary time or that God knows everything that will happen before it happens. However, again, the only evidence that exists suggests that God does.

The universe is ordered, which is proof that a design existed at the time of creation. More importantly, the very assertion of God is a claim of a supernatural force existing apart from time. This is an immensely vital aspect of the argument for the believer. If God created the universe and all that exists, God must have existed prior to the creation of the universe. If God existed prior to what we consider to be reality, then God exists outside, as well as within, reality. This effectively means God cannot be bound to time since God created time.

The skeptic would have us believe that God's creative act was directionless and meaningless, much like throwing darts at a dartboard while blindfolded. Perhaps God had a general idea in mind, but He didn't know precisely where the darts would land. This argument is, at the very least, conceivable, but it fails to explain how a creative power so magnificent that He can literally create an entire ordered universe from absolutely nothing would be incapable of knowing precisely what He was creating.

Again, this position cannot be proven by the skeptic. In fact, no evidence can be offered in its favor. By contrast, the believer can point again to the order of the universe, the mere fact that life exists, and the various scientific processes as evidence of a deliberate and successful creation. If God is throwing darts at a dartboard, He is quite good at it; for in His creation, trillions upon trillions of acts deemed by the skeptic to be random have "luckily" come together to create a universe capable of sustaining life against tremendous odds to the contrary.

Predestination

Once the skeptic acknowledges that a supernatural power must have created the universe apart from the current universe and did so knowing what would become of creation, the only logical step is faith in God. For if God created the universe with purpose and if God exists apart from time, God must know everything that will happen before it happens. Thus, at the moment God chose to create the universe and began that process, God must have deliberately chosen to create it and every event that would follow for His own sovereign, purposeful reasons.

If God desired for the universe to be created in another fashion, or for some event in history to occur differently, God could have simply created the universe in an alternative manner to achieve the desired result. The only other explanation then is that God simply doesn't care. God created the universe with the ability to blind Himself from knowing what would happen at the moment of creation. This, however, cannot be proven by the skeptic, because there is no evidence at all to support such a position. The only evidence we have regarding God's creation is the observable universe, which is orderly and contains a harmony that seems to contradict a "blind creation" approach.

The Weight of the Evidence

Even the most ardent skeptic must admit that he or she makes daily decisions without perfect knowledge. We all drive cars knowing we could die in a car accident. We all believe George Washington was a real person even though no one living ever met him, and even if someone had, we would all have no way of knowing whether that individual is telling the truth or not. The study of history is predicated on the idea that humans must trust the weight of the evidence, and this is something everyone on Earth accepts.

The food we eat, the choices we make, and virtually everything we do is based on trusting the weight of the evidence. Do I know for sure grass is green? One may say, "of course," but the truth is that all sorts of improbable possibilities exist to the contrary. Perhaps I have a problem with my eyesight and "green" to me really looks like "blue" to everyone else, and the world has come together in some sort of a massive conspiracy to trick me. Perhaps we are all living in "the Matrix" and nothing I see, feel, or touch is real. As unlikely as all of these claims are, they are possible alternatives to what we perceive as true. It was once thought that Earth is flat, and for those who believed in a flat world, nothing else made any sense at all. Today, everyone knows the world is round, but do most people really *know* that? Have you seen Earth from space yourself? Are you sure you can trust the geographers and mathematicians that claim the world is round? How do we really know anything?

Humans, in the pursuit of truth, base every decision on the notion that we must trust the weight of the evidence, acknowledging all along that we do not have perfect knowledge. Faith in the existence of God should be no different for the skeptic. Although there are alternative theories for creation, is there any scientific evidence at all to support them? Is there any anthropological evidence? Any evidence from history? No.

Skepticism in God is an odd business. On the one hand, science is held up as the primary reason for why God cannot exist, and yet, on the other hand, the skeptic can offer absolutely no scientific evidence to refute God. In fact, the only evidence that exists favors the belief in God. In the mind of the skeptic, is faith in God a 100-percent guarantee? No. However, do humans have perfect knowledge of anything? No. We make every decision based on the weight of the evidence, and the evidence is clearly on the side of the existence of God.

Competing Claims

What then of the competing claims of who God is? How can anyone tell whether Christianity, Islam, Judaism, Hinduism, or some other religion is more correct than the others?

Numerous books, articles, and movies have been made to address these concerns, and this is not the time nor the place for such a complicated question. Plenty of very good resources exist that will answer these questions better

A Treatise on the State of Man and God

than I can in this limited space. However, I would promote a few essential points.

First, only three possibilities exist regarding the various religions of the world. Either none understand God, one understands God, or they all partially understand God. They all, however, cannot be absolutely true. Only one, if any do at all, can contain the fullness of the truth. This is because each religion asserts exclusivity that would, by definition, invalidate the claims of the others. Islam, Christianity, and Judaism cannot all be correct. Either Jesus is or is not God, and if he is God, then Islam and Judaism cannot contain the full truth. There is simply no other way to look at it.

Second, as a former skeptic of all religions myself, I can tell you that if one examines each one, weighing the historical evidence each presents, some are far more believable than others, and Christianity, in my view, is by far the religion that offers the best evidence for its claims. Within the Christian tradition are contained the oldest original sources, the grandest claims (the resurrection of Christ), and the most complete understanding of God that I believe surpasses all other religious constructs.

Even for those who have not yet experienced the Holy Spirit working directly in their lives, I believe the weight of the evidence in favor of Christianity is much stronger than the weight of the evidence against it — and again, this is coming from someone who spent most of his life with a strong skepticism of Christianity.

While I cannot offer the sort of apologetic work that is needed at this point in the discussion, I can strongly suggest that even the most ardent of skeptics take the time to fairly evaluate the claims of all religions, especially Christianity. Through this process, I believe the truth can and is revealed, but only when an individual's heart is open to the possibility (and sometimes even when a skeptic's heart is not open to it).

The American Book of Prayer

It took me several years to come to grips with what I now fully and completely accept as absolute truth. So, with that in mind, I will leave you with this little bit of scripture I tried to constantly keep in mind even in the darkest days of my search for God: "Ask and it will be given to you; seek and you will find; knock and the door will be opened to you. For everyone who asks receives; the one who seeks finds; and to the one who knocks, the door will be opened" (Matthew 7:7-8).

End Notes

1. Text often attributed to Thomas Jefferson, but the Monticello.org website, operated by the same organization that runs Monticello, Jefferson's estate in rural Virginia, says Jefferson likely never gave the speech. Previous versions of this book incorrectly attributed the text to Jefferson.

2. All text appearing in the *Book of Common Prayer*, specifically the 1662 version, is in the public domain and is free to use, distribute, and copy in the United States. Some of the wording in this book has been modernized. The *Book of Common Prayer* is not in the public domain in some other countries. *The American Book of Prayer* is intended for sale in the United States alone.

3. All psalms and proverbs appearing in this publication are taken from *The King James Bible*, specifically the 1769 edition of 1611 text. *The King James Bible* is in the public domain in the United States of America and is free to distribute and copy. Some of the wording in this book has been modernized.

4. All readings from the Holy Bible are from the *World English Bible* (WEB). WEB is in the public domain in the United States of America.

5. Text taken from: http://newoxfordbible.wordpress.com/2013/05/06/prayers-of-the-presidents/ on June 13, 2014.

6. All text appearing in the *Book of Common Prayer*, specifically the 1662 version, is in the public domain in the United States and is free to use, distribute, and copy. Some of the wording in this book has been modernized.

7. *Ibid.*

8. *Ibid.*

9. *Ibid.*

10. Text taken from: http://newoxfordbible.wordpress.com/2013/05/06/prayers-of-the-presidents/. Speech is in the public domain.

11. *Ibid.*

12. From William J. Johnson, *George Washington, The Christian* (New York: The Abingdon Press, 1919) and appearing on CBN.com at: http://www.cbn.com/spirituallife/PrayerAndCounseling/Intercession/washington_prayer_sundaymorning.aspx

13. Some experts claim the short list of prayers attributed to Washington were not in fact written by him and could be a forgery of some sort. In my research, scholars seem to be at odds over this question, and as a result, many have chosen not to make use of these beautiful prayers. We will never know if these prayers truly belonged to Washington or not, but it is now undeniable that Washington's faith was as strong as any man's. For an excellent book on Washington, see *George Washington's Sacred Fire* by Peter A. Lillback and Jerry Newcombe.

14. Read more at http://www.beliefnet.com/Faiths/Prayer/2009/07/Prayers-of-the-Saints.aspx?p=7

15. Translated into English by Cecil Frances Alexander in 1889.

16. *Ibid.*

17. Prayer found in John Dear's "The Prayers of Martin Luther King Jr." posted on *National Catholic Reporter Online,* January 15, 2013. Prayer published in *"Thou, Dear God": Prayers That Open Hearts and Spirits,* edited by Lewis V. Baldwin, published by Beacon Press in 2014.

18. Text in the public domain. Taken from Dwight D. Eisenhower Presidential Library, Museum, and Boyhood Home online: http://eisenhower.archives.gov/all_about_ike/presidential/1953_inauguration.html

19. Wesley's "Covenant Prayer," which was in the past usually accompanied by a special service during which a Christian would renew his or her covenant commitment to God. The first service was held on August 11, 1755, at the Spitalfields Church in London, England; more than 1,700 were in attendance.

20. Quote is in the public domain, but a good source for Wesley's thoughts and prayers is *How to Pray: The Best of John Wesley on Prayer,*

Published by Barbour Publishing, Inc. Read more of Wesley's quotes online at: http://www.whatchristianswanttoknow.com/john-wesley-quotes-23-great-sayings/#ixzz35IKtIqtq.

21. The readings for Holy Week were selected in large part based on the *Revised Common Lectionary* provided by Vanderbilt University, but selections were also influenced by the selections suggested by the United States Conference of Catholic Bishops.

22. All Christmas prayers are in the public domain. This particular prayer was found on the following website: http://www.godweb.org/christmasprayers.htm

23. *Ibid.*

24. Selections taken based on the *Revised Common Lectionary* provided by Vanderbilt University.

25. Appears in the *1662 Book of Common Prayer* under the section titled "The Burial of the Dead." *The Book of Common Prayer* is in the public domain in the United States.

www.ingramcontent.com/pod-product-compliance
Lightning Source LLC
Chambersburg PA
CBHW021757220426
43662CB00006B/89